Prevailing OVER Insurmountable ODDS

LIFE-THREATENING CANCER CAN BE DEFEATED

25-year survivor reveals how he reversed advanced colon and liver cancers by becoming proactive and rejecting chemotherapy

Gary DeBellonia

ISBN 978-1-955156-97-4 (paperback)
ISBN 978-1-955156-98-1 (digital)

Copyright © 2021 by Gary DeBellonia

All rights reserved. No part of this publication may be reproduced, distributed, or transmitted in any form or by any means, including photocopying, recording, or other electronic or mechanical methods without the prior written permission of the publisher. For permission requests, solicit the publisher via the address below.

Rushmore Press LLC
1 800 460 9188
www.rushmorepress.com

Printed in the United States of America

Disclaimer

The information contained within the pages of this book is not a guarantee by the author of a permanent healing or cure for any condition or circumstances one may be experiencing or may possibly experience. What is contained in this book is strictly for informative purposes. The reader is hereby advised and cautioned that before embarking upon any alternative method or methods for the treatment for any condition or circumstance, they should *always* be discussed first with a qualified and reputable medical provider before deciding on any alternative anything, including products.

The reader is hereby advised and cautioned that any methods described within the pages of this book may not be construed as prescribed treatments for any disease or ailment of any type or stage, physical or nonphysical, and, if chosen to be utilized, are the individual's independent choice and responsibility.

This book is also not offering a permanent cure or healing from any type or stage of life-threatening illness and/or any life-disrupting events, whether physical or nonphysical. This includes any undesirable, serious, life-changing events one may be presently experiencing or may experience in the future.

The reader should also be aware that the author of this book *is not* a medical doctor and therefore does not practice any form of medicine or offer medical advice. He is also not involved or connected to or with any members of the medical profession, pharmaceutical industry, religious groups, or any other group(s), foreign or domestic. In addition, the author does not oppose, condone, recommend, or endorse any medical process or medications for the treatment of any physical and/or nonphysical condition, life-threatening or otherwise, whether conventional or alternative.

The decision to follow any medical professional's advice or otherwise is—and remains—the sole and personal choice of the reader of this book who is either presently or may be in the future facing the decision to embark upon any medical/alternative procedure or process; undergo any surgery; take medically prescribed or alternative medications or treatments; or follow the advice and/or teachings of any religion, groups, or beliefs, known or unknown, worldwide.

The author does not advise, recommend, or attempt to coerce anyone to adopt or follow anything that the author has done to overcome life-threatening adversities that the reader shall find within the pages of this book. Instead, the author highly suggests that you, the reader, balance whatever you decide that you may need to do for yourself, or any member of your family, or anyone you may care about, should you/they possibly experience any form of physical, mental, and/or nonphysical ailment; life-threatening illness; or other serious life-changing events.

The author suggests that the reader does not abandon the guidance of prudent medical professionals, legal professionals, and religious advisors or any legally prescribed medication deemed necessary by your medical provider.

If the reader does choose to adopt anything found useful or helpful within the pages of this book, the author suggests that you utilize what you may choose to apply for your life, in conjunction with your medical professionals, legal professionals, and religious leaders' guidance, advice, and treatments, being fully aware of what has been stated in this disclaimer.

In addition to the above, let it be made perfectly clear that this book *is not* a course on religious beliefs, miracles, etc.; and nothing in this book should be mistakenly construed as intended to judge anyone's religion or their religious beliefs.

Author's Note

What is contained in this book can make a major difference in your life. This book will not do it for you; it will only show you how. For it to work for you, you will have to put it into practice.

Contents

Introduction ix

1   What This Book Can Do for You 1
2   No Matter Your Situation, You Played a Significant Role in It. 16
3   Taking the Initiative 28
4   Why Not You?. 43
5   The Myth of the Word *Luck* 66
6   The Human Will—a Most Formidable Ally 83
7   Unwavering Belief. 99
8   The Incredible Power of Thought 124
9   What Exactly Is Inner Guidance? 137
10 Answering the "How I Did It" Question. 152
11 Self-Reliance—What It Should Really Mean to You 198
12 Your Fears Can Manifest into a Life-Threatening Event. . . . 224
13 Is My Life Over?. 237
14 Overcoming Nonphysical Life-Threatening Crises 271
15 Trust in Your All-Knowing Inner Guidance. 279
16 Trusting in Everything and Everyone but Ourselves 300
17 The Real Origin of Life-Threatening Conditions 319
18 Your Circumstances Will Change 336
19 Be the Inner Vision and Dream. 345
20 The Methods That Can Reverse Life-Changing Adversities. 374
21 The Methods That Can Develop Creative Thoughts. 395
22 The Incredible Power of Your Inner Intuition 419
23 The Beginning of the Rest of Your Life 445

Acknowledgments. 449

Introduction

"Who wrote this book, and why should I read this book anyway?" These may be the first questions that have come to your mind when you picked up this book.

Who am I? I am a person who began my life in humble beginnings, rose to the top of the hill, so to speak— enjoying prosperity on almost every level one can imagine—followed by subsequent loss of all I had achieved, due to experiencing life-threatening illnesses and other serious life-changing adversities and events that should have taken my life on more than one occasion. However, I surmounted each and every one of these situations as you are about to discover.

What sets me apart from many people who have had similar or even greater severely damaging episodes in their lifetime is that I decided to take a path that few elect to travel on. This led me to the most unfathomable and incredible knowledge one could possibly imagine that made me aware of the answers, methods, and solutions necessary to overcome all that I have and all I continue to realize for my benefit.

Now, having stated this, be assured that I know precisely what I am talking about when it comes to suffering serious life-threatening illnesses and other life-changing adversities that very well may have brought most people to their knees and who possibly may have given up entirely.

That said, I truly believe that, should you decide to adopt any of the methods that you are about to learn that are based on my personal experience, you too can have the same opportunity I had— not only to explore these methods that completely transformed my life and that I continue to rely upon but to utilize them for optimum and positive outcomes.

Within the pages of this book I demystify why so many people live a life of struggle and life-changing adversities while others appear to be free of such problems and instead live lives at every conceivable level of prosperity, virtually unexposed to seriously damaging incidents.

You will also come to learn about the *root causes* of nonphysical life-changing conditions and circumstances that seem to bind countless people to an existence of repetitive failure on every level, including financial collapse, addictions, etc., and how the shackles some seemingly wear can be removed, thus enabling a life free of any serious life-changing adversities altogether.

Although I do not possess a degree in any field of medical science or professional psychological counseling, I consider myself to be somewhat of an authority on the subject of life-threatening conditions and events, having had extraordinary exposure to such conditions. In jest, I will sometimes say that I have earned an honorary degree from the college of *personal experience* (this, of course, is a fictitious college and degree used by the author for illustrative purposes only), having majored in overcoming life-threatening illnesses and other serious life-changing events.

I consider myself to be quite unique, having chosen to do what most who have survived a serious life-threatening circumstance appear to have chosen not to do. That is to not only expose the conditions and events I personally endured, but to reach out to others who may be realizing a serious life-changing situation. As a survivor of numerous life-threatening adversities, I believe that it is not only my duty to share my experiences with these challenges but also relate what I did to defeat life-threatening illness and other life-changing adversities and events. I provide a list of some of these episodes in chapter 1.

What makes all this so worthy of note is that I was certain I would overcome these and other serious life-disruptive events and adversities. Despite medical science's negative diagnosis, I did overcome the two cancers that were deemed to be insurmountable unless I went ahead with oncologist-recommended chemotherapy treatments, which I refused. Having rejected these treatments and following this advice, I elected to embark on what I believed to be a more certain path that led me to the methods, answers, and solutions I identify in this book that I credit for my having overcome each and every life-threatening event I've experienced.

Having said that, it is important for me to also state I believe that the methods I employed and the sources I chose to follow instead were the reasons why I overcame all that I have. Now I have embarked on an exciting new career and mission, bringing to others the source, knowledge, answers, and the methods on which I continue to depend.

As a result of the extraordinary results I continue to obtain and continue to experience through what I identify within the pages of this book, I truly believe others can also catapult their self-confidence, self-trust, and self-belief far beyond their wildest imaginations. Simply by realizing that they too have the very same opportunity I had—and continue to have—to surmount most undesirable life-changing adversities and events, if they consider employing these same methods.

Here is what I told the oncologist and other medical professionals I interviewed—yes, *interviewed*—when they were insisting that I seriously consider electing to go through a series of chemotherapy treatments: "I can only be defeated if I give up or die, and I am not about to give up or die." Of course, that statement invoked a number of suspicions as to the condition of my mental health. However, my mental health was—and remains—just fine.

This book, *Prevailing over Insurmountable Odds*, should be like a breath of fresh air to anyone who may be experiencing any serious life-changing circumstance. I say this because what is contained within the pages of this book can very well be the answer to overcoming whatever life-changing disruptions one may possibly experience. However, it is important to realize that what is contained in this book requires a dedicated personal commitment if you desire to rid yourself of any undesirable life-disruptive adversity, situation, or condition and discover how to enjoy whatever level of success and good you desire in your life.

Throughout this book, you will learn how to access your all-knowing inner guidance—also referred to as one's inner mind—that contains all the methods, answers, and solutions you will ever need to utilize for good, ranging from accomplishing prosperity in every area of your life and overcoming most adversities by choosing to employ the methods identified throughout this book.

You will also learn

- how to stop depending on everything and anyone for answers, methods, and solutions that you already possess and how to access them;
- how to completely change a life you do not want, for a life you truly want to experience;
- how to recapture your self-confidence and self-trust that never really left you;
- how to achieve everything you want for good, including financial prosperity on every conceivable level;
- why the medical community is unable to offer the answers, permanent solutions, or cures for most life-threatening illnesses; and
- many more . . .

When contemplating writing this book, initially, I was focusing solely on the overcoming of physical life-threatening illnesses because as a survivor of two cancer events, I decided how important it was to reach out to others and share how I was able to overcome these tests.

After giving my initial intentions deeper thought, I decided to explore further why some people seem to draw serious illnesses and other adversities, countless undesirable situations, and failures on every conceivable level into their lives to begin with. Therefore, having spent several years researching and looking deeply into the catalysts that eventually escalate into diseases, undesirable situations, circumstances, and untold adversities, as well as serious physical illnesses, I was able to determine why some individuals encounter serious life-challenging events, many of which could very well have been avoided.

In order to properly set the stage for you to understand the *why*, I found that I must first turn your attention to some of the root causes of these undesirable and often unexpected life-challenging and life-changing conditions that millions are presently facing and how they can be avoided.

But first, be aware that it is not just about the act of fighting off some illness or life-changing adversity; instead, it's about surmounting any unexpected serious life-changing situation—e.g., loss—and a myriad of other unexpected adversities and events. This is also about being prepared and knowing, with complete, unwavering confidence, that there are no such words as *can't* or *quit* or *never have been* when it comes to any serious life-challenging and life-changing events that may or possibly have already intruded into your life. The words *can't* or *quit* aren't applicable to any undesirable situation one may encounter, not just physical life-disrupting conditions.

These words, *can't* and *quit*, have no place in your or anyone's vocabulary. They weren't in the many situations and circumstances I experienced or in the lives of anyone who overcame any serious life-changing condition or adversity. It is extremely important that you come to realize, recognize, and clearly understand that there will always be an unexpected life-changing challenge waiting for everyone just around the corner—this you can be absolutely certain. However, you can do much more about these unexpected life-changing challenges than you think or have been led to believe. The answers, methods, and solutions to dealing with these inevitable events will be found throughout the chapters that follow.

It is not just about overcoming what one's situation may be at the moment; it is about one's personal choices and actions taken. And it is about knowing where to find the answers, methods, and solutions necessary to overcome most adverse situations, not just serious physical illnesses that may possibly show up in one's life or may have already. It's about absolutely believing you can overcome any life-challenging or life-threatening condition and accessing the source, methods, answers, and solutions to problems and being completely confident that, when you discover for the first time or rediscover the incredible inner power you have—and always have had—that can provide the answers one may be seeking to surmount any adversity one may be facing, you can achieve any level of success and prosperity in your life.

Always remember this: You have always been—and always will remain—the master of yourself. It is not until you are totally committed to and continue to envision whatever you really want to occur—e.g., overcoming any tragedy, adversity, and/or loss; continued good health or a return to good health; having prosperity on every conceivable level; happiness and joy; etc.—that life becomes an unlimited beneficial actuality. It is at this point when life's self-induced shackles are released and where one becomes truly free.

Therefore, if you truly want a life where you can always access the answers, solutions, and methods you seek that can enhance your life beyond your imagination, then you should seriously make the decision to begin to free yourself now from unnecessary worry, stress, anxiety, uncertainty, and fears on any level.

If you consider ridding yourself of whatever it may be that is plaguing your life, then reading this book is an absolute must for you. Have a life full of confidence; prosperity on every conceivable level; good health; and the ability to access the methods, answers, and solutions to anything you may wish to know for your benefit that you will learn about in this book, which is the incredible innate power you already have, always have had, and always will have.

In deciding to take the initiative and take control of your life by reading this book, I am more than confident that, should you choose to employ any of the suggested methods, you can overcome almost any adversity that either may be presently disturbing your life or possibly may encounter in your journey. I further trust that the information contained in this book can open many doors for you that you may have lost the keys to—so to speak—and place you back on the path you were always meant to be on, which is the path to experiencing prosperity on every conceivable level.

Having considered this, let's now get started on your new life path, keeping in mind at all times that yesterday is irretrievable; however, this moment is yours to do with as you so choose. Your tomorrows rely solely on the decisions you make today and each and every day that you are given because you are the sole architect of your life. So beginning right now, you can choose a life free of unwanted conditions, circumstances, and lack or remain as you are. The choice, of course, is yours.

1

WHAT THIS BOOK CAN DO FOR YOU

> Everyone is at risk of a serious l*ife-changing adversity,* as one never knows what is lurking around the corner!
>
> —Author

When going through my experience with cancer, I came across this wonderful inspirational poem which I found to be extremely helpful and wish to pass it along to anyone who may be experiencing a life-threatening illness or any life-changing adversity:

Invictus

Out of the night that covers me,
Black as the Pit from pole to pole,
I thank whatever gods may be
For my unconquerable soul.

In the fell clutch of circumstance
I have not winced nor cried aloud.
Under the bludgeoning's of chance
My head is bloody, but unbowed.

GARY DEBELLONIA

> Beyond this place of wrath and tears
> Looms but the Horror of the shade,
> And yet the menace of the years
> Finds, and shall find, me unafraid.
>
> It matters not how strait the gate,
> How charged with punishments the scroll.
> I am the master of my fate:
> I am the captain of my soul.
>
> —William Ernest Henley

Here is just a brief sample of what employing the methods contained in this book can possibly do for your life:

- significantly improve your health
- overcome adversities, events, or conditions plaguing your life
- experience success and prosperity on every conceivable level
- achieve financial wealth, far beyond your expectations
- significantly improve your present situation
- find whatever you always wanted to experience for good

Why continue to struggle even one more day with any adversity, unwanted conditions, circumstances, or any undesirable situations that may be plaguing your life when you can start right here and now to begin exploring the possibilities for ridding whatever it may be that is causing you pain, stress, anxiety, depression, and any number of serious life-changing conditions or events? There is a proven way that can provide you and anyone with the power to overcome any adversity that is plaguing or may afflict your life.

My intention and mission is to provide information for anyone who is seeking to overcome adversities on every conceivable level, whether they are physical or nonphysical in nature, and for those who may wish to prevent any such occurrences and/or realize prosperity in any area of their lives. Having discovered the answers and methods to ridding myself of numerous serious life-transforming situations, I decided to share these very same answers and methods with everyone who may be enduring any life challenges.

Not only do I identify those methods and answers that enabled me to overcome serious potentially life-disruptive conditions, as well as serious nonphysical events, but I also point out the root causes of these life-threatening illnesses and how to unleash and utilize the incredible power within you that will bring forth the healing and overcoming of each and every life-threatening and life-changing events.

I want you to ask yourself the same question I asked myself when going through the critical episodes that plagued my life—"Why should I have to struggle with any condition or undesirable life-changing event that is happening to me or that may invade my life in the future?" Even if you do not have to ask yourself this question, is it worth doing nothing about whatever it is that may be disrupting your life? Begin now to substantially reduce and ultimately rid yourself of pain, fear, stress, anguish or discomfort, addiction, and any number of serious adversities, conditions, or events, including physical ailments.

Even if you have yet to encounter any life-threatening events and have achieved the success you aspired for your life, keep in mind that you never know what is around the corner. Therefore, open your eyes to that possibility, as I continue to believe "being forewarned is being forearmed," concerning practically any unexpected condition, situation, circumstance, or life-devastating event, physical or nonphysical, that may possibly appear in your life one day.

One of the first steps is to develop the insight of how to begin to accomplish all this and more and the methods and answers needed to achieve a life devoid of misery, fear, and doubting. Instead, cultivate a life of achieving prosperity on every level and beginning to heal whatever undesirable, serious, life-affecting experiences you may be dealing with.

Although we've never met, I know this much about you already—you are a person who genuinely cares about yourself and you certainly would not have decided to pick up this book and to have read this far. Sensing this about you, I also believe that you are also a person who has what it takes to overcome any adversity in your life; is seeking continued good health, free from stress, anxiety, depression, and lack of self-confidence and self-trust; and wants to live the life you always knew is achievable.

If I am right, then the information contained in this book is for *you* because you deserve it and, most of all, because *you are a very special person* who not only cares about yourself but others as well. There never was or ever will be another you.

If I could have survived all the serious physical illnesses and other life-challenging and life-changing events—in addition to the tremendous loss of practically everything I had spent a lifetime building and much more—and overcame it all, there should be absolutely no reason why you too can't overcome anything you may be coping with at this point in your life or in the future. Even terminally ill people have survived their illnesses longer than expected, despite having been told that they would succumb from their illness much sooner.

I believe that it is important to point out here that I am not a person who have never personally gone through most of the inconceivable hell life can dish out. Instead, I have lived through every moment of these events and overcame it all, and I am willing to share with you—and everyone who is interested—precisely how I accomplished surviving all the life-threatening illnesses and nonphysical life-threatening events and conditions many deem to be insurmountable.

Most people I have spoken with concerning all that I have overcome have stated to me that they believe that they would not have been able to overcome a fraction of what I have. Herein then lies a major problem commonly referred to as giving up. Giving up is a serious illness in itself. Lack of initiative and, more importantly, lack of belief, self-confidence, and self-trust are also very serious nonphysical illnesses which I refer to as root causes of most physical illnesses.

Certainly, no one can possibly speak for others who have also overcome some of life's major obstacles and challenges. However, no matter what it was others chose to do that led them to overcome whatever insurmountable odds they were confronted with—be it a serious illness, a nonphysical life-threatening event, etc.—it is my belief that the stories of some of the most incredible human survival events recorded to date indicate to me that the survivors were already in touch with what we all were born with—what I choose to call one's all-knowing inner mind. Instead of having been totally reliant upon their conscious mind, ego, and others for answers, methods, and solutions, it is my firm belief that these survivors were very much aware of their powerful all-knowing inner power that they relied upon to overcome life-threatening events.

As a man who was not supposed to be around any longer, it is virtually inconceivable for me to even begin to think how anyone can possibly go through the enormous maze and challenges that life places in front of us all without first having the opportunity to come to know one's all-knowing inner power that will always lead them to the correct path, decisions, solutions, answers, and methods necessary to resolve or to bring forth what they desire for good. This includes proper guidance, methods, direction, solutions, and answers for self-healing almost any illness, ailment, or undesirable event one may already be aware of or may encounter. This applies to anyone no matter what their circumstance or wherever they may reside in the world.

The following is a brief listing of just some of the root causes and conditions that can possibly lead to serious life-threatening illnesses, if allowed to escalate. I suggest that you take the time to look them over. Among those listed here, you may recognize one or more that you possibly may be enduring or know someone who is:

- ongoing disappointment
- always unhappy
- always afraid
- resentful
- always agitated
- nonbelieving
- prejudiced
- always mocking others
- feeling neglected
- feeling abandoned
- mean tempered

- always confused
- feeling anxious
- constantly moody
- feeling misunderstood
- always doubting
- experiencing mental stress
- feeling destitute
- feelings of guilt
- feeling unappreciated
- always sad
- always nervous
- feeling overwhelmed
- hateful toward others
- feeling betrayed
- continuous state of rage
- traumatized easily
- self-pity
- always frustrated
- conceited
- anger
- depressed
- feeling helpless
- disliking people
- jealousy
- unforgiving
- feeling rejected
- always distrustful
- exhibiting violent behavior
- feeling violated or victimized
- demanding
- always fearful
- always feeling disgusted
- feeling disrespected
- experiencing ongoing loneliness
- experiencing antisocial behavior

Personally, I am very familiar with a number of these root causes, as are others who also have faced even greater life-changing challenges and survived them. They survived not by luck, but by their unwavering belief that they would find a solution. Know this: Absolutely nothing is insurmountable—nothing. Unless, of course, you may possibly convince yourself that whatever it is you may be encountering is insurmountable. Should this be the case concerning you, know that absolutely nothing could be further from reality and the truth.

As a fellow human being, I am no different than you. It's now time to get your head out of the sand, drop the excuses and feeling sorry for yourself—if you are, as I too once did—*stop* the dependency on others or whatever it is you use as a crutch, and get back in the game of living and controlling your life instead of allowing everything and everyone else to control it for you.

Now, let's move on to learn more about these methods and your all-knowing inner mind that, when combined, can significantly enhance your reality as they have mine. Ponder this: If I overcame all that I have described thus far, armed with the methods I identify within the pages of this book, there should be no reason that you too can't try to surmount what may be plaguing you as well. The key is the quality of your existence—not how long you will live but how you choose to live it right now!

I can tell you that most people will generally say to themselves, when faced with a life-threatening illness or other serious adversity, "Why me?" and "What caused this to come into my life?" Rarely, however, will we begin to believe that, in most cases, it is we ourselves who played a significant role in bringing forth most adverse conditions and events into our current situation.

It is important for me to mention here that your changed life is not that far away. Although it has taken you years to get it to where it is today, whether you feel your accomplishments are complete or incomplete, there are no barriers concerning the word *up*, other than those you self-create, no matter if you believe you have reached the pinnacle or the bottom of your expectations pertaining to each and every area of your life.

What direction your life will take is determined solely by your total dedication and unwavering attention on what you choose to focus upon and what you truly want to achieve. This can range from maintaining or a returning to good health and ridding yourself of adversities, circumstances, situations, and related events you may have drawn to you, including most life-threatening illnesses. On the other hand is experiencing prosperity on every conceivable level, total happiness, and finding the ideal mate to share your joy and peace. It all begins with what you truly want to have manifest in your life, especially when what you are seeking for good is accompanied by *deep, inner passion* and *unshakeable determination.*

Please understand this clearly. You have a very important role to play in the achievement of any and all of the expected good outcomes you desire to happen. As a matter of fact, yours is the only role in this movie titled "Your Life," so to speak. It is not as though you can rub a magic lamp and a genie will appear, ready to make manifest instantly any of your desires. Instead, you play a major role in your expected outcome that only you can control through your total dedication to yourself and the methods and answers your inner power can supply that can lead you to the manifestation of what it is you are seeking for good. To accomplish what it is you want to exist, you can begin by making absolutely certain you are ready, willing, and able to be totally dedicated to this unseen inner power.

Once you begin to realize that you were born with an extraordinary inner power, you can control your conscious mind and your ego. This is what Wikipedia says about ego:

> The ego plays the critical and moralizing role. The super-ego can stop you from doing certain things that your id may want you to do, which is in total control of your life. The id is the unorganized part of the personality structure that contains a human's basic, instinctual drives. Id is the only component of personality that is present from birth. The id, is the part of the mind containing the drives present at birth; it is the source of our bodily needs, wants, desires, and impulses, particularly our sexual and aggressive drives.

You will then come to realize that it has been you and you alone all along, not anyone or anything else, who has been holding you back from achieving whatever it is you desire. That is also tied to lack of self-confidence, doubting, wavering, and your predominant habitual disempowering thoughts, just to name a few.

Always believe that you already have it and are experiencing it, and you'll have it and experience it.

The point being is that unwavering belief, envisioning, and expectation, collectively, are extremely powerful pertaining to the achievement of what you truly desire to occur, especially concerning overcoming any adversity that may be disrupting your life.

Because I believed so deeply and expected to overcome the life-threatening illnesses I had endured, I *innately knew* that I could heal myself and would overcome these maladies by employing the methods given me by an all-knowing infinite source, which I knew was the key to my full recovery, despite the negative odds given to me.

It is the combination of unwavering belief, self-confidence and determined expectation, and connection with your inner mind, along with the methods I identify in this book, that brings forth the eventual desired results. With these forces working in tandem, absolutely nothing is out of reach for you or anyone who truly believes they can challenge anything they choose to overcome, even if this means extending one's life far beyond any medical professional's diagnosis and prognosis. Many people who had sustained serious life-threatening illnesses and other serious life-changing events that were considered inconceivable to surmount did survive them, including me, despite being told they would not.

I am almost certain that you possibly may have seen or heard of this happening as there have been many remarkable publicized cures and deemed-insurmountable events overcome by people worldwide despite the overwhelming odds against their survival. As even more people are becoming aware of their remarkable inner power, I am almost certain that countless others will follow and they can also have the opportunity of witnessing remarkable healings and cures of both physical and nonphysical conditions in the not-too-distant future—even beyond what medical science had once thought could be expected.

In the past several decades, much of the old school of thought among medical science and the medical profession as a whole appears to be slowly changing and beginning to move toward seriously considering the incredible force of a person's inner power. There is absolutely nothing that your all-knowing inner power can't resolve and/or achieve on your behalf when you choose to believe and expect, without wavering or doubting that it can.

I have personally found that some doctors today, especially those who have recently entered the medical profession, are no longer closing their minds entirely to the significant role one's inner power plays in calming and curing the tremendous negative firestorms going on within one's conscious mind and physical body. Even my physicians have asked me how I overcame all that I have, considering all that I have been through, and wanted to learn how I did it. They have also asked me to be certain that I send them this book when it is published, containing the answers and methods I used that clarifies the "how I did it" question.

Understand that your brain is not your inner mind from which most people seemingly have allowed themselves to drift away. By doing so, neglecting to acknowledge this incredible inner wisdom with which we all came in to this world and putting it to work in their lives for their good is, in my opinion, one of the primary reasons why many people rarely solve their problems and, therefore, continue to go through life unfulfilled.

By rejecting the existence of an inner mind is the same as rejecting the fact that one needs air to breathe. Yet it has been my personal observation of many people that humanity is littered with countless pessimists and naysayers who, quite to their misfortune, may live out their lives on this planet unable to recognize any of the good others have and continue to manifest because they do believe in the existence of their inner powers. In my opinion, this is among the primary reasons for the escalating chaos, unrest, unhappiness, dissatisfaction, misery, pain, sorrow, confusion, depression, stress, anxiety, dependency, lack, serious illnesses, and myriad of adversities that people endure throughout the world today and in generations that preceded ours. Should this mind-set continue, it is more than possible that these conditions may continue to plague future generations.

If you are concerned with the intention of elevating your life from any current unwanted circumstances, situations, illnesses, or adversities, you will come to realize that you have only accomplished a mere fraction of whatever good is still in store for you to accomplish, regardless of what your current stature is in life. Your all-knowing inner intuitive guidance is the path to adjusting whatever it is you wish to exist for good in your life. Because it is connected with infinite intelligence and the infinite mind, you can continue to bring forth whatever is required to come into your life—if your desire is accompanied with *unwavering belief.*

Through the methods that are about to be revealed to you, coupled with your decision to reunite with or come to know—for the first time—your inner mind, you will be astonished by what you can achieve and what you may possibly miss being exposed to, should you choose not to explore this opportunity to reconnect with or come to know the incredible unseen power with which you came here. I am not referring to any particular religion because all religions recognize, in their own way, an infinite intelligence that created everything that claims allegiance with no religions on this planet or anywhere life may also possibly exist.

It is also important for you to realize that if you choose to believe in a thing, anything you truly believe and concentrate thought into, on a consistent basis, will bring forth what you believe over time—whether something good or something not so pleasant. It is what you choose to focus upon and think about continuously, with unwavering belief, that will eventually show up in your physical life. This includes choosing to believe that you indeed do have an all-knowing inner intelligence and also have the opportunity to have positive outcomes that you may desire.

Therefore, your persistent habitual thoughts that are contained in your conscious mind are the key, as they are the continuing messages you are sending to your all-knowing inner faculties. This is what your unseen inner mind will begin to act upon to bring forth the desired results, good or bad, as your inner intelligence/inner mind does not discriminate, judge, or argue; instead, it responds to your deepest desires' commands and beliefs, good or bad, that will be carried forth to eventually manifest in the physical.

If you will stop to think about it, this already has occurred in your life, in the lives of people you know, and countless others and others who have passed on throughout the world. The proof of this is evident in present experiences—good, not so good, full of abundance, or full of want and undesirable events; excellent health; poor health; etc. They are a culmination of what everyone dwelled upon, resulting from the primary thoughts we had concentrated on and which, over time, brought any of these conditions and situations into reality.

The very same holds true for the present moment. Because at this very moment you are creating, through your dominant habitual thoughts, what will be communicated to your inner power will eventually become reality. Therefore, if you are continuously thinking about prosperity on every conceivable level of your life, including ridding yourself of undesirable life-changing conditions, then prosperity on every level is destined to eventually become reality for you.

On the other hand, if you are continuously focused on ill health and other undesirable conditions, this is also what will become reality. Any predominant thoughts held in one's conscious mind long enough, whether for good or not, will eventually be also communicated to one's inner mind, which will make manifest every desire your conscious mind holds as true.

Then there are those whom I've met who choose to scoff at people who believe in the existence of an all-knowing inner intelligence and at anything they have yet to personally confirm and who also believe that the subject of having an inner mind is preposterous or that it can possibly contain all the answers one may be seeking for anything they wish to exist for positive effect in their life. In addition, their vast ignorance stretches as far as even condemning the very idea that the power of one's dominant and habitual thoughts as the culprit of what one will eventually have manifest in their life, for good or bad. Furthermore, quite sadly, they were also unwilling to make any attempt whatsoever to learn more about the power of their own thoughts. I did not find their scoffing unusual because countless people choose to believe what seems to fit into their perception to be the cause of their life's reality, thereby rejecting anything to the contrary that doesn't fit into the world they have molded around them. However, they have every right to do so; after all, it is the world they conceive in their conscious mind and prefer to live in.

From history we learned that numerous people who were responsible for bringing into reality the conveniences and medical breakthroughs modern societies are benefiting today had also been scoffed at, ridiculed, and some were even banned from society. They were labeled as kooks, delusional, insane, and others were even crucified for what they believed in and for even speaking aloud of the power of their all-knowing inner force, even after having demonstrated this inner power to many. Yet the ignorant among them still did not believe what was being explained and demonstrated to them. However, despite their critics' disbelief, they prevailed far beyond the imagination of all who were witness to and became ultimate benefactors of their deemed impossible achievements. Without their perseverance—despite having to overcome abuse, ridicule, and scoffing—modern men, women, and children today have become the benefactors of their knowledge and unwavering commitment to an all-knowing source of creativity that led them to the ultimate achievements of their endeavors.

Quite unfortunately, not much has changed throughout the centuries where this subject is concerned. Even to this very day, many people worldwide have not advanced much beyond their ancestors, as they themselves have accepted the handing off the baton of doubt and disbelief, so to speak, and continue to hand it off to the next generation and, by doing so, continue to create yet another generation of critics, naysayers, and unbelievers.

Therefore, unless they themselves begin to realize that the human brain alone can do nothing in the way of bringing them what they want to appear and/or achieve in life, they too will be spawning yet another new generation of critics, naysayers, and nonbelievers who will rarely achieve their deep desires for good. Sad but true. I cannot even begin to tell you how many people I have encountered, prior to and following my cancer diagnoses and other serious life-changing events, who absolutely refuse to even consider that their inner power does indeed exist.

I have also witnessed and spoken with many people who could have avoided and possibly overcome some very difficult adversities and life-changing situations that were very much aware of their inner unseen power, yet they also chose not to take the time to explore or to even make an attempt to tap into their inner power. Instead, they chose to rely upon the opinions of others who were not even aware of the methods contained in this book and who also had the very same opportunity to achieve what they were seeking. Instead, they were all relying totally upon medical science or others to resolve adversities and other serious life-challenging and life-changing experiences. Unfortunately, countless people today prefer to attempt to deal with their life-altering challenges and other undesirable conditions through these sources solely. Sadly, many have since passed on without ever have given their inner powers any consideration whatsoever.

The opinions of others are very powerful. This is because most people will first choose to seek the advice of those who are close to them and who they come to trust the most. The people who they choose to trust are family, the medical profession, close personal friends, business associates, their spouses, their significant other, etc. This is not uncommon when people become anxious or deeply stressed over something, as these are the sources they will turn to first for help and answers. We all do it, and we all seek and receive opinions and advice, some good and some not so good. However, more often than not, what you and others may fail to do is to quiet your raging mind and allow yourself to listen to that inner voice—the one that continues to beckon for you so you can access and/or to reunite with your unseen inner power.

Prosperity on all levels is not only meant to be developed and enjoyed by those who may already be prosperous; it is to be enjoyed by each and every member of humanity. This includes you who, at this very moment, may be seeking answers, methods, and solutions and who also aspires to know prosperity—especially financial prosperity—on every conceivable level of your life, which is also the primary desire of countless people. I sincerely believe that if this is your true desire, you will find this book to contain many of the answers and methods you will need to reach whatever level of prosperity you are seeking and what you consider that would make your life prosperous and fulfilled. *Merriam-Webster* defines *prosperous* as "marked by success or economic well-being; enjoying vigorous and healthy growth."

Having said this, I cannot begin to tell you just how many times I have heard the complete opposite from people, saying such things as "I can't change the way I am" or "I will never get out of this mess" or "There is simply no way for me to overcome this illness, adversity." Bananas! My response to such negative comments remains to be "Yes you can" and "Yes you will" and "Begin right here and right now." So then, let's get started on how you can begin to obtain the prosperity you are seeking in your life.

It is important that you understand that there is nothing that has manifested in your life up to now that you and all of humanity has not played a significant role in creating. This next chapter takes a deeper look into how humanity is responsible for everything they come to experience during their lifetime.

2

NO MATTER YOUR SITUATION, YOU PLAYED A SIGNIFICANT ROLE IN IT

*You were not born with negative
thoughts inside of your mind.
Instead, you learned and cultivated them over time.*

—Author

Concerning almost every area of your life and all the problem areas that you may experience, without any doubt whatsoever, know that you are part of the problem and you are also the solution.

Without any questions in my mind, you can change your life for the better—much better—should you choose to keep an open mind and be willing to believe and accept the fact that you are personally responsible for and are the creator of everything you already have and will continue to experience in your lifetime.

The following is just a brief sample of what I have overcome. Would you believe?

- I survived both colon and liver cancer eight months apart.
- Rejected post-surgery chemotherapy treatments three times and still defeated cancer.

PREVAILING OVER INSURMOUNTABLE ODDS

- Survived a morphine overdose in the hospital shortly after colon cancer surgery that, according to medical personnel, should have taken my life.
- Survived a major head-on automobile collision as a passenger resulting in sustaining head, neck and spine injuries occurring one year after liver cancer surgery.
- Overcame chronic sleep apnea, and no longer rely on medically recommended breathing equipment diagnosed needed for life.
- Survived a major heart attack having been told by the attending physicians I should not have survived.
- Overcame years of overwhelming stress, anxiety and depression.
- Overcame nonphysical life-changing conditions, circumstances, adversities, events and crises.
- Overcame and rebounded from massive financial and business loss.

Eighteen years ago, following surgery for both of the cancer events I developed, I was told by medical professionals that without highly recommended chemotherapy treatments, my chances for survival were no greater than 10 percent with surgery—at best. (See copy of medical record in the appendix.) Despite this prognosis, I continued to reject chemotherapy treatments and surmounted both malignancies.

Today, I am healthier, both physically and mentally, and much stronger than many people who are much younger than I and younger looking than many people my age. I am raising a teenage son alone, more alert and active than I have been in my entire life, walk five miles a day, earned a first-degree black belt in martial arts and became an assistant martial arts instructor at age fifty-three (two years after both surgeries), play basketball, baseball, a soon-to-be speaker in engagements related to the subject of this book, teach entrepreneur training classes, and now a writer, among other worthwhile humanitarian activities. All this despite having been informed verbally and in writing by medical specialists and other medical providers that my chances of survival were slim, at best (in other words, given a death sentence).

Not only have I accomplished all this and much more, I continue to achieve what I *choose* to for good and for the good of all concerned; and all this, thus far, has been realized through the power of my inner mind that has and continues to give me the answers and the methods it receives from an all-knowing, infinite intelligence I identify in this book.

What you and many people may possibly fail to grasp—including me, before my involvement with life-threatening events—is that you have never been broken; hence, you never had a need to be fixed. You need to realize and finally step up to the plate and take full responsibility for the fact that *you*—and each and every one of us—are personally responsible for inviting every negative and positive event that shows up in our physical lives.

You may possibly be thinking that you or no one else would ever knowingly, intentionally invite or wish to attract any life-threatening situations, circumstances, or events into your life—physical or otherwise yet. Quite the contrary, as all of us do precisely just that every waking moment of our lives unconsciously and consciously, by default. This includes not only the matter of physical life-threatening illnesses but any undesirable nonphysical events, circumstances, adversities, and hardships you may possibly develop or one day may come to know.

This book was intended for the purpose of reaching out to you and others who currently are enduring or may endure any life-threatening situations, circumstances, and/or other life-changing events, believing them to be far too overwhelming or even impossible to overcome, and who are seriously interested in learning how I overcame life-threatening events and what I did to overcome each and every one of these types of occurrences.

Someone once asked me these questions: "Are you a self-ordained prophet?" or "How is it possible that you can know all these things you speak of in this book?" The answer is this: Each and every person is and has been connected to an unseen, all-knowing force that provides the answers and the methods necessary to overcome anything anyone may desire to obtain for good during their lifetime.

PREVAILING OVER INSURMOUNTABLE ODDS

To believe otherwise is to be in total denial that an all-knowing, supreme intelligence does exist other than human beings. And no, this book is not a discourse on religious beliefs and does not delve into, promote or discuss any religious dogma or other beliefs deemed to be religiously connected.

Whether some people choose to believe this or not is not relevant. What is relevant, however, is that it is remarkable and inconceivable how some people could even possibly fathom that they are the most intelligent species in the entire universe and that the universe itself was created by some yet-to-be proven "big boom" theory, which remains just that—a theory—or that human beings evolved from some form of aquatic reptile or species of ape, which has also yet to be proven beyond any doubt and never will be, in my opinion. Instead, an unseen source has provided every member of humanity with an inner guide to call upon for anything desired for good. There are millions of very grateful recipients of this all-knowing source that can provide one with magnificent powers—myself being among them.

The mere fact that you, I, and everyone else was fortunate enough to be conceived with a conscious mind that is so complicated that even modern-day medical science has yet been able to conquer and understand how it, through its connection with an even deeper and more profound all-knowing source that can heal any undesirable human condition, brings forth untold ideas and can create prosperity on every conceivable level for anyone who calls upon it with unwavering belief and expectation. It can also permanently cure the human body from many deemed life-threatening illnesses. However, for this survivor, there has been and continues to be proof enough that this unseen force does exist, always has existed, and always will exist.

One does not have to be a religious person to know or be able to benefit from one's all-knowing inner faculties. All you or anyone needs to do is to be able and willing to recognize that you and every person has the capability of realizing substantial benefit on every level of life from this inner intelligence. All it takes is to firmly believe that you can. I cannot fathom any other source that can manifest your innermost desires for good than one's creative intelligence. In my opinion, there is no other such source.

It can and will work for you and all of humanity as well, if and only if, you are willing to place your skepticism and negative state, if you have one, in a closet, so to speak, and seriously consider making a personal commitment to never again doubt or waver and elect instead to place your complete trust in your all-knowing wisdom and incredible powers. If you choose to do this for yourself and are willing to exercise patience and steadfast belief, you can begin to know a remarkable change for the better that will only increase to the point that you can obtain prosperity in every conceivable area of your life.

Keep in mind at all times that unless you are willing to accept that you are personally responsible for drawing to you every undesirable event and situation you encounter in life, you may continue to attract more of what you do not want to have in your life that universal law describes as *deliberate creativity*. These same universal laws hold true for attracting every positive situation you desire. You can access these universal laws on the internet for your further information.

You should also be aware that all humanity was meant to live a life free of disease, stress, worry, anxiety, trauma, depression, or all types of life-threatening illnesses. Then why are so many of us suffering and dying needlessly and so early from these maladies? Know that you came into this world armed with the knowledge to turn off the *negative* fuel with which *you* continue to supply yourself, so to speak. This includes every physical and nonphysical illness and other undesirable life-changing event that has either already appeared or may possibly one day materialize in your life. Please understand that you were not born with any negative power source inside of you; instead, you learned how to build and cultivate one over time. Furthermore, it is important for you to *never*, ever give any life-threatening illness, circumstance, adversity, or any related event any power or negative thoughts. This condition is brought on predominantly through your ongoing disempowering beliefs.

You need to realize, understand, and accept that it is you and you alone who energizes this negative power habitually and unconsciously and, therefore, are the only one who can permanently shut it down and rid yourself from any disempowering false beliefs and thoughts beginning right here and right now. The beliefs and thoughts concerning what you want to become reality in your life have tremendous power contributing to the benefit of all concerned. The instant you create and continue to hold those thoughts in your conscious mind, those thoughts will be joined by similar thoughts, all of which will eventually give you back more of what you want to develop in your physical life, which will be received as instructions by your inner mind to bring forth for you. Now then, don't you think the time has finally come in your life to do something about whatever it may be you want to rid yourself of, especially if you are afflicted with a serious life-altering condition or serious nonphysical situation, circumstance, or adversity?

The false belief about being too late to do anything about your situation for the better is nothing but a lie told to you by yourself through the negative thoughts and beliefs you keep feeding and repeating to yourself over and over and over again that bring to you precisely what you do not want to continue to exist in your life. Blaming your circumstance on anyone or anything for your nonphysical or physical illness or any other undesirable adversity or events in your life is not only irresponsible—it is total denial of reality. Always be aware of the fact that absolutely no one goes through life unchallenged; and you, me, or anyone else is *not* an exception to this truth!

This world is swollen with people in offices, on the streets where we live, in malls, outdoor markets, doctors' offices, airports, public events, and practically anywhere and everywhere. So who are the real people behind all these flesh masks you may encounter? They are the faces of your friends, your family members, pedestrians, motorists, business associates, acquaintances, medical professionals, total strangers, travelers from other countries, and others we know and don't know.

Have you ever asked yourself the question *What's really behind these masked faces?* Well, for starters, there's pain, agony, anxiety, heartache, and depression; adversities on every conceivable level; addictions of every type; fear; feelings of unworthiness and hopelessness; despair, guilt, sorrow, and trauma; and, for some, true happiness and joy.

Realize that you are under attack every single day by the disempowering thoughts of many of those you know and associate with as well as the transference of their emotions, feelings, and actions. Therefore, it is vital that one becomes acutely aware of the types of thoughts, feelings, and disempowering beliefs that can and often do trigger any number of undesirable negative emotions and events in those who are around these types of personalities. Therefore, left unchecked, the negative vibrations of others can eventually lead to any number of nonphysical illnesses that, when allowed to escalate, can lead to physical illnesses.

The current world population as of May 2014 is 7,234,982,184 people and counting, according to Worldometers Real-Time World Statistics, and many of these lives are inundated with untold miseries and circumstances. Therefore, no matter what undesirable circumstances or situation you may possibly be concerned with, know that you can overcome whatever it is and be able to live the life you were meant to have. No one was ever meant to suffer deprivation at any level, especially those who do not believe they can overcome any undesirable circumstances and related conditions.

All too often, we go about our daily, almost robotic routines, with a "that can't happen to me" attitude. When we do encounter any one or more of these unwanted events, we treat the symptoms but, rarely, if ever, the cause itself.

Some people do not always seek out medical assistance for treatment when they first begin to notice symptoms of a perceived illness—unless, of course, it is so severe, it requires immediate medical attention. If this is the case concerning you, by all means, make an appointment with your medical provider. If medication is found necessary, be aware that once the treatments and the prescribed medication have run their course, what are you left with? More than likely, you may possibly say, "Well, of course, I should be cured from whatever it may be." This may be possible but not likely, unless the *root cause* plaguing you is eradicated, *permanently*.

In modern-day societies, evidence of life-threatening illnesses and other life-changing adversities when left unattended—and, worse, ignored—has reached unprecedented heights over the last several decades. This is especially true in the United States as our present-day society is facing an economic collapse as never before seen since the Great Depression, coupled with the highest cost of living expenses and unemployment, with no evidence of much relief on the horizon. Tied to these conditions, a strong belief among many people today is that government appears to have literally chosen to downplay the gravity of this real-life crisis.

Taking this into consideration, as a result, people nationwide are not only losing their homes but are also losing their jobs, savings, retirement funds, and other benefits; suffering devastating financial losses and unprecedented divorce rates; and also escalating fear and concern can be found almost everywhere due to an inability to afford health care insurance and much more.

Situations such as these and even greater events are precisely why these conditions and other nonphysical life-changing events have become the predators that very well can give birth to serious illnesses. Some people who have serious physical illnesses believe that they are precipitated by the conditions I just identified. Medical professionals search for confirmation that these conditions are hereditary or originated in our DNA, at birth, etc. Others would say that they were predestined, and others would say it's fate (kismet).

I hate to be the one who throws all these false beliefs out the window, but someone has to make an attempt to set the record straight. I truly believe that I have been led to make you and others aware that we will be dealing with a great majority of undesirable life-challenging and life-changing conditions and circumstances and that we all have and continue to play a major role in contributing to these types of conditions and others being manifested and, therefore, are mostly self-induced. Many people find this hard to believe and accept. This condition is better known as denial. The sad truth is that this is the truth.

However, as I've pointed out, you, I, and others have literally played a significant role in the creation of any unwanted conditions, situations, and adversities that cause us problems over time. Why do you think that there are so many psychologists, psychiatrists, mediums and fortune tellers, so-called life coaches, and the like treating people for untold emotional and related conditions then? I certainly realize that this is a very hard pill to swallow, so to speak. However, swallow it, we must, because humanity as a whole simply cannot continue blaming their body or others for any adverse conditions or that somehow, unbeknownst to them, one day a serious nonphysical and/or physical illness just happened to show up in their life. *No, it didn't—we certainly had a hand in creating it!*

As in any play or movie, everyone involved has a role to play; life is no different. Mankind also has a major role to play when it comes to the condition of their health, well-being, prosperity, lack, or comfort and happiness. Accept this or reject it; however, this is a fact and should not be ignored. If you doubt this, then spend a little time to take personal inventory of yourself:

- Are you always unhappy, blaming others for your circumstances and/or situation?
- Do you drink alcohol in excess?
- Do you take illegal drugs or prescription drugs in excess?
- Do you take unnecessary risks?
- Do you test the hand of fate?
- Are you always full of stress, anxiety, and experience related emotional states?
- Have you developed any or several nonphysical illnesses previously listed?

There is no one or nothing to blame, other than ourselves, for attracting and developing illnesses and/or undesirable events or, on the other hand, having prosperous conditions on every level. Furthermore, understand that only you can prevent nonphysical conditions from progressing into serious physical illnesses that can escalate into even greater catastrophic illnesses.

For those who do wish to learn how I and others escaped certain death and were able to surmount what it was that threatened our lives, we first decided to take personal responsibility for any serious life-changing illnesses and events. We chose to rely upon a much greater intelligence that led us to the answers, methods, and solutions needed to overcome and to prevent any further serious physical and/or nonphysical conditions, adversities, or events from violating and disrupting our lives again.

Some people may find some of this information difficult to accept and digest. This is completely understandable, especially if they have not had any serious life-changing adversities thus far. The primary reason why this may apply to some people is, because since early childhood, many of us were programmed to accept this as fact and to believe all, if not most, of what we had heard and learned from others that led us to accept is fact. In turn, we passed these very same teachings on to our offspring and they to theirs, and therefore, the never-ending cycle of misguided information goes on.

The end result of all this confusion and misinformation for many people inevitably led to reliance on medically prescribed drugs that have put countless members of society everywhere unable to function on their own without having to rely upon these pharmaceutically produced crutches. These artificial crutches, as I prefer to call them, ultimately spawned an entire industry which has and continues to capitalize on the millions of prescription drug–dependent victims worldwide who have given into prescription and nonprescription drugs, not to mention alternative and over-the-counter medications.

I am aware that this statement may provoke a furor from people who are either connected with or rely upon their income from the manufacture, production, marketing, and distribution of prescription and nonprescription drugs who will find every inch of self-serving justification to support their cause. And why not? Because the prescription, nonprescription (over the counter), and illegal drug industries generates billions of dollars in income a year.

No, this is not an attack on pharmaceutical corporations worldwide; instead, this is an observation of the continued utilization and dependence on "temporary fix, feel-good" drugs, which masks many symptoms people may be having but, rarely—if ever—produce a complete, nonrecurring cure. Certainly, there are prescription drugs that perform well for various serious illnesses; however, rarely—if ever—does any prescription drug alone permanently cure serious physical illnesses. The only source that can do this can be found within each and every one of us, the wise and knowing inner mind.

I have no quarrel with legally prescribed medications that serve and helped humanity and many around the world when treating serious illnesses and other ailments and, through continued extensive research, may possibly help many more worldwide with relief from pain, other conditions, and related symptoms. However, these are only temporary fixes and do not claim to be the answer to a permanent cure of any illness, especially those that are life devastating. However, for the treatment of nonphysical illnesses, there seems to be every type of drug to handle every type of nonphysical condition known to man. Many of these can now be easily purchased, either over the counter or found on practically every corner in every city, thereby creating false hope leading people to believe they could not get these cures without "artificial assistance."

While we are on this subject, let's also not overlook the massive amount of reading materials, books, psychological publications and articles, and products sold over the internet available to those who will pay the asking price for this information. Let's not forget the products that are read or used, whatever they may be, once or twice, which may make the user feel good for about a day or possibly a week but then regresses back into the nonphysical condition(s) for which they were desperately seeking a quick fix.

As if this were not enough, add Ouija boards, self-help remedies, astrological signs, horoscopes, miracle healers, palm readers, psychics, séances, disciplines such as deep meditation, and self-proclaimed religious mind/body healers. Let us not forget the high end obscenely expensive rehabilitation retreats frequented by the famous and financially wealthy people who, despite their wealth, cannot seem to find any lasting relief from self-induced nonphysical illnesses. There is an astronomically vast industry out there that literally preys on millions who suffer from their self-induced nonphysical illnesses. This includes people like me who, at one time, had also bought into some of these cleverly crafted remedies that rarely produce any significant or permanent results and later inevitably only lead to the manifestation of potentially fatal illnesses.

If you are not ready, prepared, or willing to allow yourself to open your mind wide enough without permitting it to continually retreat to its ego's gatekeeper's habitual naysaying and self-induced doubting conditioning, then I recommend that you should not, at this time, read any further. Place this book on your bookshelf until you do feel you are ready to handle the truth about your self-induced illnesses. Yes, I said "self-induced illnesses." No typo here.

However, if you consider yourself to be among those who are willing to be honest with themselves and willing to be objective and take the time to absorb what I and many others have come to discover—that includes whatever good you wish to experience—you can, if you choose to, discover the immense power you carry within you, that once activated—or, for many people, reactivated—will reveal itself to you. I did, as have others who have surmounted various serious life-changing episodes, and can also work for you just as well, once you decide to make a personal commitment to clear your mind and free it of the useless clutter that presently occupies it. Having done this, without doubting or wavering, you then can, over time, begin to benefit from a life filled with improved health, prosperity on every conceivable level, and happiness, among much more that came with you at birth.

I realize that there has been some redundancy up to this point, which you will also find throughout this book; however, this has been done intentionally in order to focus these and other important points deep into your conscious mind and all-knowing inner mind. The methods you will find in this book are the key to my having personally witnessed the manifestation of all the good I desired to be reflected in my physical life, which is also for the advantage of anyone who chooses to believe that they can.

It is important you understand that among the powerful methods I found to be able to overcome all that I have I write about in this book requires another very important ingredient—*taking action*, also known as *taking the initiative*, without which no one could possibly be able to possess most, if any, of what they truly desire.

3

Taking the Initiative

> Although the world is full of suffering
> it is also full of overcoming it.
>
> —Helen Keller

If you are not totally satisfied with your life as it is at the present moment, it is more than likely due to your lack of initiative. Most of us will wait until a situation or circumstance reaches critical mass before we even begin to give it any serious personal attention. This inaction alone inevitably can, and very well may, lead to an eventual critical event, which, when allowed to continue, can also lead to a critically devastating event that may lead to the end of life as one knows it, if not attended to. I can tell you from my own experience that anyone who refuses to take the initiative concerning whatever undesirable situation they may be enduring and allows any serious condition to continue to escalate without taking action to either curtail and/or arrest its advances is setting themselves up to becoming a person who lives in an almost vegetative or robotic state, if unable to escape from these conditions. Therefore, they're just finding themselves going through the remainder of their lives developing one or more of these undesirable conditions with no hope of escaping their self-made cage.

I've spoken with people who truly believed that they could literally meditate and/or pray their way out of any undesirable conditions. However, by way of my observations, neither meditation nor prayer can possibly have any effect on whatever matter, unless followed by taking the initiative toward ridding oneself from any undesirable adversity, situation, illness, condition, circumstance, etc. As defined by *Merriam-Webster*, *prayer* is "an earnest request or wish; something prayed for." However, prayer, without *action*, is futile at best. If you are presently concerned with any damaging condition and have not yet taken the initiative, then what that means is that whatever the undesirable situation or circumstance may not be important enough to you to rid yourself of it now, is it?

This may be why you chose to pick up this book, and if you did, you certainly made the right choice. I can think of no one who can help you with whatever undesirable condition, circumstance, or undesirable situation that you may be subjected to than someone who has already been there and had a great deal of experience with serious, adverse conditions, circumstances, situations, and other life-changing events, including serious life-threatening illnesses.

By the mere fact that I am still here and am in very good health today, I am more than certain that the methods and answers I received from the power and wisdom of my inner mind worked for me and continue to do so. They can also work for you and/or someone you care about, if you choose to seriously consider utilizing anything you find in this book you deem may be helpful to you. Keep in mind, however, to never abandon sound credible medical advice in conjunction with anything you may decide to personally choose to utilize from this book that you may find benefits you.

It is imperative that you understand and to never lose sight of the fact that it is your inaction that fails to produce the desirable results you are seeking to bring into reality. It is the initiative you choose to take instead, which is your own personal action, which will produce the desired results you are seeking—this point cannot be expressed enough or overlooked. You certainly have the prerogative to ponder what you want as the desired outcome concerning your problems; however, your life will not change one iota if you are subjected to or wish to attract an undesirable nonphysical illness, unless and until you choose to take the initiative necessary to be able to realize what you are seeking—be it a return to better health and/or prosperity on every conceivable level. *Prosperity*, as defined by *Merriam-Webster*, is the *"state of flourishing, thriving, good fortune and/or successful social status."* Per Wikipedia, prosperity "often encompasses wealth, but also includes other factors which are independent of wealth to varying degrees, such as happiness and health."

You should consider this: You have been taking the initiative and action all your life, and if you do not recognize that, that reality may never come true! Therefore, should this be the case with you, begin now—not tomorrow, next week, next month, or next year—to take the right initiative and action to bring about what you truly want. You will be pleasantly surprised how your life can change for the better and in the direction you want it to continue. However, keep in mind, prosperity does not end at a certain level; instead, it reaches as far as one desires it to reach. The key is to stop talking and begin taking the initiative and action to bring forth the results you do want. Aren't you getting tired of not getting to achieve what you truly desire for good and just settling for where you are?

The truth of the matter is that what you habitually expend all your energy and focused thoughts on every day is what becomes reality. Just examine one month of your everyday activities and keep track of where your energy is going toward and what you predominantly focus on. Then and only then will you finally begin to realize the truth of what I am saying to you here. In other words, you prove to yourself every waking moment precisely what you have chosen to emphasize and where you choose to expend your energy on most. In addition, most people will rarely accept the fact that it is themselves who cause their experiences to be exactly what they are. Accept it or reject it—this is a true fact.

As I've alluded to previously, I am often asked the question *How do you know all this?* I begin my answer with, "If you are going to listen to anyone about adversities, you should consider listening to someone who has already personally experienced numerous adversities and overcame them all." Because as a survivor of all that I have, in my opinion, there can be no better information concerning overcoming serious adverse conditions than that from people who have personally gone through that gauntlet, so to speak. Therefore, my response is always the same—"I speak and write from my personal knowledge and experience and not from something I read or heard somewhere."

It is important to realize that almost everyone's reality is hard, and some are even much more difficult than others. Sooner or later, everyone comes face to face with hardships, as not one living soul will ever be immune to the difficulties and hardships that life will undoubtedly mete out. Even the very wealthy and prosperous are not immune; their hardships are simply just on a different level but hardships just the same.

I am sharing with you what I personally encountered concerning life-changing illnesses and other serious life-challenging events and not from what I learned from the myriad of books out there that offer information pertaining to overcoming and surviving challenges. I am revealing my personal information to you in order that you and others will not have to go through what I have and/or to continue to have to deal with any undesirable occurrences. I trust that you and others can benefit immensely from what I have chosen to share with you.

What I have learned thus far is that the greater part of our lives is all about deciding what it is that is important to us and what we truly desire for good. Once that is ascertained and etched in your mind, it is necessary to then learn how to manifest these desires.

Let me ask you this: When will you finally decide to rid yourself of undesirable situations and circumstances and make the decision to change them? I ask this question because life waits for no one. As I already identified, most people will wait until undesirable conditions they may be exposed to reach critical mass before deciding to take the initiative, which begins the process of eliminating them from their reality permanently. How often have you personally witnessed adverse conditions in the lives of others you know? When and where did they decide to draw the line to begin ridding themselves of these unwanted situations? And for that matter, ask yourself the same question about your life.

What I have noticed through my contact with serious adversities is that the majority of people I've observed simply do not have a clue what is important to them. Many will tell me that they do, yet watching what they do as seriously contradicts what they say when it comes to taking the initiative and necessary action necessary to affect much-needed change in their lives. This means having the required action to bring forth the desired result for good and not evil and not relying on others for what you desire for your benefit; instead, rely on yourself. As my father once told me when I was a young boy, "If you want something done, it's best to rely on yourself if you expect to achieve it," and he was so right! That is precisely what I did; and by doing so, I overcame each and every adverse situation, condition, and event that ever afflicted me. I succeeded in obtaining everything I ever wanted for good, and to this point, I continue to do so. So can you.

Once again, what I have been saying over and over again is this: It is you—and only *you*—who can lift yourself out of any undesirable situation, circumstance, and related event, physical and/or nonphysical. If you will make the decision to take the initiative and take the appropriate action when it comes to how your life is going to go on from here and consider employing supportive methods and reconnecting with this inward sense of knowing all that there is to know, you just may find that your life can change dramatically and just how you envisioned it to be.

Among some of these situations and circumstances that have become a very serious matter are the continuing downward spiral of homeownership and the economic situation in this country that have and continue to cause many people hardships. However, taking the initiative and appropriate action and taking into consideration the methods that can be used in seeking the answers and solutions from the all-powerful and all-knowing intelligence available to us victims of this ongoing economic crisis and other serious disruptive events can be led to the solutions to turning our situation around and returning to having a prosperous lifestyle on every conceivable level once again.

I know this for a fact because I did it; and if I could, so can anyone else, as I have no greater advantage over anyone other than having been and continuing to be armed with the answers and the methods contained in these pages and taking full advantage of the knowledge that is obtained through my inner mind that is connected to an all-knowing, infinite intelligence. There absolutely is no greater weapon available that can be conceived by mankind than the inner mind to overcome any adversity anyone may face in their lifetime.

PREVAILING OVER INSURMOUNTABLE ODDS

Considering my own acquaintance and personal experience with these methods, I am a grateful beneficiary of the answers and the results I derive from this all-knowing force.

Realize that the importance of what you are now either discovering for the first time or are rediscovering cannot be expressed in mere words alone; however, just know and completely trust in the power and wisdom of the inner mind that is one with an unseen all-knowing force and that, without any doubt whatsoever, this all-knowing force can be communicated with in a very unique way, which you are soon about to learn. Therefore, anything and everything you desire can be attained when you decide to make a firm, unwavering decision with complete expectation and believe it can. You need only to believe it and then put what you believe into action in your own life, and once you do, allowing patience and time to work for you, you will have the confidence that, what you so firmly desire for good, can be manifested in your own endeavors.

This world is overflowing with people who have lived lives of quiet desperation and have withstood some of the most unthinkable and most undesirable conditions and circumstances, yet they persevered and overcame each and every adversity that challenged them and went on to become some of the most memorable and successful people in the world despite their overwhelming life challenges. Most had little, if any, formal educational opportunities or access to the medical advances humanity has available to them today.

Many of those who overcame life-altering challenges and difficult obstacles and barriers placed before them, despite the lack of having available to them all the modern tools and opportunities that we have available to us today went far beyond anyone's expectations despite it all because of their strong beliefs in what you are either beginning to discover for the first time or are rediscovering. Their efforts resulted in the countless conveniences mankind enjoys today—e.g., art, architecture and construction technologies, music, the vehicles we drive, medicines, medical scientific discoveries, surgical procedures, and other technology. They contributed a great number of discoveries that mankind is privileged to have and has improved, expanded upon, and made available to all today because of those who persevered, took action, and overcame many life-challenging obstacles.

Even today people who face even greater obstacles and challenges have overcome serious illnesses, drug habits, the ghettos and barrios around the world, unspeakable conditions, extreme poverty, racial inequity, or serious medical issues such as having missing limbs due to accidents or such injuries as a result of being in combat situations who went on to become some of the most well-known performing artists, lawyers, doctors, nurses, college graduates, composers, actors, sports figures, etc. Therefore, there should be no reason you cannot achieve anything you have a burning desire to obtain, whether it be the return to good health to accomplishing anything you set your intentions on with your inner power leading you to the methods, answers, and solutions necessary to possess whatever it may be that you seek for your good and for the good of everyone concerned.

An excellent real-life example of what I am saying here is the story of a man who had two prosthetic legs who on May 15, 2006, conquered Mt. Everest. After forty days of climbing, Mark Inglis became the first ever double amputee to reach the summit of Mt. Everest, the tallest mountain in the world. While acclimatizing at 6,400 meters (21,000 ft.), a fixed-line anchor failed, resulting in Mark Inglis falling and breaking one of his carbon-fiber prosthetic legs in half. It was temporarily repaired with duct tape, while a spare was brought up from base camp. Inglis's Everest expedition was filmed for the Discovery Channel series *Everest: Beyond the Limit* (Wikipedia).

You can believe that willpower alone could never have accomplished this phenomenal feat. However, like other conquerors of unfathomable feats, it is inconceivable—in this survivor's opinion. Although willpower played a role in their success, they never could have accomplished these feats without having called upon a much deeper inner power that revealed to them the methods, answers, and solutions needed to attain all they had set out to do, along with taking the initiative and action necessary to have overcome such incredible life challenges.

Many people throughout the world have overcome some of life's most horrendous conditions and have gone on to live remarkable and prosperous lives on every level, and still others have even beat all the odds against them and have come from near-death outcomes back to full recovery and living normal lives today. Therefore, I firmly believe that with your personal connection to this inner intelligence, you too can accomplish even more—much more.

This said, knowing the mission I had been led to, I chose to take the initiative and action, coupled with deep passion and conviction to reveal what I am absolutely convinced to be the root causes (refer to list in chapter 1) of every negative and undesirable event that can, over time, lead to physical illnesses and any other life-threatening circumstance. Also, to identify the methods, answers, and solutions, I was led to what brought me all I needed to know in order to overcome not only cancer but other serious life-changing circumstances, events, and numerous nonphysical conditions, without which, I am certain, I would not have been able to surmount all that I have.

Prior to this period of time, so many negative situations occurred, and I had always been proud of myself for being a very healthy person—well, at least, I believed I was! I exercised regularly, watched what I consumed, and did not put any drugs or alcohol into my body. Being very aware that both my parents had succumbed to two different types of cancers, leukemia and pancreatic, I was determined not to attract or pass away from any form of cancer. Of course, at the time, I believed that cancer would not invade my body and that I was invincible. How wrong I was!

Four years after my mother was diagnosed and passed away from pancreatic cancer, I was diagnosed with advanced colon cancer and, eight months thereafter, diagnosed with liver cancer that was also diagnosed to be advanced. Little did I realize at the time that I had attracted this cancer into my life via my hectic lifestyle—a.k.a., being a workaholic—and the nonhereditary root causes, as some medical people might suggest.

As a result of these circumstances, I spent countless hours scouring the internet and bookstores everywhere, seeking the initial causes of every single negative event and life-threatening illness that came into my life. However, much to my regret, I could not find many, especially those written by survivors of serious life-threatening events or illnesses or even the medical profession that even came close to what I believed were the initiators of these damaging events, both physical and nonphysical. That was until I began to realize that many books written dating back to the early 1800s did identify these root causes of serious illness and related ailments and adversities which, over time, culminate into serious physical conditions and even death.

Therefore, becoming even more passionate and vigilant about the root causes of these negative events in my life, I chose to overlook the naysayers and scoffers of this world and to boldly go beyond just being a comforter for all those who were ill with any form or stage of cancer. Instead, I choose to share how one can recognize the beginning signs of a serious, physical life-threatening situation, like I did, and the possible cause of any adversity they may be enduring. It was my reconnection with my inner mind, connected with the all-knowing, infinite intelligence, that revealed these predators to me and that began leading me to bring to the attention of everyone and anyone who is seriously interested about knowing why these root causes threaten our very lives every single day and what I did to ensure not only myself but—through this book, *now*—others that they should never again have to be threatened by nonphysical predators.

I found it very interesting and curious that over the years of researching the subject of potentially critical illnesses and other undesirable events, circumstances, and conditions people develop and having spoken with persons everywhere about their reaction to these events and conditions that affect so many lives, among the material written on the subjects of cancer, mental health problems, and other life-threatening illnesses—the majority were not written by actual survivors of life-threatening illnesses, physical or nonphysical. Survivors apparently rarely took the initiative or put forth the effort necessary to share with their fellow human beings what it was they had done to bring forth what they did pertaining to overcoming physical life-threatening and other grave nonphysical illnesses, conditions, and events.

Although I certainly do respect the authors who have written books and other materials about cancer, mental illnesses, diseases, and other devastating illnesses and events in an effort to help mankind, most of these publications were written by people and medical professionals who themselves had not personally experienced a severe illness. The majority of these publications are mostly about prevention and what to do after one has sustained a potentially fatal or grave nonphysical event. Furthermore, these materials rarely identify to the reader what the catalysts were that brought these into their life to begin with. Instead, they speak about medical opinions, ranging from hereditary to environmental causes, which I suspect may possibly have helped contribute to such negative events and illnesses.

Certainly, they are not necessarily the initial causes of why they manifested in one's life in the first place. In other words, the subject of what I call root causes was rarely mentioned—if at all. Yet the methods of medical treatments for serious illnesses, nonphysical and physical alike, were everywhere and were the primary topics. I compare this to be akin to closing the stable doors long after all the horses had escaped.

On countless occasions, I had been asked, "What exactly do you mean by you *'attracted* cancer into your life'?" What I mean is that cancer, like every other serious illness, can be one result of the actual root causes leading to a life-threatening illness. *Merriam-Webster* defines the words *root* and *cause* as "something that is an origin or source" and "something that brings about an effect or a result" respectively. I truly believe and am thoroughly convinced that nonphysical conditions that are allowed to continue, more often than not, precede a physical life-threatening illness.

I can just hear you saying "What does he mean by 'nonphysical life-threatening illnesses' when no such illnesses exist?" Well, you're not alone. Trust me. I used to think exactly the very same way. I once believed that a life-threatening event was only a physical disease. That was, of course, until I woke up one day and realized that I was "self-victimized," which now may lead you having to ask what is meant by being "self-victimized." What I mean is that *we*—all of us—attract everything that comes into our physical lives, be it a disease; an undesirable, negative event; and even an early departure from our physical bodies, all caused by our very own creation and choices. We are the captains of our own ships who choose what we develop in our lives, not anyone or anything else, whether you choose to accept this or not.

That said, instead of expanding upon the details of what I was going through when experiencing two cancer events, as you can see, I chose instead to focus upon what I discovered to be the root causes of every type of nonphysical illness such as mental, nervous breakdown, major trauma, stress, anxiety, depression, and other negative events. The initiating factor of these root causes is none other than *you* and *me*! Mind you, I've been saying *root causes* of nonphysical illnesses which can eventually lead to serious physical life-threatening illnesses that rarely have anything to do with genetics, bad luck, or other related causes. Of course, I expect to be challenged on this premise; however, there are many publications, psychological and other qualified opinions, that recognize and depict many of these root causes to be among the leading catalysts of many physical ailments.

The reason I have chosen to focus on these root causes is to emphasize to you the importance of taking the initiative and ridding yourself of any of them that you may now be able to recognize that may be disrupting your life and could very well be the beginning of serious physical illnesses that may develop.

Having now identified to you my vision, my purpose is to bring this to the attention of not only those who presently have a critical illness or are experiencing any serious life-changing event but to everyone who has yet to have any serious physical and/or nonphysical disorders as well. Among the reasons why most people hardly pay any attention to the root causes of physical life-threatening illnesses, which they themselves are cocreators, is that they disregard that they possibly are creating a root cause that, when allowed to escalate, can lead to a serious physical or nonphysical life-threatening condition simultaneously like I had.

You may possibly be saying to yourself, "I never knew any of this at all previously." Yes, you did! We all did because we all have intuitive sensations (gut feelings). However, the greater majority of people elect to ignore them and instead place them and the symptoms that accompany them, the root causes being revealed, on the back burner, until a real-life personal crisis shows up one day.

PREVAILING OVER INSURMOUNTABLE ODDS

Let me pose this question to you: Where do you think your intuition comes from? It certainly does not come from the grey mass housed inside of your skull. Therefore, it must come from what everyone—well, *almost* everyone—knows and has identified in different languages throughout the world as one's intuitive inner feelings, which in reality is your all-knowing inner mind that is continuously attempting to communicate with you. Quite unfortunately, people choose to ignore every attempt by their inner mind to forewarn them of any pending danger approaching their lives, and later they find that they are sorry that they did.

Psychiatrists, psychologists, medical doctors, and counselors of all types are said to be noticing huge increases in people seeking counseling for all sorts of problems and issues. The causes are increasing divorce rates; entire families falling apart due to economic issues; people losing total control and committing violent acts against others; and others murder their entire families and, in some cases, even themselves. And there appears to be no relief of these causes through conventional remedies for those who are subjected to these senseless acts and conditions.

Among the brief list of nonphysical illnesses and/or conditions I provided earlier in chapter 1, I would be absolutely amazed if you could not find yourself or someone you know well to either have at least one or two of these conditions. If not, consider yourself one of the rare fortunate few who hasn't and continues on with whatever it is that may be working for you. Drop to your knees and give thanks to whatever you believe in that has shielded you thus far from ever having any one of these very serious nonphysical illnesses and/or conditions. Then please be kind enough to share whatever it is you have found to work for you with your fellow men. If you choose to do this, in time, you will reap the benefit of your benevolence; you can take that to the bank, so to speak.

You're probably asking yourself what is so significant about negative emotions and how any of these could possibly manifest into a serious, physical life-damaging illness. If by chance you may have been asking yourself this question, believe it or not, those that I listed in the chart of root causes are only a few of the well-armed soldiers in the vast army of conditions that can and often do escalate into serious illnesses of every form and type.

It is possible that those who have a number of these nonphysical illnesses/conditions outlined earlier and are carrying these around with them every day are unable to rid themselves from these issues, no matter how much they try. Others who do not come to soon recognize they have been harboring any one of these conditions for a period of time may possibly now decide to take the initiative to seek out qualified professional help, in conjunction with whatever they may learn in this book that they believe may also help them. If not, possibly one day, they develop a serious physical illness.

Too many people rarely realize that they are deeply affected by a nonphysical illness/condition until, it manifests into a physical life-threatening illness. Medication, as I identified earlier, will only mask these conditions for a while; however, they can return through their continued invitation.

I have heard people say that their life-threatening illness was God's will for them. Obviously, their blatant distortion of the fact that a much higher intelligence than mankind is responsible for any negative event or life-changing illness is delusional at best. This type of blaming is not only naive and irresponsible; it is being in a state of chronic denial, which is another very serious nonphysical illness.

Whether we choose to call this higher intelligence God, Buddha, the Tao, the universe, one's higher power, etc., is irrelevant. What is relevant is that it is absurd to lay blame on any unseen higher power for our individual life's circumstances as we—individually and collectively as a species occupy and share space on this planet with the animals, plants, mountain ranges, and vast oceans—are the pilots of our separate and collective lives having free will and the ability to make choices. Therefore, we personally are responsible for whatever we create, attract, and lack by not taking the initiative to avoid or overcome such conditions in our lives.

Know that each and every person who has preceded us and the generations that follow had and will also have attracted and created everything and anything that materializes in their lives, be good or bad, period. Accept it, deal with it, and know it to be true; as there is absolutely no proof that any unseen intelligence has or will

PREVAILING OVER INSURMOUNTABLE ODDS

have anything to do with what mankind individually, collectively as a nation and the entire world, chooses to experience because all humankind was conceived with *free will* to choose their direction and path and to take the initiative necessary to actualize whatever good they seek for their lives.

I am convinced that we were all born with the ability to know everything we would ever need to know and the ability to make our own life choices. What we choose to do concerning our very own lives, individually and/or collectively is of course up to each of us and every nation. I am further convinced that I personally was responsible for having invited and ultimately attracting each and every life-threatening illness, physical and nonphysical, into my life. For me to lay blame on anything or anyone for whatever adverse conditions I have suffered in my life related to illnesses and negative events would be grossly irresponsible of me and also would be just as careless for others.

You will find that by the rediscovery of this creative intelligence, you have the power of influencing, both positively or negatively, and may be relearning how to tap into your awareness of its remarkable powers that can benefit not only you but others as well. Therefore, once you begin to recognize its remarkable power, taking the appropriate action and your willingness to reach out to help others to also discover it for the first time will become a blessing in disguise for you; and you shall find that this sharing with others will enhance your life even more than you could ever possibly imagine. No matter how wealthy or poor you may be, once you activate and/or reactivate this vital gift, your life should be enriched more than you could possibly ever have imagined.

If your curiosity has been aroused thus far about what one survivor of numerous life-threatening ailments, physical and nonphysical, did to overcome them against insurmountable odds—including conquering even greater trauma, coupled with serious physical events I was subjected to that may have caused most people to break down mentally and/or possibly never recover—then I believe you may even be more intrigued as you continue to explore the information in this book.

That said, you or anyone should never have to ask the question *Why me?* If you find yourself asking this question, you should be asking yourself instead—no matter your circumstance, situation, or life-changing challenge—*Why not me?*

Let's explore this important self-examining question people refrain from asking themselves when faced with a serious life-changing situation and what it really means to us.

4

WHY NOT YOU?

> You can do as much as you think you can,
> But you'll never accomplish more;
> If you're afraid of yourself, young man,
> There's little for you in store.
> For failure comes from the inside first,
> It's there if we only knew it,
> And you can win, though you face the worst,
> If you feel that you're going to do it.
>
> —Edgar A. Guest

As a person who has overcome very serious physical and nonphysical life illnesses and other adversities and events and who has cheated death more than once, I continue to challenge people who are dealing with life-changing adversities on any level, whether they are physical or otherwise, with the question *Why not you?*

One of the things that I could not help noticing when speaking to people who were dealing with undesirable events in their lives was that many were knee deep into what I call the "self-help publications syndrome."

I am very much aware of the myriad of self-help materials that have flooded the bookshelves of bookstores, libraries, the internet, and other sources for decades with information to help them bring forth the remarkable turnaround they need to succeed on every conceivable level. These self-help material describe aids for recovery from physical conditions, circumstances, situations, and related events people encounter. Many these endorse positive thinking to be one of the key remedies to overcoming numerous related conditions.

Having read several hundred of these types of books and related materials over the years, I can tell you from my own personal research, what I found from reading these books and related information was that the majority of the authors of these publications themselves rarely, if at all, had personally experienced the conditions they were writing about. If they actually had gone through deprivation, poverty, failures, loss, trauma, pain, illnesses, anxiety, fear, and other traumatic emotions and situations that accompany what they were depicting and advising about obtaining relief, it would have been very helpful to the reader to learn of their personal circumstances and how they managed to overcome them. On the other hand, to be fair, I do believe that the majority of the authors of these publications were making an honest and sincere attempt to reach out to others in an effort to assist them deal with whatever they were facing or to help them reach certain life goals and aspirations. In this regard, I found a number of these publications to be somewhat helpful.

The reality here is that there simply are no overnight remedies or cures to achieve prosperity on every level of one's life or for any adverse condition. Why? Because deprivation and serious illnesses, nonphysical or physical in nature, do not just show up one day in your life but instead took time to develop.

However, if you are serious, determined, and willing to be fully committed to change your life for the better, there should be absolutely no reason that you cannot achieve every level of prosperity you desire to acquire or overcome any adverse condition.

If then you are serious about obtaining prosperity on every conceivable level or ridding yourself of or avoiding any adverse or undesirable life-changing event or any of the conditions listed in this book earlier, whichever may be the case in your life, know that there are many people who have achieved success and very real life survivors of serious adversities and related conditions who are alive and well today, having acquired their heartfelt desires. Therefore, in my opinion, as a person who achieved prosperity on every level I chose to experience and who is also a survivor of numerous life-threatening episodes, it may serve you well to seriously consider reading any books and related materials these achievers and survivors have published. Whenever possible, attend speaking engagements offered by those whose experiences may be similar to what you want to accomplish. By doing so, you could be exposed to a wealth of very helpful and useful information because if these people—and I—have accomplished all that we have related to success or the overcoming of adverse situations, there should be absolutely no reason whatsoever that you cannot as well.

Ponder this: If you were seriously contemplating climbing Mt. Everest, certainly you would not rely solely upon a survivor's instruction manual, would you? The point is that you would need a seasoned guide who has climbed this mountain a number of times before, who has vast skills on surviving such an undertaking, and who has guided many others before you to successfully overcome this challenge. This should be your logical choice. If not, your chances of survival could be likened to your chances of finding a rare diamond among the ever-shifting position of sand dunes in a desert.

Concerning life-threatening illnesses, can anyone who overcame any stage of a terminal condition, event, or serious illness guarantee you that what they did to overcome their problems would achieve the same results for you? Like the example just given about the mountain guide, there could be no guarantee you would emerge successfully from your challenging climb to the top of Mt. Everest, even with an experienced guide. Therefore, the answer to this question is *absolutely not*.

That said, there have been countless people throughout the world who have conquered numerous life-changing challenges who made it to the top and back of their menacing personal mountain—figuratively speaking—as well as those who have overcome catastrophic incidents and who today are leading normal lives and have moved on.

History is full of true-life stories about people achieving whatever goals they had established for themselves, including many nonphysical life-changing circumstances, events, and illnesses against incredible odds of survival, despite being told they would never surmount those odds. Yet they emerged victorious from those situations and, again, myself included.

Imagine for a moment that none of the modern-day medical and scientific breakthroughs would have ever been possible, had those who brought them about were told "it could not be done" and had heeded all the doubters', naysayers', and critics' negative opinions. Had they listened to these scoffers and pessimists, there more than likely would be many more people meeting their early demise.

On numerous occasions, I had been in hospitals and rehabilitation facilities visiting people, both prior to and after having gone through my cancer experiences, and witnessed people who passed on from a certain illness, while others who were in graver conditions experiencing the same illnesses fully recovered and were able to walk out of the hospital and/or care facility with little assistance.

Then there were people in my extended family who were admitted to a care facility (a nonhospital environment) for convalescing, scheduled to be there for a brief period, and in no less than several months had convinced themselves that their conditions were not going to get better. Shortly thereafter, they passed away, aided by the continuance of their very own negative thoughts and attitudes and uttering words like "I do not want to live any longer" and "I will only get any worse." They literally just gave up on themselves and life and instructed their inner mind to end their physical life as opposed to *commanding* it to overcome whatever it may have been that had been threatening their very existence.

There are people from all walks of life I learned about who overcame advanced stages of a variety of very serious illnesses. Others with similar conditions expressed deep depression, fear, and manifested some stages of a mental condition; and thus their illness worsened. I also personally witnessed paralyzed people get out of their wheelchairs and actually walk and never have to get back into suffering again.

Then there are the stories of incredible healings at Lourdes, France, and other well-known shrines; and in a short period of time, people find their life change in a very positive direction. I also learned about why the Mormons so deeply relied upon the teaching and writings of a man named Joseph Smith. In Hawaii, people worshipped what was known to be the Great Kahuna who supposedly had remarkable powers over one's life. Then there were the Indians in South America whose shamans were able to perform what was said to be miracle healings on their tribespeople. These stories go on and on.

Having seen many healings deemed to be miracles, I found that the reason and difference between people who died and others with similar ailments, conditions, etc., is that the latter did not employ the method of strong belief that they would overcome whatever it was ailing them. This strong belief, coupled with the methods of having a strong will to overcome; consistent deep thoughts of wellness, steadfast self-trust, and unshakeable self-confidence; and unwavering expectation, among other methods, were employed to achieve their self-healing. Therefore, learning from those who survived, never give any of these damaging conditions any power (another effective method) and believe and know deep within you that there is absolutely nothing you could not overcome or accomplish. These methods, alone and collectively, are extremely powerful and are just some of the methods I myself utilized to overcome all that I have.

The difference between those who choose to overcome a serious life-changing situation and those who fail to do so lies within the belief in the power of one's inner mind, coupled with the infinite intelligence. Allied with strong belief, strong will, deep continuous thoughts of wellness, and the methods you will continue to discover throughout this book, you can formulate an extremely impenetrable, unshakeable bond that allows you to be able to overcome any obstacle and any adverse life-changing events and illnesses placed in your life. This is also the answer to accomplishing practically every personal goal you have for yourselves.

You may possibly be asking yourself, "What has all this to do with life-threatening illnesses and the nonphysical conditions listed in this book?" *Everything!*

In this survivor's opinion and observation, without the source of it all—the so-called infinite intelligence, from which comes the inner healing power, methods, answers, and solutions—it would be virtually inconceivable that one would overcome most potentially harmful illnesses for any extended period of time without reliance upon the inner healing power that comes from this unseen infinite source. I will even go as far to say that absolutely nothing of major significance could be accomplished related to what I am identifying here without the aid of one's extremely all-powerful inner mind that only *you* can control that can even reverse a grave illness and any other serious life-changing circumstance or event(s). I am only one among many who are living proof of its incredible capability.

History provides us with remarkable accomplishments that are referred to as miracles, as do the incredible stories of people surviving very serious illnesses and events of every type. These include incredible near-death experiences people would never have been able to overcome without the intervention of the unseen force.

I have had several people state to me that most medical recoveries and other stories of incredible survival they acknowledged were just mere good fortune and luck. Believe me—neither good fortune nor luck had anything to do with it. Neither do magic, the so-called occult, voodoo, witchcraft, mediums, or the like.

Over the past several years, I had been pleasantly surprised to have learned that medical science is finally beginning to seriously consider that there must be some truth to this inner power, having been referred to by ancient civilizations as one of the most guarded secrets by the rulers of these civilizations.

I truly believe that you and countless others who want to learn more about the incredible abilities of one's inner power and to be able to prove that it is not only everything it is said to be but more powerful and realer than anyone can possibly imagine. However, your inner power can never be known unless and until you choose to begin to place your total confidence and trust in it. Being one with infinite intelligence, which is far beyond mankind's comprehension, can bring forth every desire for good that you will ever seek to realize.

Let's face reality. As I previously pointed out, most people choose to place the greater majority—if not all—their confidence and trust in their medical doctor, people they know well, friends and family, medical science as a whole, legally prescribed medications, the opinions of others, etc. Yet more often than not, they rarely fail to place that very same level of confidence and trust in themselves, believing that they are unworthy of making major life-altering decisions for themselves.

It is important you clearly understand that only you can bring forth whatever good it is desire in your life, including complete healing, if you presently are experiencing or possibly may develop a serious life-disrupting condition in the future. This does not mean to imply that you do not listen to your medical professionals, religious leaders, etc.; what it means instead is that *you* yourself must play a major role in the recovery and healing process of any diagnosed illness or whatever it may be you are seeking to produce for good because no medical professional or anyone else can honestly profess that they are a healer or can bring forth your innermost desires. Few, if any, who are honest with you will rarely profess that they can. Therefore, *you* need to take complete charge of your healing.

Absolutely nothing can or should ever be ruled out of the realm of possibilities of survival, including any adverse life-changing event. If I and others have overcome insurmountable life-threatening illnesses and other serious life-changing events, why would anyone even believe they can't? No matter if it is a physical or a nonphysical life-challenging event—unless of course one's condition has already reached a point of becoming so critical and/or mentally incapacitated or has been institutionalized to the point that one cannot comprehend anything and/or are within moments from death.

If, however, a person is still able to think, is aware, can comprehend, understand, have deep feelings and emotions, and capable of believing and full of expectancy that one's life can be turned around, from my perspective, as a person who was given a very slim chance of surviving several very serious life-changing conditions, I cannot think of even one reason why anyone could not be the next person who will join the ranks of many who have overcome serious life-challenging and life-changing events, despite the odds against survival and the negative opinions and beliefs of others. This includes medical science's opinion to the contrary of the chances of obtaining a complete healing and/or eventual permanent cure from whatever a person may have been enduring or at some future point. This in itself should be a call to arms for those who may one day find themselves or someone they care about diagnosed with a serious life-threatening condition at any stage.

For decades, it has been determined by medical science that over time, emotional illnesses such as stress, anxiety, deep depression, feelings of hopelessness, loss of self-confidence, financial stress, and other related deeply imbedded emotional conditions when left unattended can and often lead to physical illnesses, if allowed to fester for a considerable length of time. Furthermore, if allowed to continue unattended by you, these conditions can possibly lead to a serious, physical life-threatening condition.

That said, it appears that many people who have one or more of these conditions truly believe that there is no other outlet available to them other than medical practitioners, psychological and psychiatric professionals, licensed counselors, and prescribed medications. These conditions, as I pointed out earlier, can become even more pronounced and aggravated when factoring in the present ongoing declining economic conditions that, according to economic specialists, may possibly be around for some time to come. These economic conditions, among others, are the reasons why people have to find a way to readjust to living an entirely different lifestyle than they previously would never have imagined before. I am not speaking of just people on the lower end of the economic scale but also people in the middle-class and upper-middle-class levels, including every profession and vocation and walk of life such as returning military forces, graduating high school and college students, and even millionaires and celebrities. The list is virtually endless.

In 1997, long before the present economic dilemma, I was involved with the beginning of similar problems and losses. These problems and losses at that point in time were not due to a declining economic condition (as the economy in this country was doing quite well then) but instead to grave illness and other life-changing events, a number of which were also very serious. (A list of these other life-changing events is provided in chapter 10.)

Historically speaking, having climbed the ladder from humble beginnings, a mediocre lifestyle, and working long hours for years to accomplish my dreams and goals, eventually, I reached my financial and other goals and achieved the lifestyle I had envisioned that I would one day enjoy. What I did not foresee, however, were the silent, unseen storms that were building inside me that eventually resulted in serious life-changing events that nearly cost me my life. So then, what was the lesson I learned from these circumstances?

Among the various lessons I learned, the one that stands out the most was the fact that by my continuing to ignore the earlier warning signs that kept appearing in my life, I actually believed that I was invincible. The resulting effects of this condition were the life-altering events that eventually manifested themselves into serious health issues. It was my refusal to heed the warning signs that brought me right to the front door of a living hell that I would not have even wished on my greatest foe, had I one.

Knowing my own body and also knowing that I was in excellent physical condition, I knew for a fact that the ever-increasing stress and anxiety I was developing in conjunction with other nonphysical conditions (refer to the "Root Causes" chart provided earlier), without any doubt in my mind, were the triggers I acquired from physical stress.

In addition, I had several medical doctors tell me that, based upon this intense degree of stress and anxiety related to my career and personal life at the time, they were surprised that I had not had a full-blown serious heart condition or a stroke much earlier. The condition that did eventually show up instead was cancer, accompanied by numerous serious nonphysical, life-changing conditions, if you can even imagine that.

When seeking to overcome or change any life-challenging event, it is important for you to realize that the solution and answer you seek can rarely be found in any one source in your outer world. Instead, to be able to find the answer to the *why not me?* question, the answers and solutions you seek can only come from deep within you. The results you realize begin and end with the methods of employing a strong will to succeed and overcome, unwavering belief, steadfast self-trust, unshakeable self-confidence, and expectation that all come from within, among other very important methods you shall find in the forthcoming chapters.

These and the other methods we will be looking at are among the keys for obtaining every answer and receiving the benefits you'll ever desire. It is the connecting and/or the reconnecting with your true unseen inner guide that is linked to infinite intelligence from which everything good you desire can eventually materialize in your physical life.

Unless you are willing to seriously accept that these methods are among the keys to your every desire for good, coupled with the related methods we shall explore, without any doubt whatsoever, from my perspective, you may possibly continue to suffer undesirable life-changing and life-challenging adversities. You may not get to experience the life you were truly meant to live for good from birth, and keep in mind that it is you and only you who control what you choose in this life and no one or nothing else.

It is not until you finally come to realize that unless you become closely aligned with your inner mind, your life will continue to be disconnected and incomplete. The void you are seeking to fill will always remain unfulfilled, and you will continue to seek what you may never find by relying solely upon artificial and temporary worldly remedies.

Whatever true gratification, joy, peace, prosperity, good health, etc., you may be seeking in your life, know that—as I pointed out—you will rarely find it in your outer physical world. If you believe that you can, know that whatever it is you are seeking for self-fulfillment resulting from your physical world is certain to have a limited life span, as the level of achieving overall prosperity is by way of your true source of total fulfillment. This is—and *will* forever remain—your connection to your all-knowing, all-powerful intelligence, coupled with a strong will to succeed and overcome, unwavering belief, steadfast self-trust, unshakeable self-confidence and expectation, and other methods contained within these pages; without which, all else can eventually lead to futility, loss, and a return to the void you were attempting to fill from outer sources.

As you may possibly be aware, there is more than sufficient documented medical evidence and other proof and records that people do survive serious illnesses, adversities, situations, and circumstances, as well as those diagnosed with terminal illnesses, that were deemed insurmountable. Instead of having flowers placed on their graves, survivors of these life-changing events and those diagnosed with terminal illnesses who also survived their presupposed forthcoming death sentences are very much alive today doing all sorts of normal things.

Have you ever wondered why some people survive such episodes and others who were involved in closely related conditions don't? Maybe it's time you should give this serious consideration, as one's chronological age has absolutely nothing to do with one day having come face to face with such life-changing conditions.

Now, you may possibly be thinking to yourself, *Well, it wasn't their time yet!* What does that really mean? Are we all attached to our biological clock that has a definite time and date as to when we shall depart this life? I do not mean to even come close to demeaning anyone's religion or beliefs; and by reciprocal respect, I would trust that the doubters, naysayers, and critics out there will not demean what they have yet experienced.

However, the fact is, we are not attached to any type of unseen life clock, other than the one *we* ourselves create and control—whether or not you wish to accept that it is you who determines when you choose to leave this world and not some unknown force that had predetermined your departure at the time of your birth. Your body was designed to live far beyond medical and/or insurance companies' actuarial life expectancy charts (relating to statistical calculations, especially life expectancy) predetermining one's exit based upon one's chronological age.

Tell me, do you have a life clock in your dwelling by which you live your life? I certainly don't! If you do, by all means, throw it out today. Do you accept the premise that you will be deceased before you reach age eighty-five? If so, do all the living you can before then and, for that matter, before the age of sixty-five. How absurd!

Those who buy into this manmade fallacy are seriously out of touch with reality, and you should know, you are able to live disease and illness free for as long as you wish to live. For now, let it suffice that the actuarial charts put out by life insurance companies have come about through the false beliefs millions before you had bought into and, therefore, chose to prematurely age and pass on about the same point in their chronological age as their ancestors did. How sad and ridiculous it is to have bought into this false belief, yet countless people have and still do.

This false belief was handed down from generation to generation. However, you do not need to follow the same line of thinking and believing—that is, of course, if you choose not to. Now, unless you step in front of an oncoming vehicle, take risks like climbing up the side of some sheer cliffside without proper safety equipment (even with proper equipment), risk your life skydiving, place yourself in a position to be killed, etc. No one or anything else holds the key to how long you wish to live on this planet.

It simply amazes me how most religious teachers rarely teach how to get from point A to point Z, so to speak, related to what I have been discussing up to this point. Instead, they preach from what has been learned based upon centuries of teachings from former religious teachers whose teachings are what they themselves have learned from others many years ago. Therefore, they are a carrier of a message but do not, as a rule, provide their followers with the actual *how* to surmount serious, undesirable life-changing events. Now why is this? The simple answer is that perhaps they themselves more than likely do not know.

In order to be able to lead one to the *how* to surmount serious undesirable life-changing adversities, one should first have to have personally experienced serious life-changing conditions before anyone could be credible enough to be able to teach the *how*. I believe that there is nothing wrong with faith or hope; however, these alone are not enough. Unless having actually attempted to utilize the methods I have been discussing up to this point, these methods and those that follow should not be denied, doubted, ignored, or overlooked.

Seriously consider this before going blindly following any flock over some cliff in a dense fog, if you or anyone you may know is enduring one or more of the root causes of life-threatening conditions and events that, over time, can possibly lead to serious physical illnesses and possibly even mental illness. This world is chock-full of "flock followers" ("a group under the guidance of a leader," according to *Merriam-Webster*), and the line of flock followers is virtually endless, even to the point of being unable to know for certain what the flock leaders' actual *personal experiences* are. "Follow the Leader" seems to be the name of the game, and all too often—quite sadly to say—countless people follow others who lack such knowledge and personal experience right over the cliff.

Relating to those who have researched people who survived what was deemed to be the impossible, the stories and case histories of survivors of these incredible life-altering episodes do not matter; instead, the *why* those who survived, who undoubtedly were applying what they already knew innately (the methods), matters.

Information that comes from any writings, historical or otherwise, related to overcoming anything is far from complete. Unless and until one has actually put that information into actual, actionable usage culminating in credible proven results; therefore, it is at best a serious waste of time and effort that ultimately can result in futility otherwise.

By not applying the methods in this book, which I sincerely believe to be the keys to the survival of life-disrupting adversities, this information is reduced to nothing more than hope, which in my opinion is not the same as absolutely knowing. Being in a position of absolutely knowing a thing, in my opinion as a survivor of numerous serious life-transforming events, is the difference between the survival and the failure of overcoming any adversity.

Survival is *not* a mind-set. Rarely, if ever, does one get up every day with the thought *What do I need to do in order to survive today?* Quite the contrary.

Surviving any undesirable life-changing event is to be acutely aware of the methods concerning the *how* question, long before any such event ever comes into one's life to begin with. If you already know that, armed with these methods and your creative inner intelligence, you have the distinct advantage to be prepared to deal with most serious life-changing events. Believe this and let it sink deep into your conscious mind, and should the time ever come in your life when you may possibly come face to face with a serious life-altering event, you will be pleased to have the confidence and knowledge that you will be well armed to overcome anything.

I know this for a fact as I personally have survived more than most people may ever have to experience in their lifetime. I can also attest from my personal experience and the positive results I realized that absolutely nothing, other than the methods, answers, and solutions that come from an all-knowing, unseen source can provide the answers for overcoming and surviving most undesirable life-altering circumstances.

I have heard that survival tactics are more like a habit and that you can repeat habits over time. Now, do you really have the spare time to practice survival techniques? I don't, and most people I know do not either—unless you are a member of the armed forces, a fireman, police officer, or a member of any profession requiring survival techniques. What survival techniques would you practice for? There are countless life-changing events that you could possibly come face to face with on any given day, week, month, or year. If there were such a survival practice manual ever written, it would have to be written in volumes to cover each and every conceivable life-changing condition and event one may possibly encounter, not to mention those we do not know, the sum of which could fill any professional sports stadium to the brim. It doesn't get any more paranoid than that!

Now, would you really have time to search through such a collection (if there ever were one) for methods, answers, and solutions to resolve a particular life-transforming condition, circumstance, or situation? Most people don't!

For years I continued on a path of not realizing that I really did not know myself as well as I should have concerning the real me who existed within. Therefore, I only lived in the outer material world that I did know and was quite comfortable in at the time. Although my inner world was vaguely known to me, I was aware that it existed. However, I was not interested in exploring it; instead, I was far too busy trying to satisfy my ego and my superego's constant wants and hellacious appetite for self-fulfillment and continued material gratification. I slowly began developing a number of the root causes, chief among which were doubt, anxiety, stress, depression, negativity, and various stages of fear, among the worst of the root causes that can lead to serious illnesses.

Several years later, I finally came to realize what had been missing in my life. It was at this point that I came to understand and know that I still could connect with my real self from where my real desires emanate and are brought forth into reality and from where comes what I truly wanted to exist in my life for good. I realized that before I could know precisely and clearly the *what, why*, and *how* of my desires, I first had to know where the methods, answers, and solutions were coming from that could place me on the path to realize and recognize my desires and how to tap into my creative inner mind from where these methods emanate, for my benefit and for the advantage of all concerned.

In other words, before I came to the realization that before I could utilize my inner power effectively, I needed to reach deep within to rediscover the core of who I really was. I finally began to realize that I was not just this person I was seeing every day in the mirror. Therefore, I chose to dedicate myself to learning more and more about my all-knowing inner mind where all the methods, answers, and solutions are received from the unseen source I continue to refer to that would place me in the right direction to obtain anything I wanted to develop in my life for good.

This included the eventual healing and overcoming of the cancers I had acquired, in addition to other serious undesirable life-changing events. Relentlessly, I totally dedicated myself to this personal mission and goal and reached it; and from that point forward, I knew without any doubt whatsoever that I had finally arrived at the core to finally knowing who I really was and where to go for the methods, answers, and solutions for everything good I wanted to receive and the answer to the *why not me?* question. To this very day, I continue to call upon my inner power for whatever it is I need to know or wish to bring forth.

Since rediscovering my inner powers, methods, and answers, I met many people who continue to be searching for instant answers, overnight solutions, and quick fixes to very complex situations, circumstances, adversities, and related events taking place in their lives. I find this important to revisit because impatience is among the primary reasons why people rarely find they are seeking.

What I learned through these situations is that far too many people continue to focus their thoughts primarily on material wants. These range anywhere from taking a trip around the globe, meeting the perfect mate, and being financially prosperous. To them, this seems more easily attainable than to truly getting to know themselves much better from the inside and not from the outside and what they are willing to give back to humanity in the way of services or other humanitarian outreach, before even beginning to attempt the materialization of their superego's never-ending wants list. In other words, this is equal to a "me first" attitude, which will always fail to bring forth any true satisfaction for any length of time.

That said, it remains my observation that people who are willing to give more than they ever expect to receive possess much more in life of what will eventually come back to them without once having to ask, including having prosperity on every conceivable level. Through their giving ways, they open their internal vault, which possesses all the methods, answers, and solutions necessary to acquiring anything that is for good in their outer world.

The title of this chapter happens to be one of the most-thought-about wants by people on the planet when substituting the word *you* in the title for the word *me*. At this point, I would like you to take just a moment to really ponder what I have just said. If your true intent is to be able to have the good things you desire in life, you must first be willing to understand that to achieve your wants, you must first become aware of your very own creative inner powers and how they work together and how to access them. With them, there is almost nothing you cannot achieve or experience. This is not to be taken as a motivational statement but, instead, a proven fact. I am one among others who are living proof that they do work because by activating your creative powers, the methods, answers, and solutions can bring forth whatever it may be you want for good and for the good of others.

To achieve this awareness in your life consistently, you first must be open to accepting that there are unseen forces all around you on this planet and the entire universe itself. Surely you did not believe that the brain is what will or has given you the desires and wants you may have one day or presently possess now, did you? If you did, then you could not be any further from reality with that thought. So please abandon that idea, as it is neither true nor even close to even being comprehensible.

Yet many a successful businessperson would have the world believe that they alone who brought forth their good fortune. On the contrary, quite unconsciously, they tapped into their inner intelligence *temporarily* and found the methods and answers to achieve such heights. However, maintaining that level of success for any significant period is a totally different matter, as they can just as easily take a great fall from that mountain, as many have and many more will if they continue to believe that they are the sole reason for their temporary success. Sadly, they do not acknowledge that the real reason for any success they presently enjoy came from their unseen creative mind, which without it, no one can possibly sustain their good fortune for any significant amount of time before it eventually dissipates.

In order for you to discover what good you desire, as I and many others so gratefully acknowledge, you will first need to learn how to know yourself much better than you believe by turning your thoughts inward and not allowing any negative judgment to come from your lips and to not cause harm, pain, or anxiety on any person. By turning your thoughts inward, you begin to connect with the inner source of all wisdom, which reveal to you why you are here in the first place (your purpose in life, *meaning*—"something set up as an object or end to be attained: intention," per *Merriam-Webster*). Quite sadly, far too many people have no clue as to why they are here, let alone what their life purpose is. Far more, quite sadly, depart this planet never having known their life's purpose, recognized it, or even sought it out, for that matter.

When speaking to people who appear to not have a purpose or even have a clue what their purpose in life is, the first thing I noticed about them is that they seem to be very unhappy and have little, if any, passion for life. They give the impression that life has no meaning for them and, therefore, they make life decisions without any direction whatsoever.

Most people who lack a purpose for living usually feel very alone, empty, and extremely vague; they hardly realize who they really are within or what they are here to accomplish in their lifetime. On the other hand, those who do know their purpose in life seem to have a great deal of energy, know who they really are inside and rarely depend on others to make them feel good, take good care of themselves, and seem to be at peace with the world in general. They handle adversities that show up on their life's path with complete optimism, confidence, and expectation that all will turn out for the best for them and all concerned. So if you are telling yourself "Why can't this be me?" the answer is that this can be you from this point in your life. And should you decide that it will, with the recaptured power you will obtain by connecting or reconnecting into your creative intelligence and through other methods that I will describe here, you can bring forth your heartfelt desires.

If you know someone who is reflecting any of the conditions I just described and does not reach out to help others, we can expect that eventually their prosperity can disappear. I've witnessed this happen to others whose prosperity did just that. In other words, being selfish, uncaring, hoarding, and denying others are among the quickest ways to attract loss, deprivation, and financial problems.

I have also found that people who appear to be almost robotic in their everyday actions and who routinely get up in the morning and go through their habitual routines—e.g., prepare breakfast and lunches for their children, get them off to school, get ready for work, drag themselves into their vehicles, head off to work and navigate their way through heavy morning traffic, go through their daily work routine, return back home in the evening, take care of family issues, prepare the evening meal, do those chores around the house needing to be done, etc.—do so without even the slightest inkling of what it is all for. Therefore, by not appearing to have much of a purpose in their life, other than their daily routine, over a period of time, many people become lethargic and complacent, having dug a major rut for themselves. Unless they find their purpose in life, they find it impossible for them to grow mentally—let alone in any other areas of their life—or able to attract whatever good they truly desire to exist in their lives as it becomes an endless path of habitual routines.

This leads me to why not having any direction or purpose in one's life is such a critical subject. It is very possible that you may not even be aware of this; however, living in this manner every day, month after month, year after year can develop into a health issue, beginning with nonphysical conditions such as the ones I cited in the brief list of these types of conditions earlier. Among these conditions are anxiety, deep depressive states, constant worrying, fatigue, doubting, fears, and, above all, chronic stress; any of these alone, if allowed to continue over a significant period, can lead to a serious physical illnesses and possibly a life-threatening illnesses.

Whereby the *why not me?* question needs to be seriously considered if one truly wants to experience the good they desire, which also benefits all.

The way to achieve this state of being is to reconnect with or come to know the limitless source of inner power that can and will provide the methods, answers, and solutions necessary for the life one desires. This includes possessing good heath, healthy relationships on every level, and the manifesting of anything for good one is seeking.

Therefore, considering that any one or more of these conditions could possibly show up one day in your life, it is imperative that you become aligned with your life's purpose and begin to gain direction instead of living aimlessly, which can also lead to confusion and frustration and draining all your motivation. As if this were not enough, disconnected with your life's purpose, you are unable to make a connection with your inner creative powers and therefore, that is among the greatest harm you can encounter, aside from the nonphysical, physical and emotional effects as previously outlined.

Be further aware that the methods contained in this book cannot become helpful to you without having a definite direction for your life, similar to trying to get to the East Coast from a point on the West Coast of the United States without having proper direction. The same holds true for the methods identified in this book as they are interconnected with infinite intelligence from which comes the manifestation of what you truly desire. To be able to put these methods to work for you, it is very important for you to understand that you need to come to know your life's purpose and direction, as will the right path to follow, should you not know what your life purpose is.

If you have no clue what your purpose in life is, on the other hand, then it becomes very difficult to be able to understand what you are seeking to realize and to be on the right path toward achieving your desires.

"What does not having a purpose in one's life have to do with the title of this chapter?" you may be asking yourself. The answer is *everything*! Why? For starters, it is important to be aware that countless people throughout the world have unfulfilled lives full of quiet desperation, loneliness, and despair. Why then do you think people who appear to have it all can also reach this same level of emptiness and unfulfillment and turn to all sorts of relief, including drug and alcohol abuse and numerous crutches, despite the success and "having it all together" they may display? The root causes I identified in the list provided earlier, which I also call *predators*, and many others not found in this chart do not target select groups of humanity; instead, they can show up in anyone's life, at any point in time if not prepared to recognize them in their early stages, even those who appear to have their life together.

If you have yet to be affected at any level or degree by one or more of these predators, I suggest that you continue to read on because what you will come to learn is that neither you nor anyone else are immune to these predators that can materialize in your life.

Realize that whatever it is that has been eluding you, no matter what that may be, that may be a result of your continued state of faulty thinking, doubting, lacking self-trust, self-reliance, denial of expectancy, and ingratitude for what you already have gained in your life, no matter how insignificant it may seem to be for the moment. Even if you are temporarily living in an alley with little to eat and inadequate shelter or whatever it may be that you lack, any of these conditions and others can be remedied through what I have identified thus far and by exercising the methods of self-trust, self-confidence, expectancy, and, above all, unwavering belief, coupled with enduring patience.

Since the beginning of time, not one single person born was ever meant to live a life of serious illness, oppression, total dependency upon others (with the exception of an infant, those born with maladies needing perpetual care, etc.), despair, lack, loss, misery, depression, full of anxiety, stress, or, worst of all and the cause of most life-threatening conditions, fear. These and other root causes mostly result from becoming disconnected with one's greater inner intelligence. This disconnection must be avoided and eliminated from your life and reconnected immediately—the alternative being continuing to live in undesirable conditions. An old saying you possibly may have heard or read before is "If you keep doing what you're doing, you'll keep experiencing what you're experiencing." If what you are having are mostly unwanted situations, then this condition can also be ignorance, not caring, or lack of consideration for self and/or others; and therefore, if this describes you or someone you know or care about, asking the *why not me?* question answers itself.

Somewhere along their chosen life's path, many members of humanity lost their way and decided instead to take the path so many people choose, which leads to living lives of desperation, ongoing hardships, and fear that no one was ever meant to endure. Instead, we were meant to benefit from the reverse. If you do not believe this, just watch any national cable or regular news program, read any local or national newspaper, or listen to any radio news program on any given day where you will hear and observe the seemingly horrendous, never-ending, and ongoing stories about people who continue to slide into conditions of deprivation, loss, etc. and become the so-called victims of economic conditions.

As I already identified, no one is meant to suffer or live a life as a victim or one of quiet desperation, oppression, hopelessness, deficit, doubt, giving up, and, most of all, fear. Such stories are reported every day on news programs that rarely—if at all—report on stories of people who are living the life they were meant to live with prosperity on every level, despite such conditions surrounding them, who decided to take full control of their lives and overcome any adversity they may come face to face with.

Ask yourself this question: "Why are these horrendous events happening to so many throughout the world?" The simple answer is that they are completely lost, confused, easily led, and allow themselves to be oppressed. Most importantly, they lack valuable information pertaining to how to connect with their inner intelligence that contains the methods, answers, and solutions that are absolutely necessary to lift themselves from these oppressive and other debilitating conditions.

No one could ever convince me that this cannot be done. It can, it has, and is happening at this moment to someone; and that someone can also be you—if you are experiencing any undesirable life-changing conditions. There is absolutely nothing the inner mind, connected to infinite intelligence, cannot do for anyone who truly desires to lift themselves from dreadful oppression and conditions.

Ask yourself this question: "Why are some people finding themselves in the economic mess they are presently involved in?" It is because of a loss of self-confidence and self-trust and people's disconnection with their inner source of great power, having chosen to place their trust instead in everything but this inner source and choosing to follow the flock, wherever its leaders want to lead them. In addition, they fail to see themselves as more than just a flesh suit with a brain, bones, and organs but, instead, individually and collectively, extremely powerful inner beings, connected to and supported by an powerful infinite force.

Therefore, if one truly does not want to be totally controlled and dependent upon government for their subsistence and their mere existence and totally reliant on entitlements all their lives, they can—if they choose to reconnect with their all-knowing inner mind, right at this very moment. Those who choose not to believe or are unwilling to reconnect with their creative inner powers will more than likely remain in their oppressed and reliant condition unless or until they choose to embrace this infinite intelligence.

For you or anyone who have allowed and/or continued to allow fear, doubt, stress, anxiety, lack, lack of self-trust and expectation to control your life, and continue reliance upon others for your needs and survival—you are opening your door to more dominating forces seeking to control you on every conceivable level perpetually.

This may be the reason why you're standing in quicksand, so to speak, failing to realize that the world is constantly changing and that you must be able to change with it or be left standing there watching it pass you by, before you allow yourself to be swallowed up in your self-created quagmire.

PREVAILING OVER INSURMOUNTABLE ODDS

Why not you? For the life of me, I cannot even come close to imagining why not me. Because there isn't a reason or obstacle that could ever be conjured up by any man or woman that can ever justify that you are undeserving of all the good and abundance life has to offer, regardless of where you may find yourself at this very moment.

Focusing on the question *why not me?*—I believe that no one should ever have to ask this question, considering that they are armed with the most powerful force in the universe inside them. All you have to do is to turn over any desire to this inner intelligence and to no longer be concerned about the *how* and *when* but instead be expectant of the result. Above all, exercise unwavering belief, expectancy, and patience. If you will do this and never doubt that it can, you can, like I and others, have what you desire.

Begin today by planting the seeds of trust, unwavering belief, patience, and expectation in your creative inner intelligence. If you choose to trust it and not rely upon getting lucky, watch for the signs that will begin appearing in your physical life for the good you are seeking.

The myth surrounding the word *luck* plays a distinct role in our lives, according to many who believe in this word's power. Let's now explore this unfaithful term that countless people everywhere seem to rely upon.

5

THE MYTH OF THE WORD *LUCK*

I heard a great deal about how lucky I was to have been able to overcome serious life-threatening illnesses and other serious life-changing events. My response to anyone who sincerely believes this is that luck *never* played a role in my or anyone's survival of a life-transforming event or a terminal illness—far from it.

It's critics like this who, when possibly faced with a devastating illness themselves, may place all their trust in luck or some other outside source to overcome a critical situation. However, quite sadly, they quickly learn that their total dependence on luck, medical science, or any outside source alone to bring forth a permanent healing or a total cure for a serious nonphysical event or any severe illness may prove to be a huge disappointment to not only them but to everyone concerned about them.

That said, I am not only addressing those who may currently be afflicted with a critical physical or nonphysical condition but also those who have been so fortunate as to have made it as far as they have through life having not yet sustained a grave health problem or, as in my case, both physical and nonphysical challenges simultaneously.

You should know that the so-called luck theory is brought about by faulty thinking and by events of chance, e.g. gambling. In other words, luck originates from the determined mind, which includes deep vision, concentration, and strong belief. In gambling, luck is no more than a very deep-rooted belief that one can win. Therefore, even in other games of chance, believing plays a major role in the outcome.

For those who may believe that I was just lucky, tell me, how does one survive more than I have and still be standing to tell the story? In my case, luck had nothing to do with it! If you believe in luck or even so much as to believe that manmade remedies of this world will permanently cure you from an illness, then you certainly need to be aware that medical science has never claimed or guaranteed anyone to be able to permanently cure most life-threatening illnesses.

So what was it then that I and others knew and relied upon that medical science and others apparently did or did not know about that brought us total healing from high-risk physical and nonphysical conditions?

When I talk to people about my survival of two advanced cancers, I am frequently asked why I made the decision to reject highly recommended and insisted-upon chemotherapy treatments, which decision was deemed to be a death wish on my part. I asked them this question: "Would you have the total and complete trust and confidence in yourself and an unseen inner power to make the same decision if you were in the very same position I was, despite medical advice to the contrary?"

I pose this very same question to you: Do you think you would? Do you truly believe that I am the only person to have done so and still have lived to tell about it? Do you believe that my survival was just luck or good fortune? The answer is neither.

Among one of my discoveries that I never gave much thought until after going through extremely challenging and traumatic life-threatening illnesses was that I was not just a flesh body and a gray mass in my head schlepping around this planet, taking them from place to place. Instead, beside my education and experiences, I was also capable of much deeper knowledge, derived from my inner mind.

More than likely you are aware or may have a good idea how complex the physical body is. Even today, medical science has yet to be able to uncover all the secrets of the body's so-called miraculous self-curing capabilities. Yet in untold cases, the physical body "self-healed," and those who survived achieved a complete healing despite being told that survival was not medically possible.

Despite these seemingly miraculous recoveries against all odds, the response from the medical community is usually along the lines that there apparently was a misdiagnosis of the life-threatening condition to begin with, a no comment" from some, a higher power's will, or one was just lucky. Was it? Perhaps it was something the person did or was doing all along that caused the previously diagnosed life-threatening condition or undesirable event to disappear.

There is another saying that most people have either heard of or read, and it goes like this: "God helps those who help themselves" (God being whoever or whatever one believes to be an unseen power). Then there is this one: "Physician heal thyself." This could be interpreted to mean that the one having any form or level of sickness or ailments is to take personal responsibility, initiative, and the necessary action to bring forth a healing, coupled with strong belief, focused thought, and, above all, unwavering expectation. If you are a religious person, your higher power is said to expect your full cooperation by way of your taking the initiative and taking action to do your part in the healing process and not assuming that a higher power is going to do all the work and you just lay back expecting a cure without you lifting one finger in the process. This assumes, of course, that you are physically and mentally capable and not relying on luck to favor you.

It is my belief that illnesses and other conditions need to be addressed, not only by physicians and other medical professionals but the full cooperation of the persons themselves when they begin to become aware of such conditions.

There is no intent here to be critical of the sciences of psychiatry, psychology, or the medical profession. Without their expertise and assistance, many people would most likely have had no outlet whatsoever other than family, relatives, and friends who—although wishing to be as helpful as possible—know little, if anything at all, about their loved one's afflictions. This futile effort is like searching for a needle in a pitch-black room.

The act of taking personal responsibility and action, for me, began first with a strong internal, intuitive feeling that I instinctively knew emanated from a source that could provide me with the answers and right decisions, necessary to be able to take over total control of my healing process. This was not a popular decision with my medical caretakers and others who were concerned for my well-being. I was perceived to have been making irrational and nonsensical choices when faced with the decision of ridding myself of the several cancers that had violated my physical body.

Despite their collective opinions, I absolutely knew internally, that if I was to have any chance whatsoever of overcoming potentially fatal, serious physical illnesses, I could *never* allow myself to place my total reliance upon the medical profession alone and definitely not luck, regardless of the advances medical science had made over the years.

Guided by my all-knowing, intuitive inner guidance, I knew medical science had neither advanced far enough along concerning my situation nor had the survival record improved dramatically enough. In addition, the postsurgical oncological advances were far too limited and vague for me to take such a huge risk with my physical life. In other words, I decided that it was going to have to be left up to me to heal and cure myself, and that's precisely what I did. However, I was not without reliance upon the all-knowing infinite intelligence that provided all the methods, answers, and solutions I needed to overcome this malady in my body. I decided to go forward with the methods that included rejecting chemotherapy treatments.

Making this choice proved to be the correct one, despite medical advice and insistence to elect these treatments coming from many people I knew. Although I was grateful and respectful of their concerns and opinions, it was certainly neither enough for me to trust my physical life to these nor was I going to rely on luck to get me out of my illness or any serious life-threatening situation.

There is something else that was also very clear. You see, when we find ourselves in a serious life-threatening situation, for some unknown reason—to me, anyway—we normally defer and allow others to make our decisions for us. Yes, I've already made this point; however, it is worth mentioning again. Initially, I too listened to others, just like almost everyone else does, as I am almost certain many people before me and those who will come after me will continue to do this. The fact is, we become so heavily dependent upon those who are supposedly professionals, we blindly allow them to dictate what is best for us and literally license them, so to speak, to control every step concerning our healing from our ailments or situations. For the most part, they all mean well; but it is we, not others, who must take the initiative and action, once prudent medical care has done all what it can.

Although I respect the medical community, medical science as a whole does not yet have all the answers and solutions to achieving a permanent cure for most life-threatening conditions. Knowing this, I chose not to become just another lab rat, so to speak—no disrespect for the medical community or medical science intended.

Concerning one's inner intuitive mind—those who are not certain or clear about what I am referring to, allow me to explain. *Intuition*, as most people know, means "a natural ability or *power* [emphasis by author] that makes it possible to know something without any proof or evidence"; "a feeling that guides a person to act a certain way without fully understanding why." Therefore, this all-knowing inner power is the recipient of strong, intuitive inner feelings that emanate from a much higher intelligence that I prefer to refer to as infinite intelligence and, therefore, the source from which the answers, methods, and solutions that deeper intuitive feelings transfer to one's inner mind and the conscious mind in the form of visions, imagination, and thoughts. The thoughts that are retained in one's conscious mind become one's dominant, focused thoughts.

Almost everyone has intuitive feelings—gut feelings—however, the vast majority of people are more likely to choose not to take action concerning these feelings and miss major opportunities to utilize the methods, answers, and solutions they are seeking. Knowing this, I, along with countless others, learned how to harness these strong intuitive feelings and act upon them, as opposed to ignoring them, and found that these intuitive feelings come from deep within oneself and are connected to an infinite intelligence.

There is not a person on this planet who has not sensed an intuitive feeling, knowingly or otherwise; however, as I identified, far too many people choose not to act upon these intuitive feelings and miss valuable lessons and opportunities that would have more than likely enhanced their lives. The point I am making here is for you to pay more attention to your inner feelings, as everything we do as humans is attached to a feeling. As you learn how to pay closer attention to your inner feelings, you become more intuitively sensitive and become more aware of everything going on around you in your life and are then able to make more accurate and beneficial decisions and choices for your life, as I and countless others have done and continue to do. By doing so, one will *never* have to ever again rely upon luck for anything and, instead, substitute luck with absolutely knowing. Which would you prefer, especially when it comes to any serious life-changing situation?

The questions I get asked most is, "How do you know this inner intuition is communicating with you?" The best way to describe it is to compare it to the feeling we get when we feel fear. Usually when one is fearful or senses something that makes them afraid, one gets a deep sensation of fear in their gut—the lower abdomen—and some will even get chills and sometimes cold sweats. Deep intuitive feelings are the complete opposite. When your inner mind is attempting to communicate with you, you should feel a gentle feeling and a calming effect deep within, followed by a gentle thought that will enter your conscious mind nudging you, so to speak, to act upon that thought quickly and not in the distant future.

This inner mind is so powerful that it will actually override one's ego, which will make every effort to reject any thought about an inner power, because the ego feels challenged, disempowered, and threatened. Once an inner intuitive thought is communicated, it will persist to get you to take action, until acted upon or you choose to ignore it. Even if you choose not to act upon it, it will still continue to persist to get your attention, as it is the infinite intelligence answering your innermost desires and bringing with it not only the answers but the methods and solutions to achieve your desires and hopes. This is precisely how I was able to overcome all that I have and will continue to do so, should I ever experience any undesirable event in my life again.

There have been those who scoffed at this and opted to choose to rely upon their ego and eventually found that the ego did not have the answers, methods, or solutions necessary to bring forth the desired result. Of course, this is not the ego's purpose. Over time, like me, having witnessed the results I was obtaining, others began to act upon what their intuitive faculties was repeatedly attempting to communicate to them through its intuitive powers and connection with greater intelligence; and for many of them, luck was eliminated from any further consideration.

Once again, how do I know all this? Easy. I spent a great deal of time between cancer specialists, surgeons, primary care physicians, and related medical personnel as well as psychologists who knew my case well and can tell you that subsequently, quite to my amazement, most of them eventually had asked me what I did to overcome these serious health problems despite the incredible odds against my survival and having elected not to undergo medically recommended chemotherapy treatments. When I shared with them what I did to overcome these events by way of my inner guide/inner mind and not by luck, they took this explanation to be as "serious denial" and needed psychiatric care. Even other medical professionals and my son's pediatrician asked me how I did it, who all asked if I would send them a copy of my book when published, which I am pleased and honored to do.

So what am I getting to? What I am attempting to get across to you is that it is your choice to take and you have complete control of your physical life and any life-changing condition and *nothing* should be relied on luck. By all means, always listen to your medical providers; but when it comes to decisions concerning your long-term survival, you owe it to yourself to consider other options because you do not have the luxury of allowing other people to make those decisions for you, let alone relying on "getting lucky." As opposed to what you feel from deep within, believe and know intuitively the right decisions you make for you and your ultimate survival, even if it means only surviving for five or ten more years or even less. Even if you concur with others, who could blame you, as following the advice of others is what we all have learned, been taught, and bred to do all our lives? However, concerning myself, if I had to do it over again, I would make the very same decisions and never, ever rely upon being one of the so-called lucky ones.

What would you do when you or your loved one is diagnosed with a physical or nonphysical life-threatening situation or illness? Whose advice would you follow and why? What other options do you have other than customary remedies? What is it you generally would do last instead of first? What sums of money have you or those you care about or know spent on addictive, legally prescribed medications and prescribed treatments like psychiatric or psychological counseling, expensive rehabilitation facilities, etc.? And what do you do after these treatments and medications have run their course and the result hasn't changed or improved when you first became aware of whatever it is that has been plaguing your life?

Do I have all the answers? No! Neither does the world of medical science, psychiatry, psychology, or the religions of this world—as a matter of fact, far from it. Why is it then that so many people totally recover from alcoholism; illegal and legal prescription drug addictions; deep depression; anxiety; stress; certain stages of mental illnesses; and nonphysical life-threatening situations, conditions, and related events? And if one does temporarily recover, why then do these conditions return?

Allow me to pose some additional questions to you: If you were to have a certain diagnosed condition that no one recovered from yet, why couldn't you be the first to do so? If only two had survived a certain major illness or event, why can't you be the third to do so? On the other hand, if you are free from disease or problems—for the present, anyway—are you being complacent or possibly in denial, believing that surely these only happen to other people but could never happen to you because you consider yourself to be in excellent physical condition and take superb care of yourself?

Many gallant warriors famous for their participation in sports or in the arts have fought courageous battles and shared with us their heroic efforts to conquer life-compromising illnesses. Along with their families, we have watched them succumb to their illnesses despite conventional and alternative treatments. They are role models that made a personal commitment to take control of their situation, despite the advanced stages of their disorder. Although some did not survive, they set the stage for others by their courage and actions. They helped us identify that when it comes to a life decision, one must take total control and consider every viable treatment option and have an indomitable spirit. They are accompanied by countless others who chose this same path that, although unknown to the general public, also deserve mentioning.

I cannot attest to whether or not some well-known people ever knew about or called forth their inner guidance when dealing with a life-threatening illness or related adversity and if they had a firm belief in their inner guidance's ability to heal. What I do know is that they never gave up—they took the initiative and necessary action on their own to take over total control of their lives and did not relinquish that control to anyone. I continue to be humbled by such people, and there are so many more who are unknown to the world who have and continue today to do the same. To all of them, I am extremely grateful for their gallant decisions and for being excellent examples for others.

Among the primary reasons I rejected chemotherapy treatments was, as I have already stated that, based upon my research on the medical science's track record for curing seriously advanced physical life-threatening illnesses was, *for me*, not impressive enough for me to be able to place my physical life solely in the hands of medical science.

Therefore, having made the decision instead to rely upon the methods and answers I was receiving from my inner power, I chose to combine medical science's expertise but only up to the point of my medical professional's proven and verifiable medical knowledge and with what I already knew. Since my inner mind is connected to infinite intelligence, I could absolutely depend upon these powerful faculties to bring forth an eventual permanent healing and that could supply me with all the answers, methods, and solutions necessary to overcome the challenges that I was experiencing. Beyond any doubt, this choice, for me, was absolutely correct and devoid of any dependence on being lucky or relying on any outside source whatsoever to bring forth the total and complete healing that I knew would eventually appear in my physical life. I intuitively knew that if this inner source, connected with the infinite intelligence, could not bring forth a permanent healing, undoubtedly, neither could medical science or luck.

Was this then a roll of the dice, so to speak? Absolutely not, quite the contrary! Once one has connected or reconnected with their inner guidance, there is never any doubt whatsoever as to what decision to make concerning anything for which one may need guidance and right direction.

To doubt this is to be in total denial and rejection of the incredible power of one's inner guidance, and should this be the case, without unwavering belief in this powerful force, one certainly could not expect to receive an answer or solution from this inner source pertaining to whatever it may be that they may be seeking—a resolution, healing, cure, etc. Besides, this inner guidance, connected with infinite intelligence that created everything, has a much better track record when it comes to reversing medical science's diagnosis, opinions, and predictions—even concerning terminal illnesses—and certainly has a vast track record over luck.

For example, I allowed the medical profession to perform colon and liver surgeries on me (their area of expertise) after having been diagnosed by several specialists and told how seriously advanced my condition was. However, I knew that for me to survive from that point forward, my medical professionals had absolutely nowhere else to go than to a referral to an oncologist (several, I might add) who were unable to satisfactorily answer my one and only key question—"When the chemotherapy treatments are completed, what will you be able to tell me regarding my surviving?" Their answers were all the same, "Should you survive five years after the chemotherapy treatments, we would then be able to say that the cancer had gone into remission."

Well, at that point, the ball once again was placed back in my court. My further question then was, "What does *remission* really mean?" Well, I received various explanations, but the best of all was "delayed"; "to postpone"; "a temporary remission of symptoms," according to *Merriam-Webster*. Not very comforting, is it?

This is when what I absolutely already knew through my inner mind, which took over immediately, that to have any chance of survival and be able to raise my then six-month-old son and be around to see my grandchildren one day, I would need to tune out any and all the medical profession's doomsday opinions and advice as to what to do regarding after-surgery treatments. I was also getting advice and opinions simultaneously from everyone else such as well-wishers, family, business associates, religious people, and others. However, despite all this, I chose instead to only listen to the one source that knew precisely what to do that had all the methods, answers, and solutions I needed. That source was none other than my all-knowing intuitive inner guidance.

"That's crazy you may possibly," be thinking. No! Fact is, I'm here, alive, well, and very healthy to prove it. Now eighteen years later, and my once six-month-old boy is now a very healthy, strong, 6'2", 185-pound high school linebacker. I know, I know don't even go there.

Most people know or have at least heard about the word *intuition*, right? Well, when I say the words *knew* or *know*, what I mean is we were all born with the gift of knowing everything we would ever need to know and what to do in any serious life-changing situation, if and when one came into our lives. Yes, I did say this earlier and it's well worth repeating.

So why do so many of us find ourselves scurrying, floundering, and groping for methods, answers, and solutions the moment we come face to face with a serious physical or nonphysical life-threatening illness or any other type of undesirable life-changing event, situation, or circumstance unrelated to any medical event? All we have to do is to call upon what we innately already know to do through our all-knowing, intuitive inner guidance!

A person does not necessarily need to be religious to awaken their inner power within them. The quick answer to the question of "Why do we find ourselves scurrying, floundering, and groping for methods, answers, and solutions?" is that, more often than not, many people choose to ignore their inner wisdom most of their lives and instead continue to follow what the masses are doing (what I call following the flock).

One of my favorite authors Stuart Wilde calls such people "cliff dwellers." These are people who can fall off the edge of their self-created cliff at any time and all too often do.

The primary reason you may choose to ignore what you possibly already intuitively know to do is because you simply do not want to abandon your comfortable habitual lifestyle, of course, why would you? It has always worked well for you before, so why change it, right? Judging from my own life circumstances, the fact of the matter was that neither my life simply nor my past learned remedies were no longer working for me and helping me with the nonphysical life-threatening and life-changing events and circumstances I was involved with.

However, having depended entirely upon my all-knowing, intuitive inner faculty, it was the subtle feelings I was experiencing that eventually turned into very strong consistent feelings that I knew were not coming from my conscious mind that led me to precisely what it was that I needed to do. These were harmonious feelings of calmness that were coupled with thoughts that were guiding in nature and were not conflicting in any way.

Now, before going on, allow me to tell you that I have struggled with whether I should put all the details in this book pertaining my first diagnosed with cancer, how I reached the point to go against all medical advice, and literally reject any recommended postmedical treatments beyond the two surgeries I allowed myself to become convinced by others at the time to undergo. However, the deep inner feelings I was experiencing led me to go forward with the order of events and actions leading to me ultimately overcoming these cancers and other nonphysical life-threatening illnesses and events that followed these cancer surgeries.

I fully realize that by exposing my personal medical condition and other undesirable events to the world, these become public knowledge. I also know that there are others all over the world who have been exposed to similar events and, quite sadly, have succumbed to a life-threatening illness and/or related condition, whether nonphysical or physical in nature. However, if I am willing to reveal my personal involvement with overcoming several cancers and other serious nonphysical life-threatening events and what I believe to be the reason why I survived and by doing so can help many others worldwide, then it is certainly well worth disclosing what I did to ultimately defeat these very serious illnesses and other life-changing adversities, situations, and events.

Let me be perfectly clear here. I am in no way recommending or suggesting that others follow my actions or decisions—quite the contrary. Instead, my sole and only intention through this book is to share with you and others what my personal situation was pertaining to my decisions and the resulting methods that I personally chose to achieve and successfully utilize solutions that led me to overcoming all that I have—none of which were obtained by luck, by any stretch of the imagination.

One day while doing research for this book, while perusing through numerous books in the medical and disease sections at various well-known bookstores, I came across a rather curious book written primarily for the nursing profession. This book was about how to deal with numerous life-threatening physical illnesses.

As I scanned through its pages, I found it very interesting to see the numerous brief explanations and information that pertained to postsurgical events. The book also writes how to spot certain symptoms of life-threatening illnesses by their medically known common traits. While going through this book, my curiosity peaked and led me to the medical problems that I had confronted; therefore, I went to the sections in this book related to colon and liver cancer. What I found was quite unbelievable and even incredible, considering that this was a very recently published book and considering that my two cancer incidents had occurred almost eighteen years prior. What I found under the heading "Causes" was the word *unknown*, and under the heading "Survival" was "not to exceed the medically predicted six (6) month range."

Why, you might ask, did I find this so unbelievable and incredible? Well, first of all, it immediately indicated to me, as a survivor of both of these cancers, that the medical profession was apparently no closer to learning the true initial root cause of either cancer, still, after eighteen more years had gone by and listing an expected demise (expiration date) within six months. This clearly indicated—to me, anyway—that the medical profession also had not come closer to finding a cure despite the millions—or is it now billions?—spent on cancer research annually in this country alone.

To me, as a cancer survivor, this was frightening and difficult to absorb. All the money spent on research, and nothing has apparently changed concerning these cancers in almost twenty years. This, in my opinion, should concern everyone, not just me!

This information reinforced my ongoing beliefs even deeper that indeed it was me—and only *me*—who absolutely controlled every phase of the healing and eventual curing of these cancer experiences. Not the medical profession, psychiatrists, psychologists, the myriad of professional counselors of every imaginable type and disciplines; the religions of this world, pastors, priests, rabbis, gurus, imams clerics, and other religious leaders; all the personal advisors and the innumerable ideas and opinions of people or the so-called specialists or psychics; or any of these can offer a permanent cure for any serious life-threatening illness. Therefore, the precise reason for my long-term survival was, as I had known all along, remains to be my all-knowing, intuitive inner mind—the only source that can possibly pilot my life and provide me with all the methods, answers, and solutions needed to overcome anything.

It is your intuitive inner mind that absolutely knows what you need to know in any given situation or pertaining to any adversity that may come into your life and nothing else. How could it be anything else? Science is science, medicine is medicine, and psychology and psychiatry and medical science follow certain learned and historical theories and ideas, practices, beliefs, case studies, statistics, disciplines, experimental procedures, drugs, repetitive practices, etc. Opinions come from others' life histories, but certainly and without a doubt, advice comes from others as well who received it from others who themselves received it from others and so on and on and on.

So what's left? What's left is *you*! Only the real you resides deep inside you and not physically in your shoes every day. It is you who spends every nanosecond with you, not anyone or anything else. An example of this are the people who attend religious services seeking methods, answers, and possible solutions to whatever undesirable situations they may be concerned about and who will give their undivided attention to what is being said by their religious leaders. However, based upon my observation, all too often, those sermons and teachings are easily forgotten due to people being consumed with the world's distractions. Very few religions, through their teachers, rarely teach much—if anything in depth at all—regarding one's all-knowing inner mind and its phenomenal powers being one with infinite intelligence that has no limits and how we can access our inner all-knowing inner mind that is connected with infinite intelligence. (*No limits* means "endless." *Endless* means "the basic eternal quality of divine mind." *(Divine means "of, relating to, or proceeding directly from God or a god," according to Merriam-Webster.)*

Most people who have access to a television have possibly seen so-called healings by evangelists of people who had been suffering for years with a serious ailment, someone who has been crippled, others with arthritis and respiratory problems so severe that they cannot manage on their own, etc. Although it may appear that the persons who lay hands on these people have some divine healing powers, I will not judge whether they do or do not. I personally am more than convinced that the real reasons for any credible healing through this process is primarily the result of the strong beliefs and empowering, unwavering unconscious thoughts by the person seeking healing.

Basing upon my own experience, these beliefs and thoughts were so strong they unconsciously had reached and convinced the inner mind that they believed in a cure for their ailments, which was the real cause for their temporary healing and recovery from an ailment that had been plaguing them most of their adult lives. Therefore, it is a person's strong belief, expectation, and unconscious calling upon their inner guidance—connected to infinite intelligence—that produces the healing, not the so-called healers themselves. The reason I say *temporary* is because, should those who have realized this healing discontinue their unwavering belief and their thoughts begin wavering or doubting, within a short period of time, their ailment is certain to eventually return.

In addition, it appears that medical science has no real answer and has given up on them and their religious leaders—as much as they may have attempted—and has no real answer as well (short of offering up prayers for healing from the pulpit and/or through their members). Yet they were not cured, why? Because any real healing must come from a person's strong belief and expectation. Am I saying that prayer is not helpful? Not at all. However, unless the person being prayed for unwaveringly believes they will be healed; any prayers on their behalf are being blocked by the intended recipient of prayers.

I am further convinced similarly about the millions of people who make pilgrimages every year to places all over the world where medical healing and other miracles have been claimed to have been brought forth. Some such well-known places are located in Betania,

Venezuela, and Lourdes, France where it has been said that healing miracles occur. I am more than certain that they do occur, but I am just as certain, only because of the strong belief of the person seeking healing and a cure and who strongly believe that, by taking their physical body to these places, they will be healed. However, the real healing comes from unwavering inner belief, trust, confidence, and expectation, along with an inner vision of the end result—a true and permanent healing—brought about by one's inner mind, which is connected with infinite intelligence from whence all things come. That includes what is deemed to be "miraculous healings" and certainly far from being just lucky.

I believe that once you choose to strongly accept your all-knowing inner intelligence, without doubting its incredible powers, it will bring forth strong emotions, feelings, and inner visions of any expected outcome. From this point, absolutely nothing can stop the healing, as inner mind connected to the infinite intelligence is more than capable of bringing forth anything you ask of it.

Not long ago I had a person ask me how I knew that this "inner guidance, inner mind" stuff really works. I deemed this to be a very reasonable and fair question. My answer was that any permanent healing and/or permanent cure of any medically diagnosed serious illness, including a terminal illness and a permanent curing of a nonphysical life-changing event, is convincing enough for me and also significant proof of the tremendous power of this wonderful gift that all mankind has the benefit of calling upon at any time. I went on to cite some examples, as I was one of them, considering I had such incredible back-to-back medical and nonphysical circumstances come into my life in a very short period of time (eight months apart). I reminded this person of the many so-labeled miracles that have occurred since the beginning of recorded time stated not only in the Bible but as well as medical science's inexplicable cures and permanent healings of a myriad of different types of illnesses.

In addition, how is it when one calls upon this incredible inner guidance connected with infinite intelligence that there has been the ability to communicate with a person across the world to bring forth a healing for various types of illnesses, physical and nonphysical, quite to the amazement of the person who has the illness? For me, that is all the convincing you or anyone should need, to get acquainted or reacquainted with your incredible inner guidance and understand how your concentrated thoughts, strong belief, imagination (inner vision), and full expectation play a very significant role in bringing forth any desired result you are seeking for good and for the good of all concerned.

It should be stated again here that your body is incredibly complicated. Its Creator designed it that way and with the ability to live well beyond the age of one hundred years. Certainly, if this infinite intelligence could create your body and all its organs and complicated functions that medical science has yet to understand, it can certainly heal itself. Simply put, people do not come to reach the age of a hundred plus by relying upon sheer luck or medical science, especially those who reside in the remotest areas of the world where modern medical help is virtually nonexistent and who live far beyond what is estimated to be one's expected life span on this planet.

Many people throughout history and even in these present times have exceeded the age of one hundred years and have lived productive lives. Those who have claimed the reason for living this long was due to clean living, lack of stress, anxiety, or ongoing deep depression; however, the more profound reasons were a strong belief in their inner guidance and infinite intelligence and knowing that they had total control of their mind and bodies. Let it suffice then to state that you have total control of every phase of your physical, mental, and your spiritual life, including how long you wish to live on this earth.

We continue with an important method that so many people fail to utilize for any significant period of time. It has to do with one's inner willpower and the result of neglect to accept this method as a significant force that is absolutely necessary if one desires self-empowerment.

6

THE HUMAN WILL—A MOST FORMIDABLE ALLY

Will in philosophical discussions, like generally in the English language, refers to the desire of an individual, and the acts done when such decisions are put into effect. Actions made according to a person's Will are called "willing" or "voluntary". In general the word will does not refer to one desire amongst many however, but the end result, or in other words the choice, decision, or determination which people come to about what they want. The Will is in turn important within philosophy because a person's will is one of the most distinct and recognizable aspects or parts of any individual's human mind, along with reason and understanding. It is one of the things which make a person who they are, and it is especially important in ethics, because is the part which determines how people act, at least when they act deliberately.

In general, the word Will does not refer to one's desires amongst many, but the end result, or in other words, the choice, decision, or determination which people come to about what they want. (Wikipedia)

One of the subjects I came to witness that was not being taught in most religious services or elementary, middle. and high schools, as well as our colleges was finding one's purpose in life. To have a purpose in life, one must first be able to develop a strong will before one can achieve that objective. I found that there is only one place to develop a strong will, and that is to delve deep within one's inner self and never from one's outer physical self (ego).

I have attended various religious services for years and can tell you that, apart from learning more about Christianity and other religious beliefs, I was unable to find the methods, answers, and solutions I was seeking. All that I have succeeded in accomplishing has been accomplished through my daily dialogue and connection with my all-knowing infinite intelligence—by the method I describe in detail further on in the book—that constantly provides me with the methods and answers I need and has yet to disappoint me and, from my personal conviction, never will. Therefore, it may be wise to consider coupling your religious beliefs with your inner guidance/inner mind that is one with infinite intelligence that can bring forth your innermost desires for the good you may be seeking.

I would also like to point out here that attending a place of worship is of course a personal choice. However, by choosing to do so confirms belief in an unseen power regardless of one's religious belief. This alone is only the tip of the iceberg, so to speak, as without a complete surrender and deep belief in the existence of an infinite intelligence that communicates with one's inner guidance, attending and becoming a member of any place of worship alone rarely results in bringing forth one's innermost desires for good.

Finding the right path for your life, therefore, should be the most important matter that you should seriously consider focusing on, especially if you are involved in a serious life-changing event, as it is that path that can lead you to your life's true purpose and developing a strong, impenetrable inner will.

"How does one find the right path and immovable inner will?" you might ask. Answering this question was among the primary motivators for me to write this book because unless the right path is identified and a strong inner will is developed, chances are that continuing to follow the path you have chosen instead may be among the reasons why everything may not be working for you as you had expected. That said, you need to seriously evaluate whether your present life path needs to be abandoned without further hesitation.

How do you find that path for yourself? First, you quiet your raging thoughts by finding a quiet place where you will not be disturbed for at least one hour, at the very least three times a week, on or about the same time of day. This place, for me, is what I call my safe place. And be certain that during that hour, there are absolutely no phones, texting, TV, radio, or any interference whatsoever that will take away your concentration and be absolutely certain that you leave specific instructions to anyone whom you may believe might disturb you that you are not to be interrupted during this quiet time. Better yet, a library is an ideal place. Once this is done, then you concentrate on nothing at all but what it is your desire for good to appear in your physical life and reject any negative thoughts that make any attempt to disturb you in any way. Trust me on this, they will do just that—if you allow them to.

Back when I was very young, I was not cognizant of precisely where my right path and strong willpower was coming from. All I knew was that it was just there and part of my makeup. I never gave any thought as to why I had such a deep determination and will to succeed at everything I chose to realize from childhood to adulthood. It was not until I was much older that I began to understand and strongly sense where this strong will was emanating from, and once that understanding took hold of me, I relentlessly began researching and devouring as much information as I could find on the subject of one's inner will.

It was not until I began to have a number of serious life-changing events did I fully realize the tremendous power of one's inner willpower and where it was originating from. Without my inner guidance from which I was drawing the will necessary to be able to overcome life-threatening events, coupled with the methods, answers, and solutions I was receiving from my inner guidance, my chances of overcoming and surviving these conditions may have been even bleaker than diagnosed.

It has been my observation that most people are driven by a strong will related to material things they want in life that originates from one's ego. As a matter of fact, it appears that most people are filled to the brim, so to speak, with their endless pursuit of material wants; and when they achieve one material want, they are often off and running after another material want again. Sad but true. Among the definitions for *will* is "used to express desire, choice, willingness, consent, or in negative constructions, refusal"—man's definition, not the true definition of the will that emanates from one's inner willpower, opposed to one's ego. The difference between the two are light years apart.

Most people consistently want a great deal from life, most of which is tied to material and monetary gain. However, they are really uncertain about why they want what they think they want. Having said this, it is a person's will, coupled with their ego's insatiable appetite for immediate gratification, that pushes them and dictates their very existence on this planet. In other words, a person's will, coupled with their ego and focused thoughts, creates the path most people tend to follow that results in either good or bad outcomes.

In my case, I found my strong inner willpower to be very instrumental in my survival of numerous life-changing events. However, among one of the benefits of having a strong inner will is that other attributes soon begin to show up in one's life such as unfathomable courage, self-confidence, unwavering trust, and belief.

Your inner guidance/inner mind will always lead you to a path that you must be prepared to travel on alone that stretches far beyond the capability of your conscious mind, which is ego driven. This new life path is the one that leads you to your true purpose in life, the real reason any one of us is here in the first place, where the answers, methods, and solutions you possibly have been seeking will start to appear. As opposed to relying upon your conscious mind that is often dominated by your ego to obtain what you desire, which, more often than not, is material gratification.

I learned that to resist my new life path, had I not chosen to follow it, I certainly would have missed out on the methods, answers, and solutions sent to me from my inner guidance. What so many people attempt to do instead when something is very important to them, such as their health issues, is they try to solve the matter themselves, failing to realize that they do not have the power, depth of knowledge, or the methods, answers, or solutions necessary to be able to do so, if disconnected from their inner power. All too often, most people believe they know what is good for them when it comes to resolving nonphysical and physical issues; however, most of their knowledge comes from outer sources like their medical advisors and other well-meaning medical providers who can certainly treat these conditions, but they are far removed from having what is necessary to permanently overcome and survive serious life-disrupting illnesses and/or nonphysical conditions.

You may not have been exposed to or have heard the following before. Among the myriad of things that I learned while going through the life-changing events I endured was that there comes a time when you need to relax your outer will when you begin to sense and to feel deep within that you are being led in another direction.

This became very clear to me when I realized what I wanted to achieve was not working the way I had perceived it would, despite the amount of outer willpower I employed. It was at this point I surmised that I had to change my direction, not by totally abandoning my outer will but, instead, changing my thoughts and the direction I was heading. Knowing this, I began rejecting everything that was not working for me and began allowing the strong, persistent thoughts that were desperately attempting to reach the real inner me to change the direction I was headed in that were emanating from my more superior inner will. By that point, I began combining my inner will with my new persistent thoughts that were coming to me through my inner guidance, and in a relatively short period of time, I began to notice a change in my life, including the beginning of overcoming the serious life-threatening events I was dealing with at the time.

I cannot impress upon you enough the importance of why maintaining a strong inner will is so essential in every area of your life, ranging from your everyday existence, relationships, and, especially, your good health, as well as being able to surmount any adversity that may come your way. Furthermore, I cannot even to begin to express the number of people who choose to follow and are dominated by their ego-driven will, let alone knowing the power of their inner will, when it comes to what they truly desire for good.

If you would just take the time during any given day to look around you when observing people in their daily routines and really observe what is transpiring all around you, you can't help but notice how most people appear to be wandering through life in an apparent semiconscious state, as though living in an almost robotic state and as though their daily routines had been preprogrammed.

Here is a brief example of what I am stating here:

- excessive smoking habits
- excessive alcohol consumption
- constant use of obscene language
- surfing the internet constantly for artificial gratification of every kind
- spending countless hours on social media
- texting on cell phones continuously
- exhibiting bad behavior
- lack of tolerance for others, including being mean-tempered
- impatient, rude, and uncaring attitudes
- poor eating and health habits.
- road rage

This list can take up several pages; however, given that this is not a book on psychology or psychiatry, these examples should suffice to emphasize the point I am attempting to get across to you. Humanity has become so accustomed to merely overlooking and accepting such behaviors, which, quite sadly I might add, have become part of the norm and appear to be quite acceptable to most people—which is even sadder, if not pathetic.

Now, let's take this matter of the importance of having a strong inner will up a few more notches. Following my problems with serious life-changing events, others who were also having similar situations asked me how I was able to seemingly handle these events with such calm and confidence. My response was to first forewarn them that should they choose to continue on their current chosen life path, they very well may find themselves dealing with their undesirable circumstances and situations for some time to come. Having said that, quite surprisingly to me, many were either unwilling to even consider abandoning their unproductive habitual mind-set or to even consider that they could change what it was that may eventually become a serious illness emanating from their self-defeating habitual behavior.

Instead of considering changing their present mind-set, they prefer to defend their present behaviors and thought patterns, including but not limited to excessive alcohol consumption, excessive smoking, overeating, consuming the wrong types of food, lack of exercise, refusal to remove themselves from high stress and possible life-threatening situations, etc. Their mind-set was that strong, especially when it came to addictions to alcohol, sex, smoking, drugs, and related activities that I listed in the "Root Causes" chart I provide earlier and many more not listed that could— and more than likely *would*—eventually lead to even other serious life-changing events and life-threatening illnesses. This is just a brief example of what can happen when one chooses to abandon one's inner guidance and chooses to rely upon their physical world.

This is not a medical opinion or diagnosis as I am not a doctor, psychologist, or psychiatrist; instead, this is a deep concern for anyone who is presently affected by any one of the root causes and should seriously take into consideration changing because no physical illness just shows up one day on one's doorstep. We are all creators of what we eventually come to realize in life, good or bad. You may be wondering what this all has to do with the subject of having a strong will—*everything*!

In my opinion, inner willpower is among the reasons why top athletes achieve such phenomenal feats and go on to break long-term standing records, mountain climbers conquer menacing mountain ranges, astronauts surmount risky ventures to outer space, and explorers descend into deep, uncharted caves far below the earth, seeking to uncover the unseen mysteries of the ages and to attempt to learn more about this planet's origin. Inner willpower is why missionaries travel to the remotest areas of the earth to work with the needy and bring hope and faith to them and why they stay and live with these people for years, giving up modern-day conveniences. In addition are those who choose to become a member of the armed forces choosing to risk their lives to defend freedom knowing they may not return, and those who choose to donate their vital organs to help save the life of another, and those abandoning lifelong habits and vices in exchange for living life apart from these crutches and reaching out to help others who are experiencing similar addictions to overcome them as well. I could list dozens more why a strong inner will, tied to unwavering expectation and steadfast belief in one's inner guidance should seriously be considered to become a major priority in a person's life.

I have witnessed people who felt completely abandoned by others in life lose their will to go on and life became meaningless to them. Perhaps you may have had experienced or are experiencing a similar encounter as well, either personally or with people you know or knew in the past and even close friends and/or family members. Such situations are not only trying but can become very destructive. In my opinion, there is no greater feeling of helplessness than how most of these encounters resonate with those witnessing such a condition.

So then, what about you? Have you thrown in the towel and given in to an adverse situation or undesirable life-changing problem that you needed to address but instead lack the strong inner willpower to confront head-on, whatever it may be? What then is holding you back from taking the initiative and action, which you know you need to take—that is, your personal obligation to yourself and others you love and care? By tapping into your powerful inner guidance, you then also become armed with your inner willpower that can help you overcome any adversity and achieve anything you to accomplish, including prosperity on every conceivable level.

Absolutely know that you were gifted at birth with a remarkable inner mind necessary to achieve your life's purpose, desires, goals, and results you want—reversing or overcoming a health issue, finding a satisfying relationship, raising the family you have dreamed about, overcoming any adverse conditions in your life, conquering an addiction of any kind, or any life-threatening event. Then, now is the time—not a year from now or even one more day, for that matter—as the continuance of life is guaranteed to no one, not even for one more hour, let alone one more year. Your future is today with expectation for a tomorrow! By deciding to take action now, you have everything to gain and, if not, everything to lose!

Please, do not overlook what I just said. I made that mistake and paid the price for it; therefore, heed my warning. You and only you are the captain of your ship—so to speak; you cannot afford to allow anyone to control the direction your life takes because this, if nothing else, is your life, not someone else's.

The people from whom you may be taking advice may not be in your life a year from now, let alone another day, have you ever considered that? *You and you alone are the only one who can make any decisions for your life.* And if you reject this view, then your alternative is to continue to go down the same path you've been traveling on and continue with the same results, if you are experiencing any life-changing adversity. Not a happy picture, is it? And if you are self-victimized by any of the root causes I identified for you earlier, you need to consider taking another path, if you truly want to realize what it is you want.

I've had people with serious illnesses tell me they were following the advice of others and were not proactive concerning what they could do themselves to overcome what they were experiencing. It is okay to listen to others, especially qualified medical professionals, counselors, psychologists, psychiatrists, and other licensed professionals. But even these sources can only help to a certain extent. Then after they have done all they can for you, it becomes the responsibility of the person who is having any adversity to take the initiative necessary to bring forth a healing and eventual cure. Listening is one thing; following someone else's uninformed advice, unless as I said, a credible duly licensed professional—and even then, when it comes to your survival and personal well-being—it is quite another matter.

For example, unless someone had walked in my shoes for, say, the past eighteen years—there is absolutely no way they could possibly know what has been and is currently my reality, be it good or bad or somewhere in between, now, can they? I am not someone in some professional's case files; instead, I am me and not a statistic and I don't ever intend to be, as I have and continue my separate life apart from what anyone else may have and how I choose to live it. Therefore, I choose instead to follow my inner mind that is connected to the infinite intelligence that contains all the answers, methods, and solutions I will ever rely upon to lead and live the life as I was meant to live and to have a life full of joy and prosperity on every conceivable level. Therefore, in my honest opinion, you should also at least consider that you have the same options and opportunity.

Please be aware that any givers of advice—including but not limited to those who have a plaque, certificate, a degree from an accredited university, or have a state license to practice what it is they chose as a profession—who possibly have seen hundreds of people with a similar condition that you may be having, and whom you may have chosen to consult generally base their conclusions upon their learning and the cases they have dealt with in the past. For the most part, most may be doling out the very same advice they had given to those before you; as your case, to them, possibly may not be so unique and may fall into the category of similar past or present cases.

However, you are unique and your case is not similar to anyone else's as, although it may be classified into a type of condition others are presently dealing with at some level. To allow yourself to be corralled with hundreds of others is an injustice to yourself. And as I had also said, even though you may get some useful advice and even some medication, all this is only temporary at best. Nevertheless, it is going to be up to you entirely and ultimately to rid yourself of whatever it is that is plaguing your life. Therefore, self-reliance and self-confidence, along with taking the initiative and action, are among the most important issues this book is focused on.

How do I know this? Because I have been there and have done all that and more. Although I found some of these professionals to be courteous and quite professional in their demeanor, after several sessions, what I felt deep down inside me when leaving any one of these sessions was that I was getting canned responses to my inquiries. I did not feel any different, but it was as though I was talking to myself most of the time and just venting and had learned very little and watched them watching their wall clock and/or wristwatch. And by the end of my allotted hour or so, I was a hundred dollars lighter and oftentimes more.

It is understood that these professionals are there to help, and many of them make an honest attempt at doing so. However, quite unfortunately, their help and advice is temporary. Keep in mind, they are also running a business and for the most part, a for-profit business. I realize that I may have ruffled some feathers and possibly made some angry with what I just said here; however, these are the facts, and I always let the cards fall where they fall, whether it does or does not sit well with those who may be affected by the subject I am addressing. After all, I and countless others have already been down this path, and there is absolutely nothing like having personal experience with whatever it may be to judge one's experiences now, is there?

This is not intended as an affront against any medical professional and is certainly in no way judging their or anyone's chosen profession; I do believe that in certain circumstances, these types of professionals are indispensable. However, ultimately, it rests with you; and only you who can bring forth a permanent resolution to whatever it is that is causing you pain and/or distress. Any good professional who is honest with you may tell you the same.

As for me, I simply knew, through my inner guidance, that if I was going to get myself back on the right track, it was going to be up to me and not someone who knew very little about who I really was internally to be able to give me any methods, answers, and solutions that could resolve my issues. Therefore, I chose instead to rely upon myself and my inner guidance and to tap into the methods, answers, and solutions that I found effective. The method for taping into the methods, answers, and solutions I talk about in this book will be found in the forthcoming chapters.

It has taken me most of my life to get to know myself; therefore, it is literally inconceivable how any one person can come to know me in an hour, a day, or even several years. However, your inner guidance knows everything about you and has all the methods, answers, and solutions you will ever need to bring forth the results for which you are seeking.

Please do not misunderstand; I respect any honest licensed professional, be they psychologists, psychiatrists, medical professionals, or any experienced and credible counselors who truly want to help others. I simply know that if you are seeking methods, answers, and solutions for any life-disrupting event, situation, or circumstances—know that you are walking around with all the answers that are contained within your inner mind that are at your disposal at any time, the same ones that continue to assist me to reach a successful outcome. All you have done is to be willing to tap into them through the method I discovered. Once you make the decision to do so, I can assure you the solutions and answers you are seeking can be found within you and not in some professional's office.

So be your own life counselor by utilizing the methods and the answers coming from your inner guidance that I firmly believe not only salvaged my life and placed me back on the right life path but did so for countless others, just like you and me, throughout numerous generations preceding ours who had very few, if any at all, licensed professionals to consult with and had to rely upon the most powerful force of all that resides within each and every person ever born and that will be.

Although your will plays a very important role in achieving your wants in life and is among the primary reasons that individuals have survived a serious life-changing event, it is by no means the entire answer to overcoming life-threatening events and other conditions. A strong inner will is among the leaders of the army of methods this book identifies, and although each has its own unique power, alone—unaccompanied by the others I have already cited and will continue to be discussing—they have a limited life span. Their enemies are always lurking around just waiting for one or all of them to be weakened by wavering and doubting or lack of commitment to them. This usually occurs when you or anyone may lose patience because certain desires you are seeking may not have yet taken place or within a self-imposed time frame.

You will find a number of these enemies I am speaking about in the "Root Causes" chart in chapter 1. This brief list gives you a good idea of the nonphysical illnesses and conditions that lie in wait to overtake you if and when you permit yourself to become a victim through your own self-destructive wavering thoughts. Chief among these enemies are doubt, lack of belief, lack of self-trust and self-confidence, and, the granddaddy of them all, fear. These enemies are among the reasons you also need an ever-alert and ever-present army surrounding you, led by "General Will Power" (a fictitious pet name

PREVAILING OVER INSURMOUNTABLE ODDS

I have given my inner willpower), to be on constant look out for these enemies, root causes (predators), that can and will return time and time again to make every attempt to regain control of your conscious mind, thoughts, feelings, and your life.

What may make the connecting or the reconnecting, whichever may be the case for you, to the methods provided in this book somewhat concerning to you at first is that you will be doing this on your own without any outside assistance. Should you allow outside influences to interfere with your desire to allow your inner willpower and the other methods that I will be continuing to identify to take over, preventing you from realizing your innermost desires for good, you may find yourself becoming confused and unable to allow your inner mind to take over on your behalf. This is primarily due to the conflicting information you may send or are sending to your inner mind through your habitual thoughts that follows your every command and does not judge the thoughts you are sending it. Therefore, it will deliver to you what your predominant thoughts are asking to be realized in your physical life, be it good or bad. Keep in mind that it is your most dominant, most consistent thoughts that will get the attention of your inner mind, which is connected with the infinite intelligence, better known as the Creator of the universe.

If you are not familiar with the immense energy and power that the universe generates for billions of years, I strongly suggest you invest some of your available time to research this most amazing subject, the universe, which is called by numerous other names; as it is the one and only source that is responsible for origination and continuance of every living thing you see and which provides life to everything.

Now, not to get too far away from the subject at hand, which is the will, and the other methods I will be discussing—when speaking of the universe, this subject often produces a variety of intellectual arguments about its origin, among other scientific arguments that have yet to be resolved and, for my two cents in the matter, probably never will. Why? Because the secret of its source of creation was never meant to be discovered by or divulged to mere mortal beings. If this source wanted us to know, we would. Therefore, these secrets may never be revealed, regardless of how hard and long the scientific world may fruitlessly persist.

For unscientific minds, these scientific arguments, discussions, and the obscene expense utilized in a futile attempt to discover the universe's secrets means very little. It is a fact that almost every religion on this planet has and continues to base its very existence on the belief of an unseen power, by whatever name given that created it all. For thousands of years and from their very inception, these religions have undeniably drawn to them literally billions upon billions of believers and followers teaching them, in their own ways, about the mystery of this ageless, unseen power, thereby having created and continuing to create billions upon billions more believers from all walks of life.

As for myself and millions of others around the globe, I choose to believe that these religions absolutely know how the universe came into existence and the great secret and power behind its origin that I refer to as the infinite intelligence. To add another point here on this matter, medical science has yet to be able to explain how some of the most incredible healings and survival of some of the most deadly illnesses known to humanity was achieved, yet people have and continue to overcome such adversities and go on living a healthy and joyous life. Countless people like me all over the world are unquestionable and undoubtable living proof of the incredible powers of this infinite intelligence where one's inner guidance draws its power and knowledge by whatever name it may be given or called.

Deep within me, without a shadow of a doubt, I feel and believe that none of us are here alone and none of us are without this inner guidance that can, has, and will continue to resolve each and every undesirable life-changing event we may face in this human experience on this planet. I am also convinced, beyond any doubt whatsoever, that this inner guidance exists within each and every person who has been fortunate enough to have had the opportunity and privilege to be born on this planet. Whether your personal preference is to call this unseen guidance connected with infinite intelligence the power of the universe Allah, Buddha, God, etc., any names that have been given to this unseen power by man are meaningless. What is significant, however, is the recognition of this inner guidance that resides deep within you and that you are a living part of this undeniable unseen force.

Having now said all this, I would like to explain why I believe this inner willpower is so important, aside from what I have already identified. Without inner willpower, many people would be led around like an animal on a leash being told where to go and follow others' every command. Take employment, for example. A person does not walk into an employer's facility and take up their position prepared to dictate to the employer what they will or will not do for their salary or whatever compensatory arrangement they may have with their employer. This is not what willpower means, far from it. Instead, this is blatant, outright ignorance and insubordination.

However, given the same scenario, if you were dissatisfied with your employer and your position but feel you must tolerate this situation because you absolutely need this job, here is where your inner willpower can take over on your behalf to resolve the matter quickly, if you will give the matter over to your inner guidance that controls your inner will and gives right direction and contains all the answers and the solutions to any problem or undesirable situations you may possibly encounter or are presently endeavoring to resolve. Believe me, I've been in this situation, like so many others have, and can tell you from personal knowledge that, if one elects to do this, they will see for themselves that by exercising patience it definitely works.

Remember what I said earlier, your dominant thoughts, coupled with strong belief, will gain your inner mind's attention and take action on your behalf.

It is at this point that you call upon the army of methods, led by "General Will Power," to lead the way to bring forth your innermost desires. Once you begin to concentrate and focus on the ideal job you want and maintain that thought and focus, with determination and desire, that this opportunity will appear through your inner guidance that strengthens your will to succeed—you will soon learn that, combined with your even superior willpower and with the powers of other methods—will remove all obstacles in order for your desire to be realized.

I have been asked this question numerous times—*How much time do I need before I realize what I truly desire in my life?* This is a perfectly acceptable and valid question. The answer is, it is totally up to you when you want to act on what it is you desire to show up in your life. If you take initiative and act, review the methods in this book, and include inner willpower and are willing to totally committing yourself in your inner guidance and continue to do this without fail, you will find that many undesirable situations and circumstances will begin to dissipate from your life.

I have every reason to be extremely grateful for rediscovering the phenomenal power of my inner willpower and have absolutely no reason to make any statement of fact that I myself had not personally been aware of or experienced. I also need you to know that I had few alternatives available to me when exposed to a number of life-changing events. Some of these events were very serious, a number of which were life threatening, and time was not on my side.

Chief among these methods that I relied upon to obtain a positive outcome is unwavering belief, without which any one of the other methods, alone or collectively, could not bring forth one's innermost desires.

7

Unwavering Belief

> Belief—the most powerful method
> among the army of methods.
>
> —Author

> Nothing splendid has ever been achieved
> except by those who dared believe
> that something inside them was
> superior to circumstances.
>
> —Bruce Barton

> The outer conditions of a person's life will
> always be found to reflect their inner beliefs.
>
> —James Allen

Here is the common definition of this word belief from the *Merriam-Webster Dictionary*: "a feeling of being sure that someone or something exists or that something is true." This of course is the simple definition of this extremely powerful word, but by no means is this a complete understanding of the word *belief*.

Now let's look at the word *waver*, which means "to vacillate irresolutely between choices"; "fluctuate in opinion, allegiance, or direction." Now let's look at the prefix *un*—"do the opposite of"; "reverse."

The key point here is that joined together, we have the word *unwavering* which, coupled with the word *belief—unwavering belief—* happens to be the most common condition plaguing countless people when it comes to accepting that an *inner guidance/inner mind* does in fact exist within everyone.

This being the case, it's not hard to figure out why so many people are having hardships at every conceivable level and are continuously seeking methods, answers, and solutions, where few—if any—exist in their physical world for whatever it is that is disturbing their life.

Some people will state that anything related to or said to be an unseen force is nonsense. Yet there are countless others throughout the world, dating back thousands of years of recorded time, who acknowledged and continue to recognize the existence of this unseen force to this day. This is the same unseen force that created this world's most astonishing and incredible places and sights and that provided inventors with the ideas, answers, and methods necessary to create unbelievable inventions and also medical scientists to conceive the ideas to design and create high-tech medical advances. Unwavering belief also led generations before to the methods, answers, and solutions—for those who believed in their unseen inner guidance—to overcome insurmountable illnesses and other adversities at every conceivable level and heal sicknesses and terminal illnesses. This force is also responsible for the achievement of high levels of successes that many people have and continue to reach that were once considered to be beyond the average person's imagination.

As for myself, I am firmly convinced beyond any possible doubt that an unseen inner force does exist. Without it, I absolutely know that I would not be here today—without having made the personal choice to make this unseen force a very important and significant part of my everyday life.

Furthermore, I discovered that there is a common bond that runs through all religions of the world and other teachings—such as New Age thought, Christian science, séances, voodoo, and other metaphysical teachings and just why anyone who chooses to accept and apply them to their daily life makes them work. This common bond is none other than strong and unwavering belief.

PREVAILING OVER INSURMOUNTABLE ODDS

Many people want to know why this single word, *belief,* seemingly creates what man has been labeled as miracles. This question has yet to be explained to the satisfaction of many; however know this—it works wonders, and I have absolutely *no doubt* about that. Is it magic ("the art of producing illusions by sleight of hand")? No, it is not. Instead, it is an extremely powerful force that emanates from deep within a person; and when you are focused on what you deeply desire, you can realize and actualize the very thing you believe in.

These thoughts begin to rekindle true, unshakeable belief in oneself, not on the surface but within. If you choose to adopt the methods provided throughout this book, without any doubting and wavering, this alone can release your inner powers that are necessary for obtaining all your life's most heartfelt desires, no matter what they may be that are for good and not evil in any way. This also includes the development and applying of unshakeable faith and unsinkable expectation—two other powerful methods and answers—no matter what storms may continue or may arise in your life.

I have provided the common definition of this very powerful word, belief, which in most languages is understood but quite unfortunately is not always applied in one's life when it comes one's inner powers.

My focus here and for the purposes of this book, however, is about your belief in yourself, in addition to having unshakeable self-trust and confidence in yourself. It is self-confidence, coupled with unwavering strong belief in your inner powers, that leads to successful accomplishments, which then leads to the attainment of your innermost desires that solidifies belief in oneself and nothing else.

That said, this book was also designed for you to rekindle true, unshakeable belief not just on the surface but deep within and to seriously consider adopting the methods provided for you. If you do choose to adopt any one or all of the methods provided in this book without any doubting and wavering, this act alone can and will awaken your inner guidance that you may have allowed to stay inactive. This is absolutely necessary for obtaining all your heartfelt desires, no matter what they may be that are beneficial to all concerned and not for evil in any way.

If you will take the time to really observe what is going on all around you and throughout this world today, when it comes right down to the bare bones of it all, in every area of life, there are really only two important categories of life when it comes to succeeding and reaching any level of success—the believers and unbelievers. There is no grey area. The believers succeed in all they set out to achieve and surmount. The rest are those who continue to grope in the dark, so to speak, for answers, methods, and solutions, seeking and hoping without resolution or action.

The difference between these results can be said in a word—*belief*! Why? Because without a single exception to even be considered, people everywhere become precisely what they think about and *believe* every moment of every day of their lives. Such thoughts, tied to strong beliefs, are continuously and silently nudging you in the right direction, opposed to unbelief, which is shoving you into the wrong direction, dependent on the life desires you are concentrating. In other words, your inner mind is constantly attempting to lead you in the right direction concerning what it is you desire to achieve in your life. That includes but not limited to improved health, prosperity in all areas of your life, and, above all, being able to live a joyous and fulfilled life as you were meant to. In order to do this, it is imperative that you do not rely solely upon hope and other people; instead, you must take the initiative yourself with full expectation that the results you are seeking for good, without any doubt, can show up in your life when coupled with unwavering belief in your incredible inner powers.

Why is unwavering belief so vital to what you want to experience in your life? Having a positive attitude and employing positive thinking, alone, rarely will bring forth what you may desire because they lack the necessary fuel, so to speak, needed to bring forth the desire and results one is seeking. Although these two mindsets are an important part and a good beginning toward helping you achieve what you want in life, without strong, unwavering belief and unwavering expectancy, taking the initiative, and your internal instincts (inner feelings) that come from your inner guidance—it will be an arduous and very long road toward your innermost desires, if at all. This is what separates those who succeed from those who do not. If you are not aware, practically every notable accomplishment known to mankind to date came about only because people were willing to take the initiative, action, and risk—coupled with unwavering belief in themselves and the goal(s) they were utterly determined to achieve—without giving in to any thought of defeat, fear, or doubting, despite dealing with a sea full of challenges and ridicule.

This is precisely what you will need to consider adopting into your life if you truly want to accomplish anything you desire. Whether it is maintaining and/or returning to good health; surviving a serious illness; being the first to succeed at something no one else has even considered venturing into; being in a competitive position; conquering any adversity you may be faced with at the moment or in the future; ridding yourself of any undesirable situation, event, or circumstances, etc.—you can achieve all this through unwavering belief.

All this and more, however, begins and ends with unwavering belief. Belief in what? Belief in yourself first! Unless and until you develop unwavering belief in yourself, willpower alone, already identified as another very powerful method—will be useless to you because a strong will without unwavering belief in yourself and what you truly desire in your life becomes seriously impeded.

My vast contact with all sorts of people in my personal and professional life revealed to me that most people were very capable of developing a strong belief in themselves; however, many were unaware of how to do this successfully. This is primarily due to having held false images they had of themselves and the opinions that others in their lives had about them, thereby allowing themselves to literally conform to these images, making them real. Sad but true.

This unfortunate mind-set more than likely just may have begun to develop when they were children, usually beginning in grammar school and continuing through their high school years and adolescence period. If this depicts you, absolutely know that you can believe and develop confidence in yourself in a very big way by simply beginning right here and right now and envision yourself reaching the level of life you desire and hold those images in your mind constantly without wavering or doubting.

The more you believe in this new image of yourself and the achievements you desire to realize, no matter how old you are or what your present circumstances may be at this point in your life, know that you can and will become what you steadfastly believe and focus on! I was there once and know without any reservations or doubts that not only is this possible, but it is extremely possible. Keep in mind that it is you and you alone, not what others may say or attempt to decide for you, who must make the decision to place yourself on the path toward changing your circumstances.

Having said this, I can tell you from my very own personal knowledge that belief in self is among the strongest of the methods you will find in this book. Earlier, I emphasized the importance of developing a strong willpower, which I had pointed out is also an essential method for achieving your desires and ridding yourself of any undesirable occurrences. However, as I said repeatedly, unless a strong will is coupled and tied to a strong self-belief, it is inconceivable in my mind that you can expect to gain the results you wish for your life.

Belief in self is extremely important to have in your and everyone's life, not only achieving it but maintaining it permanently. Once you decide to accept this premise, I can assure you that your life can be remarkably changed and elevated to heights and desired outcomes you possibly could not imagine were achievable. Not only are they attainable, but they already exist in your life. If you will maintain belief in self, along with the other methods we have discussed up to this point and others we will be continuing to explore together, from this point forward know that your desires can be realized in your life sooner than you can imagine.

I can tell you that from speaking with numerous people I have encountered who were beset by undesirable life-changing events, some more serious than others, the absence of steadfast belief in their lives and abilities were among the deepest problems they expressed. Many of these people did not even trust themselves, and the greater majority stated that nothing in their lives seemingly can ever go right for them. Many also admitted that they did not believe they have the confidence within themselves to pursue or be able to accomplish what they truly desire in their lives. Instead, they settled and became content with something much less than what they were and still are certainly capable of achieving.

Having had the opportunity to travel extensively in my business career, I've met people in other areas of the world who afforded me the unique opportunity to speak to them about this matter of belief in self. I found that an astonishing number of people outside this country also go through their lives on their knees, surrounded by ongoing fear, uncertainty, and engulfed with a very evident aura of defeat. Those with who I had the opportunity to speak about this subject who openly admitted to these problems were also chronically frustrated; however, none of these conditions should ever have to happen to you or anyone.

Like thousands of others, I too have personally known the hard knocks life can dish out and the accumulation of difficulties and problems that can suck the strength out of even the strongest person, leaving them discouraged and downtrodden. However, when choosing to adopt an attitude of unshakeable belief, you'll become assured you are far less defeated than you had convinced yourself you were. As a matter of fact, once you choose to adopt a strong belief in yourself, you will begin to sense, almost immediately, the feeling that you never were vanquished. Instead, you feel self-imposed disbelief and are falsely discouraged, thereby allowing your conscious mind to be dragged in that direction and for many, regrettably, for far too many years.

If not stopped in their tracks, these conditions can and often will lead to serious physical conditions. Some of these can lead to life-threatening illnesses. What I can also tell you from my personal experience is that most people actually unconsciously invite and allow undesirable events to overpower them physically and mentally long before they begin to do something about it. I did and paid one heck of a price by doing so. However, once the decision is made to choose a more optimistic thought-out path, whatever life-challenging matter can be overcome and eventually defeated entirely. How do I know this? Because, as I've been saying, I overcame serious life-changing and life-challenging adversities and events by refusing to follow a pessimistic path. Coupled with unwavering belief and my all-powerful inner guidance that is one with infinite intelligence, I continue to be provided with all the methods, answers, and solutions needed.

It is this state of steadfast belief where you will always find the total difference in choice and then be able to clearly recognize a doomsday attitude for what it really is. The answer lies in choosing to see the possibilities versus the impossibilities in any undesirable life conditions. I believe that anything is possible to achieve and/or overcome—and I mean anything—ranging from ridding yourself from continuing in a "doomsday state of mind," to choosing to overcome and defeat any undesirable situation plaguing your life, right out to bringing forth a permanent healing for an illness.

There are some people who prefer to believe that overcoming any undesirable condition was just luck, a subject I covered earlier. However, for anyone who wishes to use the word *luck*, let me tell you that luck has and never will play a role in overcoming or curing anything. A strong inner will to succeed and/or overcome—coupled with unwavering belief, steadfast self-trust, unshakeable self-confidence, and, above all, unshakeable expectation, each one singularly and collectively are proud soldiers in the vast army of methods—brings forth the desired outcome, no matter what it may be. Luck is nothing more than a powerless word and has no place in your or anyone's vocabulary, as it is permeated with skepticism and uncertainty.

As you continue on in the book, you will notice that there are no exercises that you have to do at the end of any chapter, although there are a few suggestions and activities intended to assist you in examining your individual situation. I am going to ask you to do what was a key turning point for me during my encounters with life-threatening illnesses.

On any piece of paper and something to write with, write down everything that is for you in your life, not against you. Include those whom love you, who care about you, and anything you consider an asset—good friends, children (if you have them), your residence and everything in it, what you are grateful for (another powerful method), your accomplishments thus far in life, no matter how great or small they may seem to be, your spouse or significant other who supports you, etc. If you believe in an unseen power, no matter what your religious faith may be, the fact that, if you are reading this, you still have your vision; if you have your hearing and other senses; and, the ultimate, you are still breathing at this very moment is a blessing in itself!

Where do you believe this all came from? Are you bold enough to call yourself the sole creator of all you have obtained for good and realized thus far in your lifetime? What I am getting to here is that you played a minor role with whatever it is that has manifested for good in your life. Most successful people believe that their accomplishments came from them and them alone and nothing more. However, that *nothing* can be further from reality because it all originated first from one's inner mind that one unconsciously communicated with, by way of their dominant thoughts that brought forth one's innermost desires for good to be realized. Most people who do not believe in an inner guidance and inner mind that is connected to an infinite intelligence and its incredible powers truly believe that they have accomplished all they have by their own efforts and hard work. Yet many who believe this way have also lost much, if not all, of what they believed they had accomplished and achieved alone due to their lack of belief in their inner power that sustains their prosperity. All one has to do to prove this to themselves is to take a good look at all the loss and deprivation that exist and the prosperity that has and continues to slip away and elude millions throughout the world.

Know this—if you or anyone continuously chooses to believe that something appears to be against you, it is you or anyone who believes this that is giving it permission to overpower you and to continue to hold you in its grip. This includes people who may exhibit being against you. Is this what you truly want?

Instead, you will allow yourself to acknowledge, visualize, and concentrate upon the thought that you are more than worthy, you have been blessed with an incredible gift, your all-powerful inner mind. Once you come to realize this and put it to work for you, you will know those who refuse to recognize this infinite inner power will not receive blessings as much as you will. Your only cost for this blessing is to give thanks and be continually grateful for what you have; and you will also soon find yourself to begin rising to greater heights in your life and will experience the decline of your problems, difficulties, etc., that you believed were once so overwhelming. Recall what I have been saying over and over again: it is your inner guidance, coupled with unwavering belief, that can deliver you to total victory and not anything or anyone else in your outer world.

I have been told on countless occasions by people who claimed to have placed their belief in something that nothing came about in their favor. Others have told me that they tried to believe that what they wanted to materialize in their life had continuously eluded them and, therefore, they stopped believing and just accepted life as it was for them. These situations do not depict true belief in self because what they did instead was to choose to believe in unbelief. Short-term belief is not belief at all; instead, it is wishful thinking.

Knowing what you want to materialize in your life does not equate to your actually believing you can achieve whatever it is you know you desire. By placing a deadline on the results that you want to appear in your life within a certain fixed period is nothing more than limiting your beliefs and instead placing self-constructed hurdles on your pathway, thereby obstructing the manifesting of what it is you truly want as a positive outcome.

If you do not wholeheartedly believe in what you want in this life and are not willing to allow your inner guidance time to allow your wants to materialize, you can always expect to not receive your wants.

Think of your inner guidance as your fairy godmother (fictional character) that grants your desires for good, and I believe you will then be able to grasp the picture in your mind of what I am actually saying to you here. Never forget that you absolutely must allow time to have your wants and desires develop without any doubting whatsoever. Impatience would negate your progress, and you would have to begin all over again—believing, with absolute expectation and patience (patience is another very powerful method), that your desires will show up in your life in time.

If you are going to ever be able to develop what you want to appear in your physical life, you will first need to understand and to accept that you will need to muster up the courage to shed all your long-term habitual disbeliefs and to faithfully believe—without doubting, with full expectation—that whatever it is you desire will eventually materialize when you least expect it.

So what I am saying is, take the steering wheel out of your hands, so to speak, and relinquish control to your all-powerful inner guidance that is connected to the infinite intelligence to bring forth whatever it is you wish to appear for good and for the benefit of all who may be concerned, knowing that it will arrive in your life. The only way it cannot, as I pointed out, is to insert doubt, lack of patience, skepticism, negative thoughts, and unbelief into your thoughts, which individually and/or collectively will override the positive outcome of your innermost desires.

You see, you may believe that you totally control the realization of your desires, but the reality is, you don't—no one does. Without first believing and accepting that there exists a greater and deeper power within you than your outer self (your conscious mind), you possibly may not gain what you truly want in life. As I said earlier, any success you have was not accomplished totally through your outer self, despite your belief. Instead, it came from your all-powerful inner guidance from which every good thing you have ever experienced materialized due to your inner guidance's intervention by bringing forth what you truly believed, without doubting or wavering, and would one day become reality in your life and, in many instances, did.

I have known many people who refused to believe in their inner guidance and chose instead to proceed on their own, especially those who had very serious physical illnesses. The outcome, in many of these instances, was continued failed health, total dependency on various medications, ongoing surgeries, counseling, extended stays at rehabilitation facilities, and disrupted families. This also resulted in either limited recovery, total dependency on medical science for a permanent healing, and following all types of unqualified advice from clueless people.

People have asked me, "How is it possible that an inner guidance can help me? I have never called upon any so-called inner guidance in my life and got through up to now okay?" Others also said, "I do not believe that any such power—or higher power, for that matter—exists." You do not have to call upon your inner guidance or have to believe in a higher power because these powers were gifted to you at birth. This gift does not necessarily have to hear your plea verbally or from your thought because before any verbal request or thought ever reaches your inner guidance, it feels it. Deep belief is a thing one feels, hence the beginning of the creation of one's innermost desires. When you allow doubting and disbelief to enter is when those desires begin to dissipate and go unfulfilled.

Once that feeling is sensed by your inner guidance, it begins immediately to go to work on bringing forth your innermost desires without your ever having to ask. Asking and continued deep, focused thought certainly are the key to reaching your desires sooner because focused thought, deep belief, and lack of doubting and expectation are the key that opens the inner vault that brings forth the awareness of attaining any deep desires that are for your good and not for evil.

Focus on what I just said here as this, among all the other methods you have read in this book, is one of the keys to obtaining every desire you have. If nothing else, as I've repeated to the point of extreme redundancy purposely [!], if there is just one iota of doubt inserted by you in what you are trusting to validate, your innermost desires will not be actuated, unless and until the doubting is no longer prevalent. Your inner mind requires unwavering belief in order to bring forth your desires.

Once you choose to accept this and accept that deep, steadfast, unwavering belief sets in motion extremely powerful, unseen forces that immediately begin creating your deepest innermost desires for good, you will begin to see signs of your beliefs beginning to manifest. It is here where you will need to exercise great patience and allow your inner guidance the time necessary to bring forth whatever it may be you are seeking to develop for you to experience. And as I also said, and to which I will now add, if you truly believe that you can accept this deep within yourself and decide to discard all your previous habits of harboring a constant negative mind-set—habit of self-depreciation, deep unfounded fears, feelings of unworthiness and inadequacy, and feelings of despair—you may begin to believe in yourself. If you come to realize and believe that there is more than enough in the world for you and everyone to experience, without any doubt whatsoever where you are concerned, you cannot help but realize your innermost desires.

On the other hand, if you do not believe that you can shed disbelief and change your life accordingly and choose to continue to go on day by day believing some unseen evil power is against you and that there will never be anything good for you to realize, then you can very well expect exactly that result and to continue on that same self-created, self-destructive path. However, I truly am confident that it was and is not your intent to stay on that path and instead, which is more than likely, change all that now.

I sincerely trust that you truly want to change your life for the better, whether it is a satisfactory relationship; improved health; happiness and prosperity on all levels of your life; conquering depression, anxiety, or stress beyond your capacity to cope; and/or ridding yourself of any of the conditions listed as the *root causes* (predators).

Again, how do I know all this? Because I am no different than you and have already traveled down that road—not once but many times—and from me to you, I've paid my dues and then some and am still standing and have refused to allow any of it get me to the point of caving in or waving the white flag of surrender. Never! Why? Because I've learned how to stop all those conditions dead in their tracks before they even have an opportunity to get started. By the time you reach the end of this book, my confidence is so strong in you that I sincerely trust that you can too!

From this point forward, I want you to make a personal commitment to yourself that you will immediately cease entertaining any thoughts that lead to feelings of unworthiness, doubting, fear, uncertainty, or any that are members of the "I cannot" family of doubting, no matter what they may be. These all serve as self-fulfilling prophecies leading you to not being able to ever experience what you truly desire, thereby giving you the excuse to say to yourself, "See, I was right!" No, you're not!

During my involvement with serious illnesses, I could not help noticing other patients awaiting surgery and those who had already gone through a surgical procedure and their loved ones who had already accepted defeat. Their conversations were, at best, extremely gloomy and fraught with doubt.

Keep in mind that wanting anything good, without strong and dedicated belief, can only lead to one place—that is, your choosing not to participate in your life but instead waiting for something, someone, or some other outside source to come and take away your circumstances for you. This state of mind and self-created unbelief and lack of self-trust and self-confidence and willingness to pass the baton, so to speak, on to other sources to take you over the line of victory can only lead to continued failures. No runner in any race ever expected to cross the finish line as a winner by being carried across that finish line on the back of another runner, and neither should you! Cut out what I just said here, enlarge it, frame it, and hang it on every wall of your home, office, if you have one, or wherever you spend most of your time to remind you of what this survivor just said to you here. Never forget it!

I cannot even begin to tell you how many people whom I have met who truly live this way and have for a very long time. Why? Because they're looking for a sure thing to just appear out of nowhere that will resolve their maladies for them. They will only choose to believe when they know exactly what the actual results will be. They completely live in a state of denial, believing that some superhero will come into their lives and take away their pain or undesirable problem, including serious illnesses on every conceivable level or any one of the numerous life-changing conditions that a person can suffer without steadfast belief and full expectation that they can manage any of those conditions without total dependency on any source beside themselves.

If people who are going through these types of trauma truly want to change their negative circumstances, it is going to take a dedicated initiative on their part to be able to make the decision to take a firm stand against the enemy standing before them. If they are to have any expectation of ridding themselves from whatever threat they are dealing with, they must be willing to engage and muster up the courage to face up to any obstacles that may be preventing them from living the life they are seeking to enjoy and certainly deserve.

Many people will say they have tried to shed their self-created self-destructive ways of thinking yet time and time again will return to them because this is where their comfort zone lies. Belief for them is in their negative ways and attitudes because this is where their seemingly unshakeable self-defeating beliefs reside.

If I did not believe that I could completely heal from the cancers and other serious life-changing adversities and other life-changing events, chances are that I more than likely would not be here. I am not alone in that regard, as there have been many people whom you may have read or heard about who experienced similar situations. But for some unknown reason, many have not come forward to share their self-healing involvement through what I believe to have been the power of their deep inner belief, coupled with employing most of the methods I have thus far identified—especially a strong will to succeed and/or overcome, steadfast self-trust, unshakeable self-confidence, and, above all, unshakeable belief and expectation.

If you are about to say to yourself "I tried all that before, but it does not work," and others may possibly say, "Yeah, I read all those self-help books, and I already know most of what is in them, and there is nothing new or workable for me here," really!

Now ask yourself, how often have you acted on what you say you already know and read and for how long a period of time? If you will tell me you read some of what is suggested in self-help books and tried it for a while but nothing happened, it is very possible that you just may not have believed any of this would pay off for you. However, for any of this to work for you, it first must be put into practice and to take action and made a permanent part of your life and part of your everyday routine coupled with unwavering belief that it can. Unless you are willing and able to do this, you're right, it won't work for you—none of it will, including what you will find in this book!

A good example of this would be that if most people realize that and they would just let go of whatever it is they spend a great deal of their time pondering and worrying over and instead just trust, they can receive all that is needed, if these desires and wants are allowed to be left to their inner power—one's inner guidance, connected with infinite intelligence—that can bring forth the good one is seeking. It may be possible you do not believe this deeply enough and, therefore, are afraid to take the risk. Well, believe me; you are already taking a huge risk by choosing to only believe and rely upon everything in your outer world (your physical life) where to find the answers and solutions to your problems.

Don't worry, as I was right where you and many people are before I began to totally believe in my extraordinary inner mind and am extremely pleased that I made this personal choice to believe unwaveringly, so are countless others who made the same choice. My proof, you may be asking—I am living proof of these immense powers, as I relied upon no one or nothing in my outer world to bring forth a permanent healing and overcoming all that I did, other than the methods, answers, and solutions provided to me through my all-powerful inner guidance.

It is extremely important that you clearly understand that your innermost desire(s) are only as strong as your belief in their becoming reality. If you are weak and prone to giving up quickly, should something you deeply desire not materialize in your life right away, then you can rely on the fact that you may not be able to realize most of your deepest, innermost desires, if any. It simply does not work that way for anyone, and no matter how much you or anyone may wish to choose to believe differently, nothing will change significantly concerning your circumstances, unless you choose to change it. Unless or until you personally make the decision to build your patience and accept the truth that steadfast belief, coupled with deep trust in your all-powerful inner power, can very well be the answer you are seeking.

I cannot think of a better opportunity right here and right now to make this change in your life. Most, if not all, of you will ever need to know about changing your circumstances, whatever they may be in the present or in the future, and will be bound to those concepts of steadfast belief and deep trust. Like most people, I too tried to have manifested my deepest desires through my outer worldly knowledge and quickly found that even if I did accomplish something I wanted and took the credit for it, this gain was short-lived at best. I finally learned that if it were to be and if it were to last, it was not only going to have to be up to me to believe it but for me to expect it and believe that I—like you and everyone—was gifted with an inner guidance from where all deep desires are eventually answered and made evident in the lives of all those who truly choose to believe.

PREVAILING OVER INSURMOUNTABLE ODDS

Here is what many have chosen to accept and believe instead of trusting in their inner guidance: Trusting that things in their lives are as they should be. Although there are many people who choose to adopt this as being true concerning their lives, I decided not to do that and chose instead to believe in my inner guidance, which has served me well. I decided not to accept and settle for the status quo, so to speak, and instead do something about the very serious and other life-changing events I personally encountered.

I believe that many people have gone through even more than what I had in their lifetimes. Therefore, I did not question the *why* I had to go through all I have; instead, I chose to let it all go. Not too long after I made this decision, I began noticing that a number of these life-changing events began to heal themselves and began to disappear from my life. Therefore, I chose to live my life trusting in the methods I have used and continue to identify throughout this book. From my personal knowledge, I can attest that these methods have never failed me; without a doubt, where I am concerned, they worked and continue to do so because they are connected with the infinite intelligence, which is connected to my inner mind.

There has been some ignorance attached to the serious life-changing events I sustained and overcame; some people and critics have stated that I was just the exception, not the rule. However all one has to do is to speak with any survivor of a life-threatening event or to read the survival stories of people who had no chance of surviving some of the most frightening of human episodes, ranging from airline crashes to overcoming and surviving medically diagnosed life-threatening and terminal illnesses. Despite these survivals, there are still many critics out there who truly believe that most people survived due to just being lucky. Really!

Had I relied upon luck to overcome all that I have up to now, I am convinced I wouldn't be here today. The odds would have never been in my corner and luck, as I stated earlier—if one decides to believe in such a word—doesn't happen every time someone comes face to face with a major life-challenging event, far from it. And it plays no role whatsoever for that matter.

You may be asking yourself, where does one start? You start right where you are and begin to truly believe in what you want in your life. Once you make the decision to truly believe from deep within, you will soon begin to feel and know by turning to your inner mind for what it is you need to do to make it a reality and by employing the methods within the pages of this book. Your inner guidance, coupled with these methods, will not fail to reveal whatever it is you desire to manifest for good in time, if you will exercise patience and maintain a strong, unwavering belief that it will.

If you will choose to connect with your inner guidance and to apply these methods to your life, the moment you choose to do so, you then set into motion all the powers you were gifted at birth that can make it possible for you to channel your innermost desire for good. Keep in mind that you cannot allow yourself to become discouraged; instead, truly believe and expect that what you want to materialize can occur.

Like myself, when I first began to develop the methods necessary to produce my innermost desires, I made the decision to be a role model for others whom I knew also had a need for similar results—to inspire them by example, to make this connection with their inner guidance, and to begin to believe, unwaveringly, in what they truly wanted in their lives.

Allow me to ask you these questions: Do you truly believe in what you want as a positive outcome? Are you truly happy? I believe that people ask these questions themselves silently every day throughout the world.

When speaking with numerous people throughout my travels, I was not surprised to hear that most people were not certain about what they really wanted to experience in life that would make them truly happy, with the exception of having more money which they equate to being able to acquire everything they believe will make them happy. I've already had this feeling and have also taken a very hard look at the lives of many of the rich and the famous, many of whom whose wealth has and continues to fail to achieve for them true happiness. This is not limited to the entering into and exiting from numerous unhappy marriages in a short period of time and abrupt endings to their careers due to some condition, illnesses, drug and alcohol addictions, etc., and whose money cannot help them evade serious life-threatening health conditions or be able to buy a permanent healing from any serious life-changing events.

Take it from me, money is far from the answer and is, at best, temporary happiness and can never buy true happiness. Anyone who believes that it can is fooling themselves, as it is just a matter of time before they come to realize this truth. Most who have ventured to try to buy their way to true happiness and joy have ultimately fallen and failed because there is so much more to life than reliance upon money to buy true happiness. Granted, money is an essential part of everyone's life; however, it can be—and all too often is—the downfall of those who totally rely upon it to bring them perpetual good fortune.

Among some of the most astonishing statements I have heard from people, as I previously identified as well, was that they could not bring themselves to believe something until they have first seen or have experienced it (whatever "it" means to them). Others have said to me that they could not begin to believe to trust in something unless or until they were absolutely certain how something was going to work out for them. (Crystal balls, however, simply do not exist.) Herein lies the fact that any conditional, limiting belief you or anyone may have is nothing more than wishful thinking, at best.

Giving you the benefit of my personal knowledge, I caution you once again that if you have one iota of doubt, lack of trust, disbelief, and, above all, lack of expectation about being able to achieve what you want, you certainly will not be able to bring about and enjoy the positive outcomes you are seeking. Whether you are seeking a return to or maintaining good health; an improved lifestyle; or reaching a solution to an impaired relationship, lack of trust, disbelief, and, above all—and again—lack of expectation will overwhelm your quest.

By placing any preconditions on whatever it is that you desire for good will more than likely not show up in your life because expectation without taking the initiative, followed by immediate action, is a waste of your time. Conditional thinking, attached to conditional requirements, does not register with one's inner guidance because this type of thinking is the same as telling your inner guidance that you have no trust in its immense powers. Therefore, what you choose to not believe will eventually return to you. How do I know? Because prior to choosing to adopt and rely upon my inner guidance and rely upon it totally, I too was an award-winning skeptic who kept experiencing the opposite of all that I wanted to obtain. Once I chose to allow my inner power to take complete charge of the outcome of what I was seeking to manifest in my physical life, almost everything I wanted and expected, over time, began appearing in my life and continues to provide what I seek for achieving the positive outcomes that I desire.

A decision made by you to be unwilling to let go of old, unproductive beliefs such as I just mentioned creates a self-debilitating condition that, like a circle, has no real end. These types of beliefs tend to say to you over and over and over again that the world and everything in it is totally against you, and therefore, this is exactly what you can expect to continue to reproduce in your conscious mind.

If you are to have any hope of changing your unwanted circumstances, as I said, it is going to be you who will have to take the first step to turning whatever it is you wish to change in your life for the better. You need to make the decision to want to change your circumstances and mean it. And once you do, you then need to take immediate and decisive action toward the achievement of those desires.

I have witnessed and met people who believe in faith without action. They truly believe that once they place their faith in a thing that this is good enough; they, therefore, can just sit back and wait until their faith brings them the desired results. This is prevalent in the followers of most religions. I hate to have to be the bearer of bad news, but faith alone simply does not work that way; it never has and it never will. And one can wait until the cows come home, so to speak, and their faith will still be just that—idle faith without action on their part.

The materialization of any deep desire through real faith can only be affected when doubt, fear, and limiting beliefs are no longer present and action is applied. We read in James 2:14–26, "Thus also faith by itself, if it does not have works, is dead" (NKJV).

PREVAILING OVER INSURMOUNTABLE ODDS

You are also cautioned to understand and be able to accept deep within yourself that true faith requires your ability to be able to have the intensity and the courage to absorb the methods and answers given to you by an all-knowing infinite intelligence. Should you choose to do so, faith will test you to determine your depth of patience to be worthy of what you truly want to exist.

Some people have the thought that by attending religious services regularly, they will accelerate the materializing of their deepest desires. However, belief in a higher power also means a strong belief in self and taking control of one's life by taking the necessary action, coupled with unwavering belief, toward helping themselves to achieve their deeply desired outcome.

An example of what I did to achieve my innermost desires and still do to this very moment that continues to work for me is evidenced by all that was deemed remarkable by many who witnessed my recovery from all that I had overcome. When I was told that I had a very slim chance of survival, I challenged this prognosis and immediately began to weigh the odds of my survival without chemotherapy treatments. Not having a great deal of time on my side to decide what I was to do regarding this prognosis, I made the decision to learn what the obstacles would be that would obstruct me from overcoming these life-threatening illnesses. Knowing that I had been gifted with an inner guidance that is connected with infinite intelligence that I had previously rarely sought for methods and answers, I began to consult with this infinite intelligence continuously and refused to allow any outside influences to move me in any other direction whatsoever, other than the methods and answers I was receiving. This decision, as I previously identified, and the actions taken on my part concerned a lot of people, including family, business associates, friends and acquaintances, and especially medical professionals by whom I had been receiving what I considered the best medical care within the limits of what medical science had to offer at the time. From what I have gathered, things have not changed to a significant degree, although advances have been made in diagnostic technology, surgical procedures, medications, therapy, and new stem cell research.

Among my major challenges were to shed my previous limiting beliefs and wavering faith and to yield to my inner powers. Not being a very religious person at that time in my life, I certainly had previously believed that most, if not all, my accomplishments in life were of my doing. Wow, was I way off course! There I was, face to face with not just one but two advanced cancers. So I asked myself, *What am I going to do? Should I place my faith and confidence totally in medical science and the medical community? Or should I combine my inner guidance with the knowledge of medical science?*

In the end, I followed the direction given to me by my inner guidance and refused to go forward with any postoperative chemotherapy treatments and to utilize medical science strictly for postoperative follow-up, which turned out to be the right decision.

Prior to my serious medical problems, I was accustomed to having to make very important business decisions; however, when it came to having to make decisions related to much greater matters like my health and life-threatening matters, I chose to relinquish those decisions to my inner mind. As most people are aware, any decision always involves having to make a choice. However, it has been my experience—in business as well as health issues—that many people have difficulty making a choice. They will defer critical choices and decisions to others, and more often than not, the resultant effect is that they fail to achieve what they wanted.

"If you fail to make a decision, you can rely on the fact that life will make the choice for you"—I believe this saying depicts so many people globally. We also witness this in our very own elected officials, many of which will play follow the leader and, in many instances, will follow that leader right off the cliff, so to speak. I have counseled with people about this very issue and told them that they needed to take charge of their life and to become the major participant concerning their life decisions. Having done this, one will certainly be sending out a definitive message to their inner mind and activate the right actions needed to achieve what they desired.

Contrary to this, when you make the decision to simply react to life, you will have a very difficult time in being able to achieve your innermost desires. The primary objective here is to become creative and proactive versus the opposite—indecision, which has its very own message and creative energy. The direction taken with indecision is similar to driving in a very dense fog on an unfamiliar highway, uncertain of your actual position with possible pending disaster lying ahead. What I am expressing here is that you owe it to yourself to make a sacred promise with yourself—that is, taking total control of your life and become proactive instead of being reactive. Once you make this decision, it must be immovable, without wavering or being swayed in any way by any outside influences, regardless of the source.

Keep in mind, this is your life we are discussing, not anyone else's; therefore, you need to pay very close attention to what I am saying here. The quality of your life certainly depends upon the decisions, choices, and beliefs that you choose to employ concerning your life from this point forward.

Decide that from here on, you will let go of your limiting beliefs and polluted thinking. You have now found the right path for your life and welcome this opportunity to change your former life. You are now prepared to abandon your old ways of believing, thinking, and reacting. Do this today, and you will soon begin making the right decisions to choose independently and, by doing so, have unshakeable belief.

Keep in mind at all times that your life, the condition of your health, and any successes you have are the result of the cumulative decisions and choices that you had made in the past. These now are resulting in what you may possibly currently find to be significant, as will all future choices you make for what you truly want to see realized in your life.

Ask yourself if there may be something that would enhance your life that would also be good for anyone concerned about you—be it a return to good health; a special, mutually rewarding relationship; a career of your choosing; or whatever positive results you may wish to develop. Then make the unshakeable decision and choice, with unwavering belief and full expectation, that it will soon be reflected in your life. Whatever you do, never abandon this belief under any circumstances. Once you choose to do this, you will actually begin to feel a great change come over you, and this will be a sign that you are now well on your way to having what it is you deeply desire in your life.

It baffles me how most people will believe in a thing for a while; however, when that something does not materialize in their life quickly, they are quick to abandon their belief. Then there are people who will believe in others to bring forth their desires and wants who, quite unfortunately, are deeply disappointed when others they believed ins seemingly failed them.

There are those who will place their entire faith and belief in medical science to the point of making their medical professionals gods in their life and will follow every direction and opinion given them, without question. Then there are close family and friends who will render their beliefs and opinions, which many people will choose to believe and follow. Also there are countless others who—when faced with ill health, a life-threatening event. or illnesses, for some inexplicable reason—choose not to believe in themselves. What is this phenomenon and why?

The answer is simple—a lack of trust and confidence in themselves and the inner, intuitive feelings that emanate from their inner mind.

In conjunction with the other methods and answers, self-belief is in the forefront which, when combined, forms an unbeatable, unseen, and formidable force that can only come from deep within oneself. If what has been depicted thus far may describe circumstances and problems in your life on any level, the total answer for you is to explore and develop the power of your inner mind.

It is quite amazing how many people will choose to scoff and not believe in such a powerful inner force and instead continue to rely upon everything else that hasn't worked for them and most likely will continue to not work for them in the future. There are absolutely no outside sources that can attest to being able to provide a permanent solution to the many adversities people may experience; however, in my opinion, as a survivor of numerous life-threatening conditions, there is only an inner guidance that is connected with infinite intelligence that can.

You are familiar with this guidance through your intuitive feelings. How often do you get what is commonly referred to as an inner feeling or a hunch? What is this feeling? Where is it coming from? What is directing it? Has it ever not come to you just in time and you made a decision to or not to go forth with something? Have you ever had to rely upon your intuition in an emergency situation and were glad you did?

Did you ever get insight to the right methods and answers to apply to a problem, circumstance, etc., that aided you in an important decision yet you never questioned where this intuitive feeling came from but faithfully chose to follow it? Sure you have, and so have I and millions of others and were glad we did. We just may have ignored these strong intuitive feelings that seemed to keep hounding us until we either chose to ignore them and later regret we did or decide to acknowledge and act upon them, according to what these intuitive feelings were attempting to convey to us.

This now brings us to the method that is responsible for what we choose to believe, feel, and focus on continuously—the tremendous power that our conscious and unconscious thoughts have and why they play such a vital role in absolutely everything that exists in our physical lives.

8

THE INCREDIBLE POWER OF THOUGHT

> Let us radically alter our thoughts, and we will be astonished at the rapid transformation it will effect in the material conditions of our lives.
>
> —James Allen

In popular usage mind is frequently synonymous with thought: the private conversation with ourselves that we carry on "inside our heads." Thus we "make up our minds," "change our minds" or are "of two minds" about something. One of the key attributes of the mind in this sense is that it is a private sphere to which no one but the owner has access. No one else can "know our mind." They can only interpret what we consciously or unconsciously communicate. (Wikipedia)

Thought is one of the primary methods in identifying whatever it is you deeply desire to develop in your life. In the twenty-first century, all anyone has to do is to look around them to see evidence of the immense power that thoughts contain for the creation of good and equally as powerful for the creation of evil. Thoughts conveyed to an entire nation by even one person alone, such as those during the reign of Adolf Hitler and other world leaders, were able to control entire nations that became obsessed with world domination. This phenomenon is just one example that continues to dominate millions throughout the world today.

To get an even clearer understanding of this powerful method, you should take a moment to think about this phenomenon known as thought. No one knows what thought really is, aside from the fact that thought is a mental action. Yet we see its result every day in many ways, everywhere we look on this planet.

It is extremely important that you understand and reemphasize that every thought you hold on to for an extended period of time about anything that is eventually conveyed to your inner mind is precisely what you will inevitably witness in your physical life—be it prosperity on every level, joy, good health, poverty, lack, illness, other ailments, sadness, a serious undesirable situations, etc.

Everyone knows what thought is and also knows that all of us have many of them every hour, let alone the thousands that pass through our minds every day. You certainly must realize that it is virtually impossible to be able to focus on every single thought. The question I get asked quite often is, "With so many going through my mind constantly, can I be expected to select a specific thought that I would like to concentrate on?" The answer is yes you can.

The key is deciding what you absolutely want to become reality in your life. Once you know your burning desire, then this is the thought that you begin to focus on. As you continue to focus on this thought, then begin to feel it with strong emotion and do not allow this feeling to leave you; you do this by envisioning (imagining) whatever it is you desire in your life for good.

With strong emotion, formulate a mental picture in your mind (vision, imagine) of whatever it is you desire to realize, and make certain you keep that image continuously in your mind. Having done this, be certain to believe that what you desire is already yours and has been accomplished with full expectation of it being realized.

However, should you inject doubt and/or negativity and hold those types of thoughts in your conscious mind, you will have cancelled the possibility of what it is you desired to have brought forth in your physical life, and you will have to begin all over again with that thought. The next time, focus continuously on your desire, until this appears in your physical life, keeping in mind that any dominant thought for good or evil will be transferred from your conscious mind to your inner mind that is one with infinite intelligence from which all desires, methods, answers, and solutions emanate.

Also keep in mind that you can do this with any dominant thought you habitually focus upon, but you need to be aware that your inner mind does not make any judgments and does not reason or question the dominant thoughts held in your conscious mind for any significant period of time that are conveyed to it to be carried out. For example, if you are continuously focusing on illness and/or other undesirable situations or circumstances, your inner mind can make absolutely certain that you continue to materialize more of the same. This is the desire your conscious mind believes; therefore, what is being communicated to your inner force that neither questions nor judges the thoughts you habitually focus upon, be they good or bad. However, to reverse this condition, all one has to do is to replace the predominant negative thoughts with happiness, prosperity on every level, a full recovery from an illness—as I did—a return to good health, and financial security and any other good thing you want. A very important indicator whether or not a predominant thought is what you truly want to have manifest in your physical life is the way you feel about it that will be accompanied with deep emotion.

How you determine what you want or do not want to materialize in your life is how you feel about one predominant thought over another. You can know with absolute certainty if you are on the right path, as your intuitive inner feelings will always be in line with your inner guidance. If not, your inner guidance will let you know through your inner feelings if you are on the right path or not. Most people would recognize this as a gut feeling. What you feel internally about your thoughts is the key to whether or not your pursue or abandon what you are focusing on.

It is important to understand that what you predominantly focus on, you eventually deliberately create. In other words, you will create for yourself whatever it is you set your intention and habitual thoughts upon. Pay close attention to what this means to you and pay even closer attention to what you think about and ask for, as your every desire, coupled with unwavering belief, will eventually show up in your physical life, which can change your life for the better, best, worse, or worst, depending on what it is you desire. It will always be what you choose to focus on the most and continuously that will eventually show up in your physical life, good or bad.

Why is this so important? Because to permit oneself to stagnate in any stage of adversity clearly indicates that those who choose to stay in their self-created rut are either lazy, have given up trying to change any undesirable events they have become accustomed to, or simply do not care changing their lives for the better. They fail to utilize the gift each and every one of us were born with, which is to be able to enjoy their birthright to be happy, healthy, prosperous in all areas of their life, and free from any adversities that they believe they can overcome and change. This requires self-interest, effort, and action.

In the Bible, in Proverbs 23:7 we read these words: "As a man thinketh in his heart, so is he." No truer words have ever been spoken when it comes to a person's chosen destiny over himself or herself because this relates to each and every circumstance, situation, and adversity that mankind will encounter during their lifetime. As this proverb so clearly states, there is not one among us who will not become precisely what one thinks and focuses on over time as one's character develops. Therefore, each and every thought emanates from what one chooses to plant in their conscious mind, thereby creating each and every circumstance one ultimately experiences. Whether they are thoughts of happiness or pain and suffering—all of us are precisely what we believe and think we are.

It should also be known that both cause and effect are a direct result of one's thoughts, thereby the reason why so many people destroy themselves. All humanity makes and unmakes themselves by way of the thoughts they choose to forge the weapons by which they slay themselves. On the other hand, this is the mechanism by which mankind also brings forth happiness, joy, and prosperity on every conceivable level.

Little is known about the science of the effects of thought on one's life and therefore, why so many people are having any number of undesirable events in their lives, and have no clue to what is causing these outcomes. Many of these consequences can last for years and some a lifetime, if not changed.

It is vital that you understand the awesome power carried by your thoughts, positive or negative. The primary concern regarding habitual thoughts will be believed in one's conscious mind. A person's conscious mind conveys this belief to one's inner mind, and unless changed, this inner guidance will begin to bring forth what it has received and believes to be true and will be made reality in one's physical life.

The fact that this occurs more often than not is even more concerning where serious illnesses and other ailments are concerned. It is necessary to know that we are all doctors in a sense, meaning we have the unique ability to be able to assist licensed legal medical professionals in their effort to treat a disease, serious illnesses, or any other type of ailment. Mankind's role is not medical assistance—instead, through their own initiative and personal action by way of their thought processes and strong beliefs, coupled with a vision of a complete recovery and healing and unwavering expectation. One becomes a joint participant with medical science in bringing forth a healing and eventual permanent recovery for any ailment, serious illness, and/or nonphysical life-threatening illness.

With this as our foundation, let's now delve deeper into this fascinating phenomenon known as thought.

Let it be known right here that we are never just victims of circumstances because the way we choose to think changes our circumstances in an instant, positively or negatively. Prolonged negative thinking can—and very often does—bring forth any number of illnesses, ailments, and reactions, both physical and nonphysical. In addition, these types of thoughts will affect any hopeful achievement or advancement, personal or otherwise, as well as impeding one's overall well-being. They also can and often do hinder healthy relationships with significant others and family; others we know, casually meet, and associate with socially; and in the work environment.

In addition, faulty thoughts can block the natural healing process of the body and, if persisted, may also lead to increasing deterioration of one's medical condition. These types of thoughts carry with them an army of similar thoughts that join together and impede any recovery or healing. On the other hand, healthy positive thoughts can promote healing, well-being, serenity, desired achievements on every level, financial security, prosperity on all levels, healthy relationships with everyone, and promote goodwill. In addition, positive thinking will aid in the body's natural ability to self-heal and can help bring forth a complete turnaround of serious life-threatening illnesses, prevent premature aging, add many additional years to one's longevity, and numerous other desirable benefits. Basically, when it comes right down to it all, mankind chooses their thoughts—the primary cause of the resulting effects that people, individually and collectively, ultimately experience.

It is important that you realize that the choice of thoughts has made the difference in people's lives worldwide, for better or worse, for thousands of years prior to modern-day societies, and will continue to do so on every level of mankind's lifetime.

This book is not an in-depth study on the conscious mind or the so-called subconscious mind. There are numerous well-written books available on these subjects that are available for further reference on how these two separate minds individually and collectively work. However, it is necessary and very important to repeat again that all thoughts, positive and negative, held in one's conscious mind for any extended period of time will be transferred to the inner mind to carry out the order received from the conscious mind by way of concentrated thought.

I personally can attest to the effect of both sides of how your thoughts can change your life dramatically. (By both sides, I am referring to positive and negative thoughts.) The question then becomes, "How do we possibly monitor all these thoughts to be able to make prudent decisions?" The logical answer is we can't. When I refer to being able to determine how thoughts can change our lives, I am referring to those thoughts that we give the most attention to, continuously and habitually—one's dominant thoughts, positive or negative—the ones we dwell on. These are the controlling thoughts with which we need to concern ourselves and constantly monitor.

It should be noted that every effort can be traced to a cause; therefore, every effect originates as a result of a dominant thought.

Suffice it to say that with negative thoughts, I connect a number of nonphysical illnesses that I sustained directly due to my focus on negative thoughts that I permitted to enter and remain in my conscious mind that were accepted as truth by my inner guidance and eventually manifested in my physical life.

This continued for some time, up until my introduction to very serious physical life-threatening illnesses. It was this wake-up call that brought forth my reconnection with my inner guidance and subsequently allowed myself to leave the path I had been on previously as it pertained to my thought processes. Once I made this change back to controlling my thoughts, in time, I was able to control the results I was expecting to realize from that point forward. I no longer dwelled on negative thoughts. When one did get by, I would immediately denounce it and change that thought without delay to something that I wanted to experience instead; and within a short time, by the end of a day, the negative thought that did get by had dissipated and was no longer there because I was not giving it any power to exist.

Keep in mind, if for whatever reason you are not happy with your life as it currently is, then your thoughts about your reality obviously have not been as focused on the positive. They should have been focused instead on what you want to become reality. Once a person makes the decision to change their thoughts and to focus on how they want their existence to be, this action alone begins to change everything.

When you allow yourself to believe that your life will and can change by channeling your thoughts positively and continually focus and visualize (imagine) the end result desired of what you are seeking—coupled with strong belief, emotion, and feeling and by not allowing any doubt to cancel out these changed thoughts—whatever good you truly desire certainly will appear. In other words, by allowing yourself to believe that your life will change by channeling your thoughts positively and focusing and visualizing (imagine) the end result desired, with patience and not allowing any doubt to cancel out these changed thoughts, your burning desire for good can be realized in time.

PREVAILING OVER INSURMOUNTABLE ODDS

I know precisely what I am talking about regarding the power of dominant thoughts, having experienced the life-threatening events I identified, not to mention the trauma associated with these serious life-changing incidents. I am certain that if it were not for this inner guidance I have been describing, I more than likely may not have survived. Instead, I chose to believe the evidence of the power of dominant thoughts that are conveyed to the inner guidance.

How often have you heard this before but for some inexplicable reason continue to disregard: "Human beings are what they think"? I am sure you realize that each and every convenience that people have at their disposal first occurred as a thought in someone's mind, which grew within the person with the idea (thought) who believed that it could be done and materialized. This ranges from the invention of indoor plumbing to placing a person on the moon. However, to achieve all this, inventors and other creative individuals did not accomplish these feats alone. The fact remains that the ultimate results were due to their unwavering belief—that whatever invention or accomplishment for the betterment of mankind appeared by first having a predominant thought that was ultimately conveyed to their all-knowing inner guidance that brought forth the end result in reality.

Imagine for a moment, if you will, if this very same thought process is adopted and applied to what one is seeking for good, the heights one could attain could far exceed their current accomplishments, positions, and levels of prosperity.

Therefore, these predominant habitual thoughts conveyed to the inner power, are not just confined to the overcoming of life-threatening illnesses or unwanted life-changing events but to everyday life to achieve whatever good one wants to have revealed in their life. Therefore, if people began to alter their thoughts toward anything they are desirous of achieving, beneficial results can and will be evident, especially when one combines strong belief, trust, and the ability to envision (imagine) with full expectation that the desired result has already been accomplished and will appear. That is, if one focuses their dominant thoughts on whatever it is they desire to occur in their physical lives and to remove any negativity and instead employ strong belief and self-trust.

It should be noted here that cause and effect is as certain in thought as in the world of visible and material objects. Therefore, mankind's resulting conditions are, without a doubt, the effect of their collective thoughts through which people, individually and collectively, will either ultimately destroy themselves or obtain all the joy of their desires. Whether they are for the good of all concerned—which brings with them peace, happiness, and confidence—and for which people are the originators and architects.

Here is another very important matter that you should pay close attention to: How are you feeling internally at this particular moment? Now, if you took a good look at yourself in the mirror today while preparing for your day, how do you think you looked? Did you look concerned, downtrodden, upset, gloomy, fearful, distressed, worried, depressed, and anxious or did you look happy, joyful, full of pep, a smile on your face, confident, and unstoppable? Your inner guidance always reflects on the outside what you are secretly harboring on the inside that is caused by what you are thinking consciously which—as I have previously stated—when held long enough in your conscious mind and believed will, without hesitation, be transmitted to your inner mind that will immediately bring it into your material experience.

Now, I don't know about you, but speaking for myself, I can tell you that it only took about seven seconds to size myself up when I look at myself in a mirror. How do I do it? Simply through how I felt internally. I could tell almost immediately what's going on inside me, based on how I felt and looked, which was reflected in my attitude, my demeanor, the tone of my voice (very important), how I decided to dress that particular day, my appetite, my business acumen, how I treated others, how I saw others and the world overall, how I looked to others, etc. Added to those feelings, I was able to confirm my true feelings almost instantly as well.

If you haven't tried judging yourself in this manner, I suggest you consider doing it, especially if you are feeling down about anything or troubled by anything undesirable in your life. Why? Because this is precisely how others will see and react to you, especially those whom you do not know closely.

PREVAILING OVER INSURMOUNTABLE ODDS

Keep in mind, thought and character are interconnected; they are one and the same. This is not indicative of one's entire character, however. Since they are so interconnected with a particular thought element within, these thoughts are important to acknowledge, especially if they are negative in nature, keeping in mind—and as I keep repeating—that every member of mankind find themselves where they are in life through the cumulative thoughts they have built into their character over time.

I had read that people find themselves where they are because, as an evolving being, man reaches certain levels in order that they may learn and grow and to learn a spiritual lesson which any circumstance contains for them. I further learned and wholeheartedly agree with the fact that people will continue to be pelted with circumstances as long as they continue to believe and accept that they are only an outer person subject to outer conditions—until finally the realization is apparent that they are a creative power on the inside. Until you are able to control and command your outer prevailing conditions and become the pilot of your own destiny, you shall continue to be confronted by undesirable incidents to which you are presently exposed.

If you will think of it as I learned it, a man's conscious mind is akin to a field where one plants crops. Once the seed is planted in this field, cultivated, allowed to take root and grow, and not disturbed or dug up—the seed will produce its expected fruit, vegetable, flower, etc. With this simple example in mind, similarly, once a thought is placed in the conscious mind, left undisturbed and nurtured, it will take root; and the outcome will be good thoughts that bear good fruit, so to speak; while negative and defeating thoughts will produce bad fruit. If a good thought is disturbed by a negative conflicting thought or doubting, the seed will then need to be replanted to avoid producing a bad fruit.

Although a rather elementary analogy, the point I am making here is that outer-world experiences—whether good or bad—are shaped by the inner world of thought. It is all dependent by which what a person allows themselves to be dominated, affected by their innermost desires and aspirations, good or bad, or influences of the outer world bombarded and permeated by and with all sorts of thoughts from others.

Keep in mind that no circumstances make man what he is but, instead, reveals him to himself, individually and collectively. Although undesirable situations and circumstances may have been lingering on for a number of years, they can be overcome. Although one's predominant thoughts play a very important role in situations such as these, firm false beliefs and unconscious decisions to continue with undesirable lifestyles establish a roadblock to overcoming any undesirable conditions. Author and philosopher Voltaire (1694–1778) put it this way: "We must cultivate our Garden."

Many people may express a desire to change their circumstances in life. However, most are unwilling to do what is necessary in order to better themselves in a way of improving the situations that they found themselves in and therefore, remained stuck in the same undesirable position they were immersed in.

This behavior is primarily found in conditions where people have allowed themselves to become addicted to over-the-counter medication, alcohol, and illegal substances. In addition, people can also find themselves in a range of precarious situations—often they remain mired and unable to proceed to a beneficial outcome.

So what drives these types of addictions and behaviors? From my observation, it is a matter of the strength of one's beliefs and failure of desire to set themselves apart from their peer groups. A person does not have to be a psychiatrist or psychologist to be able to find the root causes of these additions because they are everywhere. It appears that it is difficult for the medical community—despite all the tools, learning, and research they have accumulated—to make a serious and notable dent in these addictive behaviors. How can they? They need to have willing subjects first!

Medication may be a temporary fix, at best, and one-on-one counseling may be somewhat helpful for a while, dependent on the will of the addictive person being counseled to truly want to be cured of their addiction and, of course, the depth of their financial condition! Although well meaning, medical science just does not yet appear to have the answers. Even the extremely wealthy find themselves in and out of plush and obscenely expensive rehabilitation facilities, yet the greater majority are never completely healed of their addictions and over time—if not sooner—return to their addictive behaviors. Evidence of this can be found on any local and cable news programs, twenty-four seven, especially concerning the seemingly worshiped rich and famous and rogue politicians.

Having said this, the question then is, *What is the answer?* The answer is simple. It lies within the person himself or herself. They themselves need to make the personal decision to truly desire to rid themselves of their self-destructive behaviors and have the belief, desire, will, and personal commitment to do so. So how do they get this belief and will to change their self-created and self-destructive behaviors? Here is the tough part.

Although it is all well and good to talk about one's inner mind, it is not going to do a thing for anyone who insists on persisting with an addiction or habit. If a person's absolute desire is to remain in the addictive rut they have determined to dig for themselves and refuses to accept the way out of that rut, there may be additional problems. Unless and until that inner decision is personally made by them, coupled with a strong belief that they can overcome anything, they will remain in that condition because one's inner guidance will not budge unless called upon to do so by the person undergoing the situation. In this event, there is no outside help available on this planet or of an unseen nature that can do a thing to change such a mind-set. Only the person involved in such a problem can do this. Once they do, they shall have a tremendous, powerful inner mind waiting for them to call upon it at any time so that infinite mind can bring forth the permanent healing by their taking the initiative and appropriate action.

This is like anything else. No one can make someone desire to heal their self-inflicted and self-created habitual thinking conditions other than themselves. As the saying goes, "You can lead a horse to water, but you can't make it drink." The person themselves needs to do this because healing and overcoming can only come from within, never from outside a person. Strong belief, as I have said, plays a major role in anyone's healing or ridding themselves of any self-destructive habit from which they feel they are unable to break away. This not only includes life-threatening illnesses but everyday nonphysical harmful conditions as well, which if continued can—and will—evolve into serious life-transforming illnesses and related events over time.

Let's learn more about this wonderful phenomenon I also refer to as the inner guidance and why it is the best and most loyal friend anyone could ever come to know.

9

WHAT EXACTLY IS INNER GUIDANCE?

Life without acknowledgement of one's inner guidance is like an unsharpened pencil—it has no point.

—Author

Inner guidance, coupled with infinite intelligence, unwavering belief, and expectation can bring forth the manifestation of all things desired.

—Author

As I had also stated earlier, your inner guidance is the indisputable unseen power that communicates directly with the infinite intelligence that created everything, ranging from the entire universe and everything contained within it, including mankind and all things that inhabit this planet that man has named earth.

This infinite intelligence, connected with one's inner guidance, has nothing to do with any religious belief despite what one may attempt to connect it with, as it has no allegiance with any religion on this planet—never has and never will—as it is there instead for each and every being that comes to this earth to fulfill their purpose in this life. It can bring forth any desire you wish in your outer world. However, unless you learn how to contact it, you will not be able to get much—if any—benefit from it. This includes having your inner guidance manifest your innermost heartfelt desires that also need to be intended for the benefit of all concerned.

The reason why this should be important to you is that absolutely nothing outside yourself has any power to grant you anything you desire, unless there is some expectancy in return from whatever that outer source may be and has the capability of fulfilling your request. Even then, whatever that outside source may be and whatever may be granted to you will, at best, only be a temporary gain in your life. However, if you are seeking continual good to show up in your life and to have the ability to manifest consistently any positive outcome that you desire without expecting any repayment whatsoever in your physical life, then it is very important for you to realize that it is your inner guidance that can bring forth the methods, answers, and solutions needed—coupled with your initiative and action necessary to produce positive results that can meet your expectations.

From my personal observations, I can tell you that hospitals and mental institutions everywhere seem to be at peak capacity caring for those who have and continue to be self-victimized. Most of them have spent a great deal of their lives living in a state of needless deprivation leading to anxiety, stress, worry, and, the granddaddies of them all, deep depression and fear. Most have spent a great deal of their lives totally disconnected from their inner guide that has the power to bring forth a resolution for whatever they may have been seeking to overcome prior to having any serious life-changing or life-threatening events come into their life.

Even if they did not create their condition consciously or purposely, many did so unconsciously over a long period of time, through faulty thinking and possibly listening to the advice of others who were not medical professionals. They failed to listen to their inner guide and persistently followed sources in their outer world for answers, methods, and solutions to bring forth the good they may have been seeking. Instead, they find themselves in what condition they are in.

Therefore, what prohibits you from achieving what you truly desire in your life is the disconnection with your inner guidance and absolutely nothing else. I personally live by this age-old verse from the Bible: "For as he thinketh in his heart, so is he" (Prov. 23:7 KJV).

PREVAILING OVER INSURMOUNTABLE ODDS

There are many books where this particular verse appears that delves deep into the heart of this very important verse which holds one the most important keys to realizing our desires to experience for good during our lifetimes.

I do not believe I can put it any plainer than this. Therefore, I can think of absolutely no reason why you or anyone should ever hesitate to aspire to any goal you may have in life because our inner guide is more than capable to deal with anything that you may falsely interpret to be an insurmountable problem, achievement, or anything you may desire to realize during your lifetime. Your inner guide can handle any issue, concern, and whatever need.

It was not until I had made the decision to intently listen to my inner guidance that I was able to begin overcoming my undesirable situations. It all came down to what I was going to decide to trust—my outside world or my world inside. Evidently, I chose to place all my trust in my inside world that contains all the answers, methods, and solutions for the good that I was seeking.

I am aware of many people who, even to this very day, continue to suffer needlessly with all types of personal trauma plaguing their lives, much of which can be overcome. Yet the learned outer-world remedies for life's traumatic complexity includes everything but taking time to get to know one's inner guidance. Most people who have been aware that it has always been there neglect to call upon this formidable force until one day they themselves come face to face with a very serious life-threatening event, diagnosis, or, worse, a terminal illness. Unless and until you are willing to consider calling upon this powerful force you were born with, you may continue to remain a slave to your outer world's remedies, behaviors and beliefs. As I pointed out, none of these can provide a permanent resolution to any undesirable condition from which you may be seeking relief or may encounter.

Using myself once again as an example, following my surgeries, I was given a 10 percent chance of survival. Although it was deemed a chance, that was not what I thought was a great opportunity to surmount these events. I am more than certain that the only reason I overcame them was due to my decision to choose to listen to my intuitive inner guidance. That decision led me to the methods, answers, and solutions that were necessary, urging me to take immediate action on what I was receiving from my inner guide to begin to overcome these life-threatening issues.

I recognize the fact that people everywhere feel more comfortable when electing to place their confidence in everything else in their outer world, ranging from friends, relatives, psychics, religious leaders, clairvoyants, mediums, counselors on every conceivable level, family, alternative medical treatments, and modern medical science. I, however, was once also like this and misplaced my trust and confidence to sources in my outer physical world. This was until I chose to reconnect with my inner guidance. That was when I finally realized how lost I really was.

By the time I reached age fifty-one, I had already developed serious physical and nonphysical life-threatening events, lost my twenty-five-year-old business, gone through a very stressful divorce, and two major surgeries in less than one year following. In less than one year following these two surgeries, I was involved in a major automobile collision as a passenger in a vehicle that was broadsided by another vehicle whose operator ran a red light. This resulted in my being seriously injured.

Considering just these serious life-changing events alone, my answer to prevailing over any undesirable situation or circumstance you may either presently be undergoing or may ever find yourself faced with in your walk on your life's path is that overcoming and ridding yourself of any undesirable life-altering events, in this survivor's opinion and observation, can only be found through your inner guidance, connected to infinite intelligence, that contains all the answers, methods, and solutions.

Some people confuse this inner guidance as being the same as offerings of prayers. Let's define *prayer* first. A *prayer* is "an address (as a petition) to God or a god in word or thought (said a prayer for the success of the voyage)"; "a set order of words used in praying an earnest request or wish"; or "the act or practice of praying to God or a god (kneeling in prayer)." What separates *prayer* from one's inner guidance is that prayer is an *act* of asking or wishing for something from a believed in higher power.

However, when one *knows* with absolute confidence that the way to obtain any desire for good is through one's inner guidance—coupled with inner vision, strong belief, and full expectation, as it must. Unless nullified by doubting, disbelief, lack of patience, etc., the answer will be forthcoming.

Prayer is often related to asking, hoping, wishing, and, in some instances, an act of petitioning or what some consider to be pleading. This is as opposed to confidently knowing that it has already been done and will show up in one's physical existence. There is nothing wrong with prayer, as far as I am concerned. However, most people are taught to ask for a thing when praying instead of thanking one's inner guidance for the thing wanted having already been given and being grateful for its eventual materializing in one's physical life. This is different from taking the initiative and action necessary to assist the manifestation of your desires versus waiting for it to appear in your life. Such action to be taken as to what needs to be done to assist with the realization of what is deeply desired arrives in the way of strong feelings and intuition that comes directly from one's inner guidance.

Some clergy may have problems with what I am saying here, as may some of the faithful in various religions. However, there is nothing here that attempts to slander any religion or religious belief, dogma, etc.—far from it. Instead, I only wish to point out the difference between *absolutely knowing* versus *hoping, asking*, and *wishing* for something, for whatever good it may be.

This all-knowing, unseen inner guide (I also refer to as one's inner mind) acts immediately on any dominant thought and begins to bring forth the desired outcome into reality, be it good or bad. And as I exhaustively pointed out, if you dwell on the negative, this is precisely what your inner guidance will bring more for you and vice versa, as it responds precisely to what your conscious mind accepts as true and believes. Therefore, you should only focus and concentrate on what it is you want to exist for good.

It is important to realize, as I have been continuously pointing out, that your inner guidance is one with the infinite intelligence that created everything and, therefore, can remove every barrier to bring forth your expected desires, wants, and needs for you to acquire these in real life. Keep in mind that the key to bringing forth your desires is unwavering belief and expectation.

As far as I am concerned, nothing is sadder than to see young children afflicted with cancer or any other type of possibly fatal illness. I truly admire, respect, and believe that children's cancer specialists and other medical science specialists and related medical professionals treating other types of life-threatening illnesses do all that they can for these children, to free them not from only the pain that they suffer but the trauma, confusion, fear, and the unknown associated with these dreaded illnesses. In addition to all these dedicated professionals, a number of philanthropists have established large hospitals that are dedicated solely to the treatment of these devastating illnesses.

These include some of the most state-of-the-art treatments centers known to medical science in conjunction with excellent support programs for these children and their families. Some of these philanthropists have even dedicated entire ranches and experienced personnel so these children can go and learn how to be a ranch hand and work with horses and other animals and have aided numerous youngsters in so many positive ways. These are very special and totally dedicated people who understand the trauma and fear these children have to deal with at such a tender age related to the types of treatments they have and continue to have to go through.

On many occasions I have been asked, "With all these children have to contend with, how can they possibly be expected to concentrate on their all-knowing guidance, let alone to be able to understand it when having so much to deal with concerning their illnesses?" I couldn't agree more. This is where the magnificent power of your inner guidance's can answer your heartfelt and sincere request for the healing of others, other than yourselves. If you will recall, I have and continue to state that anything one may ask of their inner guidance must include the benefit of all concerned. *All concerned* also includes children beset by illnesses of any type, at any stage, who could not be expected to have to act on their own or to know how to call forth their all-knowing inner guidance. Know that your inner guidance responds to your request, in addition to answers being sought for others you are also requesting.

PREVAILING OVER INSURMOUNTABLE ODDS

How then do these illnesses show up one day in the lives of young children? I've heard medical professionals state that many are hereditary, possibly some may be. However, what about all the rest? Medical science appears to have yet to come up with a definitive cause for many of these life-threatening illnesses that invade young children and claim many young lives each year.

The good news is, the knowledge is available for anyone to know how to connect with their inner guidance that is one with infinite intelligence that knows how to bring forth healing to all of humanity.

Critics and naysayers will more than likely reject this; however, many inexplicable so-labeled miraculous healings requested for others have occurred throughout the world and recorded in medical journals and in religious records, many of which include children. Their numbers make it difficult for anyone to be able to deny that every person has an inner guide within them that is constantly looking out, not only for their well-being, happiness, and joy but also the health and happiness and joy of all those connected with them. This includes family members and all of humanity, as we are all connected through infinite intelligence, the source of all things known. Denying this would be akin to claiming one does not need water or air for the continuation of physical life as we know it.

Prior to being diagnosed with cancer I never realized the fact that we are all just hanging on by our fingernails, so to speak, in this life. This probably is not exactly what you wanted to hear or believe; however, it is the reality of life because there certainly was no separate document attached to anyone's birth certificate guaranteeing them a life for even one more day or one without illness, pain, trauma, deprivation, sorrow, or a serious life-menacing illness. One moment we are here living peacefully, and the next moment we could be face to face with a totally unexpected serious situation. Up to now, I have been describing endangering physical illnesses and serious, life-threatening nonphysical illnesses; but other life-changing events are just as critical, any of which can one day appear in our lives. And before we know it, life is turned upside down and inside out simultaneously. This may sound to you like a doomsday prophecy or pessimistic point of view on life; however, this is quite the contrary, as no one was ever guaranteed a life without hardships.

Even if illnesses and/or events never escalate into a physical life-threatening illness, know that they certainly can show up in the form of any one or a number of serious emotional problems that could possibly last for years; during which time, one's life can be one gigantic nightmare. All of us know someone who fits this scenario. Possibly you yourself had such an occurrence or you are having this condition at some level in your own life.

I have known people who have gone through an entire lifetime holding grudges against others, especially within families. This condition can become so serious and flammable that many people can and have spent two-thirds or more of their life dwelling on the past, unwilling to either forgive or forget and just let it continue, resulting in a serious nonphysical illness or worse—a serious physical condition perpetrated on themselves.

Like you may, I have known people who literally hate and/or are prejudicial of others and who will not hesitate to openly express their hatred without regard to how this may affect others. Hate is a very serious illness, and it emanates from fear that, if allowed to escalate, can reach dangerous levels, causing the hater to do things they would normally not do unless they had a serious, undiagnosed mental condition previously.

If you have not recognized it yet, due to the very serious ongoing recessionary and critical economic period affecting everyone, that includes ongoing massive job layoffs and unprecedented escalating unemployment rates and related conditions—people who once had a job they believed was secure that supported their lifestyle today are finding that not only has their once-believed job security entirely disappeared but, with it, their quality of life. This is yet another level of fear that can and may cause any number of serious nonphysical illnesses to appear in one's life.

When conditions such as these strike without any advanced warning, allowing one to be prepared, it becomes a very serious life-changing event that can cause any number of emotional problems that can and often do consume a great deal of one's life. When this occurs, those who recognize that they do have an inner guidance and strength to be able to overcome whatever unexpected storms may come into their lives will prevail over most serious adversities. However, others will panic, not knowing what to do, and there will be those who will choose to ignore this reality and just allow it to happen to them and accept it, trusting that government and other outside entities and groups will come to their aid, which is not always the case.

I have spoken with many people who had chosen to do nothing and allow a certain life-changing event to take them over emotionally and physically, and some may have even escalated to various stages and types of mental conditions. In either case, medical and other professionals would eventually be treating whatever conditions and symptoms they may need to deal with, which is by no means the total answer to the solution of the condition to which they may be subjected.

As if this were not enough, many people I have spoken with were where I once used to be until I finally came to recognize that unless I took total control of my life, especially my thoughts, I was going to remain in the rut that I had dug for myself. Day after day, people everywhere repeat—almost to the very minute—the very same routines that they have become accustomed to doing for years. Over time, they find themselves in so deep that they are unable to get out because they were totally unaware of the depth of the rut they were digging for themselves until one day they began to sense a feeling similar to that of being claustrophobic. Should this condition be allowed to persist, they very likely can become a candidate for any number of nonphysical life-threatening illnesses.

People who get caught up in these daily robotic rituals are really not living life; instead, they become slaves to their habitual routines. I could list numerous examples; however, each person individually has their own separate day to day set of routines, the difference being that some people are able to control their daily sequence of activities and avoid getting themselves into a rut over time. Unfortunately, these people represent only a small percentage who do not get caught up so deeply in their daily routine as to cause themselves undue pain and eventual nonphysical illnesses. However, for those who do, it is very important to be able recognize and be willing to admit to themselves that they are indeed in a rut they need to come out of if they hope to avoid creating for themselves any number of illnesses and conditions from entering their lives.

From my observation of many people who do not recognize this condition in their lives, it is almost as though they prefer to pull a cover over their heads to avoid having to see what they may be creating for themselves.

Here are some very important points I suggest you consider focusing on:

- Believe in your all-knowing inner guidance—once you believe, in time, methods, answers, and solutions can begin flowing to you.
- Endless methods, answers, and solutions reside within you; therefore, cease searching outside your inner guidance.
- Admit to yourself just how little you know about overcoming and ultimately defeating, life-destructing adversities on any level.
- When all else fails, you must look inward, not outward, for the methods, answers, and solutions you seek.
- Intuition—hunches, inner feelings, or dreams are constantly giving us insight and knowledge to help us make sound decisions about any number of actions we need to take in any given situation or circumstance. Intuition is the process of reaching accurate conclusions and proper direction quickly.
- Fear exists in your conscious mind but never in your inner mind, also referred to as your all-knowing inner guidance.

I knew absolutely little about the inner working of the body other than what I had learned in school and people I knew in the medical profession. Yet inner guidance intuitively knew precisely what steps I needed take to heal myself from physical and numerous nonphysical illnesses and conditions I was dealing with simultaneously. I just accepted the information that was flowing to me and took action on what I was receiving.

It is very important that you fully comprehend that intuition is something one feels within that emanates from one's inner guidance and is much more immediate versus depending upon external information. Intuition does not depend on any outer influences but communicates with one's conscious mind through strong inner feelings and hunches, so to speak, and is incredibly accurate.

Accept or reject it, intuition (some religious refer to intuition as the voice of one's soul) is actually the all-knowing inner guide and not the self-talk we all engage in every moment of our lives that provides rapid insights into negative events and can provide answers, methods, and solutions, relaying this information to our outer consciousness. Intuition allows us to be creative instead of reactive, provided that we allow ourselves to be open to receiving the information our inner guidance is sending to us.

Many uninformed people and even some scientists dismiss intuition because of where it really originates, from one's all-knowing inner guidance. They do not trust that its messages are reliable or accurate and therefore opt instead for conventional knowledge. They liken intuition to clairvoyance, being mysterious, and further believe that if such clairvoyance exists at all, only a handful of people actually possess that sort of power (insight). They believe it to be uncommon and choose to dismiss it entirely. In addition, they also choose to treat inner guidance as some sort of supernatural power. One's inner guidance is none of these things; instead, it is a very strong inner sensation coming to one in the form of a feeling, hunch, or a recurring dream (vision).

When one does heed their all-knowing inner guidance, they will eventually notice that their lives will begin to improve dramatically; fear dissipates, and the beginning of healing from nonphysical and physical illnesses can be realized, provided one sincerely believes that they will. Many people I have spoken with tell me that they regretted not heeding their inner all-knowing guidance earlier in their lives that they sensed was always there for them but chose instead to only listen to others whom they trusted, and that included medical professionals.

I relied on my inner guidance, not only to bring about a complete healing of the physical life-threatening events but to numerous nonphysical illnesses and conditions that were plaguing my life at the time.

Accompanied with these nonphysical illnesses I was realizing were haunting memories of the past that I had refused to let go, including ill feelings toward others and other negative events that I permitted to accumulate in my life. Collectively, I am more than certain, over time, these had become the cause that brought about the triggering of the physical illnesses I allowed to show up in my life. Had I learned to listen more intently earlier to the deep, intuitive inner messages and strong feelings that I was receiving from my all-knowing inner guidance, I am more than certain that I could have avoided most of the events that challenged me.

Intuition is a very strong inner feeling that has a direct effect on all our senses and cells in our bodies. Once our inner intuition is activated and believed in one's conscious mind, our outward expressions are much different. Inner intuition can be received through images, sounds, emotions, feelings, and sensations in the body that, when believed to already have been manifested in the outer self, will bring forth the desired results, as long as what is desired is for the good and benefit of all concerned.

I receive my *intuitive* messages from my daily writing communications with infinite intelligence that is connected with my inner guidance that is constantly coming to me in the form of instructions, information, wisdom, and knowledge that my outer self or conscious mind could not possibly know, supported by extremely strong feelings and sensations that I could not ignore. One needs to understand that information (knowledge and wisdom) is coming to all of us all the time from our inner guide that never sleeps.

Quite sadly, however, a number of people with whom I have spoken regarding their all-knowing inner guidance tell me they either do not believe in intuition as something they can trust and rely upon or they can faintly hear their inner guide speaking to them. This is because they never make any attempts to quiet all the self-talk and the outer noises that surround them.

I have also had people tell me that they would not even recognize their inner guide when it did try to gain their attention. To me, this means they must be among the "walking deceased," so to speak, because our inner guide is constantly attempting to communicate with us and trying to place us on the right path headed in the right direction. We know this to be true because every time we choose to jump off the correct path to health, wealth, prosperity, joy, harmony, and peace, we know and sense it intuitively immediately, even if we do not wish to admit it to ourselves at the moment. How curious it is that sooner or later we realize we made the wrong choice when all along we sensed the correct action and path to take and follow.

By choosing to ignore the valuable information that our inner guidance is attempting to give us from which all the methods, answers, guidance, solutions, direction, and correct action emanates, is as though one prefers to bask in their misery, dilemma, situation, or circumstance they or someone they care about may be going through.

The same went for me, when I was rejecting the intuitive messages that were coming to me up until the time I became ill. I *finally* began to listen to these very strong messages that my all-knowing inner guidance was repeatedly sending me.

To be quite frank about it, nothing else seemed to be working for me, and medical science and professional counseling had very narrow remedies to offer that included prescribed medications, whose effects were temporary at best, and only prescribed chemotherapy treatments following the cancer surgeries. Yet it still was not enough just to be receiving these messages. In order for what was being communicated to me by my inner guide to be of any benefit to me at all, I was going to have to take the appropriate action and necessary steps and follow the directions I was being given.

Like me earlier, most people choose to ignore one's inner intuition because initially we simply do not wish to heed what our inner guidance is trying to tell us. In other words, we are absolutely consciously rejecting what our inner guidance is trying to tell us because, as I said before, we choose instead to believe that we know better, outside sources are more reliable, or we are influenced by others we know well or too stubborn and set in our ways. Therefore, we never realize that none of us, not even those we choose to rely upon, knows the right direction and path we need to follow. However, our inner guidance does.

Cemeteries worldwide are full of those who chose solely to rely upon outside sources for cures and permanent healing. Is this to mean that, by relying upon one's inner guidance that one is guaranteed to survive a life-threatening illness of any type? Not at all. However, chances for survival and complete healing are remarkably enhanced when armed with the all-knowing guidance.

Many people around the globe have survived catastrophic illnesses and other overwhelming conditions after having been told by medical science that they only had a short time remaining or the prognosis for their chances of survival for any greater length of time was not favorable. I happen to be one of those people. If we are asked to believe in hope and faith, then there should be absolutely no reason to discard one's inner guidance that contains all the information, wisdom, right action, direction, and methods one would ever need. That is, if one would only choose to believe in this very powerful source that has taken up residence prior to one's birth. deep within each and every person that has ever walked upon this earth or those who ever will.

I found that by choosing to heed the messages, methods, and answers that I was receiving from my inner guidance that I could rely upon that this knowledge was not available to me in my physical outer environment. I further realized that if I was to be able to overcome the serious, life-changing physical and nonphysical events I was living through, I needed to take action and follow the direction I was being led to take by my all-knowing inner guidance. I had come to understand that failure to heed one's inner guide was akin to ignoring the warnings of a rapidly advancing, very powerful tornado or other menacing storm that could prove to be extremely disastrous or even fatal.

The problem with humanity as a whole is that we allow ourselves to get caught up in life's all-too-familiar routines, which I call "life's never-ending rut." We fear leaving the world we created for ourselves because we fear changing anything we have become so accustomed to as a way of life. We remain in these situations, even to the point of choosing to live with negative events, pain, and suffering and being in a place in life we absolutely despise because it terrifies us to venture into the unknown.

That said, sensing that there is something not right is a sure sign that offers all of us the opportunity to move in a direction to either choose to adapt to our problem, or to change them into opportunities that will eventually benefit us and others substantially, by being able to control the outcome of whatever we wish to change in our lives.

As I identified before, the inner guidance does not judge habitual thoughts or deep desires; it only acts upon our continuous focused thoughts, what we envision, deep desire, and commands. You may question the word *command*. Just like any good soldier, our inner guidance will follow and obey each and every command given it without question and/or rebuttal, unlike the ego that will rebut anything that even appears to be against its self-serving wants and desires. Therefore, it is extremely important when giving this inner guidance commands that one is extremely cautious about choosing the commands that are being given.

These answers to the question "What exactly is the inner guidance anyway?" are examples of what the inner guidance is and can do for your life are only the tip of the iceberg when it comes to the countless things it can do to bring forth beneficial aspects to life when one does not waver or return to disbelief in its powers. Nothing can come into reality for the positive results that we may wish to experience unless and until we truly believe it can. Taking the initiative and action necessary to produce these results that may not occur unless and until we truly believe it can and unless and until we truly utilize the methods answers that can be the most direct and expedient. This is what brought me every healing, overcoming, and, ultimately, cure of many serious life-changing condition, situations, and related events and for which I credit my still being alive today.

The following chapter deals with the answers to the questions pertaining to how I did it and how I survived.

10

ANSWERING THE "HOW I DID IT" QUESTION

Why didn't I die when I was told I would?

—Author

On many occasions following my encounters with life-threatening illnesses and related events that were deemed insurmountable, people I encountered wanted to know how I was able to overcome these life-threatening situations because I did not appear to show any signs, physically or otherwise, of ever having gone through anything like that and remain so healthy, peaceful, and accepting of it all. I more than gladly shared with them that what they are seeing before them—meaning, the person who actually survived all that I did—is only one major benefit among all I continue to receive from my inner mind that, to me, is and remains to be the answer to surviving most adversities and to experience any desire for good anyone is seeking.

The secret to the "how I did it" question—meaning, how I survived all that I have—is that it is no secret at all. The good that everyone wants to enjoy in life has always been available to people everywhere. All I did was what most people will not do. In my opinion, as a survivor of a number of serious life-threatening events, this is the primary reason why I and people like me overcame numerous adversities. For me, it was all about choosing to begin an ongoing dialogue with the infinite intelligence through my infinite mind that is one with my inner guidance. Once begun, this dialogue eventually becomes a pact bound by trust and expectation between this incredible intelligence and the person desiring to experience their innermost desires for good. This method of communication is discussed in detail further in the book.

It is this unseen source of unfathomable power that I know and believe to be the primary source that can bring forth any desire for good to be actualized in one's life. Anyone can realize the benefits that I and countless people have because this all-knowing power is not selective or favors anyone over another. Therefore, when obtaining what one is seeking for a beneficial effect in their life, they need to be personally committed to the belief that such a power exists that created everything seen on this planet and is willing to begin an ongoing dialogue with this unseen source by way of the method I am about to reveal to you.

I am extremely grateful to have rediscovered this magnificent power as it has literally cured me of what a number of medical people and others deemed to have been unachievable, considering the seriousness and stages of my illnesses. This communication continues to work for me when I decide to have manifest anything for good and for the benefit of all concerned, which is quite often, I might add.

Regardless of what name has been given to this unseen power, as I stated earlier, be aware that it is not connected to or claims allegiance to any known or unknown religious beliefs whatsoever. The key to accessing and communicating with this magnificent source begins and ends with unwavering belief, which is the very same belief that binds the people of any religion in the world. This unwavering belief is the primary reason why religions throughout the world work at all.

Having said this, based upon my personal experience and results, the key to obtaining the benefit that you desire, including prosperity on every conceivable level, is choosing to directly communicate with this incredible unseen power by way of the suggested written dialogue method you are about to discover or, for some, rediscover.

This method of communication I am referring to is not complicated and is effortless, if one elects to commit themselves to its use. This method needs to be adhered to with no alteration to maintain an ongoing dialogue. It is not only effective but only takes a fraction of one's time.

I cannot stress enough how important communicating with this infinite power can become for you because there are no words in any language worthy of describing this ongoing personal experience. The primary reason I say this is, because during your entire lifetime thus far, this force, by way of your inner mind, has been present for you to call upon it and has always been available to you. It absolutely knows everything about you and precisely what you need and all your desires and wants and wants to provide them for you.

I can tell you from personal experience with this method of communicating with this intelligence that I continue to utilize it and have realized the results and continue to benefit from them. Know that the proof of this incredible power is everywhere one looks. Learning how to establish contact with it will cost you not even one single cent and a fraction of your time. I am more than certain that there were those who are no longer with us whom I believe, had they had known this method, would possibly have paid almost any price for this knowledge which had always been available to them. For those who were aware of it, the cost they may have incurred was in not obtaining everything positive they desired by continuing to deny or ignore its tremendous power.

Everyone has two very distinct inner influences that are vying to gain their undivided attention. The one we are most familiar with is the ego. The ego is commonly referred to as one's seemingly unstoppable chatterbox or skeptic, better referred to by some as the brat that always gets its way. The other influence is one's inner guidance. The unique difference between the ego and the inner guidance is that the ego is continuously seeking to be gratified, while the inner guidance is seeking to bring forth your innermost desires for good and does not do battle with you. It has been patiently waiting to hear from us to connect or, for many, reconnect to it in order to have you realize what you are seeking and to rid you of any adversity you may be sustaining on any level, which the ego could never achieve.

Considering that many people throughout the world seem to be very busy chasing happiness and prosperity on all levels of their life, most do not seem to either have or will take the time to make any concerted effort to come to know the power and wisdom of this infinite intelligence that is one with one's inner mind that can bring forth all their innermost desires. Instead, most people will proceed along in life, lugging with them their own personal fire extinguishers, so to speak, in a futile attempt to put out as many fires in their life as they can, *alone*.

I wonder why so many people have found themselves in the dilemmas and circumstances they have created for themselves by trying to solve them through conventional worldly sources. "Why?" many people may ask. Because most people have been exposed to various ways of attempting to connect with whatever name they may have heard repetitively or prefer to give to a higher source of intelligence. However, lack of patience and waning interest, over time, are also among the reasons they rarely do.

As mere mortals, people have been taught to seek such a connection (for all those who do believe in a supreme intelligence other than mankind) by way of established religions and other ways. Some people choose to make such a connection through various rituals, forms of meditation, and dozens of other spiritual practices to connect with this unseen higher source of intelligence that they innately sense is and has been there all along. Still, others find such a connection by walking on a beach, hiking up a mountain, bicycling or walking alone on trails, or taking in nature as it truly was meant to be appreciated—all of which are beneficial when one decides to make a connection with this higher intelligence. I explored a number of these methods but found the results to be only temporary, although somewhat rewarding to a degree.

Where I received and continue to receive my best results was choosing instead to communicate with this source of infinite intelligence through a very unique writing method. Now, please stay with me and you will learn precisely what this writing method is all about and why it is so powerful and will work for anyone. You've come this far, so please have patience, and you will soon be able to see for yourself why this method can work for anyone who believes that it can and is willing to exercise the necessary patience.

By choosing to communicate with this entity in this manner, I have been and continue to be extremely successful in reaching it at will and have been able to be as open and as critical as I felt I needed to be and, at the same time, put down on paper my demands for answers to my grievances, concerns, desires, and what I want to exist in my life. I literally demanded answers to my inquiries and received them over time, all of which were very beneficial; and I also received the how-to and the methods needed to realize all that I was demanding to appear in my life for a beneficial effect.

When I first began contacting this intelligence through this writing method, I poured my heart out and actually was able to clearly see, for the first time, everything that was truly bothering me and all the positive results I wanted to produce in my life. I was able to vent as much anger and disappointment as I wished to and go back as far in my history as I wanted, in order to literally drag up everything and anything that had been so destructive and hostile to me. I also wanted to identify basic reasons I sensed why I was so miserable, and what I then came to realize had contributed to my eventual involvement with serious physical and nonphysical life-disrupting conditions and events.

I achieved and continue to appreciate remarkable success through this method of communication with this amazing unseen power. Therefore, should you decide to communicate with this all-knowing faculty, it is imperative that you continue to maintain an ongoing dialogue with this all-knowing intelligence that contains all the answers, methods, and solutions to every question, problem, illness, undesirable event, etc., that you'll ever need to know. Once this dialogue is opened through this method of communicating, it will be difficult to ignore. Because through this method of exchanging information, you should soon begin to learn the real truth about yourself in a more profound way, in addition to having the unique opportunity to achieve the materializing of your priorities, wants, and desires for good, much sooner than expected.

How do I know all this? To begin with, there probably was no greater doubter or skeptic than I, prior to finally deciding to give this type of written interaction with this superior intelligence a chance. I said to myself, "You tried everything else, yet nothing seemed to work, and if it did, it was only a temporary fix, so why not try this?" And I did.

PREVAILING OVER INSURMOUNTABLE ODDS

Keep in mind I was not seeking a temporary fix by no means; I was literally thrown to the wolves, so to speak, by medical science having insisted I undergo a series of chemotherapy treatments with no significant inference of survival, even with these treatments. What I was seeking instead was a permanent resolution to all my "why me?" issues that included ridding me of undesirable events, a complete healing of serious life-threatening illnesses, a permanent resolution to my failed relationships, and other serious events and situations I needed to deal with and bring to permanent closure.

After exhaustively searching every way and everything I knew about, I could find absolutely nothing that could bring me the relief I was seeking until I practically stumbled across this writing method of being able to communicate with this all-knowing source of all wisdom. Quite fortunate for me, I was literally at my rope's end and was extremely grateful to have found how to be able to directly contact this superior power that was able to clearly communicate with me, through which I eventually was able to completely heal and rid myself of every undesirable event taking place in my life over time. What I may be saying is hard to believe, I'm sure; but it is a fact, nonetheless.

I can truthfully state that I am completely free of all those issues, due to my decision to choose and accept to have an daily open dialogue with this higher source of intelligence that is connected with my inner guidance, despite my initial skepticism. This written communications method not only brought me the answers, methods, and solutions I was seeking but the *how*, *when*, and *where*, which ultimately resulted in my being able to attain my deepest innermost desires.

I found that by choosing a definite time every day to sit down with nothing more than a comfortable chair, a pen in my hand, and a notebook, I would begin writing everything that I wanted to come to me for good and anything else I wanted to ask or vent about. This was the most unique experience I have ever had because I was absolutely totally free to say and feel what I wanted to, with no one coaching or judging me, and I could even get angry if I chose to. I knew I was completely free from judgment and was being heard—*really being heard*—for the very first time in my entire life, not ever previously realizing that this all-knowing intelligence had always been there patiently waiting for me to establish an ongoing dialogue with it. It is difficult to even attempt to describe in words what a tremendous feeling, awakening, and awareness this was for me at first. It was euphoric, to say the very least.

This method of communicating with this higher source allowed me to unload both past and present issues off my conscious mind and be able to absolutely let go of them once and for all. These issues included, but were not limited to incidences from my past, lingering grudges, disappointments, hurts, and pent-up emotions; tons of lies I believed; failed relationships and marital problems; ranting and raving at people whom I believed had betrayed me; those whom I believe caused me untold pain, grief, and misery; and at me for allowing myself to become involved with any and all these incidents. By transmitting my thoughts in this manner, I was able to clearly see the roles I played and what I had contributed to in these situations and was eventually able to let these involvements all go out of my life and begin a new life, free of all the pent-up crud I was hoarding deep inside me. It was as though a huge boulder had been lifted off my body and I could breathe again.

Within the first week of doing these writings, I was able to clearly see my entire past as though playing on a movie theatre screen. If I cared to, I could review every undesirable scene again because it was all written down in my journal for me to refer to or remind myself of the depth of my ignorance that had led to all my self-constructed misery. Soon after this, I began receiving what I like to call infinite guidance through which answers to my previously asked questions began coming to me, accompanied by the actions to take and the methods to go along with these answers and actions.

Another extremely important benefit of being able to communicate with this supreme power was that I began to cease blaming others, circumstances, etc., for whatever was plaguing my life. This was a huge step for me at the time because like a snake when shedding its skin over its eyes and being temporarily blinded, I was finding that I had been unconsciously striking out at everyone, figuratively speaking.

As I moved forward with my personal commitment to dedicate and set aside the same time every day to continue my written contact with this infinite intelligence I began to be aware of an inexplicable peace surrounding me. Much of the tension I had been feeling dissipated, and I found myself able to cope with any undesirable occurrences with a different perspective and calmness as these situations were becoming fewer and fewer.

What many people wanted to know most with this writing method was whether or not this method of communication was responsible for my refusing chemotherapy. The short answer is yes! Not only do I believe but absolutely know without any doubt whatsoever that it was because of these written communications I was able to overcome all that I had and elected to refuse any recommended postsurgical chemotherapy treatments.

Through these written messages, I received answers to the question of what to do instead. In my case, they were, first, not dwell on these events; and, second, not allow any poisonous chemicals into my body that could possibly interfere or destroy my body's immune system, regardless of the medical community's insistence. Next, I was to return to work as soon as possible and focus on raising my then eight-month-old son. What I did next was to never talk about these events or share any medical stories with anyone and never give any thought or power to them, ever. In addition, I was led to business travel and to take on challenging exercise programs, which in my case was taking up martial arts where I ultimately earned a first-degree black belt at age fifty-two and became an assistant instructor. During all this, I never once discontinued my written communications with this all-knowing intelligence.

Another question I have been asked was, "Do you not give any credit to the medical community for the permanent healing you came to possess?" The answer is yes and no. Yes, because medical science was successful in cutting away the infected areas—their area of expertise. No, because medical science has never claimed to be a permanent healer of any life-threatening illness. Once done with all medical science knows to do, the surviving becomes the responsibility of the person involved who receives this power from their all-knowing infinite intelligence. Search all we want for remedies, we will not find the answers, methods, and solutions we seek from sources in our outer world instead, only from within.

It is very important for me to emphasize here that there is indeed an all-knowing intelligence that guides each and every one of us by way of our inner mind and responds to our every desire, if we believe strongly enough that it will. Whether you choose to believe this or not at this very moment is not relevant; what is, however, is at the very least you become aware that it does exist and is there for you to call upon at any point in your life. Whether or not you choose to ask it for help with anything or elect to deny its existence, be certain that it is always there, always has been and always will be, and awaits your communicating with it—the all-knowing infinite intelligence—for the answers, methods, and solutions you need that no person or any worldly source can provide. Based upon my personal experience, this unseen intelligence can supply us all with all the answers, methods, and solutions we will ever need and when we need them.

This infinite force and the methods and answers it can provide and how you can activate it may help guide you with a myriad of questions and decisions you are called upon to make in your life. It not only can assist you to resolve life-changing issues and adversities but any life-changing issues, circumstances, situations, and events you may need assistance with. And by knowing that you can always rely on it without question, the answers and methods that you receive from it will always be accurate. Keep in mind at all times that if you choose to put the answers and methods into action, you must do so without procrastinating, doubting, wavering, or denying in any way; replace these instead with total, unwavering trust; belief and total expectation; and, above all, patience.

As a survivor of so many undesirable events in my life, I can tell you from my personal knowledge that there is absolutely no way I could have overcome and have attained a permanent healing from each and every one of these instances, had it not been for this superior power; of this I am absolutely certain.

Even prior to my life-changing episodes, my inner guidance had been knocking heavily at the door of my conscious mind. However, all my negative thoughts and listening to others were drowning out the inner guidance's efforts to gain my undivided attention. I knew it was there as it kept nagging at me and beckoning me to listen to the answers and methods it had for me and to avoid any decision to embark upon an alternate path that I could regret having chosen instead.

People have said to me, "How do you know that this inner guidance connected to an all-knowing unseen intelligence you speak of knows everything you need to know and where's the proof?" I know because I personally benefited and continue to be the recipient of the results of its tremendous power and knowledge. I also know because, had I embarked on the path that others in the physical world had been leading me to take, I am absolutely certain I would not be here today. I was guided instead in the opposite direction, contrary to the advice I was getting from others, and elected to steer away from allowing any poisonous chemicals to be placed into my veins for any period of time. I also know it because I have tested it on the serious nonphysical events that occurred in my life, and I am more than certain it is how I overcame each and every one of these events.

In addition to all this, I rely solely upon this infinite intelligence that is connected with my inner guidance for everything, even down to the questions I continue to have. I can also tell you that not once have I been given an incorrect answer, method, direction to follow, or action to take or had the outcome of following what I was receiving from this infinite intelligence, other than my best interest and advantage.

This unseen intelligence is totally aware of your needs, desires, issues, etc., and stands ready at all times to supply the correct answers and methods to be followed for solutions when one decides to take the initiative and action necessary without doubting or procrastinating to resolve serious life-changing and life-challenging adversities, circumstances, situation, and events.

I have been asked, "By utilizing this writing method of communication, will one have to abandon their beliefs and other ways of making contact with this all-knowing intelligence?" Not at all. By exchanging messages in writing with this all-powerful source, you shall find that it will greatly enhance your other methods of communicating with it.

This writing method of communicating with this all-knowing intelligence is not meant to replace anything at all. Instead, to actually communicate with it and receive answers, you must not have been receiving or utilizing any other method you may have tried for years and bring forth one's deep desires for good and the methods and answers to deep-rooted questions and other matters. By putting one's request in writing, it allows one to have a permanent record of their ongoing contacts. One can then go back and easily see where and when they had asked for assistance, answers, and methods for anything that had been requested, including any healing being sought for an illness or nonphysical condition, adversity, or situation plaguing one's life and precisely when the answers, methods, and solutions were answered.

Someone else asked me, "How were you able to concentrate on writing to this all-knowing intelligence with all you had going on in your life with the serious issues you were subjected to?" This was also an excellent question. My response was, "Had I decided instead to dwell on these issues and allow my conscious mind to take me to places and events that had yet to happen—for instance, my situation getting much worse and/or my ultimate demise from any of these events—I am certain that eventually I more than likely would have passed on." However, I chose to stay focused on the resolution and permanent healing of these crises. This is precisely what I did, twenty-four seven, keeping in mind that if I were the creator of all these issues plaguing my life, then I certainly could undo what I personally designed and created. That is precisely what I did, relying upon the answers, methods, and solutions I was receiving.

Certainly, there will be those out there who will always believe I was just lucky. Although I do not personally believe in this word *luck* ("favoring chance"), one has to be lucky if something happens once or maybe twice. But to be lucky through all I had and survived each and every one of those serious instances, I don't think so.

It was at this very point in my life where I made my choice and elected to communicate with this all-powerful source through this writing method instead of relying upon any other methods or remedies that were available to me in my outer world at the time. I was more than convinced then, as I remain today, that this was the correct path for me to follow.

Today I remain extremely grateful for that decision and the answers and methods that were given me through this source, without which my son would have been left without his dad to raise him. Instead, thanks to my inner guidance connected with this unseen intelligence, my son—now age seventeen—has his dad with him. In my opinion, there is no greater blessing that one can receive than what I have just described.

Another question asked of me was, "Do you ever not want to write to this entity and do you really get answers and how?" This is another excellent question. I write to this all-knowing intelligence every day at a designated time that I have set aside for this purpose. Once I open my writing journal, I immediately begin my writing by first stating how grateful I am to have the privilege to communicate with this incredible unseen power being there for me and patiently waiting for me to begin my contact with it. Second of all, it allows me time to review my previous communications and be able to see for myself how many of my grievances, wants, desires, etc., were answered and when. In addition, I will begin with giving this all-knowing infinite mind thanks for what it has already done for me and others.

To answer the "Do I ever not want to write to this all-knowing intelligence?" question, the answer to this question is no, never. As a matter of fact, I cannot wait until the time of day comes when I can sit down in my quiet place and begin writing. It is at this time I can relieve myself of anything that may be concerning me and ask for the answers and methods to deal with whatever, as well as looking forward to receiving the answers and the methods pertaining to what I had previously inquired about or asked for. Therefore, the answer to whether I really get answers is yes. I not only get answers, I receive the methods and actions to take to produce what I am seeking.

Another thing I get out of writing to this all-knowing intelligence is that I can get everything and anything off my chest and complain if I need to. I can even question all the things that are taking place in my life and in the world that I am concerned about. I no longer have to worry or get overly concerned about things as I did in the past and am more than confident that my inner guidance that is connected with this powerful source of wisdom will deliver the answers I do not have that cannot be ascertained from outside sources in my physical world. In addition to all this, the comfort I get from just being able to write down everything and anything I care to on paper where I can see it is almost difficult to describe in words alone. It is a feeling of total calmness that comes over me that I have been unable to find anywhere else.

Please do not misunderstand; I do not have grievances or an ax to grind every time I sit down to write. Instead, most of the time I write about are things I just want to talk and learn about, such as the condition of this country and the world right now, personal matters like my son and his future and how I can help him with his issues as a teenager, being grateful for many things, etc., and not necessarily always asking for help with something, financial assistance, etc. It is important to recognize that continuously asking for material gratification defeats the entire purpose of being able to communicate directly with one's all-knowing infinite intelligence.

I have also been asked if there was any specific time of day better to begin this writing method. No, there is no specific time of day or night when sitting down to write. It can be any time you know you will not be interrupted at all during this extremely important part of your day or how long you wish to write and can be for as short a period of time you wish, even as little as fifteen minutes.

As for myself, when I first began writing, I was writing so frantically that I could hardly reread what I had written. This is okay as penmanship, grammar rules, spelling, etc., do not apply when performing this writing method, as you can choose to write as fast as you wish, abbreviate words, draw pictures and images—even very angry ones of someone you are writing about or whatever situation or circumstance, etc. I was furious at everything at the time I first began communicating in this manner and striking out at the world on paper, so it seemed.

I was angry about my diagnoses and all the other nonphysical issues and other serious life-changing events that were seemingly coming down on me all at once. If you are at this point or ever been there, then you know precisely what I am talking about. I felt like that fellow in the King James Version in the Bible named Job who had gone through a tremendous ordeal and further felt that his plight was nothing in comparison to what I was overwhelmed with. I actually referred to myself when speaking to people I knew as Job II.

When I first began my writings, I literally went through two notebooks and consumed three and a half hours' writing. Initially I was blaming this unseen power for most of my issues, not realizing that this intelligence has much broader shoulders and could handle anything and everything I was venting about by getting it all out on paper where I could actually see what I was feeling and what was pent up deep inside of me for years. This ranting continued for several days until one day I felt a tremendous calm come over me while writing. I sensed that this all-knowing intelligence was actually really hearing me. From that point onward, I was able to write about my issues in a more relaxed way and noticed that I was becoming less angry.

Now, to expand on the final part of the question, "Do you really get answers and how?" this is the most interesting aspect of being able to communicate with this all-knowing intelligence in this manner. The short answer to this question is yes—I have always received answers (even when I was in my teens) by way of deep, intuitive feelings. However, more often than not, I chose to ignore them and do things my way.

Over time, I learned my way was rarely the right way and paid dearly for a number of my unguided choices. As I grew older, once again, I believed that my way was the best way; and once again, more often than not, many of those choices turned out not to be in my favor. However, when I passed the age of thirty-five, I finally began listening even more to my intuitive inner guidance that is one with this all knowing infinite intelligence. This was the pivotal point in my life where things began to gradually turn around for me, to the point that I became more and more reliant upon my inner guidance. That is until one day I noticed that I was practically turning everything over to it for the answers and methods I sought. I found that once I turned any matter over to my inner guidance, I no longer worried about the outcome. I was more than confident that the outcome would be beneficial for all concerned and that I would come away with an acceptable resolution.

Discovering how to communicate with this powerful intelligence to get the results I was seeking, I never realized at the time that what I was doing was actually having a conversation with this infinite power. By the simple act of writing my wants, desires, business and personal issues that I needed answers for, etc., on a pad, my anger began to be resolved and to dissipate. Little did I realize at the time I was allowing all my pent-up feelings and emotions to come out through the pen in my hand instead of my mouth. Then answers to all my issues began coming to me. At first I believed they were a result of my wishful thinking; however, what those answers and the methods that accompanied them really were answers to my innermost desires coming to me from this powerful, unseen guidance.

Some have asked me how I really knew that this is where these answers and methods were coming from and what proof I had to confirm that. This is an excellent question. My answer, once again, was quite simple. At first, I felt it deep inside of me. It was the warm peaceful feeling and calming effect that came over me that what I was seeking was already mine and on its way and I would, in due time, sense its presence. Second, I noticed that I was no longer dwelling on the matters that were troubling me, as I had been prior to receiving this calming effect, which gave me the assurance that the matter was being resolved for the benefit of all concerned.

The answer to what proof I had—my proof was the patience that I became aware, which I never had before. I was able to shed all the anxiety and pressure I placed on myself for a resolution. This was no longer an issue with me regarding my complete confidence in the expectation that what I had so deeply desired would actually appear. Over time, what I was expecting did arrive for me.

Like myself, I realize that you possibly may be thinking that there was no way that by sitting down for about thirty minutes alone with absolutely no interference and by simply writing out your wants, desires, and problems; discussing your circumstances; talking about an illness you may have; and seeking a resolution and permanent healing could possibly occur. It sounds preposterous. I understand this because I felt the same when I first began thinking of the possibility of doing this myself for any extended period of time. However, the fact is that what I discovered through this communication method is not only real but actually brought forth the results I was seeking and continues to do so.

The key to procuring any desired result for good is to first decide to personally commit to communicating with this infinite intelligence in this manner. Set aside a specific time every day—be it fifteen minutes or for as long as you like—without any outside interferences, with your pen in hand and a pad or journal (I prefer a journal), and just beginning to write. Your writings can contain anything and everything and even off-color words, if you so choose, while keeping in mind that religious no-no's or any other rules do not come into play when you are exchanging messages with this infinite source of wisdom. It cannot be offended in anyway, extends no loyalty to any religion or religious belief in particular, and, as I said, has very broad shoulders and is an excellent listener.

Remember, you can write anything you desire, and you can go back as far in your life's history and memories as you choose. This all-knowing source was also there back then as it is now and knows everything about your past as well as your future.

As I identified, I got extremely angry when I first began communicating and blamed this all-powerful intelligence for my difficulties and even my serious illnesses and other serious life-changing events. That was until I finally began actually receiving the answers and the methods concerning what I had been writing about every day that I was getting from this intelligence that began flowing from my pen onto my journal but in a style and words that were not my style of writing. Now this may be difficult for you to believe and accept; however, if you are willing to accept it or not, this is precisely how this infinite force prefers to communicate with you.

Now here is the reason why some people who make the decision (not commitment) to try this method of communicating with this infinite intelligence will give up in a very short period of time. The reason for giving up on this method of communicating with this unseen source is because they treat this method of communicating as though they are driving through a fast-food facility. In other words, place the order, and the order is immediately filled, ready and delivered. Now to continue with this example, if the same person places their order and had to wait—in what their opinion would be an inordinate amount of time—they would either get angry, cancel their order, or simply pull out of line, believing that their order would take far too long for them to be patient enough to wait for, and, once again in their life give up. Same pattern, same results. Dissatisfaction by their own choosing.

Just so you are perfectly clear on how you should make contact with this unseen power, should you choose this method of communicating with this all-knowing infinite intelligence, the following steps are what I did that continue to work for me:

1. You should deliver any desire by utilizing this writing method.
2. You must be clear about what you are seeking and not scatter your desires for good and for the good of others like a machine-gun burst. The majority of my communications consist of anything I want to talk about to this infinite intelligence, which I treat as my best friend who will never divulge what or whom I choose to talk about, such as my concerns, family issues, my frustrations, what I am grateful for, my concerns, and the humanitarian services I want to continue to expand on that I can provide to as many people as I can.
3. You absolutely exercise patience by allowing this infinite wisdom enough time to come back to you through your inner mind with the answers and methods you are seeking. I cannot express enough the importance of this step. This is the critical step where most people decide to give up and go back to the way they were, before deciding to allow their inner mind the proper amount of time to bring forth in reality the answers, methods, and results they are seeking. Keep in mind that the matter concerning most requests one turns over to this all-knowing intelligence initially took time to materialize in one's life; therefore, this infinite source needs to be given adequate time to bring forth the desired results expected. It is right here at this point where your true test

is going to come between you and this infinite intelligence that communicates directly with your inner guidance that brings forth what you are seeking to experience.

From my own personal observation, the combination of strong belief, self-confidence, expectation, and unwavering patience were and remain a powerful combination that played a significant role in removing the adversities I was experiencing in my life, including bringing forth a permanent healing from illnesses I had, without chemotherapy or any invasive treatments whatsoever. I elected to reject these treatments because of my complete and unwavering trust in this infinite intelligence that has never failed me and am confident never will.

Can I state unequivocally that without calling upon this infinite intelligence, someone would ultimately succumb to a life-threatening illness? Not at all! However, I can state without any doubt whatsoever that if I had to do it over again, without hesitation, I would rely 100 percent on this unseen source for the answers, methods, solutions, and actions being directed for me.

Keep in mind that everything in life comes down to making a choice, one way or another, or, in the alternative, doing nothing all. Eventually, we will elect one or the other, no matter whatever problem we may face. When it comes to life-threatening matters, however, these decisions become even more important.

Also keep this in mind, by choosing to do what we have always been doing and experiencing the same result, maybe it is time to consider a different approach or path, if the result seems to always come out against our best interest. Now, if the result is positive and in our best interest, then consider staying with whatever it is that appears to be working. If not, it may be wise to consider reconnecting or connecting with your all-knowing infinite intelligence; by doing so, you enhance a positive experience, provided it is for good and for the benefit of all concerned.

Concerning religions—many people attend religious services regularly and have for many years. I was one of them. They will pray to their chosen higher source continually for their needs and for others. Those who do attend a religious service of their choosing and who pray to a higher source of their choice can be closer to having a written dialogue with this all-knowing infinite intelligence by way of the method I am describing.

The reason I say this is that faithfully attending one or more religious services each week is an indication of deep faith. However, no matter how often one chooses to attend a religious service or chooses to volunteer to assist or to work at any religious facility or occupy any appointed or volunteered position within one's chosen religion, none of these positions or service can offer any assurance they will connect directly with this infinite source of wisdom. The reason I state this is, because in order to have an ongoing relationship with this all-powerful, unseen force, one should communicate with it every day and not just once a week or month. The most direct way I found to do this is the writing method I am identifying to be able to achieve whatever good one is being sought.

The reason why is, as human beings, we are constantly preoccupied with numerous need-to-do lists every single day and further occupied with matters that are continuously coming into our lives. Then there is the need to spend a considerable amount of time at a chosen occupation, raising children, married or unmarried, taking care of everyday chores, paying bills, planning for various events, and the innumerable things that may be done during any given day—let alone any given week or month, for that matter. Therefore, even though you may attend a religious service, most of the time after leaving the service, quite unconsciously, the mind automatically shifts into its to-do list, even before they reach their vehicle or home. This is a natural and common occurrence.

Having said this and having experienced this myself, I can tell you that one cannot possibly concentrate on continuous communication with this infinite intelligence, having such interferences and occurrences going on in their lives and conscious minds every hour of every day. This is why I stated that if you sincerely desires to have an ongoing dialogue with this infinite source of all-knowing knowledge, you need to commit to a minimum of at least fifteen minutes a day—preferably thirty minutes—by way of the method that follows and not just in a silent talking way and place this communication with this infinite mind as first, not last, on your to-do list. If placed as a nonessential priority in your life, it is possible that you may receive some answers; however, the effect will not be as complete and the same when this infinite intelligence is a nonpriority on your to-do list. When you choose to prioritize this infinite force on your day-to-day to-do list and choose to dedicate the time to sit down in your chosen quiet place and allocate a set time to have a one-on-one dialogue with this infinite intelligence by way of the writing method I am introducing—or for some, reintroducing—in this chapter, this is when you can come to expect your innermost desires can be realized.

If people can find the time to get up, get dressed, get in the car, drive to the religious service of their choice, find the time to chat with others before and/or after the service then possibly go for coffee or even for something to eat afterwards, and even possibly find time to volunteer your services to their chosen religion one or more times a week, then certainly they can find the time to dedicate at least fifteen minutes—or even a half an hour—of their time every day to communicate with this all-powerful source in the manner I have been describing, in a quiet place where you can empty everything they need to unload and ask for whatever they truly desire. This assumes that the person is not so physically and/or mentally incapacitated and unable to perform this method of communicating with this infinite, all-knowing guidance that will know this and communicate instead through the inner spirit that resides within these persons and/or through anyone who communicates through the writing method on their behalf, just by including them in their daily written communications with this unseen force.

Now, am I saying that through dedicated and concentrated prayer, one's desires will not be answered? No, not at all. However, it has been my experience that they may not be responded to in as timely a manner as expected, and possibly considerable time may pass before one's prayers are answered.

I am aware and found that when communicating with this infinite intelligence in the manner I describe, what I have asked for did appear and right on time in every instance. Now, what "right on time" may mean "an instant," "a day," or "not more than a week" to some people. However, "right on time," for the purposes we are discussing here means just that—not late and never too late but will be realized within a reasonable period of time, if you choose to exercise patience.

This held true to me pertaining overcoming each and every nonphysical illness and other serious life-changing adversities and events that had come into my life. Therefore, I have absolutely no reason to discontinue my daily, ongoing written dialogue. As a matter of fact, I have increased the time I spend with it every day, ranging from my usual one hour to as long as two hours or even longer. You do not need to spend this amount of time communicating with this all-knowing source; however, I suggest that over time, you increase your writing to half an hour.

The amount of time you do allot for yourself to spend with this incredible power should not be spent solely asking for material stuff. The time I allot is used for actually talking to this infinite source, asking first for guidance I may need in any given situation. Above all else, I express my sincerest, heartfelt gratitude for everything that this infinite intelligence has done and continues to do for me and those I love and care about who have graced my life, including each and every moment and breath given me and for all mankind as well. Keep this in mind as it is extremely important, should you choose this method of communicating, expressing your gratitude is the very first thing you should do before beginning this writing method, transmitting whatever it is you choose to share with this all-powerful force.

For those who attend religious services of any types or denominations regularly, you will find that, by combining your religions belief with daily communication with this infinite intelligence, you can greatly enhance your innermost desires. With patience, over time, you should noticeably begin experiencing the good you are seeking for your life as well for the lives of others. And as I have already pointed out, keeping in mind that what you are seeking needs to be for good and not for evil. Combine this with gratitude and full expectation, without any doubting or wavering whatsoever, as any one or all of these negative states of mind will nullify any good you are seeking in your life.

When communicating by way of this method, feel free to say and request what you desire for good, within reason—remembering, as I've also been pointing out, that whatever it may be, when you have completed any session, let whatever grievances you may have shared with this all-knowing source move on with confidence, knowing your requests has been heard and, in time, the answers and solutions will be communicated to your inner guidance that brings forth your desires. Leave it there and never question the *how* or the *when* it may come about—just have complete confidence and, above all, patience that it will!

Should you decide to begin corresponding with this all-powerful, unseen guidance through this writing method, it is very important that you understand that any writings between you and this infinite intelligence should be private writings. Take into consideration the fact that they may contain very private information concerning anyone you decide to include in your writings. If this is the case with you, you may not want others to read whatever you write about, in the event of your death or illness. Therefore, no matter what type of writing tablet or journal you wish to utilize, it should be kept in a safe place where only you should have access to it, as these are your private conversations with this infinite power. Of course, this is a personal choice that can only be made by you.

This suggestion relating to keeping one's journal private evokes the question "What happens if I were to expire?" You'd think all this information would be accessible to others, and you really would not want that. Let me share with you what I did. I made the decision to place in my will that upon my expiration, my journals—every box of them—should all be destroyed and that absolutely no one is to ever have any access to them or should be read by anyone at all, including even close family members or any attorney or executor of my estate. In addition, if one chooses not to do this, then there is always the inexpensive paper shredder (a diamond-shaped, fine-cutting shredder works best). Therefore, you do not have to be concerned where to store or hide your journals as you can shred them regularly as you deem necessary.

I keep my journals because I refer to them to review everything I had requested for good and keep track of the dates I made those requests and when they were fulfilled and those that were yet to be realized, as well as being able to witness for myself the myriad of crud I had been carrying around that had disappeared from my life and no longer burdens me. I found this a good way for me to remind myself how fortunate and grateful I am for this writing method.

Some people have asked me if my journals contain rantings and ravings. As I had indicated, yes they do—well, they used to anyway. And as I identified, they even include blaming this infinite power for a number of serious issues that have occurred in my life. In the beginning, they were full of *why*s and the "why me" question as well, and I even named names in some of my writings. Boy was that a relief to get all that off my back.

They also contain some drawings and scribblings of faces of those I really had a deep dislike and others whom I blamed for a number of my nonphysical events and illnesses. These drawings, at the time, were not complimentary of those with whom I no longer wanted to be associated. Remember, these are your private communications with this all-knowing intelligence who is aware of all your hurts, anger, disappointments, illnesses, misery you have gone through; any addictions you may have or have had; any extramarital affairs, if you are or were married; etc. In other words, your inner guidance is also aware of each and every situation you have ever had, good or bad, and receives all answers, methods, and solutions you require to overcome anything you may ask of this infinite intelligence and/or fulfill any reasonable desire that is for good and for the good of everyone concerned.

Over time, during the course of my daily written messages with my all-knowing infinite intelligence, it became very clear to me that during my writing sessions, I would notice that answers and methods were coming to me related to things I had been concerned, about which made absolute sense and made me question why I had not thought of these answers and methods myself. The answer to that was, because even if I did have the answers, the methods may not have been the right way to have approached or to have attempted to solve my issues.

You see, we are mere humans residing on this planet and can never have all the answers to why some undesirable events show up in our lives. However, far too many people truly believe that they do have all the answers and can singlehandedly resolve any issue, even to the point of a serious illness that may appear in their lives one day. Now, to some extent, some people have been successful with resolving their concerns and other matters; however, for the most part, many of these resolutions have, at best, been temporary fixes, only to resurface again in the distant and even near future and, more often than not, become much worse.

I know this to be a fact as I was one of these people who not only believed that I was the sole originator and mastermind of all my business successes and did so without any help from anyone. And because of my success I, therefore, took most, if not all, the credit for these results. Little did I know at the time, however, I did not have all the answers and methods that I thought I had total control over and which I believed I was the sole architect; and one day it all came crashing down on me, much to my shock and dismay.

Now, let me ask you, how often have you seen this situation repeated over and over again with well-known public figures, people in politics, Hollywood actors and actresses, the financially wealthy and the like, and even people you yourself may know or have known? Other than myself, back then, I had known a number of successful people who thought just like I did and whose egos were so strong that they would allow no one to ever counsel with them when imminent disaster lay only a short distance ahead. In the end, they too self-destructed.

People asked me if handing one's problems over to an unseen intelligence was the total answer to resolving issues in their lives and if so, what the difference was between what is being preached and taught in some religions and what I am speaking about being able to communicate with this all-knowing guidance directly. The answer to this may possibly blow away some people. Here is the answer, and if you have problems with understanding this, I strongly suggest that you consider this before you decide to abandon this method of communication with this all-knowing infinite intelligence.

First, give it a fair chance to work for you before you choose to reach such a decision. I am certain that you do not want to ever regret you had made the wrong decision and find out that you did, long after the horse has already left the barn, so to speak, and becomes far too late for some serious event in your life for you to have been able to resolve the matter for your good and for the good of all concerned. This includes any serious or other life-changing event.

Next, try to understand that all the necessary answers and methods that you'll ever need have already been given to you and every member of mankind, to overcome any life-changing circumstance, situation, or event, as we are all connected to this infinite force. The "false us" resides in the physical world to which we are exposed and profoundly affected by every one of our physical experiences, be they good or bad. Therefore, it is we—all of us—who can control each and every situation we encounter in the physical world because we are the creators of each and every circumstance, situation, etc., in which we find ourselves—whether they are illnesses, wellness, financial, prosperity on every level, or just getting by—and which we demonstrate in our physical life. It is our inner guidance connected with this infinite intelligence that has taken up residence within you.

I have heard some people say that it is not even feasible that an inner guidance that has its own separate powers is the real them and that because they are a thinking being, they can make their own decisions and not have to ever rely upon any so-named inner guidance. My answer to this comment is, there certainly is no one I am aware of that is attempting to coerce anyone to believe that the real you dwells within you. However, you should also consider why many of your burning desires have yet to be answered or why your undesirable situation has not improved.

Not being a pastor, priest, rabbi, or leader of any church or religion, I would be the last person who would even make an attempt to try to get anyone to believe that their real self resides deep within. However, there have been far too many so-called miracles that have occurred throughout the world during mankind's occupation of this planet for anyone to be able to state that it was the brain of man alone that created all the so-named miracles that countless people have personally witnessed throughout history. This holds true for modern-day societies throughout the world.

Even the most learned and intelligent medical scientists today are baffled by what the modern man still refers to as miracles and have no logical medical answers for. Yet so many people in this era choose to believe that it is either they or medical science that were responsible and deserve the total credit for untold human survivals of some of the world's deadliest diseases and other life-threatening events.

Why is it then when many people pray for a miracle for an extended period of time or will visit holy shrines throughout the world to receive a miracle yet rarely do the expected miracles appear? And why is it that so many prayers go unanswered? Not being a person who has spent his life studying theology, I do not have the answers to these questions, and I can assure you that neither does anyone else. Maybe some have an unproven theory but not a definitive and proven answer, not yet—to my knowledge—anyway. Yet how does one explain when one communicates with this all-knowing intelligence in the manner in which I have been describing? Not only are there answers but methods to be able to achieve whatever it is one deeply desires to experience.

If I were not a living example of what I have just been stating here, then all this would lack credibility. However, having survived not only several life-threatening events against incredible odds, including numerous serious nonphysical events and other major adversities, I am more than confident none of this could have been achieved without my direct contact with an all-knowing infinite intelligence that is connected with my inner guidance that is the recipient of the methods, answers, and solutions coming from this infinite power.

Not only did I receive the answers and solutions through the method I have been describing thus far for overcoming the physical illnesses that I endured, I also received the answers and methods necessary to overcome all the nonphysical life-changing events and adversities I encountered as well, in a relatively short period of time, considering the seriousness of these events.

It should be noted, as I also had said earlier, that I am not the sole person on this planet who has achieved what some would deem to have been a miracle when it came to overcoming serious life-disrupting adversities while refusing any chemotherapy treatments, despite medical specialists' recommendations to embark on a series of these treatments. There are many other survivors who overcame much more, including some who have published their accounts about overcoming serious life-changing events and illnesses through the correspondence method I have been describing.

During my countless hours of research in preparation for this book, I encountered others who have had communications with what they call spiritual guides. These were described as nonphysical beings who attempt to guide one through the maze we all travel in our physical lives, and some have said that these nonphysical guides are present to assist us to complete our purpose here on this planet. For me, the jury is still out on this premise.

It is not my place to criticize anyone's opinions and interactions or to dissect them; however, in almost any field of work or research, one can find many who may differ with another's theories, opinions, or endeavors when it comes to how it may influence others. I have found it to be very difficult to criticize anyone's opinions or unsupported findings concerning anything to do with those who claim to be able to make contact with those who had passed on—e.g., mediums, soothsayers, palm readers, fortune tellers, and the like—who make claim to be able to interact with the deceased relatives of others still alive. Considering that I have had no such experience myself, I will rest here on this subject by stating that unless and until I personally have had such knowledge, I could not accept or rely upon such a claim. Any such decision for you, however, must be of your own choosing; therefore, I shall not render any further opinion concerning these types of claims, only to say that I can only rely upon what I have actually personally proven to myself as the reality of what I have been describing to you up to this point.

In addition, I have personally proved, as have others who have published excellent works on the subject, that communication with any unseen source does not come from the grey matter contained in the brain; instead, it comes from deep within.

I also have difficulty with even considering any paranormal communications with any former living soul. Is it possible? I really do not know! However, unless proven and not through any of the previously outlined sources, I prefer to stay right where I am with the proven methods of communication with this infinite force with which I am familiar and have been describing. These communications have made it possible for me to obtain everything that I was seeking and continue to do so, proof of which is my personal experience and results I realized through this method of communication with this all-knowing source.

When people say to me that they may possibly try ("do or use [something] in order to see if it works or will be successful") this method of connecting with this all-knowing intelligence, where I am concerned, the word *try* in itself is full of doubt. To me, trying is like making an attempt to walk across Niagara Falls in the middle of winter in freezing temperatures on a steel cable with nothing more than a balancing pole. No thanks! I preferred instead to believe, know, and trust that this infinite power will bring forth the results I was seeking for good and by trusting and believing unwaveringly, I have personally experienced all that I have for good and continue to do so. Now one might ask, "Do the results utilizing the method you have been describing come soon?" The answer is yes and no.

Yes, because any undesirable life-changing event was self-created over time. Therefore, a reasonable amount of time may pass for this all-knowing power to resolve the situation, circumstance, etc. And no, because, should a serious life-threatening adversity be the issue, it may take a while longer. However, with unwavering belief and expectancy, chances are greatly enhanced as they were for the very serious life-threatening events that I faced.

Remember, any complicated issues that you are seeking to be resolved did not just materialize in your life one day. The majority of serious issues took years to develop; therefore, you should not expect the matter to be resolved overnight. If you will commit to undoubting, unwavering belief, trust, and full expectation that it will, the matter can be resolved in your favor within the right timing that only this all-knowing intelligence controls. I personally have yet to have any of my requests go unanswered or unresolved, including my serious physical problems. I attribute the healings I received were a result of my total daily dedication to the method of communicating with this incredible power that I have been using and by never doubting its superior power.

I was once asked if the method I have been describing had even once not met my expectations. The answer is, yes—when I first began to utilize this method and began to doubt this all-knowing influence for what I truly desired to have manifest in my life. Other than that, I cannot recall a time when it did not respond to any of my desires or to resolve any issues through my inner guidance, after this short period of doubting.

Much to my chagrin, I have read that astounding results should not be expected anytime soon when first corresponding with this all-knowing infinite intelligence. Not true, by my personal experience anyway. When I first began this method of dialogue with this force, even the most insignificant requests were answered much sooner than I expected. I was astonished at the prompt responses I was receiving, accompanied by the methods I needed to follow to have my issues resolved.

Another question that I get very often is, "Do you accept every answer that you receive and act upon it immediately?" Yes, but only when I deeply feel the answer and the method I am receiving—without hesitation. If, however, I do not get this deep inner feeling, I am confident that the answer I received was coming from my conscious mind and not from this infinite intelligence, which is the ego attempting to interfere with the answers being received by this infinite power. "How can this be?" you may be thinking. Because the ego is constantly making every attempt to dissuade you from accepting any idea, answer, or method that goes against those coming from the conscious mind by way of the myriad of thoughts that are continuously passing through one's conscious mind. Keep the thought that your conscious mind and your inner guidance—your unconscious inner mind—are not one and the same, and therefore, you must learn to guard against and be able to determine where any and all answers are emanating. The key to separating the two is to always follow your strong inner feelings and emotions and not listen to that small voice that nags at you constantly, your ego.

It is important to know that you should never question what you write to this all-knowing intelligence or ever go back to second-guessing yourself. By doing this, you begin to doubt what your first writings were attempting to say with passion and feeling which are coming from deep within you and not from some outside source, as is the case with the ego and conscious mind, which will question and critique what your first emotions, wants, and desires may be and may attempt to change them. However, *don't*.

The method I have been describing, as I said before, does not require perfection in writing, paragraphing, punctuation, spelling, penmanship, etc.; instead, express your true, innermost feelings; wants; and burning desires that you need right answers for and methods than can help rid you of undesirable events and illnesses and to be able to heal serious illnesses. Furthermore, this method of communicating with this all-knowing force does not require years to learn how, judge anything or anyone, lay blame on anyone, including yourself, or how you need to try to impress this infinite all-knowing power. That would be a major error as your inner guidance is one with this all-knowing intelligence and cannot be impressed because it already knows all there is to know about you. No one could ever impress or fool it, no matter how much you try, as mere mortals cannot compete with this superior power; to believe one can is a display of total ignorance.

Remember, you are seeking answers, methods, and solutions, not a jousting match with this infinite intelligence. You must never lose sight of this when sending or receiving messages with this incredible guidance, as it is there for you always, as opposed to the relentless, never-ending need for satisfying its tremendous desire for material possessions, which is there to feed you its unending wants.

Another question I am asked is, "Do the answers and methods always come from the writing method alone or do they come in some other form as well?" In my case, the answers and methods I was seeking came and continue to come through my writings and the strong feelings I receive from this all-knowing source of wisdom. I have yet to personally experience any beneficial answers and methods that come from any outside source. I found that this writing method works for me every time and, therefore, would never have any reason to seek any other method of communicating with this infinite wisdom.

Does this mean that you can never achieve what you truly desire to experience for good and for the good of all concerned unless this method is utilized? I cannot personally attest that the same result cannot be achieved through the use of other methods of communication. What I do know is that prayer, if believed in wholeheartedly, has worked for many people; however, few people are consistent with prayer. It has been my observation that prayer is generally utilized when one is seeking help with critical situations, dire need, and often a petition for healings—as opposed to the writing method where the person is in continuous contact with this infinite intelligence. Prayer is utilized when a need arises or as repetitious, memorized affirmations which are utilized in various religious beliefs, primarily in group settings and services, but rarely when they are away from this type of environment, thereby having only limited connection with this al- knowing infinite intelligence—with the exception of those who are totally devout and dedicated to their religious beliefs.

Assuming that you may choose this writing method, you must be totally committed to selecting a specific time of day every day, without fail, when you can devote a minimum of at least fifteen minutes of your time—preferably more—with this infinite intelligence through this writing method. Notice I said *writing*, meaning that everything you write—every complaint, hurt, request, question, blame, deeply imbedded feelings, grudges, hateful feelings, disappointments, your deepest desires for good and needs—is what I am referring to when I say writing.

Once you begin writing, do not hesitate at all, unless you feel ill or there is an emergency you absolutely must attend to; otherwise, just keep writing. At first, it does not matter what you write, just keep writing without taking time to think about what you want to write about. Just let whatever flow through your pen to paper as fast as you can, without giving any thought whatsoever to what is coming out of you. Know that you do not have to have any subject in mind that you wish to write about, as any subject shall do.

Also understand that for the first week or two, you should not expect any answers to come to you at all from this method; so whatever you do, *do not get frustrated*. However, after the fourth or fifth week of dedicated writing, having not missed one appointment with this all-knowing guidance, you may find during one of your writing dates that what you're writing will be something you are unfamiliar with and may not even recognize the style or form of the writing coming from your pen to paper. Just keep on writing and do not stop until you have completed your writing session for at least thirty minutes but not longer than an hour at a time; as before long, you will find that you may be writing as long as two hours at one sitting. I myself may write up to two hours; however, it is not necessary for you to write as long, unless one day you feel you wish to do so and only if it becomes comfortable for you. This writing method is not meant to be an arduous chore but one of enjoyment and love for this all-knowing infinite intelligence and, above all, for yourself and others you may be writing and care about or love.

When you are done, if you wish, you can then go back and review what you have written previously, but do not change anything you wrote, because what you wrote was coming from deep within that needs to be addressed.

In the beginning, the answers may not be complete; however, the total answers and methods will follow if you exercise patience. Keep in mind that you should allow yourself to write whatever comes to you and not hesitate to take time thinking about it. Therefore, when you begin your writing session, do not stop and think about what you are going to write about—just begin writing and you will be amazed what comes flowing out of your pen.

I emphasize once again, it is very important that you do not stop to think about a subject to write about or how you wish to phrase your writing because the key to communicating with this all-knowing guidance in this manner is to get it all on paper as fast as you can and to just allow yourself to vent, rant, and rave; complain, blame, wish, or cry; or scribble or draw anything you wish—even if it doesn't make sense at the moment. Whatever comes, allow it to flow onto your paper without questioning what is coming from you, with no erasures. What is coming from you is precisely what you need to see and acknowledge, as it may be experiences in your life as far back as early childhood where some issues had never been healed or had been brought to closure.

Remember: Do this at the same time every day, *without fail*, as you continue your writing; and by doing so, you shall find, over a period of a month or two, that the answers and the methods you are seeking will slowly begin appearing in your writings and will make perfectly good sense to you. You will wonder why you could not have thought of these answers and methods yourself. In essence, you did, through your real inner self—your inner guidance. Keep in mind that this writing method is the strongest, most expedient, and surest of all the ways you can receive the answers, methods, and solutions you are seeking.

It is important that you are aware that you should not miss even one day of your commitment to your daily writing appointment with this infinite intelligence—unless, of course, it is absolutely unavoidable. In this event, just continue as soon as you can. If you do have to miss your daily writing appointments in your chosen quiet place, consider doing what I do. Carry a notebook with you in your car, briefcase, pocket, or purse—if you are a woman—and to always keep one handy if you missed your appointed writing time for any reason and just do your writing for that day, even if it only for a little while, right where you are, and resume your selected writing time the following day. You can do this when waiting for a doctor's appointment, dentist's appointment, or anywhere and use that time to write as much as you can, even if it is not for the entire thirty minutes.

As I said, you will experience the beginning of answers to your inquiries, questions, needs, and desires coming to you through your writings. Do not question it, fear it, judge it, or doubt it—just keep writing. And at the end of your writing session, go back to where you first began your writing, and you will be astonished at the answers you have been seeking that are slowly beginning to be revealed to you as well as the methods that are coming from this infinite guidance. These writings will contain the wisdom you will recognize could not have come from your physical mind or most worldly sources, and at this point, you should begin to get very excited. I certainly did.

By writing at a specific time every day, this infinite power will come to recognize that you will be there at the appointed time every day and will be ready to assist you with the answers, methods, and solutions you are seeking, as well as to guide you in the proper direction with anything you may ask or desire for good.

PREVAILING OVER INSURMOUNTABLE ODDS

Remember, that nothing presently exists in your life or will in the future with which this infinite guidance is not familiar or is without proper guidance, answers, solutions, or methods you may be seeking. In addition, aside from any desires you may be asking to be manifested in the physical, as you continue to communicate in this manner, you shall soon find that your inner guidance, which is one with this infinite intelligence, has become your best friend and confidant and the best listener you have or will ever encounter during your lifetime.

I know this to be true as I have been fortunate enough to be able to communicate with this unseen intelligence as though it was sitting right beside me in the same room where I am writing and talking to it through my writings and as though it was a very close trusted friend, which it truly is, who would never betray my confidence and would console me when I needed consoling, provide me with the wisdom I need that had been missing in my life, provide that warm and gentle smile that we all long for from others but rarely receive, will hug me when I need to be hugged, and wipe away my tears when I am sad and feeling all alone at times.

So you see, this infinite intelligence is not there just to resolve your issues and provide the answers and methods you are seeking, but it does so much more when and if you make a personal choice to give this infinite guidance the chance it is beckoning you to give it, as it has been extremely patient waiting for you to call upon it—in some cases, for years. Quite sadly, many go through life on this planet not having even once called upon this all-knowing infinite power and so many more, living lives of quiet desperation and depression and experiencing a myriad of other undesirable conditions.

Therefore, considering all I have said thus far, should you choose to begin a dialogue with this infinite intelligence, the following information describes how I first began communicating and receiving answers, methods, directions, and solutions. Take a minute here to review these easy-to-understand steps and make a note of them for future reference:

1. *Purchase an inexpensive lined or unlined notebook and several pens.* If you are more comfortable with using a computer, this will also serve the same purpose. Those who prefer

to utilize a small handheld recorder, this is acceptable but not preferable and should only be used when absolutely necessary but not as a substitute for your writing when you communicate with this all-knowing source of wisdom during your regularly scheduled writing session.

2. *Always begin your writing with a thank-you to what you perceive to be the all-knowing infinite power, and give this power a special name.* Should you choose to do this, the name you choose to give to any unseen intelligence you prefer will do. I start out by writing, "Good morning, infinite intelligence," and thank this intelligence for all the answers, methods, and direction that will be given to me and those that will continue to be given to me. Being grateful is the key to receiving the answers, methods, and solutions you are seeking. Then and only then will I begin my writing.

3. *Some people like to utilize soft music prior to beginning their writing session.* I am told music seems to place them in a relaxing mood and lessens any stress they may be experiencing. I find no problem with this or meditating prior to beginning the writing method, if this is what one feels comfortable with or has become accustomed to doing. However, do not listen to hard, loud music or music that contains any negative messages or listen to any music or perform any form of meditation when you begin your writing; you should not have any outside interferences whatsoever when you begin your writing. This will not be of any assistance to you, and it can cause your communication to be confusing and far removed from what you had intended to write to this all-knowing power.

4. *Make a brief list.* The evening before you begin communicating, write down all the questions, concerns, issues, etc., you wish to communicate about. There are no rules, protocol, etc., necessary when communicating with the all-knowing infinite intelligence. However, do not bring this list with you to refer to when you are ready to begin your writing session. By preparing such a list and reviewing it before you retire, what you want to talk about with this

infinite wisdom will be conveyed to your inner mind; therefore, you will be well prepared to continue writing and gathering your thoughts or remembering what it was you intended to write about, as your inner mind will convey whatever it was when you are ready to begin your writing session. I have found this to be the best method to utilize, prior to sitting down every day to write; and by doing so, my writings are uninterrupted and flowing and go directly to the point.

5. *Begin writing.* When you are ready, begin writing the very first thing that comes to you that will trigger other thoughts. Those thoughts will trigger many more, until you will soon notice that you are writing with incredible speed, wanting to get all these thoughts down on paper as fast as you can. As I had instructed, do not be concerned with your penmanship—as long as you can read it, that is all that matters. Use abbreviations whenever you so choose, draw pictures or signs, or do whatever that helps you at the moment while you are writing; but by all means *do not* cease writing or erase anything once you begin. Just allow whatever is coming to you to flow through your pen and the paper you are writing on, and you will see that it all make sense. If you are dealing with the past and suddenly jump to the present, so be it. Do not be concerned with it at all and just keep writing. If you feel some remorse, sadness, or joy, *allow it.* If you cry, *allow it.* But *do not stop* writing or interrupting what is coming from deep within you onto paper during your writing session. Even if you have the urge to reread what you just wrote, don't.

6. *When your writing session is over, just close your journal and do not be concerned with what you just wrote.* Later in the day, should you still wish to review what you wrote, go back to your journal but only when you are alone with it and have absolutely no interruptions; and by all means, as I said previously, do not change what you wrote as these were—and remain—your private, personal true feelings, wants, desires, questions, etc., which have already been

communicated to this infinite intelligence to handle for you. Afterward, place your journal in a safe place where no one else can read it, as this is your private communication that is not meant to be shared with anyone. You can choose to, this is but not advisable.

7. *Whatever you do, do not make up any answers you may want to hear.* Instead, be very patient, and in time, the answers will come to you in various ways. Some may come through your writing, where you will be writing answers coming to you from questions you had previously asked that are now appearing on paper, which you will recognize not being either your style or the way you think or write. Answers, methods, and proper direction will also come through intense, intuitive feelings. Do not ignore these feelings. Once you receive such intuitive feelings, it is important that you act upon them. Other forms of answers can be very strong, and these continuous thoughts become predominant thoughts—that is, these thoughts will overshadow the thousands of thoughts that pass through your mind every day, for good. These too should be acted upon without procrastinating, should the answers make perfect sense to you.

8. *Refrain from asking choices.* When writing, don't ask for choices, as you should never assume that this infinite guidance will make any choices for you. Any choices you decide relate to what we all have that is commonly known as free will. If you feel you need to have choices, petition instead for advice and proper guidance with whatever it is you may be seeking choices for. Always avoid any yes-no questions because this infinite power will always provide you with the right direction to take, no matter what the issue may be that pertains to what you are writing about.

9. *Trust only on the inner guidance.* Once you begin this writing method, *never* consult with a third party like a medium, palm reader, psychic, or anyone claiming to have direct contact with the spirit world. Your inner guidance is connected with the infinite intelligence and is not to be confused or to be connected to any deceased being such as

a family member or any such source that may be rendering advice or answering you in any way. The entire purpose of this writing method is for it to communicate with you directly, not relying upon or going through any third party whatsoever for confirmation of the answers you receive. What you are seeking through this writing method is inner wisdom and the right answers, methods, and solutions that matter to you and not to hear or receive information from someone in your distant past. Therefore, it is not *who* but the right direction and the right answers that should be important to you. Know that any answers and guidance you may receive is not coming from your conscious mind but is being conveyed to you through your inner guidance/inner mind that is one with infinite intelligence.

I cannot emphasize this enough: It is extremely important that you are totally undisturbed during your writing session. Make absolutely certain that all outer noises are cut off, all telephone devices are silenced, and there should be no interruptions from others, including the children. Be certain you use the restroom first, if needed, as you are embarking on a matter that is of uppermost importance to you personally.

Keep in mind that once you have decided to begin communicating through this writing method, over time, you will begin to develop you own preferences that best suit you and which you are comfortable with, as not everyone who chooses to establish contact with this infinite guidance in this manner maintains the same method. This is one of the most remarkable parts about connecting with this infinite intelligence, as you not only can gain direct access to it but can design how you wish to share messages with it during your writing sessions every day. Your results and style of communicating may vary, and if you know or find someone who is also making this link with this all-knowing intelligence, no matter by what name they may have chosen to give this connection with this unseen all-knowing intelligence, keep in mind that you should *neither* divulge anything you write about to anyone nor they with you. The information you are receiving is to be your personal information and is to remain solely between you and this all-knowing infinite intelligence. Therefore, sharing with anyone what you divulge and write about may nullify whatever it may be that you are seeking to realize for good.

The very purpose of communicating with this infinite intelligence in this manner is to have a very personal one-on-one conversation every day. This needs to be a high priority for you and needs to be treated in a very confidential manner. Here is one very good reason. Suppose you chose to share your daily journal with someone you believe you can trust. And suppose this trusted person decides to disagree with you or attempts to convince you that this is not real and it should not be pursued. This thought then becomes an implanted thought in your conscious mind, and the possibility is great that you will either consider that thought or dwell on it for a period of time.

In either event, you may decide to cease communicating in this manner for a time or permanently and follow this person's guidance or the direction of others who you may have chosen to share your personal writings with as well. I have not—*and will never*—share my personal writing to this infinite intelligence with anyone, no matter how close a person or others may be to me.

This is the one thing I consider sacred, very personal, and extremely valuable to me because I have experienced the results that, in my opinion, could never have been achieved through any other source and as timely as they were made manifest in my physical life. To consider ever abandoning this method and/or this infinite intelligence is not even on my consideration chart and never will be!

Considering the fact that this-all knowing guidance has yet to let me down, I know that this one-on-one communicating method is personal and confidential; therefore, those written exchanges shall never be divulged. They will remain with me always and never to be allowed to fall into the hands of anyone, as this is a solemn promise this infinite intelligence and I have made to each other soon after I began communicating with this incredible power.

I rely upon this infinite guidance the majority of the time, in conjunction with my common sense. Therefore, using a 100 percent–scale scenario, I rely upon my all-knowing intelligence, 100 percent.

PREVAILING OVER INSURMOUNTABLE ODDS

During my daily writings, I have learned to rely on it for the right answers, methods, solutions, and direction. Of course, everyone is not the same, and therefore, some may choose to rely upon it more or less. This depends upon the individual and their trust comfort zone.

The reason is because we have all become accustomed to receiving information from others in our physical environments and choose to follow the greater percentage of such information and advice, especially when those rendering this knowledge and direction are professionals like doctors, lawyers, etc.

Some people tell me that they are unsure whether to do this communicating method or not. This is a perfectly normal reaction to most anything new that one has not previously been exposed to. My question, however, is this: If you are presently experiencing any undesirable events in your life or have been for quite some time, are you better off remaining with these conditions in your life or would taking the step needed to rid yourself of these undesirable events be worth the effort to at least making contact with this all-knowing intelligence? Furthermore, have the remedies you already attempted to seek and/or the advice you have received from whatever source you have chosen been helpful to the point that your undesirable circumstances, situations, and/or events are no longer in your life? If so, then my suggestion would be to stay with what is working for you.

However, it would do you no harm and do you every good if you would still pursue a dialogue with this infinite all-knowing power. Because as each day appears on the horizon, there are always different challenges for all of us. No one passes through this life undefeated and will always need direction one can rely upon, with confidence to be able to deal with whatever life hands us. Therefore, why not be prepared in advance to also be able to rely upon this all-knowing power that is connected with your inner guidance that can and will keep you armed at all times with the right answers, methods, solutions, and proper direction?

It certainly would not hurt to set aside at least thirty minutes of your time a day to explore what this infinite source of wisdom can do for you. And once you do, I can assure you that you more than likely may never rely 100 percent again on any outer source for your needs, desires, and resolutions to any life-disrupting situations, events, or circumstances that may come your way.

It has been apparent that when people get easily frustrated, desperate for an answer to their questions, and seeking resolutions to any adversity they may be experiencing, they will begin to become impatient and desperate for answers or try a perceived remedy in the outer world, hoping this will bring forth what they are seeking. This, of course, is known as impatience. However, if you do choose to communicate with this all-powerful source through this writing method, do not attempt to do this at all costs, if you have chosen to dedicate yourself to communicating with this all-knowing intelligence. The reason is that when one tries to receive an answer from their outer world sources, as well as from this infinite force simultaneously, the result usually is no result whatsoever. Therefore, it is imperative to maintain total confidence in this infinite wisdom, coupled with unwavering belief, expectation, and unwavering trust, knowing that whatever you have petitioned this infinite intelligence to assist you with is already done and on its way for you to realize if—and only *if*—you will exercise the patience necessary to experience whatever it is you are seeking for good.

In the beginning, I too was not that comfortable relying totally upon an unseen all-knowing power because, in the past, I had always been a skeptic and needed everything proven to me before I would accept whatever it was that was important to me. Therefore, when I first began communicating with this infinite intelligence through this writing method, I was somewhat still doubtful to the point where, when I first began receiving answers and the methods I was asking for, I believed that they were just my wishful thinking coming through my pen, emanating from my conscious mind. However, when things began to materialize in my physical life that were precisely related to what I was requesting, over time, I was able to trust this intelligence more and more, until I had developed enough trust to expect that the responses to all my questions and requests that were for good and for the good of all concerned would eventually be reflected in my physical world. Most importantly, I always received answers I could rely upon, and this continues to be so.

I've had some people tell me that they were not receiving any answers from this all-knowing infinite intelligence. When hearing this, I will ask asked how long they had been petitioning this intelligence through the writing method I have been describing. In most cases, I had been told anywhere from one week to not more than one month. As I said earlier, patience, unwavering trust, and expectation are the keys to receiving answers, methods, and solutions. Anything one may convey in private to this source—it already is aware of and knows your every concern, need, and grievance, even before you begin any dialogue.

Now, for those who, like me, have admittedly spent practically a good portion of their life as a skeptic, trusting that answers, methods, and solutions are really coming from an unseen force is the most difficult part in the process of developing a dialogue through this writing method. I should know—I was there once myself. And being the skeptic I had always been, I too had a very difficult time deciding to give my trust to this method. So you are not alone by any stretch of the imagination, as anyone who first makes the decision to consider communicating with this unseen source of wisdom by this method goes through the same thing as you probably are right now and as I have as well. What it took for me in the beginning was adopting the famous Nike slogan, "Just Do It," or spend the rest of my life as a card-carrying procrastinator and skeptic, so to speak.

Unless and until you make the decision to go forward and try this method of communicating with this unseen power, how will you ever know if it will work for you? As for me, I decided that I was no longer going to have to place my life in the hands of anyone to make any life-altering decisions for me, especially critical decisions. Some *credible* advice is okay, but when it comes to my life, I made the irreversible decision not to allow anyone to make life-altering decisions for me, especially when it came to my health, my future, or anything dear to me. For me, I know without any doubt whatsoever that I made the right decision for my life and am here to tell you that I would have it no other way, had I had to do it again.

As a matter of fact, I staked my entire physical life on this unseen force with not just one but several life-threatening illnesses and the decision to refuse highly recommended, insisted-upon chemotherapy treatments. Now, if this is not unwavering trust and confidence, then I have no idea what is!

In addition to this, there is a great deal of wisdom coming to me through my writing dialogue with this infinite intelligence for me not to trust it. Had this wisdom been available to me coming from my conscious mind, there certainly would be absolutely no reason or need for me to have to communicate with this infinite intelligence that is one with my inner guidance.

Now once you become relaxed with this all-knowing source, begin first by handing over smaller matters and ask uncomplicated questions. After having received answers and methods and personally witnessing the answers, methods, and directions being received and they were helpful, it is at this point that you can then begin to ask and deal with more serious matters for which you seek a resolution.

To give you an idea how powerful this infinite power is, I have chosen to allow my readers to view the list below of some of the issues and events that I had turned over to this source, which were all resolved within a reasonable period of time. Considering the immense complexity and seriousness of these issues and events, the permanent resolution of these issues was a significant result, considering that they were not completely resolved by worldly sources or remedies but by this infinite force from which all answers, methods, and solutions have come to mankind for centuries and will continue to do so, to follow for those who choose to seek it.

Here are just some of the personal mountains I found my way down from by way of the methods, answers and solutions that came directly from this all-knowing infinite intelligence:

- Major depression
- High anxiety and stress
- Extreme trauma
- Fear
- Continuous doubting
- Loss of self-confidence and self-reliance
- Distrusting others
- Skepticism
- Blaming others
- High levels of frustration
- Always nervous

PREVAILING OVER INSURMOUNTABLE ODDS

- Advanced colon and liver cancer
- Abandonment
- Loneliness
- Total financial collapse
- Loss of most assets, home, and property
- Loss of a twenty-five-year-old business
- Insurmountable debt obligations
- Betrayal

"Me after embarking on a daily dialogue with this infinite intelligence."

Always believe and trust in this infinite intelligence.

Should you make the decision to develop a daily dialogue with this infinite intelligence through the writing method, you can then judge for yourself the benefits you may discover by allowing yourself to get onto paper what may still be lurking in your mind, e.g., undesirable memories, unresolved issues that have been plaguing you and asking the questions you have been harboring within you for some time or about your life, and any other issues plaguing you, including physical illnesses and nonphysical conditions.

I have to note that some people will start out with the intent of communicating with this infinite force that is one with one's inner mind in the manner I have outlined for you. However, shortly thereafter, they would find a myriad of excuses for giving up and not continuing.

I can identify for you any number of excuses for their giving up, some of which are the following, but the list goes on and on:

- They did not see anything immediately taking place in their lives or anything different than what they had been experiencing.
- Really could not find the time to do it.
- Too many other important matters on their plate that had to be attended to.
- Got bored with it.
- Lost faith and saw no sense to it.

Some people to whom I taught this method chose to just give up on themselves. Although they represented just a handful of people to whom I've taught this method, they chose to give up within the first several weeks, thereby failing to realize whatever it was that was plaguing their life had taken almost a lifetime to develop. However, others, who chose to exercise patience and to stay committed to this all-powerful infinite source that is one with the inner mind, over time, obtained far more benefits than they had expected, just like me.

Therefore, unless you consider discovering the benefits that can be realized through this method of communicating with this unseen power, you more than likely may not realize the benefits you are seeking for your life by choosing to only employ remedies you are seeking from sources in the outer world. The methods in the chapters that follow are also needed and necessary for manifesting what you desire in your physical life. They work in tandem with one another, as they must, to bring forth results expected to be obtained in order to alleviate problems and produce benefits. They will continue to do so, as long as you are dedicated to them and choose to apply steadfast belief, patience, and unwavering expectation that originated from this infinite force.

Keep in mind at all times that communicating through this writing method is a very personal matter and should be treated as such. Embarking upon this writing method with the intent of sharing your communications would be the wrong reason to consider utilizing this writing method and should not be pursued. It would only be a waste of your time as the results you will be seeking may not appear.

Having gone through the writing method as it pertains to establishing a connection that I exclusively utilize when communicating with this powerful source of all knowledge, methods, answers, and solutions, should you choose to utilize this writing method when desiring to personally connect with this force, you now have everything you need to begin this process. As you progress, you will soon begin to develop a system of your own after choosing the time of day, a quiet place, and the length of time you choose to spend exchanging information with this all-powerful infinite mind.

Having now identified how to communicate with this all-powerful infinite source, what you need to understand and begin to believe is that you contain deep within yourself the most vital and powerful source of knowledge and wisdom that has been and continues to be overlooked by countless people since mankind first inhabited this earth. Therefore, there should be no intelligent reason why one would not want to open or reopen an ongoing dialogue with the one source that is capable of resolving most of, if not all, your innermost desires and adversities.

Another very powerful method I utilize with great success is self-reliance, a formidable foe against any undesirable life-changing situation.

11

SELF-RELIANCE—WHAT IT SHOULD REALLY MEAN TO YOU

What you decide definitely matters, concerning your health and overall well-being.

—Author

We are a species who are heavily reliant upon others for our personal well-being, success, and other gratification that we seek in life, whether we are willing to admit it or not. Having just read what I just said, some may be temporarily wounded by this statement. However—stay with me—reflect on your own life and not others and ask yourself this question: Upon who and/or what have you been heavily depending in your life in order to make your life work for you? Go ahead, take a moment to reflect on this right now, as it is very important for you to understand the point I am attempting to get you to see here for yourself. No, do not go and get a pen and something to write on to make a list as you already know upon what and/or who you're heavily reliant.

For some, it was a job; others, it was a spouse or significant other; and for others, the stock market, their 401k retirement plan, their much older (and now rarely seen) children, a family member, a medical professional's advice, medications, friends, business associates, a counselor, financial advisor, stockbroker, banker—this list can go on and on, can't it? Of course it can! These are just some of the myriad of life crutches, so to speak, that people everywhere have and continue to rely upon in their physical world and become so habitually accustomed to in their everyday life. Deny it you may; however, for the greater majority of people, this is a fact of life that most people, for whatever reason, will not own up to.

I am certain you can think of at least three things you are heavily reliant upon to make your life work for you that if they were to disappear tomorrow, your life, as you know it, could begin to unravel; and for some people, it already has. Therefore, for those to whom it may have already happened, I am almost certain they can easily relate to what I am attempting to get across here. It may even be you, the reader, that I am referring to.

Know this: there is only one leaning post you can rely upon that is dug in so deep that not even a direct hit from a category EF5 tornado or hurricane could displace it. That leaning post is the real you within, not the outer you—your ego! Therefore, it is you and only you, when everything and/or everyone else are no longer there for you, to lean on that you can truly depend upon. This is especially true when whatever it was you were so heavily dependent on failed you or your expectations turned out not to be as reliable as you once believed they were.

Do you realize that most people—you and I included—have become so reliant upon the advice and leadership of others, so much so, that we have literally become ridiculously addicted to this condition, which I refer to as a "chronic need for dependence on others"? Having become acutely aware of this condition in my own life at one time, identifying this condition was a key turning point that led me to be able to overcome some very serious ugly events that I actually created for myself. This included several very serious physical illnesses that were diagnosed to lead to my demise if I didn't do this or do that—in other words, a life expiration date! However, what I said to myself was, "I don't think so, medical science, or you, choir of naysayers!"

Have you heard of a TV program titled *I Shouldn't Be Alive?* Although my experiences had nothing to do with being lost in a jungle in some remote area of the world, trapped in some menacing deep cave with no apparent way out, surviving a plane crash, or have actually had to deal with critical circumstances related to these types of survival experiences,—without any doubt in my mind, to survive these ordeals, in my opinion, most who did possibly had believed in an unseen force that was responsible for the guidance, answers, and methods that led them out of their life-threatening events or they possibly could have perished.

Believe me, luck had nothing to do with these extreme human survival stories. And if you ever have the opportunity to ask any of them directly, I believe that the greater majority would more than likely tell you the same—unless, of course, some just may actually believe luck or they themselves were the reason they survived their ordeal. It's possible but, in my opinion, doubtful.

As I've already pointed out, with all the instability, frustration, and out-of-control worldwide economic issues going on today, not just in the USA, it will not be long before people everywhere—even you—may possibly be struggling with life-disrupting conditions. It may happen, more than likely at a highly elevated level, as things become increasingly more difficult to cope, with these serious, rapid changes going on in the world today appear to be affecting almost everyone, especially the rapidly disappearing middle class in the USA. Some people may hide it well—temporarily, that is—but eventually, even they will begin to undergo some of these conditions at some level and possibly a number of them simultaneously.

Sounds like some wacko's doomsday prediction, doesn't it? Well, it's not. It is the reality, and it is on millions of people's minds and doorsteps knocking at this very moment, possibly even yours. Maybe that's the reason you may be seeking relief and wanting to prepare yourself for whatever is coming in your direction or that of someone you know and care about may already have been burdened with these situations to some degree.

Before coming to my senses, I too was heavily reliant upon many things, especially upon others for advice and even for emotional support and uplifting. At one time in my business career, I placed heavy trust upon the professional opinions and guidance of others whom I had come to know and respect, not realizing at the time that this confidence and trust was misplaced. Eventually, this misguided dependence and reliance placed me in a very serious life-changing situation that I eventually also overcame but not without having a terrible price to pay. It has been said that our toughest circumstances in life are our best lessons. There is a great deal of wisdom and truth to this as I am certainly living proof of it.

I've had many people say to me that they cannot break their dependence upon this or that or whatever. They tell me that if they did, they would not know how they would be able to cope or know what to do, should they have to face their undesirable situations without their life crutches. Many further stated to me that they were not that strong or not as strong as other people are. Little did they realize at the time that this opinion of themselves was not even close to being accurate. It may have appeared that way to them on the surface; however, mastering self-reliance and self-confidence is to be on a path of true freedom—a path much unlike one has ever imagined, if they had not been there yet.

There are truly no adequate words that could ever describe this freedom once you decide to become self-reliant and rediscover your self-confidence. The euphoric feeling that occurs when self-reliance and self-confidence have been recaptured and put into action once again—through the help of the immense power of their inner mind—is indescribably intense. It is at this point that everything changes gloriously, and from this moment on, your life will no longer feel as though they cannot survive without being heavily dependent upon temporary inadequate remedies as one had once falsely been led to believe they needed to be.

It's amazing that, lest we forget, the people we permit to render advice to us, lead us, preach to us, or tell us what is right and what is wrong with our lives and the direction we should be heading had to get their information from somewhere or someone. But from where and who? And the bigger question is, what research was conducted by those who give advice for the information they pass on to others? What I mean is that they are not walking in your shoes—you are! Advice is only as good as its source and the source that advice came from originally and prior to that. For me, the only source I choose to place trust upon is what comes from infinite intelligence that I refer to as infinite mind. Short of that, I rarely, if ever, act upon any other advice, unless and until I consult with this all-knowing force first that has yet to fail me—and never will—as without it, as I have said, I am more than certain I would not be among the living today.

Even at my age, I can still go back to school and learn how to become an informed psychologist, crisis counselor, or be whoever or whatever I choose. I can read hundreds of books on these subjects, work in clinics, work as an apprentice or understudy in one or more of these fields, and so forth and so on. So may I ask then, who wrote all these books we learn things from? Where did their information come from? From where did those writers' information come? From where did those initial texts obtain information? "What came first, the chicken or the egg?" is an ancient question that has yet to be resolved. However, the answer is quite clear to all those who choose to trust in this all-knowing infinite intelligence that is one with the inner mind.

Now, of course, this statement may be disputed by critics of anything unseen, especially the infinite intelligence. Yet dispute this unseen force if one may; however, for me and countless others, we are living proof of its incredible power. And proof is all everyone needs to substantiate any belief and to determine where one's self-reliance and self-confidence emanates.

I wanted to know where all the knowledge, wisdom, and textbooks came from in the first place that contain the information that we seemingly continue to pass on to each other and continue to pass on to generation after generation, with nothing more for proof of their correctness and accuracy than those who say it is correct. To me, the only true and reliable answers, wisdom, and knowledge come from an all-knowing source and not from mankind's physical brain that was created by this very same source. Take a minute to reflect on what I just stated here. If you choose to do so, I truly believe that you cannot possibly help envision the reality of what I have just stated.

Therefore, that said, it is very clear that the majority of mankind seemingly relies upon the hundreds of thousands of diplomas, certificates, and plaques hanging on office walls everywhere of those rendering advice to us which we take as reliable fact and act upon it without any further consideration given. Sit back and ponder this for a while, and you possibly may find the irony to all this advice and opinion giving. Okay, I get it, math is math and science is science, medicine is medicine, etc.; however, where is the reliance upon oneself and the desire to really know where all this information came from in the first place?

Self-reliance and self-trust in one's inner mind is rare and seemingly becoming almost extinct. Don't believe it? Well, just take a moment to ask yourself how much mankind relies upon others, their egos' never-ending wants, government entitlements, and the pursuit of material gratification.

Have you ever really sat down to do any reflecting on those seemingly important things you allow yourself to rely upon? Have you ever done any real soul-searching, so to speak, before choosing to rely upon what we label as professional opinions? If not, it may possibly be time for you to seriously consider doing so before relying on everything others say. Reflect that this infinite mind that I continue to identify contains every answer, method, and solution you will ever need to get through to life's adversities, before deciding to turn your back on this source that created it all and can bring forth your deepest desires for good.

In my case, I chose self-reliance over medical science's opinions and diagnoses when it came to rejecting chemotherapy treatments. Did I believe I knew much more than they did? Not hardly—far from it. However, what I did know was that I was blessed with a more dependable source, which I knew that whatever guidance I was receiving was coming from an infinite, all-knowing power that has all the methods, answers, and solutions one would ever need to make a totally informed decision. Many people may balk at this; however, none, not even medical science and medical professionals, can deny the proven results I and others experienced (and continue to experience) by our total reliance on this all-knowing intelligence.

I did not allow myself to believe that I had become another medical statistic because I never considered myself among the others to begin with. Therefore, I absolutely refused to include myself in the ranks of the ones who had passed on from what I too had been diagnosed with. I didn't then and don't now. I absolutely refused to allow any medical professional to decide for me when I would depart from this world or to tell me that I had an expiration date.

Am I some miracle as some people had labeled my survival to be? Not even close. My survival of all that I have overcome emanated from with my unwavering belief and trust in my inner powers that come directly from this unseen source I continue to speak about, coupled with my unwavering self-reliance, confidence, and self-trust. I have and continue to baffle medical professionals with my survival of very serious conditions and other life-changing adversities when I tell them that my survivals and experiences of what I desire for good—including experiencing prosperity on every level—were and continue to come about by my believing and relying solely upon this incredible force.

As for miracles, who am I to say that they do not exist? If I am to be considered a miracle due to all I have survived, I reject this premise as I believe that my survival of these physical problems could only be because I was totally reliant upon self and completely trusted in the guidance I was receiving and nothing else for the decisions I had made, which unnerved many people at the time. Medical science played a significant role surgically; the survival part, however, was the result of my deep belief and unwavering connection with what I have been describing.

Now is this to be considered arrogance or ignorance? Nothing I have presented in this book is meant to be arrogant, let alone ignorant. Instead, I only meant to share my involvement with some of life's most serious life-changing events and what I was led to do to overcome each and every adversity I experienced. I am not advocating that you or anyone should do what I did and continue to do—not by any stretch of the imagination. What I am saying, however, is that you begin to become, if you are not already, dependent upon yourself and to seriously consider what I describe throughout this book, as opposed to relying upon others and the opinions of others, when it comes to your life and any life-changing condition you may be presently dealing with or possibly may be confronted with in the future.

This is not to be interpreted as to shutting anyone out and not listening to them or that text materials are not valid, important, or useful because they certainly are. Instead, I only wish to bring to your attention the importance of taking full control of your own situation or circumstances and awareness of the source of any information, written or otherwise, and rely upon yourself to make important and critical decisions as they pertain to your life through your silent relationship with your inner mind that will never lead you astray and will always give you the right answers to whatever it may be you need to know. You have everything to gain and nothing to lose by becoming totally aware and self-reliant and by developing and maintaining an impenetrable self-trust.

I believe that I had every right to ask questions about anyone's opinions, diagnoses, and/or both when it comes to my life, and so do you, if you are so inclined. I sensed that my medical professionals, although they never said it to me directly, silently disliked my questioning them. This was evident in their demeanor. And herein lies the problem. Countless members of humanity are akin to cattle led to the slaughter—quite willingly, I might add—as opposed to choosing to become more self-reliant (the one black sheep, so to speak, in the herd). However, more often than not, they will follow the flock right off a cliff.

This is not to say we ignore commonsense laws and prudent medical advice. Understand that to be self-reliant and to listen to one's inner mind that will never fail, opposed to being led around like a horse with a bit in its mouth, is a prudent choice. However, what it comes down to is choice—your choice—as to what you wish your life to be like or to continue to be like.

The age-old truth about human life is that we are all continuously seeking something, aren't we? Usually it is gratification of some type on some level—be it financial prosperity, security, happiness, the fulfillment of some dream or wish, the ideal life partner, acceptance, power, etc. However, the only real wealth, happiness, and total gratification should be taking total control of your own physical and spiritual life first (whatever *spiritual* means to each person) and benefiting from continued good health, without which, all else is nothing more than like venturing into a very dark forest during a menacing storm. It may begin as a very nice day in the forest; however, with very little advance warning, one can find themselves having a sudden loss of direction, confused, and having to rely upon others to rescue them.

If this is the type of situation you want to prevent from ever becoming a part of your life, then the path to escaping the storm can be found within you, not in your outer physical world. In the end, however, the choice, as always, is yours and yours alone, isn't it? When it comes to the quality of your life and the manifestation of what you truly want and not what others want for you, then it is you who must be the pilot of your life.

Most people go through life not knowing exactly what it is that they truly want and wander through life focusing on what it is that they do not want, which brings them more of the same through continuous thoughts about what it is they do not want. This is a luxury one simply cannot afford, as this is also the beginning of continued indecision and unhappiness. For example, when people suffer a life-threatening illness, they almost immediately become fixated on the worst-case scenario. This is what is deemed as negative thinking. Negative thinking is among the primary leaders of the nonphysical illnesses that I had listed earlier. This fixation on the negative among those diagnosed with a serious life-threatening illness is not uncommon; quite the contrary, it's very common. This is primarily contributable to the immense power the word *fear* carries—fear of dying, fear of having one's career coming to an abrupt end right in the peak of success, fear of leaving loved ones behind, fear of the unknown (this is the biggest among all fears), and fear of facing the reality of their medical condition and the related untraveled road ahead.

Understand completely that for you to achieve what you truly want, you will need to reorganize your thinking to include full expectation and having complete confidence and trust in your real self within. You must also be willing to embrace and commit yourself to becoming totally self-reliant and trust in the answers, methods, and solutions your inner mind is sending to you continually that you will experience through your instincts, emotions, strong feelings, visions, dreams, and, most of all, your dominant thoughts.

Most people have heard or read the saying "If you keep doing what you are doing, you will keep getting what you are getting." Not only is this true for undesirable conditions but desirable ones as well, because we receive in the physical world precisely what we give our attention to the most. Again, this is nothing new. However, it is really that simple, yet many people refuse to accept this truth and instead elect to continue to facilitate what they do not want in their lives and, as I have identified, continue to be heavily reliant upon others for methods, answers, and guidance instead of turning these matters over to their inner power and inner mind to be resolved.

You are here on this planet to advance in your life, not to be or remain stagnant or live in deprivation, illness, ongoing strife, etc. No. Instead, you were meant to be prosperous on every level of life, happy, joyful, and free from disease, life-threatening illnesses, or negative events, which are all unnatural experiences.

Understand that relying upon one's inner mind in no way is meant to replace proper medical care and advice but to be used in conjunction with proper medical care and credible professional advice. Never disregard prudent and trustworthy necessary medical advice. I didn't, and by combining credible medical advice with self-reliance and total confidence in this all-knowing infinite source, I know for a fact that this is precisely what led me back on the path to totally trusting it, coupled with strong belief and self-confidence. Having done this, I was then able to eventually overcome what I did, in addition to other serious nonphysical illnesses and events.

As you continue on this journey with me, you will come to realize that you are more powerful and unique than you ever realized. The mere fact that you are in this world at all proves that you are not just a physical being—you are also a very powerful one-of-a-kind spiritual being. Know it, believe it, and, most of all, feel it with deep emotion. Yes, you've heard and may have read this before, but for some reason, most people have forgotten this, may have chosen to disregard it entirely, or never knew this before. I know I disregarded it up to the time I had my great reawakening and am extremely grateful that I rediscovered it.

The Messages and Advice We Choose to Rely on Instead

The latest in a long line of "youth recovery and enhancement" products are the various male enhancement products. If this is what it takes today to attract a mate, if you are a male, then you certainly have lost your self-confidence and self-trust. Even more than that, it does not necessarily require sexual attraction to attract the right mate; instead, absolutely knowing that you can and knowing and trusting that artificial substances, injections, pills, etc., are not the answer to any real and true long-lasting relationship. Only you—and you alone—can attract the right mate into your life without any artificial anything to make it happen.

And if you find the person you believe is right for you and they require you to utilize such enhancements, do not walk away. Run. Any relationship that is judged by the level of one's sexual capability and performance is unworthy of continuation because it is not true love. The truth of the matter is that far too many of us have lost our self-confidence and self-trust in who we really are and instead want to become who we really are not or what others want us to be for them.

The industries that produce these products, along with the cosmetic and pharmaceutical industry (an eight-hundred-billion-dollar-a-year industry alone and growing, according to an NYU School of Medicine report) literally has a major chokehold on millions of consumers worldwide. Why then should anyone lack the confidence when they were already gifted from birth with all the knowledge they would ever need that provides all the power they will ever require, not only to have and maintain what one deeply desires for good, and is waiting for everyone to call upon it, twenty-four seven?

This infinite source I refer to makes absolutely no demands upon you whatsoever and never requires you to open your wallet! "You mean I do not even have to open my wallet? Can you be serious?" you say? Yes, I am!

To prove this, I suggest that you to begin paying closer attention to advertisements, particularly on TV, and pay particular attention to the subliminal messages they are sending across your TV screen to you and, if you have a family, what your young children and significant other are paying attention to. Do this beginning today.

This brings me to some very interesting words such as *robotic*, *easy prey*, *hypnotized*, and *subliminally controlled* (i.e., "existing or functioning below the threshold of consciousness"; "subliminal advertising"). These are just a few of the many words that could be used to describe how humanity is corralled and duped into a false sense of security by these cleverly contrived marketing schemes and ploys. Yet humanity appears to have failed itself miserably by not realizing just how unique and special they really are, individually and collectively.

All the good health, peace, happiness, healthy life style, healthy relationships on all levels, and freedom from all sorts of ailments, diseases, and life-threatening illnesses can only be found within, not outside of you, and not in any pill, potions, drugs, cosmetic surgeries, makeup, or the like. Unless and until you are willing to call forth this inner power that you control, you will remain a victim of yourself, with a strong possibility of attracting self-inflicted emotional illnesses, especially when these artificial enhancements begin to fail you; and over time, they certainly will.

In my considered opinion, one's inner mind should be cherished as a very special gift. Some religions would call it a blessing. However, we are not referring to or discussing religions and their beliefs in this book. To be able to do so, one would need to be a theologian (a person who is an expert on theology), which this author is not. Your inner mind certainly is capable of bringing forth the necessary methods, answers, and solutions that can arrest most, if not all, forms of illnesses and any adversity and bring forth your innermost desires for good. I am living proof of this, among many others. This is not any form of psychic or demonic power, as one person once suggested to me—quite the contrary.

Ask yourself this: why do people go to doctors, psychologists, psychiatrists, mental health specialists, family, drug and alcohol counselors, and other medical professionals? Because they knew something is out of tune with their body or mental state and were convinced and trusted that these professionals can fix it—whatever *it* is—and that they have the answers and the cure for their ailments. "No they don't!" you might say. Did you ever ask yourself where these professionals go or turn to, should they personally experience a serious nonphysical or physical life-threatening illness? Surely they are not going to make an appointment with themselves. Therefore, the obvious and logical answer is that they may see someone within their own profession and, if they are religious, they may possibly seek counseling and help there as well.

However, those who are aware of their inner power will inevitably turn to it for answers, methods, and solutions every time because they know that it contains all there is to know to deal with any life-disrupting conditions, situations, or circumstances that they may attract into their lives. That said, all we have to do is to trust in it and patiently await its instructions. When you learn how to trust it, you will find that all the answers and solutions to whatever it is you ask will come.

My medical professionals' answer to the possible solution for curing the two cancers I experienced was surgery, followed by a regimen of chemotherapy, period. This was all they offered, as this was all they were trained, required to recommend, and know to offer their patients. I chose surgery before I realized that I should have heeded my inner knowing. It was soon after surgery when I decided to seek out the real answer to my survival as I sensed that surgery alone was no assurance or no guarantee of a total cure. The first thing that I was led to, through my inner mind, was not to accept any chemotherapy treatments. How, you might ask, did this come to me? It came to me soon after I summoned it forward in the form of a deep inner feeling within me to do so. After a short period of time, this feeling became stronger and stronger; and soon after that, it became all I could think about, until it became a living part of my life.

Consequently, as I stated earlier, I went against the medical opinions and insistence of some very well-known experienced surgeons and other medical professionals and trusted friends, clergy, and family members. As a result of my decision to forego any chemotherapy treatments or any other type of continued invasive postsurgical treatments, I was told by these medical professionals that I was in serious denial, wasn't thinking clearly, emotionally clouded, did not trust the medical profession, had a death wish, and was lacking personal responsibility, not thinking of my immediate family—which, at the time, consisted of a new six-month-old baby boy and three stepdaughters ranging from age five to thirteen—and also had a flourishing business. I even rejected the idea of meeting with any recommended crisis counselors at any level.

I have often been asked if I ever regretted that decision. My answer was and remains *not in the least*. In retrospect, had I had called upon my inner power sooner, I more than likely would have rejected the cancer surgeries. You may possibly be thinking to yourself, "Is this guy nuts or what?" Okay, a fair question. To the best of my and medical science's knowledge, I'm not.

Let's see, was Nostradamus nuts? How about Gen. George Patton? What about Gandhi? Mother Teresa? How about the vast number of inventors and famous painters throughout the history of the world? The great Babe Ruth, those who were instrumental in placing man on the moon, those who walked on the moon, and others who also had unwavering inner visions, self-trust, and confidence? These people and many more history has memorialized had one thing in common, although they lived in different times and places throughout the world. What they had in common was the gift of absolute knowing and the gift of being able to actually envision, through their inner mind, the end result of their individual burning desires, coupled with focused thoughts, deep beliefs, and expectations. Therefore, their vision and imagination were manifested in their lives. Do we call these great people and many more like them we have read or know about nuts too? I don't think so. They absolutely knew what they wanted to attract and experience and summoned it forward from within, and so did I.

Just think about the seemingly impossible athletic feats most of us have been able to witness in our lifetime by Olympians and athletes participating in basketball, football, baseball, tennis, hockey, cycling, racing, skiing, ice-skating, boxing, swimming, and soccer, just to mention a few among many more throughout the world, who broke all kinds of previously thought-of-impossible athletic records. I had one person suggest that these athletic accomplishments were a result of supplements these athletes were taking that enhanced their ability to achieve such remarkable feats. This type of conduct does not apply to the vast majority of competitive athletes but just a few misguided competitors. I am still amused by that statement.

Most people were not born with the abilities and talents that they demonstrated but either consciously or unconsciously called upon their inner power and inner mind, time after time, to attain what they did, coupled with envisioning their greatness. Some may and some may not acknowledge this to be true; however, anyone who may doubt that that an all-knowing inner force was called upon by those who reached such greatness and notoriety seems improbable. But such success is obtained by people throughout the world who unconsciously or consciously have also called upon the same inner power to achieve whatever they desired for good. And so should you, because anything you ever want to obtain for good in your life—and did—was accomplished in the very same way, even though you may not have recognized or acknowledged it at the time.

Similarly, people who choose to rely upon this incredible inner power to realize what they were seeking to experience for good—whether it is something they have always envisioned or whether it was to heal and cure themselves of a physical disease or life-threatening illnesses—and not rely solely upon any medical professional to bring forth a complete cure and have overcome whatever it was they were seeking to defeat, in my opinion as a survivor, also have an obligation to share their knowledge and experience with this unseen inner power with all of humanity. Anyone who has overcome any potentially fatal illness and/or life-changing event, circumstance, or situation who believes that any such accomplishment was brought forward from an outer source only is certainly in denial that an unseen inner infinite force exists. However, it is never going to be too late to recognize that an unseen intelligence other than the human species certainly exists, as many people who are in denial of this fact come to realize after having contracted a very serious life-threatening illness or event. Therefore, I will trust this denial does not apply to you and that you can and will come to acknowledge that an inner mind that is one with infinite mind does indeed exist and can and will bring your innermost desires when you decide to believe and begin to call upon it with complete expectation, trust, and, above all, patience.

Keep in mind that it is very important that you carefully consider and evaluate the sources from which the advice you do rely upon in your physical world is coming from and from whom these messages and advice are coming as your life may very well depend upon what you choose to accept, follow, and act upon. Seemingly impossible achievements and self-healings are not solely an act of one's outer physical self, faith, or hoping—not by any stretch of the imagination. They are absolutely and without any doubt examples that those who attained such successes knew internally first, before ever accomplishing what they did, that they were already going to accomplish these great feats, self-healings, and cures.

This all-knowing power, when summoned forth, completely takes over, if—and only if—the person who asks for this knowledge believes in it and fully trusts its remarkable powers. In addition, having confidence that it can and will bring forth their innermost desires and also fully trusts it to take over and to then let go of any and all of their external, ego-controlled, futile attempts of trying to surmount any obstacle, circumstance, event, and/or any disease or life-threatening illnesses presently plaguing one's life can realize what they are seeking for good.

As for any medical support, if medication for severe pain is absolutely necessary, it should be discontinued once the prescription has elapsed—unless renewed by your doctor and deemed absolutely necessary to continue—and not to be continually or habitually depended upon, unless medically ordered by a credible, legally licensed medical professional. If surgery cannot be avoided (such as I was led to believe in my case), you should consider allowing your inner mind and infinite force to bring forth the healing during recovery process after your elected surgical procedure and not rely solely upon your medical professionals to bring forth a permanent cure of a life-devastating illness. And if they are honest with you, as they should be, they should tell you that they are not the total answer or ultimate healers.

As I have attempted to make very clear, medically recommended treatment for acute physical conditions that have escalated should always be seriously considered but never be relied upon as the sole range of treatments for a complete or permanent healing, since no medical procedure or medication is a guarantee of a permanent cure. In my case, recommending chemotherapy treatments is a good example of what I just stated because the medical profession knew that surgery was not the total answer to a permanent cure; instead, it was a chance at remission. However, you—and only you alone—have the power to choose to listen to the internal messages you are receiving continuously from your all-knowing guidance.

Never forget that there are options for you to consider beyond your medical professionals' suggested treatments. It behooves anyone with a serious physical life-threatening illness to do some very serious soul-searching and research to make certain that all options are explored and clarified before considering surgery—unless, of course, the condition is so serious that surgery is the only immediate option. And even if it is not cancer but some other serious physical life-threatening illness, one owes it to themselves, their family, and loved ones to take the time to inquire and research other options and alternative treatments before going under the knife.

If incapacitated and unable to do this on your own, have someone you trust do this on your behalf. Of course, there are always going to be those events where time is not on your side. In the event this is the situation and surgery cannot be avoided, then one must alternatively research their options regarding permanent healing, including what is contained in this book.

To achieve a permanent healing, a total lifestyle change may be part of the healing process, including your diet, a change of environment, choosing a less stressful career, and even eliminating some people from your life who may be contributing to anxiety-provoking situations. This includes how you choose to think, and this means getting rid of negative thoughts at all costs and any other obstructive behaviors preventing a permanent healing. Remember, it is your life we are discussing here, not someone else's. Keep this uppermost in mind as well.

When people die, those left behind eventually move on, and moving on may include the remaining spouse eventually finding another mate and formulating a new life change. Therefore, considering this reality, you have an obligation to no one—significant other or otherwise—other than to yourself, to make sure you stick around much longer than any medical diagnosis may be telling you differently. The last time I looked, I could not find any termination date stamped anywhere on my body or birth certificate, and I do not believe that you can locate one on yours either.

Remember, life waits for no one. What time is it in your life? Do you truly desire to avoid and/or overcome physical and emotional diseases and life-threatening illnesses or do you prefer a medicine chest full of pills to mask your symptoms, all other dependent drugs and prescribed remedies, and other invasive methods that temporarily ease pain and/or agony of a disease or life-threatening illness?

Do you think that the medical or pharmaceutical communities are going to miss you or your money if you leave them? Not likely. Because you are easily replaceable by an endless line of humanity standing ready to take your place in the appointment registers of medical professionals, counselors, psychiatrists, psychologists, pharmacies, and a host of others. When was the last time you received a call from your pharmacy or medical professional asking where you have been and why haven't they've seen you in a while?

You may say that you don't believe it. Should that be the case, ask any citizen needing medical attention in Canada and England for openers and now right here in your own backyard. As I have intended to make perfectly clear, a medical professional should never be shunned or ignored. They should be utilized if and when it is absolutely a necessity; but they should also not be relied upon as your last line of defense, advice, and total reliance and definitely with caution for a complete cure and/or permanent healing.

To prove that many people have harbored self-induced emotional diseases and other ailments that they are suffering from, medical professionals will occasionally give some patients what is commonly known as a placebo medication (a usually pharmacologically inert preparation prescribed more for the mental relief of the patient than for its actual effect on a disorder). Some of the results have been remarkable when patients having taken the placebo have reported a complete absence of their symptoms. Some would deem this temporary recovery a miracle. A miracle is defined as "an effect or extraordinary event in the physical world which surpasses all known human or natural powers and is ascribed to a supernatural cause" or "such an effect or event manifesting or considered as a work of God or by whatever name one calls, identifies, this infinite intelligence/infinite mind."

A great majority of humanity, quite unfortunately, forget that they have been preprogrammed since birth to believe in a certain way. If a person anywhere recovers from a life-threatening illness, having been diagnosed as being serious enough to cause certain death, humanity is quick to jump to the conclusion that this survival is a miracle or, as the medical community calls it, "a spontaneous recovery" but isn't.

Now, let's review that definition again of the word *miracle*. It is "an effect or extraordinary event in the physical world which surpasses all known human or natural powers and is ascribed to as a 'supernatural' cause." Now, let's look at this word *supernatural* by definition, which is "pertaining to or being above or beyond what is natural"; "unexplainable by natural laws or phenomena"; or "abnormal." Considering these definitions, it is reasonable to state that one's inner mind is certainly all this and more. *More* because there is no reliance upon a onetime event but, instead, an ongoing, never-ceasing happening deep within all of humanity that can, does, and will manifest into the physical any burning desire for the person who fully trusts and holds on to that thought with absolute trust that this unseen power definitely exists through their total and unwavering acceptance of simply trusting that it does.

This inner all-knowing guidance is unending, perpetual. It has existed before time as we know it itself existed and will be far beyond what infinity is conceived to be by the limited minds of man. It needs not summon anyone to it or battle for its recognition, simply because *it is*!

It is humanity's sole responsibility to call it forward into their lives and to embrace it. It calls not to you because it is the most significant part of you. All you need to do is to be aware of its existence within you. Your conscious mind does not perform the function of your inner mind; instead, it is the receiver of its directions, answers, methods, and solutions, not the originator. All you need to do is to remember and continue to remind yourself that all you need to do is to summon this inner power forward into your life and to follow its all-knowing guidance, if you truly want to experience all that you desire for good.

Let's now look at the word *disciple*. This word means "someone who accepts and helps to spread the teachings of a famous person." Examples of this are the followers of John the Baptist, the man called Jesus and the apostles who followed this man, Gandhi, Buddha, Mother Teresa, and others who more than likely followed their all-knowing inner guidance that gave them all they needed to accomplish their memorable accomplishments. I have also seen this following referred to be connection, intention, and inspiration—all members of the same family of meaningful words that reside in harmony with *overcoming* and *inner knowing*. For the purpose of this journey, however, "all-knowing guidance" refers specifically to the belief of preventing and eradicating of diseases, ailments, nonphysical events and circumstances, and life-transforming illnesses through the infinite source.

Many of those living in obscurity today throughout the world who achieved a state of excellent health and are today free from physical and nonphysical life affecting illnesses, I believe, have and continue to do so—by rejecting any suggestions or thoughts that would attempt to convey anything contrary to their steadfast belief in the all-knowing infinite source. All these people, including myself, would never entertain exchanging this infinite intelligence for any worldly possessions.

If this were about religion, it could possibly be refuted by naysayers. However, since it is not about any religious belief whatsoever, not even the best in the medical profession or the scientific community can question it because, other than their professional opinions, there have been no medical or scientific fact to yet be able to either support or credibly dispute the so-called miracles that have occurred since recorded history, concerning the recoveries from terminal and other said to be nonreversible medical and even mental conditions.

Most survivors of life-challenging events and serious illnesses are visionaries and have future plans for accomplishments they want to achieve, their purpose in life. They are goal setters who aim high at reaching their potential. Life-threatening and terminal-illness survivors own a burning and unwavering knowledge and vision in an absolute victory over their illness. Ernest Dimnet (1866–1954), a French clergyman, stated, "Everyone has a success mechanism and a failure mechanism. The failure mechanism goes off by itself. The success mechanism only goes off with a goal. Every time we write down and talk about a goal we push the button to start the success mechanism."

A very wise man once said that speaking "useless, damaging words is like piercing yourself through with a sword, but words of wisdom and encouragement are healing to your body" (King Solomon). The point being here in these brief examples is that rejecting anything that just may be helpful in completely curing anyone of a medically terminal and/or life-threatening illness borders on a state of serious denial and lacks being reasonable.

As I have identified, I survived several cancers without any chemotherapy treatments by my choice. I envisioned, without any doubt whatsoever, being with my then-six-month-old son when he would have children of his own, my embarking upon yet another exciting humanitarian career helping my fellow man, and, in the interim, attracting the right life partner. These continue to be my visions, along with my "already accomplished" visions. I have many more future visions, and everything is headed in that direction toward the manifesting of each and every one of them because of my strong belief and dedication to my all-knowing inner mind and their materializing into my life right on time. And you can as well.

For those of you who possibly may have been diagnosed with a life-threatening illness, after you absorbed the initial shock of hearing this, did it not later make you angry to be told this and that you possibly may not recover? I know I was. As a matter of fact, I was angrier than you could possibly imagine. Why? Because I resented the fact that anyone could possibly infer that they had the right to place any thought in my mind as to when I would expire and from whatever cause.

Just because someone went through years of medical school and graduated with a 4.0 grade point average does not entitle them the right of predicting anyone's time of demise. That choice belongs to and only to the occupier of the body that houses their inner guidance that is one with infinite intelligence that created everything. Therefore, the person having been diagnosed with a possible unfortunate situation related to a serious illness is aware of what they have done over time to contribute to their serious condition.

One person said to me how I could possibly know I may possibly die from some illness or event. Good question. Well, here's the response. There isn't a person who ever lived who did not have an all-knowing, inner intuitive moment cautioning them to be aware of an action or something they were intending to do at a certain moment or point in time which they chose to ignore, ranging from a risky adventure, placing themselves in stressful situations, to potentially life-threatening poor eating and health habits for years. Yet they chose to go against their all-knowing, intuitive inner guidance, knowing that they should not do a particular thing; and as a result, many facilitated the ultimate undesirable result by doing so. We've all done it; some of us survived. and others had nothing occur. Therefore, because nothing did occur or we did survive and ignore this inner guidance, we habitually continued to ignore it until one day we attracted the thing we chose to ignore, knowing prior that we should have listened to our intuitive inner guidance. (Some people refer to this as "intuition.")

A very good example of this is people who decided at the very last moment not to embark on a certain flight which resulted in a major air disaster. Others chose not to be at a certain place at a certain time where a major disaster caused by nature wiped out an entire town or coast, killing thousands of people. Others decided not to get into an automobile at the last moment and avoided being killed in a major auto accident. Others decided to forgo a cruise they booked and later learned that the ship capsized and ran aground, killing many of its passengers. Others continued their poor health-related habits and eventually contracted a serious illness or life-threatening condition. This list can go on and on.

Your inner power is not a hope, a wish, a prayer of want, or an asking for but, instead, an absolute manifestation and that it has already been done and has already materialized in your life, despite not presently appearing in the physical at that given moment. (This is not related or based upon any religious belief, as all beliefs are infinitely and collectively tied to only one unseen force.)

Therefore, hoping, wishing, or asking for something is the very same as stating doubt and that you lack something when in fact you have never or ever will lack anything good you desire—not anything—that is also for the good of all concerned, should you live in a constant state of expectation. To entertain thoughts of anything less is the same as summoning forth in reality what is less. Never should one say I *know* a thing may or might happen but, instead, that I *absolutely know* it has already happened for my benefit and for the benefit of all concerned and is on its way (again, not connected to any religious belief).

Let me be absolutely clear here that what I am describing is not absolutely knowing the outcome of a horse race or the result of some game of chance or if there is infidelity taking place in a relationship. These and anything related fall under instinct, clairvoyance, psychic opinion, the resulting investigation of a private detective agency, etc.—none of which is the direction or intent of this journey.

If you have traveled this far in this book, I trust that you surely understood before now that this type of knowing, as I just described, is not a part of the subject matter of this book. I am sorry if you may possibly be disappointed. However, the value of the inner guidance's power to you I speak about far outweighs any outer physical reward you could ever possibly dream. Especially where it concerns your personal overall well-being and health, no amount of prosperity or other material gain on any level could possibly surpass the immense value that this inner guidance can provide in anyone's life.

The inner powers I have been referring to will not only change your life but will change everything in and surrounding your life for good that you want to influence—and I mean *everything*—and you will come to notice that all sorts of people will gravitate to you, to have you share with them how they too can tap into this marvelous inner power, and to have manifested whatever good they desire manifest in their lives as well. Hence, you are no longer the pupil but, instead, become the example and the teacher.

This then demands that you never utter the words "I can never"; just the mere utterance of these three words insures that you never will, no matter what it may be, and are denying the existence of your inner power. By speaking out in this manner is a clear signal to anyone that this is precisely how you are thinking and feeling. Therefore, thinking and feeling in this manner acts as a direct order given to your all-knowing inner intelligence that, in turn, will return to you precisely what you have ordered.

Remember that you have the power to know all there is to know concerning the real you and much more. The path that leads you to this absolute knowing is for you to simply state to yourself, "I absolutely know that whatever I want to manifest for good and for the good of all concerned will happen, in infinite intelligence's timing," over and over again to yourself silently; and once you begin to do this, through the power of your inner power, what you desire for good must appear in your life. This manifestation may show up in a matter of days, weeks, or months; however, you may rest assured it will come because it always does. The reason that it does is because absolutely knowing is absolute and, therefore, cannot do anything other than to deliver your burning desire for good into your life and the life of others because of the fact that it is absolute.

Related to this is the subject of the messages and advice we choose to rely upon instead, which are subliminal messages ("existing or functioning below the threshold of consciousness"; "the subliminal mind"; "subliminal advertising") which play a significant role in the decisions we make every day.

Let's now look at the tremendous power subliminal messages have over our everyday life and why it is so important that you become more aware of how the decisions you make every day are deeply affected by these messages that we are bombarded with constantly. These cleverly crafted, hidden, subliminal messages are the key to the success of all advertising, resulting in the choices people throughout the world make consistently.

The Hidden Power of Subliminal Messages

For decades, mankind has allowed themselves to be unknowingly hypnotized by well-constructed advertising campaigns promoting every type of medication, from the common aspirin to quick-fix, over-the-counter nonprescription remedies for all sorts of ailments ranging from insomnia, pain of every imaginable type, salves for deep-muscle aches, arthritis, allergy medications—you name it. Yet people everywhere remain gullible enough to buy into these products and are more than willing to open up their wallets to purchase these temporary-fix remedies.

These cleverly designed advertising campaigns are commonly referred to as *subliminal messages*—which mean "existing or functioning below the threshold of consciousness"—and they usually snag countless people annually in their net, ranging from the very young to the elderly. These subliminally designed advertisements are purposely designed that way because it's all about the money! Once people finally wake up to this reality, they will be able to see that they and they alone can remedy any condition, circumstance, or any other undesirable event they may be having or may have in the future, including improving one's looks, sexual dysfunctions, self-esteem, and any undesirable event one may possibly sustain in life.

The fact is, short of medically prescribed medications, many of these products are not necessary to produce the results one is seeking. Yes, you read that right. And the results can come without having to pop pills for years, go to any type of head doctor, any type of counselor, rehab facility, etc.

Self-trust and self-reliance have all but evaporated in modern civilizations. In this humble person's opinion, these conditions have reached epidemic heights. One cannot turn on a TV, listen to a radio, read a newspaper or magazine, or surf the internet; drive down any highway; or go into any grocery, convenience store, or pharmacy without being bombarded from every imaginable side by advertisements and products of all sorts that purport to take care of a myriad of ailments—some of which we may never have heard about!

Health food stores are not off the hook either as they too promote good health, not by injection or radical medical procedures, but they are somewhat more subtle in their approach by placing placards and photos of very healthy people in strategic places. Most of what are being presented are models who got that way through physical training and more training and, of course, taking excellent care of their bodies and who are generally in their late teens or early twenties who comprise the minority, not the majority of humanity, who are nowhere near in that good a physical shape and, if even close, rarely reach or return to that level of physique of the models being displayed. Granted, some may; however, they represent the exception, not the rule.

Therefore, these facilities use this advertising technique to promote all sorts of healthy ideas through the use of vitamins and herbs of every type imaginable, concoctions you can mix and drink, all sorts of products designed to assist clogged bowels, pills to slow down the aging process, creams and lotions to bring your aging face back to look like some seventeen-year-old model, powdered drinks that will shape and enhance your muscles into some menacing football linebacker or beach volleyball superstar, and other stuff that will allow you to eventually soar through the air like some famous basketball player. The sad part about all this is that people, especially young people, buy into these illusions to the tune of millions—no, billions—of dollars annually.

The truth of the matter is that far too many of us have lost our self-confidence, self-trust in ourselves, and, if I might add, our self-respect in and who we really are. Instead, we want to become who and what we really are not. I find this not only sad but remarkable as well. This industry, along with the cosmetic and pharmaceutical industry, still continues to maintain a chokehold on millions of consumers worldwide and will continue to do so, unless people begin to come to rely instead on their all-knowing inner guidance that can provide all this and much more and will deliver any desire for good being sought by anyone who summons it and believes that it will.

We will now explore why many people choose to live with fear and what they can and should be doing instead of living with this self-created emotion, which is one of the most serious among all nonphysical illnesses.

# 12

YOUR FEARS CAN MANIFEST INTO A LIFE-THREATENING EVENT

Fear is the one luxury you simply cannot afford and ranks high among the nonphysical illnesses in the chart provided in this book. The word *fear* on its own is meaningless. Yet it has the false, undeserving power we human beings give to it.

Here is the meaning of this word according to the dictionary's definition: *fear*—"dread, fright, alarm, panic, terror, trepidation"; "painful agitation in the presence or anticipation of danger"; the most general term and implies anxiety and usually loss of courage (fear of the unknown). Within this definition is "anticipation of danger." *Anticipation* means "visualization of a future event or state."

Relative to the perhaps false and undeserving power that this emotion evokes in human beings is the visualization or anticipation of danger. The phenomenon known as fear implies anxiety and loss of courage. This is also to anticipate something and can either be experienced suddenly or gradually and to varying degrees.

You certainly have heard the term "I am scared to death of . . ." and the term "I am so excited about . . . ." These are two extremes on the opposite ends of the scale of human emotions. Concentrated thought on an illness or any undesirable life-changing event only acts to further the condition—compared to concentrating on anything that will result in good, joy, and happiness. In other words, we draw to us what we want to be reality, good or bad, through what we continuously dwell upon for any significant length of time. Herein lies one of the primary reasons why a person cannot seem to ever be able to get well or to overcome a life-changing illness, situation, circumstance, or event.

Therefore, once fear grabs hold, it seems to be like being in the grip of a great white shark about to be devoured. This word *fear* is the poster phrase that immediately follows "you have cancer." This statement seems so big at the moment it is uttered that we cringe and seemingly seek shelter as soon as its impact strikes us.

Statements such as "You have cancer"; "You may never be healthy again"; "You will never find a good job again"; "You mostly likely will not recover"; "You are going to lose your house, car, and other material possessions"; "No, we are not going to be able to bail your business out of its financial problems—we stopped lending to small businesses"; "I'm leaving you if you do not get our financial situation taken care of" (for some, this may be a blessing in disguise); "There is no cure for what you have"; "You're fired"; "I do not love you anymore"; etc., are indicative of what can and often does strike deep fear in a person. Keep in mind, everyone is afraid of something. This is not a statement; it's a fact! For anyone to deny this is certainly to be in denial.

It is our fear of the unknown that cripples so many people everywhere. To make it even much worse, for some unknown or inexplicable reason, once the fear seed is planted in our minds, we go into autopilot—if we immediately allow our conscious mind to begin to dwell on these fears, which feeds what they need to continue to survive and grow in one's mind—allowing the fear to become even more powerful. This action alone aids in the development of the actual thing feared.

Know this: it is you who gives your fears power, no one else, unless you give someone else your permission to feed your fears by allowing them to do so. By your acting out in your conscious mind every worst-case scenario, you are actually playing these yet-to-materialize scenes in your mind over and over and over again until you have thoroughly convinced yourself that what you fear most finally shows up in your life one day. If you do play these fear scenes out in your mind continually, they will show up in reality, at your invitation—believe it! This includes fear of a life-threatening illness, a major life-changing event, a loss, a negative financial situation, etc.

No matter what it is, you need to face it head-on and know the truth, which is that it is you and only you who can control the level of anxiety and fear you allow to enter into your mind. No fear is permanent, unless you choose to make it permanent! Remember the saying "Negative thoughts eventually become negative images, which eventually become reality."

As I said earlier, one of the primary things that I did to overcome life-endangering illnesses, other adversities, and events, in addition to the writing method—which I continue to utilize to communicate with this all knowing infinite intelligence that is one with my inner guidance—is that I refused to give any continuous thought whatsoever to the crucial events that I sustained—*never*—and neither should you. It is like feeding a stray cat; once you begin, the cat expects you will feed it again and again and again, until one day you own the cat and the cat now finds a home and literally owns you. Therefore, do not ever feed the fear and do not invite fear into your life, period!

Remember, you are in total control of what you allow to come into your life. Only you can invite a fear and a serious life-changing event into your life. Most people believe that a life-threatening illness just suddenly materialized one day in their life—no it didn't! You invited it to appear in your life over time. Here is where most people get all bent out of shape because they refuse to accept personal responsibility for their role in having any life-menacing illness or event suddenly appearing in their life. So they will look everywhere else for the reason other than themselves! Did I strike a nerve here?

I've spoken with many people who had a catastrophic illness surprise them and can tell you that the majority of them actually believed that the reasons it appeared ranged from hereditary to fate. Rarely, however, did they accept or take any personal responsibility, having to do with it materializing in the physical; and a good number of them are no longer with us today.

I sincerely believe that anyone who refuses to take any responsibility whatsoever for why a devastating illness or life-disrupting event unexpectedly occurs in their lives that more than likely would also reject the fact that it is they and they alone who can play a significant role in their healing. This is a very sensitive subject with many people and with families of those who are critically ill and quite understandably. It certainly was for me and my family at the time I was diagnosed with not just one but two advanced cancers within eight months of each other. Think about that shock.

We all exhibit what is known as *learned behaviors*. What is a learned behavior pertaining to what I am identifying here? It is what we learn to do from others in times of crisis or when we become aware of a major life-changing event that seemed to take place with no warning. We usually will do what our parents and others have done or do or we follow the crowd, so to speak. We accept medical science's word as the final analysis; we listen to opinions; and we follow the advice of those who do not have a clue about what a particular life-threatening illness really is. We do this because we never learned how to become self-reliant in these areas of life. Take it from one of the former flock followers—me.

You need to become self-reliant, more personally involved, and take full responsibility for your own personal health and well-being. When a life-threatening illness or life-changing event comes into one's life, believe me, it is the one who is experiencing it who is truly alone with it, regardless how many people you may have around you for support. It is when the well-wishers begin to taper off and family has settled in with the acceptance of your condition that the most damaging emotion of all, fear, has its greatest opportunity to take over your conscious mind with fear thoughts.

There are numerous books, articles various other publications, seminars, and Internet sites, etc. concerning the subject of negative thinking. However, from my personal knowledge and perspective, of all the people I have spoken with, counseled, or whose behavior I had observed, who had life-threatening illnesses or suffered undesirable events, rarely even consider the serious consequences of the negative thoughts they continuously allow themselves to think. Know that you need to start paying serious attention to how you perceive life and your circumstances, because the mere act of continual dwelling and thinking in a non-positive way (habitual negative thinking) can eventually manifest into a paralyzing state of fear.

If you are going to dwell on anything then, let it be the positive outcome and not the negative. Remember, by allowing yourself to dwell on the negative aspects of any life-threatening situation for any given period of time day after day, month after month and year after year, what you are actually doing is sending a command to your inner guidance to stay in the same existing condition. You are literally inviting fear to escalate and are negating any possibility of overcoming whatever it may be.

When allowed to brew, negativity can cause very serious future consequences if not controlled and arrested permanently. For some people, negativity is similar to the addiction of smoking and other vices. In other words, it is addictive and becomes a serious habit that, like other well-known habits, is extremely difficult to overcome.

You may be thinking,"How you do you know this to be a fact?" Good question. The reason I know is, because I have had a lot of personal exposure to the addictions known as negativity and fear. In addition, at one time, I surrounded myself with like-minded people. Eventually, my negativity finally caught up with me; and when it did, all hell broke loose in my life, beginning with developing one nonphysical life-threatening illness after another, with extreme negativity, skepticism, and fear being the leaders, which was later followed by another very serious physically life-threatening illnesses.

I am not the only person to ever have experienced these conditions. I say this is because people everywhere are assailed by or have any number of the nonphysical life-threatening illnesses listed in the chart I provided in this book, among which negativity and fear being the leaders—fear being the more severe of the two. Negativity winds up as a habitual scenario that is played out in someone's life day after day and is a habit that is difficult to break. Yet it can be broken and discarded for life, just by replacing it with other habits. The habits you need to replace it with are the habits of continuously telling yourself that you are in total control of your life and that absolutely nothing can harm you or manage your life—better known as self-confidence and self-trust.

The only way any habit can possibly stay around is when you give it permission to remain in your life. What I am saying is this: giving your fear permission to allow a bad habit to inflict more negative thoughts into your conscious mind and, eventually, into your physical body. This is possibly why you—if this applies to you—still have the problem you have to deal with, whatever it may be, physical or nonphysical. It is like watching reruns of old movies over and over and over again, yet you are so accustomed to seeing these the movies, you rarely make any effort to even look for any newer movies that you may like better than the reruns you keep playing in your mind continuously.

Have you ever given even the slightest consideration to experiencing an entirely higher level of prosperity and happiness in your life? You can, if you are just willing to change your thoughts. This is not only a choice but an obligation to yourself to do so. What do you have to lose by committing yourself to begin thinking the possible instead of the impossible? The alternative is to continue as you are and go deeper and deeper into the worlds of negativity and fear, thereby eventually inviting very serious circumstances and situations to be able to just walk in and take total control of your conscious mind and eventually your life.

If your choice is to allow this to happen, then you have chosen to allow yourself to reach even greater misery or illness that can and will become permanently a part of you for the remainder of your life. The result then is robbing you of all the joy and happiness you are entitled to, which is your birthright as a member of humanity.

Had I allowed myself to remain in the same negative, fearful mind-set prior to and soon after both cancer events, I more than likely would be spending the remainder of my time in an asylum somewhere, weaving baskets. Instead, I am alive and well and can attest to the fact that there is nothing realer than having had a personal association with life-threatening nonphysical and physical illnesses events and surviving from them. By doing so, it is possible for me to reach out to my fellow man and to share with them the confidence, faith, belief, and expectation that they too can envision overcoming anything that they do not want to come into or remain in their lives.

Keep in mind that the overcoming does not just benefit the person seeking healing and a permanent cure but each and every one who is concerned as well, in order that they too may be the recipient and benefactor of the expected healing. Unless this is the true intent, their inner guidance knows not to allow any selfish motives to prevail. As I keep repeating, the inner guidance—connected with the infinite intelligence, which will only respond if what is being asked of it through one's infinite source—is also for the good of all concerned as well. Your positive response will be reflected in the attitude of those who interact with you.

A distant cousin of negativity is imagination. It is here where one can either conquer their affliction or be conquered by it. It is this word, *imagination* (inner vision), that has given mankind every modern convenience enjoyed in the world today and every tool and idea given ancient and prehistoric societies to develop, construct, and overcome some of the greatest challenges, feats, and accomplishments that continue to baffle modern mankind to this very day. It also allowed prehistoric man to survive, armed with nothing more than crude handmade weapons they carved out of stone and trees, which they used against the threat of prehistoric beasts that hunted them for food. Imagination also gave us one more thing—*fear*!

I can go on and on about the subject of imagination, but I believe you get the picture. Therefore, instead of imagining the worse that can grow into fear, imagine instead the best and allow your all-knowing inner guidance to change your negative imaginations to positive ones and to bring forth the healing and permanent cure only your inner guidance knows how to bring about. To conquer any life-threatening illness or life-changing event, you first must know and absolutely trust that there is no illness or event that is so great that your inner guidance that is one with infinite intelligence cannot conquer—absolutely know it, trust it, imagine it, and believe it! Once you do, never turn back.

Whether you are aware of it or not, your inner guidance has brought you through many nonphysical life-altering events and circumstances in the past and will continue to do so in the future, if you call upon it. However, in order for it to rid you of physical life-threatening illness and/or any other life-changing events, you must take total control over all your negative thoughts, not just some of them, as it is the negative thoughts and self-destructive habits that nullify the desires for good that can be realized through your all-knowing inner guidance.

Begin right here and right now to discipline yourself not to permit any negative thoughts and self-destructing habits cancel out what your inner guidance can and will do for you to assist you to heal impending life-threatening illnesses or events.

We all have either heard or read at one time that fear is the greatest foe of mankind. Not being a medical professional myself, I can tell you through personal experience that fear is the primary catalyst that is responsible for the escalation and rapid advancement of many illnesses affecting countless people all over the world, which shows its ugly head in everyone's life at one time or another. Fear is the condition that causes one to fail at something, relationships to come apart, people to stay away from other people, fear of losing one's youthful looks, fear of losing a significant other, and fearing we cannot survive with them out of our lives, as well as reaching one's sixties and older. The greatest fear of all, however, is our very own eventual, inescapable demise—how curious! Rarely does one take the opportunity to explore what fear really is. Fear is nothing more or less than what we allow ourselves to think about; in other words, we fear our very own self-created, self-induced dominant thoughts.

It has been said—and medical science has proven—that some deeply embedded beliefs can create deeply fixated fears on almost every level. When some children at an early impressionable age have been exposed to some fictitious characters they may have seen in a movie they viewed or possibly a sibling had portrayed which caused the child to have internalized this scenario, they can carry such memories with them through adulthood.

I myself know of a teenage boy whose his sister would constantly scare him by portraying some ghoulish character and would dress up in scary outfits when they were very little. Although she believed her actions to be a harmless prank, to this day, he still will not go to sleep with a closet door open or unless his bedroom door is wide open. This fear in this young boy's mind is very real indeed, almost as though there really was a real threat of some menacing monster coming out of the dark.

With the exception of the fear of noise and the fear of falling that people are sometimes born with, mostly every fear we respond to in life came from anyone or anything that may have influenced our childhood. Some of our strongest fears exist due to our imaginations running wild that we literally invite into our lives. Most people know that we can eventually attract in reality what we fear most by continuing to dwell on them.

Despite the fact that we choose what to fear, most fears do not materialize unless we make the decision to bring them into existence. And before we know it, what we had feared is staring us in the face. In other words, from the King James Bible, "For the thing which I greatly feared is come upon me, and that which I was afraid of is come unto me" (Job 3:25). Continuing on this path, one may also be inviting nonphysical illnesses such as anxiety, stress, and depression, among others. Remember this: Reliance upon your inner guidance can free you from ongoing fear of anything—permanently.

By focusing only on your true desires and becoming deeply engrossed with them, you shift from your fears to your inner world of imagination of your deep desires, which not only will build your confidence but will lift you out of the place you were in and position you on the path to peace, happiness, and expectation, thereby knowing that you are now allowing your inner guidance to bring forth that which you desire and to rid you of any false imaginations and unfounded fears. Each and every person ever born has been and is connected with this inner infinite power. Although it cannot be seen, touched or felt it is always there with us just the same. This is where one needs to focus their imagination on continuously and not on unfounded fears.

Indulge instead in thoughts and imaginations of happiness, wellness, peace, and prosperity for not only yourself but for others—despite your present medical condition, situation, or circumstance. Because if you do this and do this continuously, you can witness your present situation, condition, and/or circumstance begin to change for not only your good but for the good of all concerned.

It is your inner power that is one with the infinite intelligence that brings about the permanent change from fear to freedom of all

PREVAILING OVER INSURMOUNTABLE ODDS

fears. It is also important to recognize once and for all that only the inner you—your inner guide—can rid you of your fears.

It almost seems natural to jump to fear, anxiety, and stress that can lead to eventual depression when one is involved with any serious life-changing condition. To add fuel to this campfire, as identified earlier, fear is strengthened when supported by others, such as medical personnel, families, significant others, and friends and acquaintances, turning controllable tinder to a huge, blazing forest fire, making it more difficult to extinguish. I realize that these situations in themselves are accompanied with the natural feelings of anxiety and stress. I should know because not only was I that person who had several life-threatening medical events, but I have had personal firsthand association with loved ones, immediate family members, friends, acquaintances, and others who were also passing through serious life-changing conditions, situations, circumstances, ailments, and very traumatic life-threatening illnesses that ranged from confusion, disorientation, fear, extreme anxiety, and other stressful conditions, as well as becoming chronically depressed.

What we all fail to realize is that none of us are prepared for the possibility of the fact that one day we too just may find ourselves faced with any life-changing events and/or life-threatening illness or conditions. Therefore if and when such a situation does show up in our lives, many of us will almost immediately shift our imagination machine into negative gear, imagining the worse versus the better, completely forgetting that what we fear most and dwell upon can eventually come upon us. By giving way to our fears, we leave the door wide open, inviting every imaginable condition to occur instead of imagining and believing (not hoping) that this too shall pass and we shall continue on with our life, as this is nothing more than a pothole on our life's path, so to speak.

We inevitably unconsciously decide not to shut down our negative thinking and opt to believe all the diagnoses, prognoses, and opinions from our outer world—sources that, as I had previously stated, at best, are basing their scientific findings and opinions on learned and historical data, in addition to what some test results may have indicated, which may indeed be accurate from where they are standing and coming. However, what are you and your inner guidance saying about it?

Are you sitting back and accepting this medical conclusion or are you going to thank them for the information like I did? I made the decision to believe and to state to myself instead, "What I fear most I no longer fear as it does not exist, contrary to any scientific findings. Neither does fear, anxiety, stress, doubt, nor or depression at any level, as none of these are the real me who resides deep inside me. Therefore, I reject them and do not accept any of these opinions to be transferred to my all-knowing inner guidance or to continue to manifest in my outer physical self. Instead, I will only rely upon my inner power, inner guide, that is connected to a divine all-knowing source that can bring forth the methods, answers, and permanent healing I know is already in progress of healing every cell, fear thought, and negativity that have made an attempt to violate my body." I have also said this continuously on behalf of anyone other than myself, if they may have been subjected to a life-changing event in their life, until a healing has been effected on any level or to any degree, keeping in mind that our inner guidance works best when you are asking and believing for the good of all concerned as well as for yourself.

One's first reaction to this may possibly be "Sure, easy for you to say, but you are not in my situation!" Yes I am! Recall, if you will that I was there and I was that person who was also chock-full of doubts, fears, anxiety, stress, and depression and the dealing with a myriad of nonphysical illnesses at the same time. That said, I am just as subject to having yet another life-changing event as anyone else. The only difference is that I am thoroughly prepared for any attack against me because I've been there and have an entire army at my disposal, through my inner guidance and all-knowing infinite intelligence/infinite mind that supplies me with any answers, methods, and solutions I shall ever need to ward off any attacks against me physically or otherwise. So do you.

Rarely will one find a book like this one written by someone who has actually been there and done that. Yes, there are others out there like me, some of who have come forward with their life-threatening survival stories, but not many compared to the number of survivors of life-threatening illnesses and events. This I can assure you.

I certainly am very grateful for the few survivors of any life-threatening event who had the courage to come forward and tell the story of their survival by writing a book or speaking to others who may be experiencing a life-changing event, in an attempt to help others who may now be facing a similar or related situation. It takes remarkable courage for them to come forward and bare their soul and life to the entire world in an effort to reach out and help their fellow man, woman, and child. I am very proud to be counted among them, whoever or wherever they may be on this planet today.

Take it from me—in the final analysis, it is going to be you and only you who can deliver you from any negative or health-related life-changing event that may or has already occurred in your life and/or the life of anyone you love, know, or care about. You see, no one resides inside you or is in your mind or shoes but you. Others may say they understand, feel your pain, know what you are going through, etc. No, they don't! Only you can know any of this for sure, as only you reside inside your skin and mind; therefore, only you truly know what you are feeling, sensing, going through, doubting, desiring, wishing for, etc., as your thoughts and feelings are just that—your thoughts and feelings and not anyone else's.

That said, you and only you can access your inner guide that is guided by an infinite power from which all wisdom and knowledge emanates. The sooner you grasp this truth, the sooner you will realize that despite any medical diagnosis that is said to be absolutely unavoidable and requires an invasive medical procedure (hopefully, you have gotten several additional medical professional opinions and diagnoses first), you and only you control your survival. Fears, anxiety, stress, doubts, negativity, skepticism, denial, and confusion, among many others you can absolutely control without heavy reliance upon medication. Unless, of course, a condition without prolonged medication is absolutely medically unavoidable. To place your trust in anyone or anything else for your ultimate survival is to allow yourself to be misguided and misdirected.

Now we deal with one of the most common disempowering thoughts that many people have when diagnosed with a probable life-threatening illness or other serious life-changing adversity. Combined with doubt and skepticism, this can be lethal if such a thought is not arrested before having any chance of escalating to that point in one's life.

13

IS MY LIFE OVER?

*If you tell yourself repeatedly you're defeated, you are.
If you tell yourself repeatedly you'll
overcome whatever it is, you can.*

—Author

The title of this chapter was the first question that entered my mind when I learned that I had cancer. Included in this chapter are two very important conditions, skepticism and doubting, that together can lead one to ask the "is my life over?" question when experiencing a life-threatening condition.

When undergoing my ordeal with cancer the sensations that raced through my mind were so intense that mere words could never describe those moments. Had I not noticed mucus covering my stools, I probably never would have gone to my family physician and, as a result, not be here today. My primary care physician recommended an immediate colon examination be performed. I reluctantly agreed while all along not believing I could possibly have anything wrong with me because I had been very healthy up to that point and was very energetic.

I had the colon exam, and when I learned the results of this examination, colon cancer, my first thought was "How do I tell this to my family?"

At that time in my life, I was raising three stepdaughters ranging in ages from four to thirteen years old and my six-month-old baby boy, and to make matters even worse, I was the sole provider of my family. I trust you can imagine the reaction of my family when they learned this news and the trauma associated with such a sudden life-changing event.

You see, when anyone is told that they have a life-threatening illness, it is not only they who have the illness but everyone who cares about them as well. The lives of everyone who are concerned are literally transformed almost instantly. Unless anyone has gone through this situation, there is absolutely no way to describe it in mere words alone. I shall never forget that day, as it has been permanently etched into my mind.

As if this were not enough for one human being—having elected surgery for this condition at the insistence of my medical providers, family, and others I trusted at the time—eight months following this diagnosis, after undergoing a follow-up MRI, CT scan, and needle biopsy for a suspected metastasis to my liver, I was told that the result of those examinations were that a rather large tumor in my liver was located and, worse yet, that it had been there all along and, sure enough, I had been misdiagnosed earlier for a metastasis of cancer from my colon to my liver, which was diagnosed to be advanced liver cancer.

If you think my family was traumatized after learning about the colon cancer diagnosis, imagine the shock when they were told about this new cancer discovery. I was told at the time of this second cancer that I would once again have to undergo immediate surgery and needed to follow that up with immediate chemotherapy treatments if I were to have any chance of extending my life. Having never had any previous experience with surgeries, with the exception of having my tonsils and adenoids removed when I was a very young boy, I had no idea what to expect.

What these very serious physical illnesses did to me in a positive way was to force me to dig deep into my past in search of the cause of why cancer had invaded this once-perfectly healthy body. Believe me when I tell you there is no deeper soul-searching, in my opinion, than staring your possible demise directly in the face. After having been confined in the hospital following these surgeries and convalescing at home after being discharged, I had plenty of time to search deep inside my mind to find the answers I was seeking.

Before long, the methods and answers I was seeking finally began to slowly surface—and surface they did through my all-knowing inner guidance. What I began to learn was that cancer did not just show up one day in my life; instead, it showed up, believe it or not, at my personal invitation, through what I have previously identified as nonphysical life-threatening illnesses that, over time and allowed to escalate, can manifest into a physical illness. (Please refer to the list of some of the commonly known nonphysical illnesses provided earlier in chapter 1.)

As you may have already noticed, I talk about these nonphysical illnesses often. The reason being, in my personal opinion, is that it is these nonphysical illnesses I truly believe are the root cause of physical illnesses, especially cancer, heart disease, massive coronary arrest and strokes, and certain levels of mental illness, to name just a few.

For those of you who are fortunate enough to be free of any potential dangerous life-affecting physical illness, you should pay particular attention to these nonphysical illnesses and learn not only how to avoid them but control them. Should you find at some point in your life that you suspect that any one or a combination of these nonphysical illnesses has shown, be absolutely certain you do not ignore these as, without any doubt, they will manifest into a physical illness.

For those who may presently be subjected to a physical or a nonphysical illness, you will find a wealth of information in this book pertaining to what I refer to as your inner powers that are a vital part of your marvelous internal guidance which I credit to my having been able to achieve a permanent healing. My mission is to reach out to others who are either presently dealing with a potentially life-compromising event and those who should be aware of how I dealt with numerous critical adversities and how I surmounted them all personally and permanently.

Whether you choose to consider what I believe can bring forth positive results is, of course, your choice to make. However, no diagnosed life-threatening event waits for anyone. Procrastination is not an option, regardless of what choices you may make in dealing with any illness or adversity. On the other hand, if you have not experienced a severely damaging nonphysical or physical life illness, this information should be even more important and valuable to you for learning how to prevent most nonphysical illnesses and a related life-threatening event. I obviously was not concerned enough to call upon my inner guidance, which was available to me long before becoming afflicted with these cancers. If I had, I can assure you I would have been extremely attentive to it much sooner than I did.

Please keep in mind that I wrote this book especially for you—yes, you—as you need to know that you are the most important person in your life. There is only one of you on this planet, and there is never another quite like you and will there ever be again. Don't believe it? Well then, if may be the case concerning you, let me prove it to you so we can shed this doubt and/or skepticism you may possibly have once and for all.

I want you to begin thinking about something that most of us rarely or ever think about at all. It is about the greatest battle and struggle you ever faced. It is the battle you fought before you were even born into this world. Now when I say this to people, they have no clue what I am talking about. What I need you to know is why you are the most important person on this planet. The answer is, because there were numerous battles you had to fight and overcome in order to be able to come forth into this world, the most important of which is the greatest battle of all, the greatest race of all—the race between millions of sperm cells whose single and only objective is to reach the egg that contained a nucleus no larger than a pinhead. And although not being able to be seen by the naked eye, only microscopically, millions of sperm raced to be the first to be able to pierce the egg. Therefore, being the fastest and mightiest among the millions of sperm competing to reach the egg, it was a particular sperm that was victorious over the greatest of all insurmountable odds of survival—you.

I need you to think about this for a moment and reflect on how fierce that battle was as it was taking place in the microscopic world. What were the odds of winning that battle against other very determined sperm that were going to do what it took to be the first to reach and penetrate this precious egg? It was at this point that the life of the most incredible person you know or will ever come to know had begun.

And with this victory over the most staggering odds, through this accomplishment alone, you inherited all the possibilities and awesome power you would ever need to achieve any goal or objective you would set out to accomplish. Because you were the champion of all champions, no matter what obstacles that you may encounter on your physical life's path, none of them will ever be as great as the one you already overcame prior to your birth. If this accomplishment does not resonate with you, it should, as it is one of infinite intelligence's greatest wonders and mysteries.

I believe this means that victory over anything you may encounter in this world has already been achieved through your birthright, as at that point you had become forever and perpetually connected to your all-knowing inner guidance. That power has all the methods and answers necessary for you to draw upon to overcome and survive any adversity of any type or stage that you may possibly encounter on your journey through your life on this planet.

Whether you are aware or not, you do have options, calling upon your all-knowing guidance is primary among them, coupled with knowing precisely what it is that you really want to experience for good in your life.

If you would choose to place your total and complete trust in your inner guidance, you would soon begin to witness the tremendous power that your inner guidance can manifest in your physical life.

Among the benefits to connecting with your all-knowing inner guidance is that you will never be required to have to open your wallet because, as I have already said, it is what everyone was born with, therefore no charge. You'll never receive any billing statements in the mail, never have to produce any insurance information, pay any up-front copayment charges or any other doctor charges, and never have to wait for medical services or appointments and never receive an unexpected humongous hospital and/or laboratory billing.

If you would take a moment, you may recall in your life you had unconsciously called upon your inner guidance and gave you the answer(s) you needed at the time. The good news is that nothing has changed. The only thing that has changed is time itself, as your inner guidance never has or never will abandon you.

I sincerely believe that the majority of people who develop a life-threatening illness or related event, especially when it has escalated to a very serious stage, rarely seek, recall, summon, or are even aware of the awesome power of their inner guidance. If they did, this valuable information would have reached many people who very possibly were never made aware of the tremendous power they control that lies dormant within them, waiting to be called forth.

It is my vision that countless people throughout the world experiencing a life-threatening event will one day become reacquainted with their inner guidance and begin to personally demonstrate what many deem to be a miracle. However, it would not be a miracle. Instead, it would be their inner guidance connected with infinite intelligence that they were endowed with at birth that would bring forth whatever they desire for good to manifest in their physical life and possibly for the lives of those they love and care about.

Once again, I am not advocating abandoning proper and prudent medical advice—quite the contrary. Instead, I am identifying for you that there is also an alternative option for healing to be explored and considered, in which one can place their confidence and trust, in conjunction with conventional treatments for treating serious illnesses and other undesirable adversities, which is one's all-powerful and all-knowing inner guidance.

As a survivor of not only two cancers but numerous serious nonphysical illnesses and events as well, I am concerned that medical science may possibly continue to reject the fact that a person can bring about a permanent healing on their own concerning a serious illness and/or nonphysical disruptive adversities that, in addition to modern medical treatments for these ailments, is very real and has power to return people back to good health. I'm one of those people!

Personally, I believe that I will live to witness the day that medical science joins hands with the idea of individuals being able to heal themselves from serious physical and nonphysical life-threatening conditions that include the use of one's inner guidance, enabling and encouraging a person the opportunity to take an active role in their own healing. Some medical practitioners have already turned that corner and are beginning to see the immense benefits when conjoining medical science with one's own participation in the healing process—be it for a physical or nonphysical illness condition. If this were to take place on a greater scale, it is my belief and vision that the survival rate of many physical and nonphysical life-threatening illnesses could increase significantly. I further believe that this type of doctor-patient joint participation in the healing process has rarely been discussed in-depth by their medical practitioners with their patients with critical illnesses and/or seriously advanced nonphysical illnesses.

If you or someone you know or care about may be sustaining a physical life-compromising illness or nonphysical condition or has been told that their illness is terminal and were never made aware that they have the power to begin to bring forth a joint approach to healing for their ailments within themselves, in my considered opinion, it is not only irresponsible but inconsiderate of anyone who is aware or who knows that these powers certainly do exist.

As a survivor of life-altering physical and nonphysical illnesses, calling upon one's inner guidance when faced with an undesirable event is not considered an act of desperation; it is relinquishing total control to one's all-knowing inner power with complete trust, belief, total confidence, and expectation.

Complete denial of the existence of such an inner power could prove to be very costly in the way of an escalation of an undesirable event or even an early termination of life, in the case of a serious physical life-threatening illness that very well may otherwise could possibly have been avoided, extended, or permanently healed. At the very least, coming to know or to rediscover the all-knowing inner power certainly merits serious consideration, preferably prior to and/or especially when all medical science's remedies seem to have been exhausted.

However, only the person who is actually realizing a life-threatening illness themselves can make that decision. But it should never be a decision arrived at through the influences from others who may mean well yet have little, if any, training or knowledge and base their judgment and advice on historical data, cases, and opinions who suffer from the "follow the flock" syndrome—meaning, what other people chose to do in this situation—excluding knowledgeable medical specialists.

Once again, remember to never abandon prudent and credible medical advice. However, do not ignore the fact that, after receiving such advice, other options should also be sought out, explored, and considered before embarking upon any invasive treatments, risky surgeries, and other treatments that can carry with them some very serious side effects which can last for years, chemotherapy being among them.

Always keep in mind when considering conventional treatments and listening to the advice and the opinions of others who are not medical professionals that you are not *other people*; you are you and as so and you owe it to yourself and no one else to explore and research any viable and credible alternative treatment options. And as I said earlier, if you are unable to do this, by all means have someone you trust and can rely upon to do it for you. If the person themself is unable to do this, then it is incumbent upon their caretaker to do so and not ignore this responsibility, as it just may prove to be the decision you are being led to by your inner guidance that can and will bring forth answers to achieving the healing being sought.

As for myself, like so many others exposed to life-threatening events, I chose a much wider field—opposed to the much narrower field of options offered by medical science—to pursue a complete and permanent cure. Was this a wise and intelligent decision to make? First of all, I did not make the decision from my conscious mind. The decisions I made came directly from my inner power, in conjunction with knowing precisely the results I wanted, and focusing on nothing else other than the expected end result, which was a permanent healing, that I ultimately achieved.

The key point here is knowing exactly and very clearly what it is that one wants to achieve, without wavering. It is right here where some people become separated from those who get it and who are willing to pay very close attention to the fact that every single thing that happens to all of us during our lifetime is the direct cause of what we focus upon the most that ultimately attracts that exact situation to us, causing it to eventually materialize into our outer physical life—be it good or bad. Believe it because it is true.

Would I choose to make this same decision again to pass on highly recommended chemotherapy treatments? My answer to that question is without any doubt, I would make the very same decision without the slightest hesitation. Remember, we are discussing *you*, not other people or anyone else with a nonphysical or physical life-threatening illness.

A decision regarding one's physical survival and well-being, in the final analysis, comes down to the person themselves who has a life-threatening illness, not the observers, medical professionals, and/or religious advisors. As for myself, I refused to allow anyone to make this decision for me. I even regretted having elected to undergo the cancer surgeries that were recommended by others, including medical professionals, family members, those I had known for some time and trusted, etc. Had I summoned my all-knowing guidance back into my life sooner, I am absolutely convinced that I would have also refused these two surgeries and elected instead to follow my inner intuitive guidance for the methods, answers, and solutions necessary to obtain a permanent healing.

As a matter of fact, I initially did cancel the first surgery. The surgeon was furious and continued, telling me that without the surgery my chances of survival were, at best, very minimal. I failed to realize that this decision to cancel this surgery was coming to me from my all-knowing inner guidance by way of very strong feelings that I elected to ignore at the time. Having a six-month-old son to think about, I caved in to the surgeon's and others' relentless nagging me to get the surgeries. My original decision was the correct one because the first surgeon misdiagnosed a cancerous tumor lodged in my liver that metastasized from my colon, which had been there all along, who insisted on performing the liver cancer surgery. I opted to decline and elected instead an experienced, well-known, world-renowned liver cancer specialist and head of surgery at a hospital who specialized in cancer treatment and has a superior track record.

It was precisely when I attempted to cancel this surgery when my inner guidance was attempting to get through to me. However, I chose to ignore its continued attempts. Despite this decision, my inner guidance never quit and kept communicating with me relentlessly by way of the strong internal feelings that were coming to me continuously, making them impossible for me to ignore. I finally woke up and allowed my inner guidance to take over, and having made that decision, I have not regretted it ever since. I agreed to have the surgical procedures but refused the chemotherapy.

For some inexplicable reason, we seem to place our total confidence and trust in our primary-care physicians and transfer our trust in a higher intelligence to medical science, religious leaders, and people we choose to trust instead—our governments, criminal justice system, elected representatives; prescribed medications, psychological and psychiatric opinions; significant others; the products we choose to use, media advertising, and infomercials of every conceivable kind; aircraft, trains, cruise ships, public transportation systems, and their operators whom we know nothing about or never met. Yet we seem to place very little trust in our real self, the real person who resides on the inside, our all-knowing guidance.

Most people are not cognizant that we are not just that person on the outside whom we see every day looking back at us in the mirror or our reflection in a still lake or pond; we are connected to an inner guidance associated with life in a physical body. As much as some would prefer to discredit this fact or discredit the existence of anything that even comes close to an unseen inner power, it should go without saying that there are far too many inexplicable events that have taken place for generation to be able to deny the existence of an unseen energy that contains all the methods and answers that mankind has sought after and experienced since recorded time. To deny that such an unseen power exists is to deny our very existence.

There are literally hundreds of books, articles and publications, if not more, written on this subject, each with its own interpretation. Some of these writings are based upon historical information handed down over centuries, others contain religious beliefs and related information, some are expansions of writings of others, and some from personal knowledge and experience.

Not unlike others throughout the world, up until the time I discovered my inner power, I too had placed my trust and confidence in everything but my all-knowing inner guidance from where also comes inner intuition Although inner intuition has been given many different names, such as subconscious mind, the soul, etc., it really has little significance what label is placed on it. What is significant, however, is that it is always right and renders methods and solutions we receive from our inner guidance.

When we were very young, we acted based upon what we learned and were taught, not what we knew because as small children what did we know? Everything we do or have done is the result of what we were exposed to, beginning with our parents and/or childhood caretakers, up to our adult experiences. However, the only true knowing comes from deep within oneself—one's all-knowing inner guidance. Even as children, we always had this inner all-knowing inner guidance to rely upon and did unconsciously, which we used in many ways to get what we wanted.

As we grew older, however, our outer physical life interactions were and continue to be controlled primarily by our egos. Let's face it, we all encounter situations and circumstances for which we are seeking methods, answers, and resolutions and do not always know or are certain where to find them. Almost consistently, we seek out these answers and methods from every conceivable outside source first before we ever even begin to consider listening to our inner self—our all-knowing inner guidance, the person who we really are, the one who resides within all of us. We fail to realize that everything begins with a feeling—call it intuition, sixth sense, a hunch, an inner reaction, etc. Everyone has and continues to sense these feelings that are directly connected to our inner guidance. Too many of us, including myself, chose to ignore these feelings and instead went head-on into disastrous and regretful circumstances and situations.

If what I did by refusing chemotherapy is considered to be crazy or living in denial, then I had plenty of company, as there are many of us so-labelled crazies out in the world who chose to follow our inner intuitive guidance that communicated the methods, answers, and solutions to us that we were seeking. We have a choice, just like anything else we do in life. We either choose to accept this feeling as being the beginning of the answer to our situation and/or circumstance or to ignore it entirely.

Understand that it is not a matter of why you are so overwhelmed by whatever it is you are aware of in the way of negative and/or undesirable events or an illness. The fact is that you yourself are the *why*! The real question is, What are you going to do about it? To agonize and/or dwell on it can only lead to attracting more of the same.

Some people believe that they can hear this all-knowing inner guidance giving them the answers and the methods they are seeking while surrounded by people who are busy at whatever it is they do for a living or are around any other interferences or disturbances that consume the greater part of their daily routine. Believe me—they can't! Receiving resolutions to whatever negative or undesirable event you may be consumed with within your conscious mind while performing daily functions is light years apart from actually listening to your inner mind that is one with your inner guidance that is receiving the answers, methods, and solution being received from this all-knowing infinite intelligence.

To be able to really hear your inner guidance, as I explained earlier, first, you absolutely must find a quiet place where you will not be distracted for at least a minimum of thirty minutes where you can be alone with just you and your all-knowing inner guidance—your real self. Keep every negative or disturbing thought away from the personal time you choose to set aside for solely this purpose and just listen to what is coming to you, and you certainly will hear. This quiet time with your inner guidance is not to be confused with the separate time you devote to the all-knowing infinite intelligence through the method I identified earlier. Being alone with your inner guidance can be as short a period as five minutes or longer. It is at this time you should quiet the ongoing chatter coming from your conscious mind and outside disturbances and allow your inner guidance to speak to you without interruption.

It is extremely important that when awaiting for your inner guidance to bring forth the answers, methods. and solutions you are seeking being received from infinite mind, being *patient* with yourself is extremely important as not all the answers, methods, and solutions you are seeking will come to you all at once but eventually will come, as you continue to set aside the time once a day, just for you and this infinite intelligence to communicate and to also communicate with your inner guidance. As you do this, in time, you will begin to realize and begin receiving answers, methods, and solutions to whatever it may be you are seeking, along with the right direction and path to follow. Note that I emphasized the word *patient*. Patience is the key to your being able to connect with your inner guidance and all-knowing infinite force and to eventually perceive whatever it may be you are seeking to manifest in your life. Under no circumstance should you allow yourself to become frustrated if you feel that you have not achieved any results at first. Just continue on. Soon you will begin realizing amazing results that will first come in the way of a strong feeling, followed by receiving in your conscious mind the proper action and direction to take concerning whatever you are seeking.

It is at this critical point that most people become frustrated and literally give up on themselves. But don't! Do not give in to frustration, impatience, doubting, skepticism, negativity, or any related emotions that will keep you from connecting with your all-knowing inner guidance. I cannot stress this point to you strongly enough as it is the key to your breaking out of your habitual negative thinking syndrome and entering into the world of unlimited possibilities. I should know because I did it and continue to do it every single day of my life, and it works for me. Therefore, there should be absolutely no reason, other than your own negativity, doubting, skepticism and disbelief that would prevent you from communicating whatever it may be for good and for the good of all concerned that you are seeking.

As I pointed out earlier, I was the biggest skeptic you would ever want to meet when it came to wanting to even attempt to connect with my inner guidance. But then I had to ask myself this question, "Who are you listening to for the answers and methods you are seeking and what have been the results that benefited you from whatever those sources are? A fair question, right? The answer I found, once I thought about it seriously enough, was that I am listening to sources such as other people, medical professionals, family members, friends, acquaintances, and the like. When I finally began to consider what I was getting back from my inquiries, having to do with the numerous issues I was seeking resolution for, I found that not much in the way of real benefit was coming back to me from these sources I had chosen to rely upon.

That was my first clue and a huge wake-up call for me. The result of this exercise for me was to choose to either continue to inquire and listen to the advice from these sources in my physical world or to begin to listen to the messages and strong feelings I was receiving from deep within myself, my all-knowing inner guidance/inner mind that is one with infinite mind—a force that undeniably contains all the methods and proper direction mankind will ever need to know by simply asking and placing total trust, belief, and, above all, expectation that the methods and answers I was seeking would come along, with right direction and the proper course (path) to follow. For me and thousands of others, this decision was the right one. Having overcome all that I have, which was deemed to have been beyond insurmountable odds, is proof enough for me and those who also believe in the incredible power of this infinite power and inner guidance.

Many people have inquired of me if meditation would be a way to connect with one's inner guidance. My answer to this is that although there are various forms of meditation, some of which I have tried, I believe that meditation could possibly be a way to connect with your inner guidance. For me, however, I preferred the writing method that I outlined earlier as I can connect with the infinite intelligence that is connected with one's inner guidance at any time and only requires fifteen minutes—or more, if desired—of silence in an undisturbed environment. If you wish to do this in a group where other people are performing meditation, I have found this to be an uncomfortable setting for me, but do not rule this out entirely, as many people can meditate comfortably in such surroundings.

Realize that intuition and inner feelings are interconnected with your all-knowing inner guidance. There are feelings all of us relate to that continuously come directly from our inner guidance that is connected with infinite intelligence, but many people appear to ignore them. Listening to the inner mind, however, separates the conquerors from the defeated. Therefore, it is very important that I emphasize again that once you do choose to begin to listen to your all-knowing inner guidance, be certain to do so when your attention is not diverted and be certain to set aside a calm and relaxed time for yourself to allow all the continuous interferences to dissipate in order that you can connect with infinite intelligence that is one with you inner guide. If you do this, you can begin to realize this infinite intelligence communicating with you.

The trouble with seeking outside sources for a permanent resolution for undesirable situations and circumstances is that their advice and treatments are generally learned information and in-depth experience with numerous cases that can produce temporary results. However, this cannot promise you a permanent cure of a serious or life-threatening illness. And although others may be well meaning, their advice may possibly not be the information you are seeking that may bring forth a resolution or the answers and methods to whatever it may be you are seeking.

The answer to conquering any negative event or illness, as I have been repeating, is to intently listen to your intuitive inner guidance that is always communicating with you, awake or asleep, in many ways—e.g. feelings, intuition, and through the writing method with infinite mind I have described that can reveal the right answers, methods, and solutions you are seeking. Once you finally make the choice to quiet your conscious mind, you can then allow your inner guidance to receive the answers, methods, solutions, and right direction being received from this infinite intelligence. At this point, you can learn all there is to know concerning the answers and methods you are seeking to know, as it is your intuitive all-knowing inner guidance that is the recipient of all the knowledge and wisdom from this infinite intelligence that created everything, including the entire universe and everything contained within it. Man and earth are only a very miniscule part of this unfathomable force.

I am confident to state that in many cases, people intuitively knew and sensed the possibility of placing themselves in harm's way prior to engaging in situations that were likely to bring forth an undesirable outcome by sensing strong inner feelings and forewarnings that came directly from one's all-knowing intuitive guidance. This holds true for all of types of situations that contain inherent high risk.

You may possibly have known of people that had an inner or bad feeling about something that kept them from embarking on certain trips at a particular point in time and, by doing so, avoided becoming a fatal statistic. Others sensed that they should not get into a certain automobile with someone, and because of their inner intuitive feeling, they too avoided a serious situation. Still, others had an inner feeling not to embark on a certain skiing outing to a place known for hair-trigger avalanches and later learn some people perished at the very same place they had originally planned to go at the same point in time. Coincidence? Not likely! A deep inner intuitive feeling that came from one's inner all-knowing inner guidance? You bet, without a doubt!

What Do Skeptics and Naysayers Think They Know That Survivors Don't?

Let's define some terms first. The word *skepticism* is defined as "an attitude of doubt or a disposition to incredulity either in general or toward a particular object; "the doctrine that true knowledge or knowledge in a particular area is uncertain"; "the method of suspended judgment, systematic doubt, or criticism characteristic of skeptics"; and doubt concerning basic religious principles (as immortality, providence, and revelation)."

For those skeptics who possibly may be thinking to themselves, "Sure, you may have survived some life-changing events, but what about those who didn't?" My response to this type of question is that I am convinced that why I survived, without any doubt, is attributable to my ongoing deep trust, expectation, and unwavering belief in my inner guidance and infinite mind that I am more than convinced brought forth the healings I desired and ultimately obtained. What those who expired from a life-threatening illness did or did not do is unknown, as only they themselves knew if they had such a deep belief, trust, and expectation in their inner guidance, whether or not they ever called upon it for the answers to overcome any life-changing event or life-threatening illness. No one may ever know. What I do know is precisely what I personally experienced, as have others who have come to know the immense value of connecting with one's all-knowing inner guidance that is more than capable of resolving any life-changing event.

Medical history supports the fact that there have been many survivors of illnesses with a grim outcome like myself, including those who survived terminal illnesses. I absolutely know why I survived two serious cancers and a myriad of other serious life-changing events. If and until when other survivors choose to share their survival stories with humanity and give others the same opportunity I am attempting to share with my fellow man, woman, and young person, I guess we shall not learn how they achieved their healing. Of course, that would be a shame, in my considered opinion as a survivor of numerous life-threatening events; however, what I am sharing should be contributed to assist others who may need supportive accounts of positive results.

Did anyone know what was going on inside the minds of people before they died and left this world? Does anyone know for certain if they may have chosen or willed themselves to die or believed all the talk of succumbing to their condition, especially the medical diagnosis and prognosis (the prospect of recovery as anticipated from the usual course of disease or peculiarities of the case)? The correct answer is an obvious no. How could anyone possibly have known what they may have been thinking unless they communicated it to others?

Why is it then that skeptics/naysayers won't even consider that the possibilities for overcoming any diagnosed life-threatening illness and/or serious life-changing event are endless? Certainly it is easy to say anything, especially if you do not presently have any signs of having any life-threatening illness or disease in your body or are having a serious life-changing event. Yet skeptics out there may want to consider that they are not bulletproof or are guaranteed that they won't find themselves experiencing a serious life-changing event/life-threatening illness or serious condition at some point in their lives. At that point, they just may wish to redirect their attention to those who did survive a serious life-changing event or life-threatening illness and take a page or two out of their book because they will never know when they may wish to refer back to it one day. I should know, as I myself was once a longtime card-carrying member of the skeptics' anonymous club, so to speak.

Do you actually believe that cut (surgery), burn (radiation), and poison (chemotherapy) are the only solutions to ridding cancer? Have you ever sat down with more than one cancer survivor and asked them how they believed they survived when all the cards were supposedly stacked against them? Do you realize that this a perfect setup for attracting and inviting diseases and all sorts of nonphysical and physical illness into one's life with the type of fast-paced lifestyle societies we live today?

Are you absolutely certain that you are not next to be diagnosed with any form of serious disease or life-threatening illness? Maybe it's high time you consider coming down from that branch in that tree you are perched on and have a serious discussion with yourself and not with others who know less about you. After all, whose life is it anyway if not yours?

Denial, doubting, emotional diseases, fear, and close-mindedness are the calling card for most skeptics. They may possibly say such things like "well, you were just lucky" or "that could never happen" or "there's no such a thing" or "statistics say that . . ." or "no one could possibly survive that" or "the surgery saved you, nothing else could have." Really!

Skeptics are strongly opinionated people and are adamantly opposed to change or don't fit into their way of thinking and believing, as change makes them nervous and uncomfortable. They prefer to live their lives at a much lower vibrational frequency as opposed to a higher level. Most possess a "Thomas mentality," the "I won't believe unless I can see and place my finger into the wound for myself" kind of faith. Thomas was one of the disciples of the biblical prophet Jesus who doubted the resurrection (John 14:1–7, 20:19–29). They appear to be extremely firm in their attitudes and insensitive the majority of the time, relying upon their embedded beliefs instead. They seem to want to grasp others' attention, hoping to pull them on their side. As the saying goes, "Misery loves company."

Skeptics will label people much like me as delusionary and losing touch with reality, having a death wish, or dreamers. They may also attempt to try to convince anyone who will listen that surviving a terminal illness of any type is extremely unlikely or just plain luck. Skeptics usually view themselves as an authority on every subject that does not agree with their way of thinking. They became an expert on all life-threatening illnesses virtually overnight by voicing their negativity. And they get this skeptical knowledge from the "University of Jack of All Trades and Master of None" (a fictitious university). They are often immobilized by the thought of "there might just be another way."

Skeptics appear to believe that they are in a war by exemplifying an "us versus them" mentality. If you ask them why they feel this way or that way about the subject of this book, they would be able to fill the Grand Canyon to the brim with all sorts of reasons and excuses. If you have ever been in the company of a skeptic, you may have noticed by the look on their faces that they are usually unhappy people who appear to feed on conflict, doom and gloom, and pessimism.

I have noticed, when speaking to many skeptics, that most of them fear the subject of death, which is an inevitable conclusion to everyone's mortal life, because it represents something final to them. It appeared to me that for every positive, they had a negative. To me, their reluctance to accept any other possibilities exemplifies fear and doubt (two of the most serious nonphysical life-threatening illnesses I had outlined earlier).

I have run into a number of skeptics and naysayers who were so steadfast and rigid that it appeared that they would fight to the death if they had to, to defend their position without giving any ground to considering any other way is possible. In their world, conflict appears to be the only way. Everything to them is measured by the standards of the external world and their ego, and to them, the internal world does not exist. Talk about serious nonphysical conditions! This condition of being close-minded, another nonphysical condition, ranks extremely high among nonphysical illnesses.

In my discussions with numerous skeptics about a possible alternative to medical science's answer to reaching a cure for very serious life-threatening illnesses, they appoint themselves as judge, jury, and executioner by insisting that a person diagnosed with a terminal and other serious life-threatening illnesses cannot possibly recover and their demise is imminent. If I were able to take a journey inside their minds, I am certain that I would find all sorts of thoughts living there such as "can't"; "impossible"; "never will happen"; "out of the question"; "no one ever has"; "not in this lifetime"; "I doubt it"; "it's never been done before"; "I'll have to see it to believe it"; "very unlikely"; etc. These types of thoughts stand ready to pounce on anything that would even remotely suggest differently.

Now, here's the knockout punch: Let's look at a very real possibility that, should any one skeptic one day find themselves face to face with a serious life-threatening illness, they will need to either choose to call forth their skeptical thoughts that have been so active in their minds for years and/or rely upon medical science for a permanent cure. Or seriously consider another path. Challenging, isn't it?

There is much to talk about and explore in-depth concerning the reasons how people like skeptics and naysayers of this world got this way to begin with. It is not the target of this book, however, to go into the depth of the skeptics' and naysayers' deeply embedded thought patterns and their motivation for being this way most of, if not all, their lives. I can, however, share with you this much: The reason I know so much about the traits of the skeptic/naysayer is because I was formerly the chairman of the board of the world-renowned Skeptics International Club (used for illustration purposes only and of course this is not a real organization, so please do not look for any membership applications on the internet!)—that was until I finally surrendered my seat on that board of directors and decided to join Skeptics Anonymous (used to illustrate a point only and is not an existing organization).

This was back when I was an up-and-coming young businessperson. I thought I knew it all and also was exactly like the image of the typical skeptic and naysayer that I have outlined. How else could I be so intimately familiar with their character traits if I was not a member of this family of skeptics and naysayers?

Since my departure from this world-renowned fictitious club, it is still going very strong—worldwide, I might add. To validate my membership in this fictitious club, I made absolutely certain to surround myself with an army of real skeptics and naysayers just like me. Anything we found that we did not agree with, in our opinion, was reason to shoot it down, and there rarely was less than a 100 percent agreement. We were a happy group and, for the most part, were all healthy; so we believed anyway. This was a real group of businesspeople and acquaintances with whom, at the time, I associated and today am very grateful I broke those ties years ago.

We were very adept and successful in drawing numerous skeptics and naysayers from other parts of the globe into our group. Quite to our surprise, we quickly learned that in their part of the world, they too had many skeptic-naysayer friends and business associates who were more than pleased to introduce our members. Over time, we became a very gleeful, cohesive group (actually, a very gloomy group, I might say)—despite our futile attempts to wear our arrogant, happy masks and proudly display our skeptic-naysayer shields and coats of armor, so to speak.

As time wore on, many in our ranks succumbed to various types of serious life-changing events, diseases, and physical or nonphysical life-threatening conditions. Despite these illnesses, it appeared that we held on to our deeply embedded beliefs and refused to yield to any alternative remedies (not medical) other than what they firmly were attached to—medical science's remedies. Any alternative or detachment to our previously learned remedies, for us, wasn't an option.

As the years passed by, I and a number of others began to realize that all this negativity was in fact resulting in the very opposite of what we had always believed was what had kept us going. Never realizing what was correct, little by little, what all this negativity and skepticism was really doing was, like cancer, slowly eating away at all of us and disempowering what we thoroughly believed was empowering us.

This may be the part that I have had the toughest battle with, and to some degree, this old foe continues to make every attempt to break down the barrier I have built to make certain it never enters my life again, as it played a significant role in practically, if not all, my nonphysical illnesses and other life-changing events that eventually led to very serious physical life-threatening illnesses.

Probably the greatest formidable opponent a man, woman, and young person has ever encountered and ever will whose cunning attacks emanate from inside us, not from our outer world. Its attacks are so relentless and constant that it can and has caused a myriad of nonphysical illnesses to surface in the lives of many people, including me. This enemy I am speaking of is responsible for most stressful and anxious conditions, and we all know it well—it is that other voice that we so often hear nagging at us, the voice we all know so well as doubt.

Realizing this, those of us who came to our senses after witnessing many among our ranks checking out of this world—just as arrogant and unyielding as we had been—slowly but surely began to seek alternative ways to live our lives. Although many are no longer among us today, those of us who still are finally found alternative ways to live and left the ranks of the diehard skeptics who went on to spawn many more like themselves. It is disheartening to have to say that these ranks of skeptics and naysayers have grown exponentially worldwide. However, just as strong, I am pleased to say that people everywhere are beginning to rediscover their true power, their all-knowing inner guidance.

In time, medical science worldwide may find themselves yielding to this undeniable inner guidance that has lived within all humanity for as long as mankind has existed. To doubt this is to question that you are alive at this very moment. If you happen to be among one of these skeptics and naysayers, do not be overly concerned because your inner guidance is extremely patient and allows you to make your choices. It will never cause you to choose between your present beliefs and your dormant all-knowing inner guidance that absolutely knows that you have had and continue to have glimpses of its immense power.

Your inner mind also knows that you have not accomplished a thing on your own. It also knows it nurtured you as an infant and knows that you know where your real home is and that before long you will once again summon it forward. But this time, when you do, you will never abandon it again, as you will come to finally realize that this guidance is all you really ever needed on your present life's path, being your truest friend, confidant, and provider of your innermost desires for good, among so much more that you will soon come to relearn once you chose to reconnect with your all-knowing inner guidance.

PREVAILING OVER INSURMOUNTABLE ODDS

I can guarantee, if you are one of the skeptics and naysayer you may possibly be today, one day soon you will also want to rediscover your inner power. And when you finally make this choice, you'll ask how you ever allowed yourself to live your life that long without it. The answer is, you didn't. It's been with you all along. Those of us who already know all we need to know about the outcome of any of our desires that will benefit all concerned have no need to ask for anything ever because we are already grateful constantly for what we know has already been done and what will be done for us in the future. All we have to do now is call it forth into reality.

What I am suggesting is for the skeptic and naysayer to seriously consider reconnecting with their own inner power so they can also experience what I and so many others have already discovered. (It does not matter by what name they may choose to call this inner knowing.) All anyone needs to accept for themselves is that it exists within each and every one of us. To choose to disbelieve or suggest this is not true is to deny your very own existence. Once one makes this choice to reconnect to their all-knowing inner guidance, know that all anyone needs then is to exercise patience. If you are a skeptic and naysayer and choose to make the decision to reconnect with your absolute inner power, you will begin to recognize having your desires that are for the highest benefit of all concerned manifest into the physical in your life. And when you do, you will want to take off that skeptics and naysayers' mask you have been wearing for far too long so that the real face of your inner guidance can finally be visible for all to see and share. Afterward, you will want to keep on sharing this priceless gift with all you come in contact with, including other skeptics and naysayers, family, friends, and associates. I say this because I know that I know, and soon so will you know.

This chapter began with the question, "Is my life over?" This thought in itself, if allowed to continue, unless replaced by life-enhancing thoughts, can permit any life-threatening illness or nonphysical adversity or event to escalate and, more often than not, happens at a rapid pace, if not arrested and contained. I firmly believe that no one's life is over unless they themselves decide it is over. On the other hand, unforeseen senseless acts of violence, natural disasters, and serious vehicular accidents defy explanation.

GARY DEBELLONIA

The Great Danger of Doubting

The word *doubt* means "a lack of confidence"; "distrust [has doubts about his abilities]"; "an inclination not to believe or accept [a claim met with doubt"; and "a state of affairs giving rise to uncertainty, hesitation, or suspense [the outcome is still in doubt]."

We now come to the part that I have had the toughest battle with, and to some degree, this old foe continues to make every attempt to break down the barrier I have built to make certain it never enters my life again as it played a significant role in practically, if not all, my nonphysical illnesses that eventually led to very serious physical life-threatening illnesses.

I am talking about the greatest formidable opponent man, woman, and young person will ever encounter that emanates from inside us, not from our outer world; and once allowed to take us over, its attacks are so relentless and constant that it can cause any number of nonphysical illnesses. This enemy I am speaking of is the mother of all stressful and anxious conditions, and we all know it well; it is that other voice that we so often hear nagging at us—the voice of doubting.

In order to dispel all doubts that we are continuously plagued with, we must first understand that practically every negative experience that occurs in our physical lives occurs for a reason. And you are that reason. Unless you are able to shed the doubts that continuously haunt you, they will become etched in your mind and become that part of you which accepts and believes them to be fact and true, thereby rendering it difficult to be able to think about them differently. By doubting, we are reenforcing the belief that whatever it is, is not possible or will not occur.

Banishing doubt is not a simple task as it has taken years of daily practice to perfect it. I have read and heard people say it is as simple as just trashing it and getting up one day and choose to no longer be doubtful about anything. I will agree with choosing to no longer be doubtful about anything. There is absolutely no doubt in my mind that doubt is as dangerous as swallowing gasoline; however, ridding oneself of this horrible habit (a bad habit continued for any prolonged period of time becomes a nonphysical illness) needs to be treated like any bad habit that has a strong grip on us—e.g., smoking, taking drugs, consuming alcohol in excess, lying, cheating, stealing, being ill tempered, constant use of profanity, sexual promiscuity, etc.

By beginning to eliminate doubt we can then start to become more reliant upon the possible as opposed to the improbable. This then becomes trusting that we can or that something can be done, without a doubt. It is at this point that things appear to us to be possible and the things we thought could not be accomplished can be, and the solutions to our doubts begin to become clear and then can begin to become creative, surpassing what we had once believed could not be done. Now an entirely new world opens for us before our eyes.

That said, on the other side of the coin is the alternative—that is, by choosing the deadly path of doubting, should anyone choose to continue living in the world of doubt, they may be assured that absolutely very little will ever be accomplished. How can they? The moment they run into any obstacle or difficulty, they will choose doubt every time over possibility. Cemeteries are full of people who lived their entire lives this way. Let's examine just a few examples:

- "It is not possible to find a cure for what I have."
- "There are no remedies for this situation."
- "No one has been able to accomplish this ever before, what makes you believe we can?"
- "I will never get any further in this job."
- "Terminal illnesses cannot be survived, especially this type."
- "They'll never put a man on the moon again."
- "It's not possible."
- "Run a mile in under how many minutes? Ha!"
- "A flying machine—what are they drinking?"
- "Sail this vessel around the world?"
- "Open heart surgery isn't possible."
- "I don't think so!"
- "I'll never graduate high school or make anything out of myself!"
- "Their marriage can't possibly last."

Instead, had you been exposed since your childhood to a society that was free of doubting, just imagine what you could have accomplished and created for the good of mankind and yourself. What if you never heard "it's impossible" or "it can never be done"? What if you were never criticized for attempting to do what no one else had ever tried or tried and failed and never tried again? Instead you did, and you became known for your great accomplishment. What if you were able to use your mind unclogged with uncertain thoughts and doubting influences from those you are around, those who raised you, and others who are or were always mistrusting or negative or even your very own infected mind through the cage that entraps you that you self-created by continuing to associate with negative types?

Had I not reconnected with my all-knowing inner guidance, without any doubt in my mind, I would have convinced myself that everyone around me was right and that I should listen to them. Had I done that, I am also convinced that I would be nothing but a memory today to those who cared about me. I would never have been able to reach out through the pages of this book in an attempt to help my fellow man, woman, and young person and would have missed this great opportunity to help others, which I firmly believe is one of the key reasons I am still here today.

By refusing to undergo any chemotherapy treatments, it was considered by many that I was in a state of denial and doubting, the possible benefit of these treatments. However, I was absolutely confident in my decisions to forego any such treatments and not to put into my body what I knew would interfere with my body's ability to ward off any disease I could possibly contract at some future date.

The questions as to whether I would survive without these treatments, however, came from the medical doctors, family, friends, business associates, acquaintances, medical social workers, oncologists, etc. It was like running away from a posse of skeptical ghouls. This was absolutely more frightening than the diagnosis of both cancers combined, if you can imagine that. It was creepier than most scary movies, to be blunt about it. Never in my life had I witnessed such a collection of skeptics and naysayers, and it can't be done choir (my vision of this group).

PREVAILING OVER INSURMOUNTABLE ODDS

This is not meant to be disrespectful of the genuine concerns of everyone concerned with my welfare. However, it was overwhelming, to say the very least. Because in conjunction with the trauma connected with these two cancer events, it was enough to deal with, let alone the added anxiety. Although I survived all this and much more, these memories stayed with me as a constant reminder that, armed with my inner guidance, there wasn't anything I could not conquer.

I can state from my own personal experience, perpetual skepticism is not only dangerous but can also be mentally crippling and, if allowed to continue, can often turn into a serious nonphysical life-threatening condition. When this happens—and it happened to me—it can take years to extinguish from one's life.

Let me refamiliarize you with another chronic form of doubting. You may have been around or know people who thrive on having to talk about their poor health. You may even have been around people who will describe every detail of their operations as opposed to any benefit they may have derived from such a procedure. And maybe you know or have known people who always look for symptoms of illness on their outer body—as well as inner—and if they cannot find something, then they will invent one or more to talk about to anyone who might want to listen. Then there are those who will buy into every type of new health product and gizmo they truly believe will cure whatever they believe they are experiencing, only to later learn (after having spent good money for these products or medications) that these so-called remedies do not work, were being investigated by the FDA (Food and Drug Administration), and were useless. Then there's the all-too-familiar hypochondriac. These are the folks who imagine and/or fear sickness of all type and continue to discuss having these symptoms long enough until they actually do "attract" the condition they most fear to themselves.

Medical science has pointed out that countless people bring on illnesses and conditions of all types through the overactive negative thinking in their own minds, especially when they bombard their minds continuously with such thoughts. This is better known as psychosomatic illness that has its beginnings in the mind. This is what I have been referring to as nonphysical life-threatening illnesses.

This is caused when one's mind never is at rest and in continuous conflict with thoughts of good and excellent health. Some of these conditions may be but are not limited to cramping, (not necessarily menstrual), continuous feelings of indigestion and heartburn, chronic headaches and migraine, poor circulation, infections, skin rashes and hives, kidney and bladder problems, varying levels of ulcers, and, for men, impotence. The list is virtually endless. Many of these and more are the end result of severe tension, anxiety, and stress, which can lead to various stages of mental problems.

Dwelling on illness and chronic distrust is the path that can lead to an endless list of illnesses that can spawn from these conditions, which eventually are turned into beliefs by both the conscious and the unconscious minds. Once accepted as true, these may manifest into serious physical illnesses, some of which can lead to one's eventual demise. The mind is extremely powerful, and when one focuses on a negative condition long enough and formulates a picture of this condition in the mind, this condition may eventually appear in reality as pictured.

I have been an expert at developing such negative images and thoughts and can tell you from my perspective, having lived through a number of nonphysical and physical life-threatening illnesses, that what I just described to you is real and is possibly happening to someone somewhere on this planet at this very moment.

Then there is the converse[?] of these self-imposed conditions. If the subconscious mind tends to accept these negative thoughts and images as real, then the same process will also accept mental pictures of excellent health. The result is the person (you) who is free from any of the previously described symptoms and nonphysical life-threatening illnesses/conditions that you created for yourself.

What if you should attract a flu virus or the common cold, sustain an injury or some disease, or any other adverse event and absolutely know that you will overcome it? The mind, occupied with thoughts and visions of excellent health and vitality and confidence, coupled with one's all-knowing inner guidance, sees far beyond any condition and can help in healing them all. Including the serious illness of doubt? Yes! Doubt is a serious nonphysical illness.

PREVAILING OVER INSURMOUNTABLE ODDS

I can hear some of you saying right at this very moment, "Sure, easy for you to say, you are not going through what I am right now." You're right—I am not going through what you are going through. I've gone through worse, much worse!

If you keep telling yourself you *are*, then the chances are good that you will continue to go through whatever you are going through right now. Your negative thoughts are providing the fuel these conditions need to continue to grow—whether it is a physical, mental, or some other life-changing event that has taken the joy and trust out of your life. However, may I remind you, I've been right where you are right now and am no stranger to life-threatening illnesses and other life-disrupting adversities and overcame them.

Please do not expect anyone—other than close family, loved ones, or close friends—to sympathize with you. This is not a right of yours or mine or anyone else's to expect people to have sympathy for any of us who have or are now going through any type of physical or nonphysical trauma or event. The total responsibility is ours and ours alone to overcome whatever it may be we are experiencing. Let's face it, we are the ones who played a role in attracting these plagues us and, therefore, the only ones who can bring forth a total and complete self-healing for ourselves, and not anyone else! Therefore, do not seek sympathy—seek complete self-healing instead through your all-knowing inner guidance that is one with infinite intelligence.

Ask yourself whether you are willing to continue with habitual doubting if this is the case with you personally. Do you really want to do something about this negative behavior that even you are so accustomed to that you hardly recognize this condition that occupies a substantial amount of space in your conscious mind?

The word *fear*, as I stated earlier, is chock-full of synonyms and has an array of definitions. Fear is very closely related to doubt. If one can rid themselves of fear, then they rid themselves of doubt and replace it with total confidence and knowing. By freeing oneself from fear, we are at the same time freeing ourselves from our very own self-constructed evil.

How much energy is spent worrying about things that we have very little control over and how much energy do we spend on fear of our own death, financial security, bad health, and loss? I will step out on a limb and be so bold to say that a great deal of our time is spent in harboring silent fears and doubts. Imagine, if you will, shedding that useless and wasted effort by replacing it with confidence and trust that there is nothing to fear and less to doubt, especially when one firmly believes in their inner guidance.

In the USA alone, there is an abundance of everything. Why do you think people from all over the world want to live and continue to flock here year after year? The USA has even built huge fences and placed thousands of security personnel on the borders to try to at least slow down the illegal immigration flow. If we think we have it so bad in the USA, why not try living in countries where its citizens are flooding to the USA, especially to take advantage of the most advanced healthcare programs in the world? See if we are or are not better off right where we are, despite the seriousness of the economic problems the USA and most of the world is presently undergoing.

Regardless of what situations and circumstances you possibly may find yourself confronting at this point in time, you cannot afford to not separate yourself from your self-made fears and doubts. This is an absolute must for self-preservation and placing yourself back on the path of self-reliance and self-confidence.

Unless you can recapture these very important states of mind and until you make the personal choice to do so, you may very well stay exactly where you are now, if you are experiencing what I just identified related to fear and doubting. There simply are not EMS services or self-confidence and self-reliance hospitals to help you with the issues we have been discussing regarding doubt and fear. There are numerous for-profit local-, state-, and government-run mental facilities and rehab centers that are more than happy to relieve you of your hard-earned money or the funds from your insurance provider. If your insurance provider will cover such illnesses or events, and if they do, you can rely upon your annual insurance premium skyrocketing toward deep outer space.

Most people are so deeply entrenched in the state of skepticism that it has become part of their daily routine. I have been told that to doubt something acts as a person's safe haven; and it is when they are proven wrong, oh well, just a coincidence that it turned out the opposite of the habitual uncertainty and they just go on in the same way day after day. I was no exception and know this nonphysical illness well, as I have spent a good portion of my life as a doubter.

To be able to reverse this illness is no easy task, and there simply are no quick fixes for anyone. This nonphysical illness is especially dangerous for those who may have a serious illness or experiencing any serious event, situation, or circumstance.

However, unless you begin and are willing to commit to yourself that you will change your thinking once and for all, it is very likely that you will remain right where you are. There are no pills or medications that can change one's mind from doubting to acceptance and then to trusting themselves that they can overcome any adversity.

It is extremely important that we understand that we are where we are and who we are because of our habits and thoughts, followed by the resulting actions we take. It is extremely important that you pay very close attention to how you think and act and your learned habits, negative or positive. If it's more of the latter, you shall find them more enriching and uplifting and will transfer you from where you may find yourself today to where you really want and need to be in your life, despite being affected by any adverse conditions you may be faced with at the present moment. You need to continuously remind yourself that your prolonged thoughts on any matter, good or bad, will eventually be translated into the physical equivalent as they respond to our burning desires.

By controlling one's thoughts and having the will to control habitual doubting, humanity can and should control their destiny and follow the true path they were placed on—the path of abundance, excellent health, happiness, and giving, just to name a few of the myriad of good things humanity was meant to experience in this life.

Always remember, you are to give no prolonged thought to any adverse conditions, circumstances, or events that may come or have come your way, as to do so is to empower these habitual thoughts, which can only lead to continued misery and despair.

When I was lying in the hospital during the separate cancer events, for the first time in my life, I was able to witness what once were very strong people reduced to childish states when confronted with the reality of being afflicted with a serious life-threatening illness such as cancer. What became even more prevalent was the tremendous conversations coming from these people who were, for the most part, fraught with doubt and then paralyzing fear.

Almost every conversation with medical personnel, family members, friends, and other well-wishers contained obvious doubting and fear of the possibility of death on the horizon. If faith was previously a part of their lives, one would never had known it, as they appeared to require constant reassurances that all is well and that they would overcome their illness. Paralyzing fear and strong doubt are the two necessary ingredients that often takes a person down to a point of no recovery. Add to this a negative prognosis and weeping visitors and not-so-encouraging immediate family members. All that is lacking is the clergy, followed by the funeral director.

I apologize to my readers for being seemingly too harsh; however, let's face it—we all contributed in some way to attracting any serious physical and/or nonphysical illness or condition into our lives. It is we who decide to own up to this truth or not. And to be even more frank, most of us will not own up to having had any role in having such an event coming into our physical lives.

I also would lie there in those hospital rooms and in ICU and believe that I was all alone in the world; and when in that situation, when all the well-wishers and family have gone and there is almost dead quiet on the hospital floor outside your room, with the exception of an occasional calling for a nurse or the noises from the various medical apparatus, I was. So then what? Then you are alone with your thoughts, which you and only you can control, as this is all you have total control over in that situation, and I experienced this twice in under a year.

One evening after colon surgery, I resigned myself to the fact that if I was going to survive, depending on these medical people, that was not going to be the answer as I had my hospital room door closed several times a patient had succumbed, which only made me reach deeper inside myself to find the solution to how I would survive these physical attacks on my body. Once I realized that I was not going to cease finding the answer, I knew immediately when I made that decision that I was in fact not alone at all. This knowledge came from deep within me and continued to feel that I was surrounded with all the love and knowledge I would ever need to overcome anything I decided to overcome and had access to all the methods and answers to what I needed to defeat this and any physical attack on my body.

Once I absolutely knew I was not alone and understood that I was my own healer, any doubting or fear I may have had left me and was never allowed to return, as this inner knowing made doubting and fear impossible to return. As I grew stronger day by day in knowing I was no longer alone with this physical affliction, I refused to allow anyone to refer to that physical condition by its medical name and refused to give it any power or thought whatsoever. The mere fact that I absolutely knew that I was not alone made it impossible to allow me to have any disempowering thoughts about this temporary physical condition.

It is important that you focus on the fact that once you make the decision to abandon doubting and fear from your life, it becomes an improbability for either one to be allowed to reenter your life again. You then would have already begun developing an inner confidence so strong that will take over, which at that point allows you to be absolutely certain of what needs to be done in any given circumstances you may possibly be dealing with in your life. In short, this inner awareness—your inner guidance—will guide you in the right direction to accomplish your mission, no matter what it may be. What I learned from this was that being in a state of fear and doubt, over time, actually became a self-constructed prison. By reaching deep inside yourself mentally, you will find that any and all doubting and fears soon disappear from your thoughts, replaced by absolute confidence and knowing.

I understand that by saying to you that any adversity, mental or physical, that you may be experiencing or may possibly affect you has been placed upon your life's path for a very specific reason; it would be futile to question why. I have been asked, why then do some people go through life never getting anything more than a common cold or flu and others have to suffer with very serious illnesses? What I learned is that to question anyone else's predetermined life's journey is only that you doubt you have been as fortunate as they because you feel that you are less fortunate, not realizing that, to get to the place you were meant to be. These things are all part of your life's plan.

By accepting this, you can transcend to a much higher level on your life's path once you stop comparing and judging and just stay focused on your absolute knowing that you are special and that all is well, regardless of what physical appearances may try to point otherwise.

Always remember, you are to give no prolonged thought to any adverse condition, circumstance, or negative event that may come or have come your way, as to do so is to empower these habitual thoughts. Ask yourself this: "Is this truly what I want to continue to experience?"

Let's now explore how nonphysical adversities can be avoided and overcome.

14

OVERCOMING NONPHYSICAL LIFE-THREATENING CRISES

In the beginning of this book I provided a partial list of nonphysical illnesses to demonstrate some of the root causes of most life-changing illnesses and conditions.

On or about the year 2007, not only the US economy but the global economy began unraveling and demonstrating serious financial problems. Considering the fact that most all of the news-reporting agencies have and continue to report about this apparent ongoing situation, there is no need to expand on these conditions here, as most everyone is aware of the horrendous conditions we are all affected by and predicted by economic experts to extend past the year 2016 and possibly even longer.

As identified earlier, people everywhere seem to be at a loss to know precisely what to do to survive this unprecedented economic storm, let alone how they would be able to recover from catastrophic financial losses and loss of jobs and material possessions they had worked for and accumulated for most of their lives. Entire families are faced with major hardships, marriages are threatened, unemployment continues to escalate with no end in sight, personal and business bankruptcies are on the rise, home foreclosure's continue to escalate, small businesses are failing and many have disappeared, and prosperity on all levels is fading into the horizon, along with confidence and trust in government that is also declining at a rapid pace. What's amazing about all this is people's complacent reaction to these circumstances. This is probably a large pill to swallow for many individuals but an inevitable reality, and unless people begin to seriously address these conditions and take action to recover from these events, instead of acting like bystanders, chances are that they may even get much worse, with the possibility of causing even deeper stress, anxiety, and fear and begin to reflect any number of the conditions listed in the chart provided earlier.

When circumstances in life change drastically, such as just described, and begin approaching critical and even crises levels, in order to be able to overcome and/or avoid serious health issues, one must place themself into survival mode and be prepared and determined to survive, no matter what comes their way. People who choose to survive anything life may throw at them and refuse to cower and give in to adversarial circumstances belong to a very unique group. Those who are true survivors did not one day find themselves in an unexpected situation and then simply pass through another door and their adversity, situation, or circumstance was overcome with no effort at all on their part. Quite the contrary.

True survival of any adverse circumstance or unexpected situation or crises takes dedicated personal involvement, a focused effort, and, above all, being completely convinced that one has already survived and overcome whatever it is—with no exceptions whatsoever—and be able to envision themselves having already overcome these trials. The only way to not survive anything is simply to do nothing and just hope for the best. I already addressed the word *hope*, which, without action, is powerless in itself.

Although I find absolutely nothing wrong with hoping, which is akin to expectation of fulfillment or success, I found that there are numerous modern cancer treatment centers and other magnificent institutions dedicated to cancer patients and ongoing cancer research that emphasize hope. Among some of the most recognized founded by philanthropists are the Huntsman Cancer Institute Salt Lake City, Utah (founded by Jon M. Huntsman), Cancer Treatment Centers of America, and St. Jude Children's Research Hospital (founded by Danny Thomas).

PREVAILING OVER INSURMOUNTABLE ODDS

As a cancer survivor myself, I applaud the superior efforts and dedication of the founders of these magnificent modern-day facilities and others and all the work and dedication they do every day to help those who are diagnosed with any stage of cancer. That said, having personally witnessed many people who were treated for various types and stages of cancers and listening to what they said and continued to focus upon, I am more than convinced that life-threatening illnesses originate from what I call nonphysical life-threatening illnesses.

As I stated, these dedicated modern-day facilities certainly play an important role, as far as medical science is concerned. However, these institutions and their very dedicated staff and highly skilled medical personnel treat patients after the disease has been diagnosed—which is their primary function—and, for the most part, do a magnificent job in medical science. They also have important adjunctive professional aspects that support medical-surgical treatment and psychosocial preventive measures.

There have and continue to be countless theories and medical science opinions about the origin of various types of cancers supported by cancer research. My personal experience points specifically to what I am convinced are the root causes of physical illnesses of all types. These root causes I call nonphysical life-threatening illnesses begin at very early stages of a person's life, which, if left unattended or unrecognized, can and often develop into physical life-threatening illnesses.

Among the numerous statements made by the medical professionals who were treating me were those emphasizing that I definitely needed to avoid any type of stressful situations or risk the possibility of a recurrence. This advice in itself makes a very powerful statement by recognizing that stress and anxiety, among many severely affecting nonphysical conditions, are chief among the reasons for any number of physical illnesses, providing eventually grim results.

That said, what I have come to witness through my observations to date is something that seems to be rapidly disappearing among a vast majority of people in the USA, especially this country's youth (ranging from grammar schools through universities)—faith, confidence and trust in self, and religious belief (the apparent leader)—and is being replaced with lack of faith, disbelief in religions across the board (especially Christianity), lack of self-confidence and self-trust, and, might I add, taking the initiative.

There is nothing wrong with the words *hope* and *faith*—both are excellent to add to one's arsenal when it comes to overcoming life-changing and life-threatening events, crises, and illnesses. However, each of these words offers expectancy of a cure. Having my personal choice, I knew innately and intuitively that if I was going to dispel the medical opinions and historical medical statistics given me against my odds of surviving, I was going to need much, much more than just hoping that I was going to survive. And to be blunt about it, time apparently was not on my side, according to medical science's opinion. How did I know I made the right choice? Given only a 10 percent, at best, opportunity of survival without chemotherapy treatments (which the medical profession placed in writing and which I rejected) and now still cancer free eighteen years later is all the proof I need!

Some people have asked me, "What about those who are in a coma and not coherent or cannot hear?" First of all, what proof is there that they are not cognizant or cannot hear? Medical science, as advanced as it is, is neither always correct nor is it perfect. It is a science, and science is not absolutely perfect or flawless. How does anyone really know that by uttering the right words a comatose person is not hearing and responding inwardly and may one day recover? It has happened. Here's a news article from the *Daily Mail*:

> I screamed, but there was nothing to hear: Man trapped in 23-year 'coma' reveals horror of being unable to tell doctors he was conscious. Rom Houben, trapped in his paralyzed body after a car crash, described his real-life nightmare as he screamed to doctors that he could hear them - but could make no sound. 'I screamed, but there was nothing to hear,' said Mr. Houben, now 46, who doctors thought was in a persistent vegetative state. (2009)

PREVAILING OVER INSURMOUNTABLE ODDS

We don't! Left on a respirator and other life support apparatus in a room alone, no visitors or family or anyone who cares about them, with no more than medical people monitoring their vital signs, and not having anyone to communicate with them could leave them with little reason, if any, to recover. Medical science has been baffled more than once when people in deep comas, diagnosed not to recover from that condition, one day wake up or were awake all along but unable to communicate. This type of recovery has medical science perplexed as to what caused the person to recover from a condition determined irreversible. If you do not believe this, the internet is full of these types of recoveries. I suggest you take a moment to scour the internet the most incredible coma recoveries recorded by modern medical science for more information on this subject.

Medical science has its role to play, and you have yours as well. As I have been saying, sole reliance upon the medical profession for a total healing and permanent cure is simply wishful and faulty thinking. Unless you have realized it yet, medical professionals are not anyone's higher power and, therefore, should not unfairly be relied upon to be miracle workers. Once the medical professionals do their part to help overcome and defeat any potentially serious illness, affliction, or other serious events, you must then also perform your part. Unless you do, you can rely upon a continued steep climb with your illness, affliction, or other serious life-changing event or crisis.

Far too many of us place the total responsibility for our recovery from illnesses of every known kind, physical or nonphysical in nature, on the medical profession and others. But very rarely, if at all, do we shoulder responsibility on our own shoulders. We even go so far as to place the entire burden for our recovery upon a higher power, regardless of one's religious belief.

Isn't it high time that all of us take full individual responsibility for our very own recovery and survival after medical science has done all they can? I did and so have others. In my opinion as a survivor of serious physical and nonphysical illnesses and events, doing nothing for yourself beyond medical care is precisely what you can expect in return.

From years of observing people who find themselves in a serious life-changing and life-threatening situation or crisis, many exhibit or are engulfed with a pessimistic outlook when it came to life presenting inevitably negative conclusions and circumstances. As I pointed out earlier, an illustration of this is when I was hospitalized. I was surrounded by a number of pessimists. To make matters even grimmer, others were surrounded by family members and friends, the majority of whom were award-winning pessimists instead of life-enhancing optimists. At best, this was depressing to witness. If I did not elect to tune these people out, I sincerely believe that I too would have joined the pessimist antisurvival choir, so to speak. How fortunate because I can't sing!

There are many religions that place a great deal of emphasis on the words *faith* and *hope* as well. It has been reported down through the ages that what are referred to as miracles have come about for those who subconsciously and consciously lived by these two words with unwavering belief and loyalty. The key here is *unwavering belief* and *loyalty*.

Those in modern-day societies who have overcome serious illnesses and other serious events in their lives that are convinced beyond any possible doubt that due primarily to strong belief, no one can dare challenge this as the proof of survival against all odds. I agree because unwavering belief in anything good or bad can very well bring forth the result being sought. I am among those who unwaveringly had and continue to believe that unwavering belief in my inner guidance and the power of my infinite intelligence, despite given a very slim chance of survival. I went as far as making the choice to refuse any chemotherapy treatments and have the written document (see the appendix) to prove my chances of survival without such treatments.

Any honest medical professional would tell you that it is the patient themself who plays the most significant role in the healing process. Without the patient's complete trust in their innate ability to bring forth a complete healing and eventual permanent cure, there can be no permanent cure. Sounds simple, doesn't it? However, the fact of the matter is that the majority of patients who have a serious life-changing and/or life-threatening illness event do the complete opposite. They choose instead to place their total confidence and trust exclusively in prescription drugs, invasive surgical procedures, poisonous chemicals poured into their veins, radiation treatments, etc.

Therefore, it is at this point where the correct path to choose when coming to a fork in the road heading toward a complete healing and permanent cure becomes most difficult for most to choose which path they should follow. For others, they aren't even close to even being on any path whatsoever. How do I know this? I know this because I have spoken to countless people who had serious illnesses and/or life-changing events. Many trusted that surgeries, prescribed medications, counseling, and/or other such purported remedies were the total answer. Others did not have a clue what to do and allowed themselves to be led and relied upon others. This is akin to the lost leading the lost.

You see, the power to heal anything you may possibly be experiencing is already yours because you own it (the power). It lies in the knowing that you already know what to do. It is a matter of shifting your trust in everything but yourself—meaning, *self-reliance* versus *reliance* (*reliance*—"something or someone relied on")—and knowing, without any doubt, that you are able to bring about a complete healing and possibly a permanent cure for whatever it may be your illnesses. Guaranteed? No. Possible? Definitely.

A permanent healing and ultimate cure begins and ends with unwavering dominant and habitual thoughts, coupled with envisioning overcoming any condition. It simply is not good enough to accept a "one day at a time" attitude. If one is going to trust themselves to be able to bring forth a complete healing and possibly ultimate cure, one absolutely must—as I've already described—be able to envision it as though it has already happened and they are enjoying a normal and healthy life, completely free of any illness or event, serious or otherwise. (It may be a good idea to highlight this and write it down and put it where you can see it all the time until it becomes a part of your every waking moment.) Today, you or someone you love or care about deeply may be in perfect condition; however, life offers none of us any guarantees of continued excellent health or absence of a serious illness, life-changing event, or crisis to come into our lives. A doomsday comment? No, it's reality and a fact of life.

Why do so many well-known hospitals that focus primarily upon a certain life-threatening illness emphasize *hope* and *faith* as an important part of their recovery programs? Because hope and faith are "future valued," not short-term gains. Yes, short-term gains are victories; however, they are far from a complete healing and a possible permanent cure.

You see, only we as individuals can bring forth a healing and eventual possible permanent cure. For anyone or any medical professional or those involved with alternative remedies to state otherwise is a deliberate, misleading falsehood. Now I am almost certain this statement may draw some criticism; however, it is what it is—the will to survive lies deep within the individual who has the illness or event.

The medical part plays a role in the overcoming of an illness or life-changing event after it has already shown its ugly head but cannot be relied upon to be the reason for a total healing or possible permanent cure, unless it is a broken bone or non–life-threatening illness or wound. And even then, it is the body's internal healing function that brings forth the healing, not the doctor.

As I stated earlier, the healings and permanent cures I have personally learned about have been said, ranging from pure luck to a miracle. I myself absolutely know and am certainly convinced that by tapping into and choosing to absolutely trust my inner intuitive guidance, its indisputable power can continue to be relied upon. As I also stated before, the words *hope* and *faith* have no power in themselves. The power they have can only come from the fuel you provide them.

Let's now explore why it should be extremely important to trust in one's inner guidance instead of relying and placing confidence in others and everything else other than ourselves.

15

Trust in Your All-Knowing Inner Guidance

People who spend the majority of their time attempting to deal with serious life-changing conditions through their outer world sources are among those who unconsciously disregard their inner guidance. Instead, they allow their ego and others to dictate how to deal with their life-changing events. Yet through their inner guiding power, they already possess and know everything they will ever need to know.

By allowing to receive the guidance coming from one's inner power that is one with the infinite intelligence, everything anyone may need to know when it comes to life-changing conditions and events can be known through the answers, methods, and solutions that can be provided. By allowing this all-knowing inner guidance to provide the answers, methods, and solutions to any problem being sought and expecting to realize whatever it may be for good is on its way, those who do choose to trust in the power of their inner guide will have conquered their ego that has had total control over their life. When this occurs, this is when one is finally in total control of their life—not the power of the selfish and insatiable ego.

Knowing this, never allow yourself to be enslaved or intimidated by anyone, anything, or any circumstance when it comes to controlling your life, as there is always a better way. Know that and only allow thoughts to come to you that will light up your path to total peace and especially complete happiness. There is no one or nothing that can ever keep you from the happiness and the joy you have always been meant to enjoy. However, we simply allowed the external physical life to rule and take us over.

As I and most others have done and continue to do—even to this very moment—face your limitations, embrace them, master them, and do away with anything and everything in your life that will keep you from the totality of this inner power deep inside you; this magnificent gift with which that you came into this world.

I am willing to venture that you sensed that there is more to you than just your outer self (your ego), and that you finally have made a personal choice to control your life under your own power because of the mere fact that you picked up this book. Is it possible that you could achieve every desire you ever wanted, including conquering any adversity, illness, ailment, crisis, or any undesirable event you may possibly be having? Not only can you obtain it; it's already yours for the asking through the infinite intelligence that is also infinite energy that will never dissipate. Neither will you as you too are energy and, as such, will never dissipate.

Remember this well: Always allow your intuitive inner feelings to be your guide, as your intuitive feelings will dictate everything you do in your life. These intuitive feelings emanate from your all-knowing inner guide, which is one of the ways this all-knowing guidance communicates with you. Never forget this.

It is the wise person who knows deep within what feels right and who knows that it is their divine gift that lies deep within them—one's inner guidance—that is the real wise one. It is your inner guide that possesses the only key that opens the vault that contains your real treasures.

To know this gift completely is to feel every dominant thought for the good you want to experience until it is felt deep within the core of your being. Do not overwhelm yourself by wanting the totality of your conscious mind to open all at once; instead, allow it to open through one thought at a time that is transferred to your all-knowing inner guidance to bring forth for you to realize.

Allow me to emphasize that knowing something through a strong feeling coming from deep within one's inner self is not going to be much use unless one is willing to put the methods and answers being received into action. Unless and until one applies this knowledge to real use in their life (taking action), without hesitation or procrastination, the knowledge that has been brought to them would be incomplete and useless.

After all, the knowledge that is being given is to be applied by taking the action one's inner guidance has led them to take that may benefits all involved. Once the answer is received through a strong, intuitive feeling, taking action is the difference between succeeding and not succeeding in order to procure the desired results. I have known people who realized strong inner feelings that brought them the answers they were seeking yet failed to take any action whatsoever once the answer arrived. Therefore, the desired result was never achieved and they went on to experience the same undesirable condition they were seeking to rid themselves of. Their inaction allowed doubting, disbelief, and faulty thinking to impede achieving their deepest, innermost desires.

You must take the appropriate action regarding the answers and methods that are received from one's inner guidance, if you truly desire to achieve the results you wish to have materialized in your physical life. Taking or not taking action is the entire difference between gaining and losing a desired result and could possibly be the difference between living and succumbing to a life-threatening illness, should this be the case.

Taking no action once the feelings are coming from one's inner guidance is similar to getting dressed to go out but never getting in the car to drive oneself to their destination. This could also be likened to a batter in a baseball game coming to the plate to face the opposing team's pitcher and having no intent to even swing at the pitches delivered to him. The point being, one must take action if one is expecting the desired results to show up in their physical life. As C. S. Lewis once said, "Telling us to obey instinct is like telling us to obey 'people.' People say different things: so do instincts. Our instincts are at war... Each instinct, if you listen to it, will claim to be gratified at the expense of the rest."

Here is the dictionary's definition of this word *instinct*:

- "a natural or inherent aptitude, impulse, or capacity (had an instinct for the right word)";
- "a largely inheritable and unalterable tendency of an organism to make a complex and specific response to environmental stimuli without involving reason"; and
- "behavior that is mediated by reactions below the conscious level."

Now here is the dictionary's definition of the word *intuition*:

- power or faculty of attaining to direct knowledge or cognition without evident rational thought and inference; and
- faculty: ABILITY, POWER: as innate or acquired ability to act or do b: an inherent capability, power, or function.

Author Laurence Gonzales of *Deep Survival: Who Lives, Who Dies, and Why* quotes what a survivor is: "A survival situation brings out the true, underlying personality. Our survival kit is inside us."

In his *New York Times* best-selling book *The Survivors Club* by author Ben Sherwood, he describes *instinct* as follows:

> You have a remarkable gift that isn't learned or taught. You have the innate power of instinct and intuition. You don't need to think very hard-you don't panic or obsess-you act. Your inner feelings come naturally and automatically. You trust yourself to do what's necessary. Often you don't know why or how you make a particular decision. It just feels right. Sometimes you notice warning signals that other people miss. Again, it's not logical or intellectual. It's instinctive. In a crisis, you gain immediate insight into your challenge and know what to do. You sense when things aren't right and act on your hunches. In certain situations, you trust your instincts. You're attuned to everything around you. You see signs of danger before anyone else.

PREVAILING OVER INSURMOUNTABLE ODDS

Author Gavin de Becker, in his best-selling book *The Gift of Fear*, observes that the root of the word *intuition* comes from the Latin *tuere*, meaning "to guard, to protect." De Becker is one of the world's top experts on threat assessment and runs a successful firm that helps companies and individuals predict and manage violence. The cornerstone of safety and survival, he believes, is your intuition. He says, "Like every creature, you can know when you are in present danger. You have the gift of a brilliant internal guardian that stands ready to warn you of hazards and guide you through risky situations."

That said, I have no idea what C. S. Lewis was thinking about when he penned his opinion regarding instinct. However, what de Becker and Sherwood wrote sums up everything I have been telling you about that I had and continue to acknowledge through my inner intuitive guidance.

It should be noted that Mr. Sherwood's book was copyrighted in the year 2009. I began writing the initial draft for this book in 2006 and had no knowledge of Mr. Sherwood or Mr. de Becker until Mr. Sherwood's book came to my attention when Mr. Sherwood was a guest on a very well-known cable news program that I often view to keep abreast of current events.

Being realistic about the seriousness of life-threatening illnesses, I recognize the fact that it is very difficult for anyone who may be experiencing a serious prognosis of illness of any kind and at any stage to accept the suggestion that they need to begin to place their reliance in their inner guide when face to face with a very uncomfortable and threatening situation such as a life-ending illness. I too had the very same difficulty until I realized that my options at the time were limited to what I was being told by the medical professionals who were treating me. Frankly, I too did not want to listen to anything concerning inner anything. It wasn't until it finally came to me that I could leave my six-month-old son fatherless that I began to realize, if I was going to survive, it was going to be up to me to find a way.

I was finally able to fully comprehend what the medical professionals were telling me—modern medical science had done all that they knew to do for my serious condition, short of my accepting their recommended remedy for a possible remission. This was the critical turning point for me. It was either I find a way out of that mess or follow the medical doctors' recommendations for chemotherapy treatments.

Based upon my knowledge and knowing others who chose to follow their medical doctors' recommendations to go through chemotherapy treatments, witnessing the end results of those treatments and radiation treatments to which members of my own family elected to submit, there was no way I was going to go through that experience. Knowing the risk of making this decision, I decided to follow the strong feelings I was receiving that carried a very clear message to pass on the chemotherapy treatments and to seek other options. Of course, this decision was considered to be very dangerous. As I identified earlier, I even had people extremely upset with me, including members of my immediate family, all believing that my decision to forgo chemotherapy treatments was irresponsible and inconsiderate. However, despite very strong opposition against my decision to pass on chemotherapy treatments, I forged forward and proceeded down a less traveled path that I was led to by my all-knowing inner guidance.

I chose instead to stay with the deep conversations with this infinite intelligence and my own body commanding it to do what I wanted it to do and what results I knew that I had already achieved, despite not yet seeing it in the physical at that point in time. I refused to recognize that I ever had any debilitating disease in my entire body or to give it any thought whatsoever and rejected its very existence, went to work every day, treated my encounter with cancer as nothing more than a flu that was already cured, resumed business travel, got back into my business routine, and refused to discuss anything to do with this situation with anyone. Knowing that if I did, it would be like opening the locked door of a caged monster seeking to break out of its captivity with the intent of devouring me. I began martial arts training and adopted a regimen of discipline and mind-set associated with these disciplines. I literally became a vegetarian overnight and never looked back once I began on this path.

The primary discipline I follow every moment of my new and completely changed life is to heed my inner guidance's messages that are being continuously sent to me through deep inner feelings I sensed directing me to what I need to do in any given situation. I realize that you wish to rely upon family, medical providers, and others you trust—this is completely understandable and quite common. However, in conjunction with that, do not overlook yourself. Make absolutely sure that you strongly consider also relying upon yourself as well. Remember, this is your life and not someone else's.

Also keep in mind that many people give in to the opinions of others because they have had a long-term association with them, especially family members and providers of medical services. I did the very same thing, much to my regret.

There is nothing wrong with listening to the opinions of all those who are close to you and care what happens to you. However, taking yourself out of the decision-making process when it comes to what to do regarding the treatment of an eventual healing of any ailment, life-threatening illness, or life-changing event is an injustice to yourself, which is a luxury you certainly cannot afford in any situation. Therefore, you should seriously consider your own decision when it comes to these very important and serious matters.

Aside from highly recommended surgeries, patients also become subjected to variable prescription medications that are deemed necessary pertaining to certain medical conditions. Although initially necessary, most medications run their medically prescribed course, yet countless patients, over time, allow themselves to become heavily reliant on these prescribed medications. Unless and until a credible, duly licensed medical professional deems it absolutely necessary to continue any prescribed medication, individuals must seriously consider they themselves play the major decision-maker in their total recovery and healing of anything they have been treated for and should be knowledgeable about their medications.

For those who may not be informed, as I also identified earlier, the worldwide pharmaceutical industry is an enormous financial giant that has a tremendous appetite for profit, not unlike any megacorporation throughout the world. Therefore, it is in this industry's ongoing best interest to manufacture and sell as much legally prescribed medication they can—after all, they are a for-profit business like any other megamanufacturer worldwide. Now, this may not sit well with many, including medical providers, who rely heavily upon the pharmaceutical industry and/or anyone who may rely upon their income from the manufacture, production, distribution, and sale of prescription and nonprescription (over-the-counter) drugs and most likely find every inch of self-serving justification to support their cause. And why wouldn't they? This business generates billions of dollars in earnings a year worldwide anyway.

Medical science has its place in our society and does serve humanity well however, up to a certain point that is. As I also had stated, we are a worldwide mass of humankind that have become totally dependent upon—and many literally addicted—the innumerable drugs that are legally prescribed and have become so heavily dependent upon and overdrugged to the point of almost catastrophic and epidemic levels. If you aren't aware, you should, because of the fact that once a legally prescribed medication has run its prescribed course, instead of looking for substitute drugs from your medical providers, counselors, or pharmacist to rely upon, know that there is an alternative—your inner guidance that is one with infinite intelligence for healing of any level of adversity you may be experiencing.

This is not an attack on pharmaceutical corporations or medical science as they all do provide a very important service to humanity. The pharmaceutical community is not responsible for the number of prescriptions any medical provider may write on your behalf and is entitled to earn a profit from their respective legal industry. Keep in mind, this is all about you. It is you, not the pharmaceutical industry or your chosen medical providers, who must wean yourself off your continued utilization of artificial temporary-fix, feel-good drugs, which for the moment may mask any symptoms with which you may be suffering. You will also need to stop your dependencies on other people's opinions about your recovery, if they are not legally licensed medical providers, and do it now. If you are not a prescription drug–dependent person, then you certainly are miles ahead of many people who, quite unfortunately, are.

Although I have a certain level of respect for medical providers who genuinely wish to help those who are suffering from all types of nonphysical/physical illnesses, keep in mind that you are still relying upon another human being just like you. However, do not lose sight of the fact that humans are not without issues and problems and possibly even deeper than some of their patients because they are constantly exposed to people with deep emotional issues and chock-full of negativity. Therefore, it would be unfathomable, in my opinion, that they—being so exposed, could escape—over a period of time could find themselves becoming afflicted with a nonphysical and serious physical life-threatening illness.

I have no quarrel with legally prescribed medication that is used when treating life-threatening physical illnesses and certain psychological and psychiatric conditions that help people get through the various stages of their illness. However, I do disagree when dependency upon these medications become a dangerous addiction. They become crutches to the point of leaving a person almost totally helpless of ridding themselves of nonphysical and/or physical life-threatening illnesses because they have become so convinced that medication, counseling, etc., is the total answer and solution to their individual ailments. All medications should be discussed with your physician or medical provider regarding their continued dosage requirement, action, or effect.

There are many hazardous careers out there that people chose to pursue that physical risks. Those who choose these types of careers are usually very much aware of the hazards and risks and, therefore, are outside the circle of the majority of humanity. Quite remarkably, however, many who do choose these types of hazardous careers adjust to these harsh and dangerous environments and survive many years without developing a serious life-threatening illness or event. However, they are among a very small minority who do.

The nonphysical life-threatening illness for this condition I believe best fits this type of personality is denial—a psychological defense mechanism in which confrontation with a personal problem or with reality is avoided by denying the existence of the problem or reality. Sometimes people like me, in the past, chose to close their eyes or to turn their backs on the reality of a given situation knowing intuitively that their alternate choice may place them in a dangerous and/or extremely high risk situation that they may possibly come to regret at some later time.

Denial is among the most serious of the myriad of potentially harmful nonphysical illnesses to which one can be exposed in life.

Denial is a very sad condition to witness. Those in denial—like I was for far too many years—become absolutely convinced that what they are denying is a reality they either chose not to face or reject its existence altogether. The truth, however, surfaces eventually through one's inner feelings, and this is the point where the conflict between absolute truth and denial meets. An example of this is when there is a loss of someone close, either through death or leaving one's life.

For many people, the inability to accept the reality of either of these two situations becomes impossible for them to overcome because this is the mind-set in which they choose to stay.

It is also very sad when one has received information from a medical professional that they have contracted a very serious physical life-disruptive illness—or worse, a terminal illness—and given a projected period of time before their life would end due to the illness that has been diagnosed. I can easily relate to this example because I was among those who were given such a death sentence. Not only denial but a boatload of other emotions invade one's mind when hearing a diagnosis such as this.

Just having to deal with these emotions that practically seem to all hit at once is a monumental task in itself, not to mention having to also deal with the devastation, trauma, and fear instilled in the lives of those who care about the person having been diagnosed. Unless and until one chooses to take full control of their emotions and be able to become the rock for all others concerned at the same time, which I do admit is difficult to do—a situation like this can easily escalate and become uncontrollable. In my case, once I chose to accept the reality of what was staring me in the face, it was at that point that I stopped thinking of myself and focused on all those around me who were affected by this diagnosis. I realized that although I needed to find a way to overcome this situation, unless I could control others' emotions, it would become extremely difficult for me to be able to focus on overcoming my illness.

Envision a room full of mouse traps. Now picture each mouse trap with a ping-pong ball carefully placed on it where normally a piece of cheese or food would be placed for the purpose of luring a mouse or other pesky rodents. Now picture you are standing at the door of that room holding one ping-pong ball in your hand and you toss this ping-pong ball into the center of this room. The resulting action would begin a chain reaction on all the traps, set off by just this one action on your part, causing other ping-pong balls to be launched into the air, setting off almost all the other traps. This is the same reaction humans experience mentally when receiving devastating news, such as I have just described. In this example, to avoid such a chain reaction, do not throw the proverbial ping-pong ball into the room.

Therefore, to avoid an out-of-control emotional outburst from occurring when devastating news appears in your life, although easier said than done, you become captain of the ship who must take control of their situation, even though you're experiencing the life-threatening illness. Here is a prime example precisely where one's inner intuitive guidance comes into play. It is here where one's inner guide takes over and supplies the answers and methods needed to be able to take full control of the situation. Therefore, by doing so, you begin to immediately strengthen all those who are also affected by this disruption, who could have fallen totally apart otherwise.

I've heard people tell me, "But I do not think I would have the strength to handle this for others, let alone myself." My response to this is this: Yes you can. Even if you have to live with the physical discomfort for any period of time, unless you decide to take control of *what* and *how* you think and say to others, then you are right—you won't be able to handle that. And by doing so, you would cause substantial harm to others as well. It is not the person with the illness who needs to come up with the *how-tos*. The how-to comes when one turns the how-to over to their all-knowing inner guidance that knows exactly *how* and *what* to do.

Do you think I knew *how to* in my situation or do others in similar situations? Heck no. Most of us didn't. And if we were to state that we did, we would be lying and also be in denial of reality. Understand that fear grabs everyone by the throat when faced with a situation such as the diagnosis of a life-threatening illness. Having personally participated in this situation, anyone who tells you differently is not human, that's for sure. All sorts of thoughts run through one's mind when face to face with the unknown and the reality of such a situation. No counselor or medical professional has anything more at their disposal than what they learned and have been accustomed to saying to people suddenly introduced to such a condition in their lives, and they couldn't do any more than this, with the individual's families and others who care about them. So who can then? *You* can!

You are the only one who can bring calmness, peace, and assurance to all concerned and no one else. Why? Because if you are not in control of yourself, you certainly cannot expect others to be in control of themselves either! Do not depend upon your medical professionals for grief counseling. They are exposed to these conditions every day and some may become inured to all the emotional drama and trauma associated with serious illness situations. The responsibility falls right on the person with whatever the illness may be and not anyone else, not even a religious leader or group of religious people at your side—just you. The sooner you understand this reality, the sooner you can get on with the healing process. And remember, you are not alone because you have your all-knowing inner guidance that is one with infinite intelligence leading you every step of the way. You can take that to the bank and cash in on it!

I found that most books, written by the few cancer patients who published them, were based upon the word *hope*. As I identified earlier, I also could not help but notice that many cancer hospitals and treatment centers also express the word *hope* as a key motivator for overcoming cancer. As I also have previously stated, the word *hope* is among the words upon which people rely. Although I believe that this word carries with it a great deal of trust in the expectation of a complete healing and eventual total cure for those who chose to rely upon it; as for myself, however, I needed more, much more than just hope. I needed something definite and reliable, and I found it. There is no bigger proof than the fact I am still here.

I asked the people I've interviewed when doing my research for this book this very simple question about the word *hope*: Why do most people believe so strongly in the word *hope* when dealing with serious life-changing adversities? Most did not have a clue why. I found that most people will tolerate serious life-changing events and just *hope* that they will go away.

Many cancer treatment facilities also promote hope in their program as one of their remedies to assist with overcoming this life-threatening illness. I have heard people with serious illnesses state that they hope that the treatments they are undergoing will heal their illness and will go away. Yet they themselves appeared to be doing very little or absolutely nothing to help themselves and do not explore available alternatives for their healing and a possible permanent cure. I tell people who are dealing with a serious illness or life-changing event that have come into their physical lives, if they are relying on hope for an excuse for their reason not to take any action on their part, they are only sinking deeper and deeper into inaction, as apparently the word *hope* has a very strong hold on them.

As in my case with serious life-disrupting events, I neither focused on any of these conditions nor did I dwell on them. Instead, I focused on the cure and ridding myself of any thoughts that would allow me to think about the events I was facing at the time.

Surely one can always hope their conditions or situations will improve; however, by not taking specific and ongoing action to bring forth the desired result, hope alone just won't do it for you or anyone else, for that matter. It is the action you take that is the catalyst (a person or event that quickly causes change or action) that initiates the beginning of experiencing the result you are seeking. Hope, in my opinion, can work *against* you and *for* you, unless it is coupled with ongoing action on your part; without which hope is actually working against you and definitely not for you.

To expand on this further, how many times in your life thus far have you heard people say the word *hopefully*—hopefully this or hopefully that? I cannot begin to tell you how many times I've heard medical people say this word to their patients openly. As you can see, quite habitually, people use *hopefully* to replace the word *hope*. If you think about it, the word *hopefully* is an action word as opposed to the word *hope* which is a passive word. Therefore, how did this word *hopefully* go from being an action word to a passive word? It certainly appears that this has become a habitual trend among the majority of people.

My concern for you and all humankind is that people throughout this world will not permit the word *hope* to prevent them from taking the action they need to take. Therefore, by combining the word *hope* with taking action, then they become an extremely formidable team. Together, they join with calling upon the all-knowing inner guidance, connected with the infinite intelligence, to bring forth the desired results, for whatever it may be that one is desiring to secure for their highest good and for all concerned.

American editor Edgar Watson Howe (1853–1937) says it this way: "There is nothing so well known as that we should not expect something for nothing, but we all do and call it hope."

As a survivor of serious life-changing events, what I tell people who are so heavily reliant upon hope is that they need to take the bull by the horns, so to speak, and become an active participant in their own healing process of whatever it may be they are involved with, life-threatening or otherwise.

Among the reasons I have problems with the word *hope* is that most people depend on the use of this word and believe that by doing so, their situation may go away—e.g., "I hope things will be better soon"—which in itself is a denial that one will get rid of whatever they are "hoping" will disappear from their life. Here is another instance whereby hope is utilized to the point of nausea: "Prepare for the worst and hope for the best." This not only indicates disbelief but is evidence of passivity, as stagnation and denial are really saying that the situation being hoped for will not come out okay.

What you need to seriously consider is, if hoping may possibly describe what you may be doing about any life-altering adversity you may be aware of, then you need to wake up immediately and begin to take an active role in overcoming whatever it may be that is plaguing your life. Begin instead to believe in expectation and focus primarily on getting better and abandon just hoping the matter will go way. Hope is not belief or expectation of a healing or ridding of whatever is interfering with your life and keeping you from living the life you were meant to live.

In addition, in our culture, there is visible evidence everywhere of a limiting type of hope that people repeatedly verbalize outwardly or silently to themselves which has become almost (if not already) a habitual condition of the constant use of the word *hopefully*—e.g., "hopefully our flight will be on time"; "hopefully, the storm will not come this way and destroy our property"; "hopefully he or she will survive"; "hopefully the company will not close down leaving me without a job to support my family"; etc. And to show the dependency upon the word *hope*, many people will frequently and often unconsciously say "I hope." By utilizing the word *hope* in this manner, this stops most people from doing what they should and need to be doing; instead, take action and combine that process with complete trust, strong belief, and full expectation that whatever it is that is being hoped for has already been resolved and the results will materialize and not "hopefully" appear.

If there are circumstances, situations, or life-disrupting events in your life, whether it is a nonphysical or physical life-threatening condition, and you may be relying on the word *hope* in place of your lack of taking action or have become lethargic—then this hoping has taken a very strong hold on you and instead should be replaced with "I know"; "I expect"; "I am certain"; "I am confident"; and "I am already healed."

I am quite aware that I have been continuing with this subject of hope. However, the reason is because it has become an unnoticed epidemic among people who appear to rely and lean heavily on this word—which, as I identified, in itself is powerless. I realize there are skeptics who will not accept that an inner intuitive guidance exists that can lead them to the methods, answers, and solutions to the life-changing adversities in life. However, no one can honestly say that they have never sensed or felt within themselves a strong feeling (intuition) that is attempting to communicate with them. If you have yet discovered this in your life, then you need to take time to quiet your conscious mind and cease all busy thoughts that run through it. Just ask the infinite intelligence to provide you with the answers and methods you are seeking for something you need to resolve or desire for good, through the method I provide in this book. Even if it is not an illness or inevitable negative results, keep in mind that whatever you are asking this infinite guidance for is also for the highest good for all concerned and not just for yourself. Try it. What do you have to lose?

If you ask your infinite intelligence to bring you the answers and methods you need in order to resolve whatever is plaguing your life, realize and accept that you may not always get an immediate response. By exercising patience, you will find that, when you least expect it, the answers and methods will come to you. When they do, be certain to write them down; and as I also said, most importantly, be certain to act on the answers and methods swiftly, without hesitation or, worse, procrastination. If you do hesitate or delay, you can fully expect that your inner guidance will believe that you are no longer in need of what you have asked it to resolve for you and do nothing until you summon it again.

If you do doubt that this all-knowing intelligence cannot or will not bring forth what you ask of it for good and not evil, then you can rely upon the fact that, at that very instant, you will have nullified any chance for obtaining whatever it is you deeply desired to have manifest. Should this occur, your inner guide will not act on your behalf—unless and until you shed all doubt that it can.

Doubting, wavering, disbelief, and lack of patience are all negative actions that will nullify any desire asked of this infinite force. Therefore, you will have to begin again—this time, with firm belief and expectation, along with patience, deep emotion, and gratitude, thereby giving your inner power the opportunity to produce whatever it is you desire. Visioning and believing you already have received and in possession of whatever it is you want are primary keys to experiencing whatever you are seeking.

If you remember nothing else, remember what I just said here, as it is the golden key to whatever you desire to become reality for the highest good in your life—in other words, firm belief and expectation that you are taking the correct action to resolve your need.

There isn't a person alive who doesn't have direct access to the all-knowing inner guidance. The reason they do not access it is because they have chosen not to make it a part of their daily routine. People who are religious practice prayer every day all over the world. Similarly, beginning to talk to this infinite intelligence and asking it for the solution and methods for your needs, as long as they are for beneficial reasons for all concerned, shall begin to be made available over time. You will be totally amazed at the incredible power that your inner force has that carries out what is being desired for good that you may have possibly been ignoring.

PREVAILING OVER INSURMOUNTABLE ODDS

To my surprise, I have interviewed or have casually spoken to many people who never even realized that they possessed an inner resource able to direct their bodies to good health, rid themselves of undesirable events they may be having or desiring to avoid, and direct their lives in the right direction toward the attainment of their innermost desires.

Why is this so important? It is important because it is what you are telling yourself precisely what your life will be like. Instead of talking to yourself or grumbling about something that may be bothering you, keep in mind that whatever it is, you had a role to play in it. Seek instead your inner guidance and allow it to handle the matters concerning you and others.

If you would try this, beginning with just little things first, you will find that if you would trust and not waiver that your inner guide will respond in a beneficial way, it always does. Even if the answer you receive—be feeling or thought is not exactly what you wanted, follow it and do not kick it to the curb so fast. Why? Because the response you get is the beginning of something much, much better, if you will continue to trust your all-knowing inner guidance.

I have spoken with people who were ill who did not wish to even think about having a dialogue with this infinite intelligence. However, once they came to trust in their inner power, they began receiving beneficial information and methods they were seeking that neither they nor others had received from the outer world or those they trusted for advice. This is indicative of just another major contributor to the life-threatening nonphysical illnesses family—and a very serious one at that. People who may be trapped in this type of behavior, whether they realize it or not, need to be able to recognize this conduct before it reaches a critical stage in their lives.

Although I have no quarrel with board-certified and licensed psychologists, psychiatrists, or counselors; it has been my personal observation with my very own psychological problems and from speaking to many people who had also been aware of similar issues when it comes to healing these types of nonphysical illnesses. And in the final assessment, one has to take over full control of their situation, circumstance, illness, and/or life-changing event. I have found that the best way to do this is self-analysis—taking an inventory of oneself for the purpose of revealing the actions that precipitate the conditions with which they found themselves dealing.

Once one is willing to take this very important step and commit to it, they will begin to find that they can consequently be able to clearly see for themselves a number of reasons why these situations entered their life in the first place. Coupled with their willingness to seek out their all-knowing inner guidance, they will have the opportunity to receive the methods they need to bring their situations and circumstances under their total control, followed by an eventual resolution of the matter with which needs dealing.

In my dealing with the numerous nonphysical illnesses I had to resolve, and my observance of others who had similar or much greater nonphysical illnesses, the methods needed to resolve and to rid myself of these illnesses came much earlier than any counseling could possibly ever achieve—and, might I add, at no out-of-pocket expense for counseling, rehab center, or medication of any type.

These were the preliminary steps that I use in overcoming not only my life-threatening physical illnesses but those that affect my critical nonphysical illnesses as well. What you learned up to this point is precisely how I rid myself of all these conditions. I realize that you may possibly find this to be far removed from the ordinary, and you are correct in thinking that way. However, what I did and others also have done to recover from serious illnesses, is not ordinary or mainstream—far from it.

Do you honestly believe going against medical advice and opting to travel on another less traveled path is what most people and medical science consider as normal or ordinary? Hardly! If what I did and what others who had experienced a serious life-changing event have done—utilizing viable alternative options at our disposal—was considered normal, then of course, like following medical science's answer to a possible healing, everyone would be doing it now, wouldn't they?

The primary reason people do not choose to select an alternative path in conjunction with medical science's proposed remedies is primarily due to their lack of knowledge, in addition to being easily influenced by their peers others and the medical community and their fear of the unknown. However, the unknown exists regardless of which path one chooses when having to deal with a catastrophic illness. Think about it!

What I can tell you is that I and others were confident enough to not only question mainstream medical science's remedies for healing but also fully trust what was being felt internally and intuitively to be the correct path to follow toward a permanent healing. There is not a soul alive that can possibly challenge anyone's decision to trust the inner guidance and intuition because the choice to follow the inner intuitive guidance proved to me, without any doubt, to be the right decision, considering I am alive and well and continue to share this experiences with this infinite intelligence connected to one's inner intuitive guidance with all those who are willing to at least listen with an open mind. The only thing hard about it is what one chooses to make difficult for themselves. After all, there has been no suggestion in this book that tells anyone to abandon their medical professionals—quite the contrary—yet there are a myriad of medical professionals who would not recommend that their patients even consider anything other than what modern medical science has to offer when it comes to the healing of life-threatening or any type of illnesses.

Notice I mention the word *healing*, not *curing*. The reason for this is that medical science cannot offer a remedy for a permanent cure. But your inner guidance, connected with infinite intelligence, contains many methods, answers, and solutions that can be utilized in conjunction with medical science as an alternative approach for healing, if trusted fully without doubting or wavering.

As I've identified, I was told that without chemotherapy treatments, my survival chances were minimal at best. Yet I am still here despite having refused these treatments. Why? I am thoroughly convinced I am here for the reasons I have previously outlined and because my inner guidance led me to the path that indicated how I was going to accomplish that feat.

I am also convinced that numerous survivors of serious life-challenging illnesses and other life-disruptive events also survived their ordeals because they too had drawn from something extremely deep within themselves, consciously or unconsciously, in order to have been able to survive what may have been deemed as virtually inconceivable to survive. So then how did they? If these people survived, others can too, despite of others' opinions because this is precisely what they are—opinions, a generally held view.

This is not meant to be an offensive remark toward anyone or any licensed medical or other credible professionals; instead, I am only meant to make an important point. That point is that no one on earth can possibly state to you that anything is impossible. So by what provable, credible knowledge by which this impossible or "not likely" verdict is supported? People do survive the so-called impossible and/or improbable, and I for one am living proof of this fact.

Man walked on the moon, and there are many other examples of what was once considered to be impossible, not likely, inconceivable, etc., that have occurred, including survivors of some of the deadliest illnesses and crises known to mankind. Therefore, what I have stated is virtually unchallengeable, unless and until modern science can disprove—beyond any reasonable doubt—the existence of a person's all-knowing inner guidance, which is connected with infinite intelligence.

Although not included in the previously listed life-threatening nonphysical illnesses, I consider attitudes by others who openly use such word as *impossible, not likely, inconceivable*, etc., in the doubting family to be among those who belong to skeptics who, as I had also stated, are themselves exposed to nonphysical illnesses such as exemplified by the usage of these types of words and attitudes on a continuous basis. Skepticism in itself is a serious nonphysical illness. I should know—I used to be a skeptic.

Diseases do not emanate first from a healthy cell or millions of healthy cells in the body going haywire. Instead, it does just the opposite—they begin by becoming unhealthy. I believe that nonphysical ailments play a role or serve as a trigger so that these absolutely normal cells turn from healthy to eventual life-threatening cells. Ongoing stress, anxiety, depression, etc., sustained continuously over time will eventually show up as a serious ailment and can escalate, unless these harmful, life-changing nonphysical events are eradicated.

Therefore, the key to taking back control of your life is to first follow your intuitive guidance that is constantly speaking to you.

Fully commit yourself that you shall never again allow anyone or anything to interfere with your right to control your life.

I know for a fact that the reason I became very ill was emotionally at first, followed by two life-taking illnesses was primarily due to my inability to stop allowing others to control me, which is known as codependency—"a psychological condition or a relationship in which a person is controlled or manipulated by another who is affected with a pathological condition such as an addiction to alcohol or heroin"; "dependence on the needs of or control by another"—and my refusal to listen to my inner guide. Had I listened to my inner guide long before becoming physically ill, I truly am convinced, beyond any doubt, that I would have avoided cancer entirely and had been able to rid myself of any life-threatening illness or related undesirable events that had plagued my life.

I trust that this thumbnail sketch gives you a fairly good look at just how people can and do attract nonphysical illnesses leading to life-threatening physical illnesses. Of course, there are countless more examples that can be listed, some of which you probably know about.

We proceed now to explore the factors that most people use unconsciously that enhances a lack of self-confidence and self-trust. When allowed to continue, they open the door to numerous undesirable conditions.

16

TRUSTING IN EVERYTHING AND EVERYONE BUT OURSELVES

It was not until I finally learned to trust myself and begin to listen—I mean, *really* listen—to the voice most of us hear continuously that comes from deep within us all, which many people and religions refer to as the soul, that everything for good began turning around for me.

Surviving anything like a life-threatening illness begins and ends with trusting yourself. Trusting what you may be asking yourself? Okay, let's begin with some examples. It is far beyond my understanding and baffles me that people will place their entire trust in climbing the highest and most dangerous mountains in the world relying on nothing more than their gear, climbing expertise, and an experienced guide. Even with all this as their false security, they could very well meet with misfortune and may perish without other climbers to help ensure their survival. However, when it comes to trusting that one can overcome and survive a life-changing or life-threatening illness, well, that is an entirely different matter now, isn't it?

I have personally witnessed a number of people who, when told that their illness was very serious and may even possibly get much worse, they opted instead to place their complete trust in what they heard and learned from others, instead of trusting that they had the inner power to help overcome their illness or adverse circumstances—these included medical professionals—and the result of which was that they indeed got much worse. And today, most of the people whom I knew are no longer among us. Cemeteries across the world are full of people who made the decision to trust everyone and everything other than themselves and if they had, many of who would possibly still have been here today. I realize that this statement will be challenged. However, it is not only I who may to be challenged; instead, it is all the survivors of any serious life-threatening illnesses or events who were told that they would not survive and to get their affairs in order.

Most people diagnosed with a serious illness can live longer than predicted, if they only would believe it and envision themselves actually living beyond any life expiration date given to them by medical science that they accept as fact and then begin to live and act out that thought. I don't know what is worse—those who put that thought in their mind or those who actually accept that thought in the first place. Each and every one of us forget that our being here in the first place was nothing short of a miracle. Yet do we consider ourselves a miracle? The majority of us don't! We are far too busy surviving day-to-day challenges now, aren't we? And what do we trust primarily? We trust in our ability to earn that dollar and climb the familiar material-gains ladder to success.

Oh yes, we are very, very good at the "survival of the fittest" game. We have all the self-trust and self-confidence when it comes to winning at this game at any cost, especially matters of money. Yet when it comes to the survival of a life-changing illness or event, it's an entirely different matter now, isn't it? We are no longer so self-confident and self-trusting, are we? And in almost the blink of an eye, most people who first hear such a diagnosis are instantly transformed into very weak and extremely humble dependent specimens who, just days prior, were full to the brim with self-confidence, self-trust and, for some, arrogance. Of course, no one likes to hear this about themselves being that way.

However, for most people, the all-too-familiar rat race is all life seems to be about. Per Wikipedia, a rat race "is an endless, self-defeating, or pointless pursuit. It conjures up the image of the futile efforts of a lab rat trying to escape while running around a maze or in a wheel." I should know, as I too was once very much caught up in that contest—so much so, that I was relentless when it came to being the very best I could be and to gain as much material assets and toys as possible while I could. Was I unique in this regard? No!

The majority of people in the business world now, and long before us, were doing the very same thing. This doesn't pardon those who are not in that highly competitive world, not by any stretch of one's imagination. Those who are not involved in the dog-eat-dog business world are just as guilty of the very same thing. ("If a situation is dog eat dog, people will do anything to be successful, even if what they do harms other people. In show business it's dog eat dog—one day you're a star, the next you've been replaced by younger talent" [*The Free Dictionary*].)

Has the mirror finally exposed the reality of what I just depicted? Only a handful of people worldwide are the exception. Those are the ones who already have and/or who very possibly will survive a life-threatening illness and/or life-changing event.

Understand this: once we are visited by a severely damaging illness, physical or nonphysical, we can either choose to place all our confidence in others or realize the reality of the matter. When everyone has rendered their opinions, professional or otherwise, it is you who is going to be alone with the illness or circumstance threatening your life. Therefore, how you choose to deal with it will be the determinant that will place you either on or off the path to overcoming and an eventual total healing.

"Physician, heal thyself" is a phrase that alludes to the readiness and ability of physicians to heal sickness in others while sometimes not being able or willing to heal themselves. This also suggests that physicians, while often being able to help the sick, cannot always do so and, when sick themselves, are at no better place than anyone else and in fact may not even identify that they are ill or need help. Another phrase suggests something about the cobbler, which "always wears the worst shoes—that is, cobblers are too poor and busy to attend to their own footwear." These phrases hit the nail directly on the head.

I cannot emphasize this point enough. Unless you are willing to make every attempt to heal yourself, no matter how much medical or other attention you presently are receiving or may receive in the future, it will do you little good if you do not become an active participant in the healing process. The body and its cells, which contain memory, respond to whatever instructions given to it through the all-knowing inner guidance. If you tell it something for its good and completely trust in what you habitually and repetitively command it to do, the body can eventually respond accordingly. However, many people allow themselves to continue absorbing negative messages, pity statements, doomsday medical diagnoses, unfavorable medical statistics, and the like or permit themselves to be surrounded continuously by what I call "people in the premourning stage," if an illness is in the critical stages. These and other self-induced conditions open one to receiving the perfect storm by not being able to overcome or to effect a permanent healing for whatever is threatening one's life.

I realize that this is a lot to absorb and accept; however, ask yourself this question—"What are the alternatives?" As I said before, do not abandon any credible medical treatments; instead, combine them with the complete understanding and self-trust that medical science, prescribed medications, credible professional counseling, and the like are not the total answer to a complete healing. You are!

If you are a Christian and believe in the Bible, Jewish and believe in the Torah, or whichever you may have faith in, do not abandon your beliefs; combine them with complete trust in yourself first and, above all, total confidence in your all-knowing inner guidance. Your inner guide is not connected to any religion originated by man but is your life's gift given you at birth by an unseen, nameless force much more powerful than any religion or man that simply cannot be claimed as belonging to any one system of worship.

By combining the previously outlined power words, *faith* and *hope*, with any religious belief you may have with your all-knowing inner guidance, you will have created an unstoppable force. A power that can remove every obstacle preventing you from overcoming and eventually totally conquering your affliction or any undesirable event that may be plaguing your life. Believe it, become it, and, like your faith in anything in reality, commit to it totally without any doubting whatsoever. This all-knowing inner guidance is your connection to an indisputable, powerful, unseen power. It takes commands received by way of your dominant thoughts, for the benefits you wish to produce that are contained in your conscious mind, unless instructed by you otherwise. This means that every time you have a dominant thought or inner vision, your all-knowing inner guide is always prepared, listening and ready to act on your dominant thoughts.

Another important fact to keep in mind that most people fail to realize and accept is the fact that absolutely nothing is forever. This holds true for relationships, careers, suffering and pain, financial wealth, excellent health, fame and fortune, material possessions, nature, and, oh yes, one's *natural* youthful looks. (Please note that I emphasized the word *natural*.) Yet all of us seem to believe that these things will go on forever.

You've probably heard this phrase "what you focus on continuously, with strong feeling, steadfast belief, and expectation will eventually come about, good or bad" before. Instead of dwelling on the bad, only focus on the good and the possible, as though it has already materialized in your life. There are literally scores of material written on this subject. It is not new, and I am not the first or claim to have brought this to your attention either. However, I am among those who experienced back-to-back life-threatening illnesses and numerous life-threatening nonphysical conditions and events who did survive and can attest that this is not a theory but a fact and a reality and absolutely works for those who choose to believe it will for them as well.

How do I know this to be a fact? Because I actually lived it, and I still do to this very day. It is still working for me, and I am thoroughly convinced that it always will and can for you as well. I truly believe most people would probably not have survived the very serious life-threatening adversities, events, and circumstances that simultaneously appeared in my life that I overcame, despite the odds, against my being able to overcome them. Why do I say this? Because I have personally witnessed many people who, instead of believing that they could overcome a serious life-damaging adversity or even a nonphysical condition, just gave up and allowed whatever misfortune they were concerned with to consume them mentally and physically.

The Attacks Will Never Cease Unless You Choose to End Them

As for me, I decided to end the attacks I was plagued with. I knew that if I continued on my present path, I would continue to be attacked by more adversities. Just realizing that the result of having allowed these life-threatening nonphysical illnesses into my life and to remain there, which ultimately brought about a number of life-threatening physical illnesses, was reason enough to make the decision to take a much higher road and set out on an altogether different path—the path that my all-knowing inner guide had been leading me to all along.

Today, I am free of each and every serious life-changing condition I was assailed by, and yes, for each one, I sought out medical professionals to aid me medically. The mistake I made, however, was that I had totally forgotten about my gift of inner guidance and finally realizing that the only one who could heal me was *me*. Although grateful for advancement in medical science my medical providers had at their disposal at the time, I came to the realization that medical science could not guarantee my survival—or, for that matter, offer a permanent cure—but I knew *I could* through my all-knowing inner guidance connected with the infinite intelligence.

Some people may believe that I was the exception in overcoming these serious nonphysical, life-destructive illnesses and that the odds are far too great against most people ever surviving illnesses I endured at the time and that those who did was a result of medical science's intervention and knowledge and nothing more. If you are in agreement, know that nothing could be further from the truth. I elected to go through two very traumatic surgical procedures, and prior to each surgery, I was required to sign a lengthy statement stating that, in general, there was absolutely no guarantee I would even survive either surgical intervention, let alone that the surgery would be successful at all for completely eradicating the cancer sites in my body.

I am confident and convinced that I healed myself of a number of life-altering events like others who also overcame and obtained a complete healing from their ordeals by also combining medical science and their total confidence in themselves that a complete healing from within is not only possible but definitely achievable. I further believe that future generations will adapt to their inner guidance and realize that they can heal themselves from any serious illness as they *finally* come to discover that it is they—who believe in the healing power of their inner guidance that is one with infinite intelligence and who also participate with medical science for the real answer—can bring forth a permanent healing of any serious life-changing event. Do you recall this saying I identified to you earlier, "Physician, heal thyself"? The question becomes as follows: How many physicians and people really do place all their faith and trust in medical science to come up with a complete cure for a particular illness instead of realizing that it is they themselves who are the cure?

This brings us full circle to what I identified earlier that is going on in this country right now. It was not too long ago that Americans were prospering and living the great American Dream which has appeared to have disappeared: Most people were employed, the greater majority of middle America owned a home, two cars or more in every driveway, could afford gas, food and clothing were at affordable prices, banks and finance companies were lending to people and small and new businesses, home mortgages were available and affordable. Most people had at least one, if not more, credit cards; retail sales and the economy and unemployment rate were stable; small business owners were enjoying profitable business and hiring new employees; corporations' employment levels were on the rise and everything appeared—on the surface, anyway—to be doing just fine; and government was not micromanaging American businesses and entrepreneurs and prying into private citizens' affairs.

Then all hell broke loose somewhere around late 2007, and this country's economy began taking a turn for the worse—much worse than anticipated. I have no intent to venture into the depths of the financial situations that have invaded and continue to disturb the good people of this country as this subject alone is best left to economic and related experts to deal with. I believe that the everyday reality of life in this country today is more than enough for people to have to understand, knowing the truth and gravity of their very own situations and what they are becoming aware of.

The common denominator among all people—rich, middle class, or poor—is that absolutely no one has been able to escape the repercussions and reality of the fact that this country is having one of its worst economic crises ever in history and people's lives everywhere are being destroyed because of it. The majority of those who have become affected by this massive economic nightmare are hopelessly watching practically everything they had worked for all their lives slipping away. This not only includes assets; but it also encompasses the loss of small businesses, medical coverage, millions of jobs, economic stability; families being torn apart; anxiety, fear, depression, blame, feelings of hopelessness; and many other real-life circumstances that literally came into their lives practically overnight. One day people woke up, ready to begin their routines as usual, only to learn that hundreds of thousands of people were literally losing their homes to foreclosures and their jobs almost simultaneously.

People all over this country are literally panicking and have lost trust in their government and their financial institutions. Like being in a dense fog, people are figuratively wandering aimlessly, not knowing in which direction they are headed, as day by day the economic situation seems to get worse with no apparent end in sight. What was once known as confidence and stability has rapidly turned into confusion and uncertainty. What this ultimately leads to is a myriad of life-changing events showing up in people's lives, which could lead to a life-threatening nonphysical condition that, if left to grow, could eventually lead to inevitable, grim physical consequences and real illness.

This is where the true test emerges. In a situation that is skating dangerously close to the events that people faced during the Great Depression era is where you will have to rediscover your inner guidance and know that although you did not create these events, you alone cannot turn it around on a dime either. What you can do, however, is to remove the real you from the entire fiasco as though it has never happened. So what do I mean by this?

For far too many years people have allowed themselves to be controlled by others. They allowed others to tell them what they were worth; how far they could advance in their lifetime based upon "set in stone" societal standards; how their educational level dictated their ranking in society and what they would amount to; what types of diseases they may have that transform their lives because certain members on their family tree had several generations previously; and that they were certain to age, grow old, and then then wither away in their sixties or, if they were so fortunate, age ninety—and they believed it. And quite unfortunately for countless others today, they *still* believe it! The sad thing about all this is that humanity actually bought into it—most still do.

Now, here you are, possibly facing the worst financial mess in the history of this country (and the entire world), and what are you doing about it? Well, many people are melting down, giving in and giving up, and have chosen to rely upon the federal government to bail them out of their dilemma by chasing innumerable entitlement programs of every possible kind and looking everywhere and anywhere for help instead of looking deep within themselves for the answers, methods, and solutions they need to climb out of the dark pit in which they are finding themselves.

I once was told by a former owner of a small company I was working for when I was very young to "look down at my shoes" when I asked the owner of this small company about my future with his company. The person who said this to me was a seasoned self-made entrepreneur who, at the time, was around the young age of eighty-two. What he meant by this statement was that the only security I would ever have as long as I was still breathing could only be found in my own shoes. How right and how big that statement became as the years passed!

Many people in this country have been and continue to be heavily reliant and dependent upon others, especially the government for their livelihood, their mortgage payment, car payment, utility bill payments, clothes, food, children's education, and almost every basic necessity imaginable. As this dependency became rooted in people, many began to become even more reliant upon government—local, state and federal—which became the greatest stranglehold placed upon them. To add to this dependency issue, the concern and burden continues to be immense when they must take care of their family financially and are saddled with the expectations of meeting the needs and wants of everyone but themselves, under very stressful conditions.

Then one day the economic crisis hit their lives. This crisis ranged from the company they had worked for most of their lives suddenly closing, and *poof!* There goes that long time job. Along with it, possibly, their perceived retirement income at an age where they are virtually close to being unemployable was also gone. In addition to the loss of their homes, some lost their marriages and everything they worked for and had spent a great deal of their productive years building for what they believed was their future, not to even mention any health insurance benefits they may have had for themselves and their families.

It is right here at this point where the medical science community is acutely aware that such disastrous circumstances will certainly eventually create a flood of people heading straight for their doors, seeking relief. This relief could be in the form of all sorts of counseling—psychiatric or psychological—and medication to ease the conditions of stress, anxiety, depression, and feelings of hopelessness and a boatload of other emotional symptoms.

Recently, on a very well-known cable news program, a medical professional made a public statement stating that due to the restrictions of his overwhelming current patient load, if he had more time to spend with his patients, he would prefer to first counsel them pertaining to prevention, among other issues he shared with the news commentator. (This is not word for word but close to it.) This is interesting because controlling, preventing, and overcoming serious life-changing events and avoiding the causes of life-threatening illnesses should be an integral component of medical care.

The root cause of practically every type of life-threatening condition and illness—physical, mental, or otherwise—is not necessarily the environment in which one lives, caused by air pollution by manufacturers, automobile emissions, or other pollutants that go into the atmosphere. And neither is it any particular work environment, a hereditary issue, fate, just plain bad luck, etc., as we have been led to believe for years, although some of this may possibly be a contributing factor but certainly not the sole root cause. Many root causes stem from nonphysical life-changing illnesses and events and could prevent further damage, if identified and treated early.

It is important for you to understand that what you and most people are seeking are answers, methods, and solutions to questions concerning any adversities you may be subjected to or may possibly develop. Not one of us on this planet, including all those who came before us, has or ever had all the answers, methods, or solutions to resolving life's adversities. The real question then becomes "What is it that we are exactly seeking? Why didn't those before us have the answers, methods, and solutions to what we are seeking to find?"

What most people are looking for is the answer to what will bring to their lives total peace, perfect health, wealth and prosperity on every level, and, above all, happiness because all of us are what I like to label "temporaries"—meaning, "lasting for a limited time." Rarely in anyone's life are we truly satisfied for any length of time with most things that come into our lives before; and one day we become disenchanted, bored, or feel a need to fill some void that we believe will bring us a sense of fulfillment—be it a new career, new car, new relationship, new accomplishments, continued education, travel, changing our appearance, environment, spouse, significant other, etc. (better identified as the insatiable appetite of the ego)—for continued gratification.

Why? Because for some inexplicable reason, we never seem to be quite there yet—wherever *there* means to anyone individually—as not one of us is the same in any way. But as much as some may wish to reject the idea, we are all connected—believe it—because we are!

The answer to all this can only be found in one place, and that place is within each and every one of us. All the answers, methods, and solutions one is seeking for their life for good can only be found through one's inner guidance that is one with infinite intelligence, without which one will continue seeking through their outer world or their conscious mind, which, at best, is an effort in futility.

We can go on for a lifetime and never find what we truly are seeking. However, if we would just wake up, we will find that all the answers, methods, and solutions needed and being sought can be found within the all-knowing inner guidance I have been describing. Unless you choose to make the decision to at least make contact with it, you more than likely could spend a lifetime seeking what continues to elude you. Compare this to a beachcomber seeking treasures in the sand who, for years and years, seek in this manner, for his effort could only find just a mere few treasures. None of which could or would sustain his hunger, hoping that one day he will finally find that hidden treasure that had eluded him for years that he believes would fulfill his life's dream. Ask yourself this question: "Is this how you too choose to continue living your life?" I don't believe your answer could possibly be *yes*, unless you choose to live a mediocre, unfulfilled life. Your life is like a menu—you literally order what you want to experience.

Let's now look at the most abused word of all as it relates to life-threatening illnesses and events that just seem to appear one day in our lives, and when they do, we are so quick to label ourselves as a *victim*. Let's take a closer look at this word.

Victim, as defined by *Merriam-Webster*, is "one that is injured, destroyed, or sacrificed under any of various conditions [a victim of cancer]"; or "one that is subjected to oppression, hardship, or mistreatment." This subject of being a victim can and often does draw a tremendous amount of pain into the lives of people, families, and others concerned who are legitimate victims of crime, abuse, and any number of serious events, including murders, violent crimes, rape, etc.

For the purpose of these observations, however, the word *victim* is confined to serious life-changing events and not those having to do with any other subjects outside the scope of these issues. There are many people throughout the world who have been characterized as legitimate victims—e.g., casualties of senseless wars and oppression beyond what mere words could never possibly attempt to describe man's inhumanity to man—which continues to exist to this very day throughout the world. However, this is a subject for the experts who know much more than I do pertaining to that type of victimization and also that having to do with every level of discrimination and abuse.

That said, let's take a look closer at what I believe to be a very important matter concerning nonphysical illnesses and life-threatening physical conditions and events either occurring or waiting in the wings to materialize at the invitation of the recipient, which many people prefer to label as being victimized.

When speaking to numerous people over the years, I discovered generally shared impressions in those who were suffering from life-transforming illnesses and events and those about to cross the line from a potentially serious nonphysical illness to a life-threatening physical illness. I also found that the common denominator among them is that each and every one I had spoken to, with the exception of a handful, consider themselves to be victims having lost their homes, jobs, savings, valued relationships, pensions, hard-earned assets, etc., resulting from, according to them, an unforeseen, out-of-control, downward-spiraling economy.

The majority of those I have spoken with openly displayed an "it is not my fault" attitude in addition to the "I am not responsible for whatever problem at the time" mind-set. My response to this is that aside from the types of victimization I just outlined, assumed victimization has to do with any nonphysical life-disturbing events (refer to the chart of nonphysical life-threatening illnesses provided earlier). Therefore, if one is unwilling to take personal responsibility for their role in contributing to a life-changing event coming into their lives, they will continue to remain and believe they were and/or are a victim. Nothing can be further from reality.

Rarely can anything successfully substitute for one's personal experience, regardless of the subject. I am referring specifically to physical and nonphysical life-challenging conditions, events, and illnesses. I have met and interviewed my share of so called victims who had these types of conditions, and even to this very day, I continue to run into people who have yet to realize a life-disrupting physical illness but who openly demonstrate their "victim role" quite unconsciously and quite remarkably—to me, anyway—has been allowed to become a permanent part of their everyday lives.

Why is this so easy for me to recognize? Because at one time in my life, I too had considered myself a victim of adversities I experienced. Therefore, I see the reflection of my former self in those who consider themselves a victim of whatever it may be that they certainly played a role in having shown up in their life.

The big cousin to victimization is self-pity. I am prepared to take a great deal of flack on this one from those who have yet to recognize themselves playing the victim role when it applies to nonphysical illnesses. Yes, there are many who became victims of a disastrous event related to an automobile accident, an airliner going down, a sports-related accident, a brain injury caused by any number of occurrences, and the like. However, when it comes to life-altering nonphysical illnesses, this is a completely different matter altogether. Most, if not all, life-threatening nonphysical illnesses that I identified earlier are controllable by those developing them. Any credible psychologist, psychiatrist, and experienced, qualified, licensed counselors and also medical doctors just may agree.

Self-pity rates high among life-threatening nonphysical illnesses and among the most addictive. Self-pity allows the so-labeled victim to obtain temporary relief, thereby separating them from reality. Self-pity is self-validation in action.

What I have noticed that stands out in many people who are afflicted with an ailment is that they have convinced themselves that they have limited and even seemingly no control over their life. They are easy to identify because they are continuously feeling sorry for themselves. Some even reach the point of paranoia believing that everyone everywhere is against them, thereby constructing a mental box that they are unable to get out of and driving them even deeper into self-pity and, worse, becoming deeply depressed.

Once one reaches this state of mind, they become reliant for help on those close to them and others who may be concerned about them. This is a normal reaction; however, at best, it can only offer temporary relief because those being relied upon—other than immediate family members—sooner or later begin to detach themselves because it eventually becomes a full-time effort on their behalf.

Self-pity has another side effect—the false relief one feels when choosing to sidestep taking personal responsibility. They believe that they are not required to do anything about their self-induced condition or have to take any action whatsoever on their own behalf, thereby avoiding taking any accountability for their own lives and discarding a serious effort on their part to rid themselves of the ailment or making the tough decision to do so. Instead, they prefer to take the easy way out by ignoring any action to take control over their lives.

What this mind-set really boils down to is that those who are stuck in the world of self-pity need to make the choice to terminate it and end it immediately before their condition turns into something much worse that can possibly lead to eventually developing an "it's no use" attitude, which can possibly manifest into suicidal tendencies and an untimely death. It can get that serious. This, of course, is not a medical opinion by any stretch of the imagination, as I am not a medical professional but a personal observation from my own contact with numerous people with this condition. I have known members of my very own family who chose to take this path.

So what should you do? For openers, choose a much different mind-set, one that begins with a "yes I can" attitude. No, it's not easy. However, the alternative can be devastating, not only to those choosing the self-pity path but to each and every one who truly cares about them. Yes, I am aware that it is easier said than done. Why? When someone is deep into the "victim and self-pity" stage and has become comfortable right where they are, considering that they may be getting a lot of attention from others, they do not have any reason for having any incentive to change their now habitual behavior. In other words, why change when getting all the attention and validation justify their self-induced state of mind? Yes, I said *self-induced*; it's a behavior that people adopt when they do not want to do what is necessary to rid themselves of this state of mind. Self-pity is a dangerous illness and state of mind because it can—and often does—reach levels of blaming others for a condition and can grow even to reach a level of seeking revenge over others believed to have harmed or caused the condition to materialize in the person's life.

In my considered opinion as one who has gone down this path, all the advice available to anyone on what to do in order to change their mind-set and turn it around and head in a positive direction is absolutely useless. Why? Because the only voice the person who has this condition absolutely must listen to first and foremost is that of their very own all-knowing inner guide speaking to them continuously. This requires calm to quiet their mind and allow the right instructions, methods, and answers attempting to get through to lead anyone to how they can rid themselves of these horrid conditions.

Rarely, if ever, does one who is subjected to either or both of these conditions simultaneously come out of it through their dependence upon others who are simply being kind and thoughtful. However, those being relied upon are unknowingly reinforcing this behavior, which can—and often does—become a form of addiction.

I believe that neither of these conditions is ever permanently healed through prescribed medications or alternative treatments alone because drugs were never meant to be a total cure for such conditions and alternative treatments have not yet been able to make any acceptable, credible claim to reverse these disorders as well. This statement will, of course, raise some eyebrows; however, it is not meant to offend or accuse. I instead only want to state the reality of this matter since the healing process begins and ends first and foremost with the individual. If not, then reliance upon other people, counseling, medical science, or alternative treatments will eventually only prove to be a great disappointment, not to mention a good deal of out-of-pocket expense resulting in little, if any, significant results over a long period of time.

Further on, you will find that I discuss blaming and why we all must take responsibility for our own lives. This includes spouses, offspring, siblings, close relatives, friends, acquaintances, etc. When we choose to finally become able to clearly see this, then—and only then—will anyone having either or both of these two serious conditions, victimization and self-pity, finally be able to begin the recovery process.

Blaming others for our problems, circumstances, and events that we have recently in the past or may be personally involved with at the moment creates an extremely damaging situation. Examples of this include the possible destruction of a marriage, dividing an entire family, pushing away friends, isolating coworkers and acquaintances and the closest people to one who had valued their loyalty, etc. It can also literally disintegrate dreams, goals, and even ambitions, as well as destroy achievements.

Now let's take a very brief look at another very interesting sentiment that most people know but seldom embrace with any depth of sincerity and, most of all, longevity. From my personal knowledge—once again observing many people who have dodged a bullet, so to speak, by overcoming a very serious life-changing illness or event—the reaction that follows has either been taken lightly or became an extremely important part of one's everyday life.

I am firmly convinced that when this deep emotion is found to be absent in one's life that any level of recovery from any serious life-threatening illness or life-changing event will be short-lived. Not only do I firmly believe this, I've witnessed it with my own eyes on numerous occasions in many different environments. What I am talking about is gratitude—"the state of being grateful" or "thankfulness: conscious of benefit received, for what we are about to receive make us truly thankful," per *Merriam-Webster*.

Thankfulness—what a concept! I can tell you that not only I but you as well have possibly witnessed and have been around people who were very fortunate in many areas of their life, ranging from business and personal successes, to overcoming some of the most serious life-threatening illness, events, ailments, and life-changing events known to man. People who seemingly—rarely, if ever—know how truly thankful or grateful they were for their good fortune. How sad it is to have had or still have to witness in the modern day all the financially well off among humanity who appear to have it all yet turn to greed instead of gratitude and benevolence for and with their fortunes. These are the folks I call "self-appeasers" who, instead of appreciating their successes, cannot wait until they reach their next level of financial conquest at whatever cost, including at the expense and harm of others along the way.

Then there are all those who have been so fortunate to reach a level of success and carry an air about them that nothing is enough. I only used these few examples of these types of people who truly believe they themselves made it happen for them. Perhaps you may know some people like this, possibly within your very own circle of friends, associates, acquaintances, family, and/or perhaps yourself.

I've been fortunate enough when I was engaged in business to be able to meet and speak with many people in my travels that drove themselves into an almost addictive state working twelve to fifteen hours a day chasing success, achieving it, and rarely, if ever, showed any gratitude for this success. I've also met people who had recovered from very serious illnesses, despite the odds heavily stacked against them, who never expressed gratitude/thankfulness for their recovery. When they started feeling better again and returned to their old, domineering, and selfish selves, they still failed to recognize or reached out to those less fortunate or who did not recover from the very same or other serious ailments.

There are people in governments all over the world who, despite their highly elevated stature in society, fail to be grateful/thankful for much that has fallen into their laps or that they may have achieved. Most of all, they consistently fail to reach down to help elevate those less fortunate and, on an individual basis, show how they recognize and appreciate their particular fortune. I will concede, however, that there is possibly a handful that do not fit this mold. Sadly to say, this is not the greater majority.

Why is this subject of gratitude/thankfulness so important? If this is even a possible question churning in your mind, please allow me to bring something to your immediate attention. First, I did not promise hearts and flowers or even rose-colored glasses—far from it. I didn't promise or expect that you would like some of the things I discuss. However, as a survivor of much more than the average person I have come to know in my lifetime thus far, I truly believe that I have a solemn obligation to every person to share what I believe to be valuable information and my experience with those who may develop any stage of a serious life-changing situation or circumstance and/or life-threatening illness—be it physical, nonphysical, or some catastrophic, traumatic, unforeseen event.

That said, it is with great sincerity and obligation that I identify that without gratitude or thankfulness on a continuous, constant basis, you risk the inevitable crumbling before your very eyes of every single achievement you may have realized and any you ever hope to achieve. Believe it—I've been there and personally can attest to this, as so many others have as well.

This information that describes an inner guidance that is one with an unseen all-knowing infinite intelligence, does not cross the line into religious beliefs, dogmas, scientific opinions, theories, etc. However, somewhere deep inside each and every one of us, we intuitively know that the opportunity for gratitude needs to be acknowledged constantly and consistently, ranging from each and every time we arise in the morning and are able to draw yet another breath and for any level of success and achievement, no matter how minor or major it may be.

Let me tell you that I have seen fortunes disappear, relationships dissolve, material possessions vanish, former serious illnesses return, happiness into grief, negative events multiply, entire families torn apart, businesses dissolved, and dreams shattered overnight, to name just a mere handful. On the other hand, I have seen poverty turn to wealth, loneliness turn to enriching relationships, serious illnesses disappear, financial difficulties resolved, new relationships appear where all hope was once abandoned, etc. Of course, there are so many more that can be listed on both sides of this matter of being thankful/unthankful.

In my considered opinion, those who are ungrateful intuitively know that they need to make the choice to get off the path they are presently following because their present fortune may one day come to an abrupt end if they do not take the time to realize this. Therefore, knowing this intuitively, it would behoove those to whom this applies to begin becoming extremely appreciative for even the food they are able to have each and every day. Deciding to embrace a thankful attitude can only multiply more good to come into one's life, unexpectedly and unannounced.

Quite sadly to say, this is also true for those who fail to acknowledge their all-knowing inner guidance because they choose instead to live the way they presently are. For them, the sky may be blue and the sun may be shining today; however, to ignore gratitude/thankfulness for any considerable length of time can only eventually prove to be risky and, over time, possibly disastrous.

Let's now explore why everyone is responsible for bringing forth any life-changing adversities one may presently be enduring or may possibly acquire, whether anyone is ready to admit it or not.

17

THE REAL ORIGIN OF LIFE-THREATENING CONDITIONS

*If you keep going in the direction, you are going
you're certain to end up where you're headed.*

—Author

Medical science can probably fill a professional football stadium with volumes of medical books containing medical and scientific theories as well as research and opinions in response to this question. Some of it is considered to be fact and the rest theory, experimental data, and opinions. However, all too often, the one ingredient that seems to always be missing in medical science is that there is rarely, if at all, any mention that it is you and I who give birth to any life-threatening condition and negative events we do or may develop. Why? Because we both attract and invite them into our lives, and medical science gives little credence to this as being anywhere near a possibility for these conditions.

How often have you heard a medical practitioner say the diagnosed life-threatening condition was brought on by something you or someone else personally did to bring it about? Not very often, if ever; from personal experience, I can assure you that. Instead, we are told that we either caught it from someone or somehow; it was hereditary; caused by our surroundings and lifestyle; exposure to certain catalysts such as coal dust, asbestos, chemical exposure, smoking; fate; etc. From that point, the experimental treatments' trial balloons begin appearing on the horizon, and you and I become the experimental human lab rats.

Having been through a number of devastating conditions personally and surviving each and every one of them and having spoken to scores of people for years who either had cancer, heart disease, tuberculosis, mental illness, drug dependency, nervous break downs, etc.—I believe life-threatening nonphysical conditions are the root cause of many life-destructive illnesses. I perceive that the shared characteristic is, was, and always will be all of us, not circumstances, which may cause harmful conditions, adversities, or negative events we have or ever will have in our lives. Our failure to recognize this is, as I said earlier, to be in a condition of serious denial.

It is at this point the critics begin to come out of the woodwork and begin raising their brows. A common question asked of me is, "How can it be me causing any serious life-affecting conditions to come into my life?" Others have said to me, "But how can infants and small children be held responsible for attracting life-degenerating conditions into their innocent little lives?" This is a great question and deserves to be answered. So here is the answer: They're not. Instead, their ancestors, going back thousands of years, are! What? This just may be one's response to this statement. So then let's look at it with an open mind, shall we?

You can easily see in your own circle of family, friends, acquaintances, associates, and others you may know that their children have already adopted most of their parents' traits and habits—be it worry, anxiety, fear of all types, negativity, a sense of hopelessness and unworthiness, poor lifestyle, low self-esteem, bad behavior, etc. Yes, there are the exceptions to this; a person who's learned behaviors is the complete opposite.

These behaviors come directly from who and what these children are exposed to in their earlier years. For those whom I mentioned first, however, these are not hereditary, as we are all too often led to believe; instead, these are learned behaviors, which, if not corrected early in life, will undoubtedly be passed on to their children and their children's children, throughout the generations. If the chain of these learned behaviors is not broken, chances are very high that children raised under these circumstances and environments will more than likely realize one or any number of nonphysical grave conditions that can—over time and very possibly may—manifest into a life-threatening physical illness.

As for infants, the answer to this question can only be ascertained from a higher intelligence and power much greater than mankind. This all-knowing unseen intelligence, therefore, has yet to be revealed to mankind; and if and when it does, the answer to this presently unanswerable question will may be revealed.

Let me make something very clear at this point. This book is not about dwelling or focusing on the medical profession, pharmaceutical industry, or religions and their individual beliefs; instead, this is a wake-up call for all humanity. This is especially true for all members serving at any level in the medical profession who face highly stressful conditions each and every day who also need to take inventory of their very own lives. Not even members of the medical community worldwide are immune to avoiding any number of nonphysical life-changing conditions which, if not kept in check, can and very often do manifest themselves into serious, life-menacing physical illnesses—of this I am convinced. As a matter of fact, people in these positions are even more vulnerable than most just by the very nature of their professions, which are permeated with very high levels of stress and anxiety.

I myself do not lay blame for any of the life-threatening conditions I have endured on anything or anyone but myself and only myself, as I said earlier. I have come to understand and realize quite clearly that I—and only I—created each and every condition I personally attracted and invited into my life. So did or will you, if you haven't already, if you do not wake up and pay closer attention to yourself.

The critics can criticize, the naysayers can naysay, and the doubters can doubt—that is, until they one day may possibly come face to face with a serious life-compromising condition. If they already have one or more in their lives right at this moment, they need to stop and reconsider the source of their conditions. The greatest among them are the disorders of fear, high stress, pessimism, anxiety, depression, and always being in a state of constant doubting, criticizing, and seeking to constantly discredit anything and everything out of their outer world. All can eventually lead to serious, unsustainable physical conditions.

However, it is entirely up to you, isn't it? Not your doctors or other medical professionals you have so heavily depended upon or continue to plan to rely upon. Yes, they are necessary to a certain degree. But they are certainly not a higher power, and they certainly are not you.

The choices you make from this point forward concerning your life will determine precisely the level of life-threatening conditions you may or may not attract into to your life—or, if you are currently having one or more serious illness, then how you will choose to deal with it/them from this point forward.

Therefore, the answer to what the real origin of devastating conditions is, from my prospective as a survivor of numerous major life-threatening conditions, to understand that it is you who attracts any and all such disabilities into your life or those waiting for your invitation to enter it. The primary reason is because you ceased listening to your inner guide and instead chose to listen to everything else, including others' opinions.

People who have any combination of negative emotions are at high risk of inviting into their lives very serious physical conditions and even an untimely death. This is why it is so important to recognize the disempowering feelings and emotions you are currently aware. It is vital that you rid yourself of what you may be experiencing before they are allowed to consume your entire life and possibly affect the lives of many others.

It is evident, as recorded, that I did not set out to do battle with the medical, psychology, psychiatric, or pharmacological professions or to tear them apart. After all, I elected to go through two major surgeries placing my trust in the medical community. However, despite my actions, I was told by these medical professionals, unequivocally, that unless I further elected to have a regimen of chemotherapy treatments following these surgeries, my chances of survival were not good—less than 10 percent—based upon statistical records of many of those who came before me with the very same diagnoses. Remember this: "I am not you or you me!" I was not any of those people in that historical, statistical record group to which these medical professionals were referring now, was I? And neither are you.

The world is permeated with masses of humanity all around us every day at the office, on the street, in malls, at a doctor's office, and practically anywhere. So who are the real people behind these flesh masks? They are the masked faces of your friends, your family members, pedestrians, and others we know and encounter every day. And what's behind these masked faces? Well, there's pain, agony, anxiety, heartache, depression, addictions of every type, fear, feelings of unworthiness, hopelessness, despair, guilt, sorrow, abandonment, trauma, and, sometimes, true happiness and joy, just to name a few.

The majority of humanity worldwide is sleepwalking through their lives totally unconscious of the tremendous control they have over their own lives. Only *you* have total control over any life-injurious illnesses that will possibly threaten your life or already have. Not the medical profession, the pharmaceutical industry, your family and friends, religious leaders, nontraditional treatments, alternative medicines and treatments, or counseling of any type—your healing solely up to you and you alone!

It is not either fair or even close to reasonable to expect others to be responsible for your total healing and/or overcoming of a life-changing event. Yet of all the people I have spoken with, who had either a life-disruptive physical or nonphysical illness, most expected others to cure them totally from their ailments (primarily their medical providers). They saw no personal responsibility on their part to contribute to their healing. I was not amazed to hear this from so many I had spoken with because this is precisely how many people who are undergoing a life-altering illness or event think.

I have personal experience with this as I heard it over and over again when I was being treated for cancer. Not only is this ludicrous; it is also a condition of completely irresponsible thinking and denial. It is comparable to expecting someone to dress you every day before you go about your daily activities—unless, of course, you are below the age of six or are disabled or incapacitated.

There are many people throughout the world who believe that a higher power will come to their aid. They are also aware that a higher power is also expecting the individual afflicted with a serious ailment to help themselves and to not rely totally upon their higher power to do it all. In other words, yes, humanity should believe in faith. However, it is the individual who also needs to contribute to the expectation of a total healing and/or eventual overcoming of any undesirable condition they may have.

What I want you to understand and realize is that what I am and have been expressing thus far is, this is not all about me and my survival. Instead, it's all about your life, and everyone you know and care about, and the millions you'll possibly never meet or know.

It's about what we all once knew yet forgot. It's about those life parameters that we create for ourselves, our self-induced pain. It's a about choices—our choices—and it's about every type of life-threatening illness, physical and nonphysical, known to man, and it's about choosing a life of expectation. Most of all, it's all about the choices you make when faced with adversity. It's about how we attract each and every illness or event that already has or may ever come into our lives.

It is also about absolute knowing—knowing everything we need to know, when we need to know it, and how to alleviate any possible negative event that has come or may ever come into our lives. It's all about you and your right to live a joyful, fulfilled life. For those of us who already know and for those of us who are about to learn, it's a about rediscovering the immense power of this this all-knowing inner guidance.

This is not about fiction or science fiction or religious beliefs or medical science. Instead, it is about the gift, your inner guide, given to all those yet to have discovered their gift and those who already have known about it but chose to let other life influences (their ego) control what happens in their lives. Absolutely know that you are creating your circumstances every moment of your life, through what you focus on and believe to be true; and by doing so, you are creating your own reality.

I believe that being grateful for the learning that we derive from our life process is extremely important. Once one comes to realize this and begins to include gratitude for what we do have, the lessons learned from any experience, whether positive or negative, are most valuable.

PREVAILING OVER INSURMOUNTABLE ODDS

Gratitude—the Key to Achieving All Desires

*Being grateful for what you already have
cannot be emphasized nearly enough.*

—Author

If you may be saying to yourself at this point in your life you cannot find much to be grateful for, then find *anything* to be grateful for. Begin with the next breath of air you are about to take and the one you took a moment ago for openers. What about your having reached the age you have and are not lying in some cemetery on this day or that wherever you are residing is an absolute blessing? As millions worldwide live in third-world countries, have dirt for floors and tree branches for covers, tin for roofs, mere rags for clothing, no shoes, inadequate or poor nutritional food, and no medical care—surely you have *something* for which to be grateful.

In these times of severe financial hardship and uncertainty, many people have said to me that it is very hard to be grateful when they are seeing everything they have worked to achieve now beginning to crumble all around them. This is certainly a valid point and needs to be addressed. Certainly, financial collapse and the threat of loss of material things people have worked long and hard to have, including their homes and careers, is devastating and shocking. You are not alone. Millions of Americans have and continue to be face to face with this very same concern.

Many have already lost their jobs and homes, and others have collapsed financially to the point of having to file for bankruptcy and having to relocate to other states or forced to move back with their families. Everywhere one you look, these circumstances appear to be a mirror image of what is occurring in the USA and worldwide.

Now here comes the most controversial statement you will see considering these negative events. Even though millions are on the brink of total financial collapse—and among these millions, many have already reached that point or have lost it all financially—this is the precise time when each and every person on this planet absolutely needs to be grateful for everything that comes into their lives, positive or negative. Easy for me to say, right? Wrong! Why? Because beginning in 1995, my downward spiral began with the disappearance of everything I owned and continued with the loss of a twenty-five-year business, followed by two devastating life-threatening cancers, two failed marriages, and losing hard-earned assets and almost every material possession I had earned.

So what did I do through all this loss and negative events that seemed to arrive suddenly one right after another and many actually appeared in my life, one on top of another? It was not until I was diagnosed with a life-compromising illness that I realized why I was going through these experiences.

What I discovered was that I rarely had given thanks for things that materialized as I was far too busy building a business and accumulating material stuff, enjoying lavish vacations and living quite well. Little did I realize at the time, when I was prospering materially, that all that could disappear as quickly as it had appeared. I thought I had it made and finally arrived and had it all, but the huge mistake I made was that I neglected expressing gratitude for all I had accumulated. It did not take long before things began crumbling around me until one day all I had worked for was gone, including a home valued over $1.3 million at the time.

Despite all this, having realized why my life was falling apart, I began being grateful for everything that was on my life's path, including the bad. When I tell people this, they ask me if I lost my mind. The fact is, however, I actually found it—finally!

It wasn't until after I began being grateful for everything that had come into my life that everything began turning around for the better. I even began being grateful for any previous negative events that had come into my life and changed how I had initially reacted to them. As I came to realize that, it is our reaction to negative things that come into our lives that affects our feelings and attitudes. Our deep negative feelings are the cause of most, if not all, life-threatening nonphysical and physical illnesses that many have come to realize. For me, even though I was enjoying the achievements of my labor, I was never totally comfortable. As time marched on, I began to have more and more stress that I later realized was attributed to my lack of gratitude, which ultimately led to the physical events I developed—of this, I am convinced.

Of course, not everyone's circumstances are/or have been as dire as mine. However, it may be time for you to seriously consider taking personal inventory of the circumstances that may have already or may possibly be leading to negative situations in your life that can very well teach you something about yourself and the life path you have chosen to follow.

Let's face it—it is unlikely that most of us will get out of this life without realizing an undesirable event or adversity. You might not know why these things come into one's life at the time they do. However, giving gratitude for the knowledge they bring—regardless of how painful they may be—you will have learned a very important lesson. Like me, you may possibly begin to understand and come to know the reason why the undesirable situation happened to you.

Giving thanks for all the good things that come into our lives can bring forth more prosperity in life. However, being grateful for the valuable lessons learned from the not-so-good things that may appear in our life may be possibly difficult to do but can bring forth valuable lessons that we may not have otherwise learned. You will find that by being grateful for everything, positive events can show up the more your gratitude continues to grow.

I realize that many persons who have been affected by the present economic tsunami can't help continuing with ongoing negative thinking and that the last thing they want to do is to express or be in a state of gratitude. However, without a state of gratitude, nasty and negative thoughts will continue to easily get through. Without the barrier of continuous gratitude to diffuse these negative and destructive thoughts, these types of thoughts can, over time, destroy a person's life.

I would have never accepted anyone telling me when I lost everything I worked so hard to achieve—followed by the two life-threatening events—that that was the best thing that could have happened to me. I probably would have dismissed this and asked them to leave. However, in retrospect, it was! Since what had seemed to be devastating problems, as I was passing through them, actually proved to be blessings in disguise. What I learned from my misfortunes was to be grateful for what I had previously taken for granted—return to good health, a body having all its limbs and faculties, the fact that I was still inhaling and exhaling, etc. Surely, we all have much to complain about. Yet we have so much more for which to be grateful.

Another question I am always asked is, "To what or to whom should I be grateful?" My short answer is that, if you are a religious person, then you already know the answer to your question. If you are not, then begin by being grateful to Thomas Edison for being able to find your way at night without breaking a leg or an arm stumbling over something or down a flight of stairs; Henry Ford for the automobile; the Wright brothers for air travel; the water company for the water you get from your tap every day; the oil companies for the gas that powers your car; the farmer who grows your food; etc., etc., etc. However, it is not to whom or to what one should be grateful; instead, it is the *actual feeling* of gratitude that really matters, and it costs you absolutely nothing to be grateful now, does it?

You will be pleasantly surprised when you begin being totally grateful for everything in your life, about how good you will begin feeling about yourself, and the amount of mental weight you will drop, not to mention the stress and anxiety that accompanies not being grateful. If humanity were truly grateful for everything that came and will come on their life's path, we all would have little, if any, time to entertain any negative debilitating thoughts now, would we?

You can possibly be grateful for your teachers, your parents, your sisters and/or brothers, your relatives, your children (if you are a parent), your provider (husband or wife or significant other), the roof over your head, food you get to eat, clothes you get to wear every day, furnishings and beddings you get to sit and lie on, the television you have to entertain you, your car (if you own one), your job (if you are fortunate enough to even have one these days), every breath and day you are given, even for this book and books by other authors who are also reaching out to help humanity, etc. Once you begin to do this, you then will have opened the previously locked gate to receive the myriad of positive outcomes you will, without any doubt, surely receive in your life. You will soon find that the gift of receiving is the result of the gift of gratitude.

PREVAILING OVER INSURMOUNTABLE ODDS

Do it and do it now, starting with anything you know you should be grateful for. As you add to this list, you will continue to find relief from any anxiety, stress, doubt, and paralyzing fear that may be disturbing you. I should know as I was virtually paralyzed with all of this and more when I began losing everything I earned and worked for all my life, which seemed to disappear virtually overnight when diagnosed with two fatal cancers.

I have known people who absolutely reject this idea of being grateful for everything they have—their cumulative assets, spouses, children, careers, bad conditions which were no more than things and people who were meant to come into their lives to teach valuable lessons to draw from, and even diseases and serious life-changing events/life-threatening illnesses. Yes, even these as well.

The real you exists deep inside you, and it is here where all knowledge resides in each and every one who was ever been born since the beginning of time itself. Therefore, gratitude plays an extremely important role in everyone's lives.

I can tell you from my own personal experience that any burning desire that I have trusted to my all-knowing inner guidance became actuality, over time, when I first thanked that intelligence within for what I desired. Therefore, you are no different. Once this all-knowing inner guidance is summoned into your life, you will begin to be aware of a sense of peace, calm, and serenity that comes over you.

That aside, maybe—just maybe—you need to accept, realize, and know that you are a very powerful being who can achieve overcoming life-changing adversities, physical and/or nonphysical. Keep in mind that your all-knowing inner guide already knows everything that there is to know; all you have to do every single day—or as often as you can—is to thank your inner power for your desires.

Do not concern yourself about the *when* because your all-knowing inner force knows the precise and correct timing as to when what you want it to materialize. Pushing the "When button" when deferring to your all-knowing inner guide signifies to this knowing that you have doubts and reservations, which is the easiest way to nullify whatever it is you are seeking. How do I know this? Because this is precisely what I did and each time I did. I wound up realizing I was pushing what I desired away from me instead of attracting what I desired. Just know and trust, and you will witness that your all-knowing inner guidance will respond.

The most difficult fact you are going to have to accept is that the true cause of any of these conditions is you! Tough to swallow, isn't it? But it's true. I had the same feeling when I learned this truth, and yes, it was also very hard for me to accept as well. As discussed, any medical professional is aware that life-damaging nonphysical illnesses, left to fester for years, can and often do manifest themselves into life-devastating physical illnesses. A good example of this is the nonphysical illnesses of stress, anxiety, and depression and that these alone can bring on many life-threatening physical illnesses.

If you did not know this before now, be grateful that you now know this and can now do something about it. Unless you do something about it, you can expect that if you choose to continue on this path that you have selected for yourself, over time, this possibly could lead to your ultimate destruction, mentally or physically.

People have asked me, "What is it I can do right now to begin to heal myself?" Without hesitation, I tell them that if they are serious about ridding themselves of a life-destructing illness and/or condition, physical or nonphysical, then they need to begin with the healing of the distortions of their disempowering thoughts and to never allow anyone tell you anything that would even remotely move you off your newly discovered or rediscovered inner knowing and self-healing path—no one!

Through my all-knowing inner guidance, I knew that that every organ, vessel, and cell that make up my body was working just as it was designed to work. Further, I said to myself—as I do every day—"I am very grateful for my life."

I further knew that even though I chose recommended invasive surgical procedures that the outcome would be the same—no further disease would be found anywhere else in my body's organs, lymph nodes, or anywhere, for that matter—and it wasn't. I also knew that I would never accept any chemotherapy treatments whatsoever. Hence, I refused chemotherapy treatments on three separate occasions and gave thanks for these decisions prior to and after the surgeries and for the all-knowing inner guidance that led me to the decision to refuse chemotherapy treatments.

Some have said it was luck, others called it stupid, and more called it insane, inconsiderate, careless, and being in total denial of an inevitable demise. None of these opinions—professional or otherwise—mattered. What mattered was coming directly from my all-knowing inner guidance. This was, is, and will remain my only guide to anything to do with my life as long as I draw a breath on this planet. Why? Because I am living proof of its power and unlimited knowledge.

I would like to take a moment here to say a word about how being grateful is so important and plays a major role in being able to possess what it is you desire in your physical life. I am more than convinced of the significance and extreme importance of this state of mind, of being grateful for everything.

In my personal involvement with the state of mind of being grateful, one of the key methods, is having been fortunate enough to have discovered this undeniable unseen power that I absolutely know I can rely upon at any point in time for whatever good I wish that materializes in this life—whether it is prosperity at any level, peace of mind, happiness, excellent health, or the right relationships. This has nothing whatsoever to do with having to commit to or rely upon any religious teachings, dogma, or the like. I do support and respect anyone's beliefs and choice of any religion because all religions are connected to the same unseen infinite force, whether they are willing to recognize this or not.

Be grateful for you have in your life at this moment and recognize that there are millions throughout the world who may not have even a quarter of what you or others may have and/or have access to directly and freely at this point in time. What stands out most is the fact that in this country, everyone has the freedom—including all the other privileges that living in America provides—millions throughout the world have never and may never acquire in their entire lifetimes.

Know for a fact that whatever good we may desire in our physical lives is already at our disposal when employing right thinking, unwavering belief, trust, expectation, and being grateful for our all-knowing inner guidance that is one with infinite intelligence, among other methods thus identified.

Being in a constant state of gratitude by trusting, knowing, and expecting means that whatever good you want to have in this life is already available to you. Believe that there is absolutely no lack of abundance or prosperity at any level you may desire to obtain in your life. It has already been made available to you through your all-knowing infinite intelligence, which contains all the methods and answers necessary for you to be able to secure whatever good you expect in your life and the lives of others to whom it may concern.

It is important to realize and for me to reemphasize that survival of any adverse circumstances takes personal involvement, along with medical science, a focused effort, and, above all, completely conviction and envisioning oneself having already overcome whatever one sincerely desires to conquer, with no exceptions whatsoever. Always *express* **gratitude in advance,** even though the adverse condition may not yet have left your life. The only way to not survive whatever you are dealing with is simply to do nothing and just hope for the best. Good luck with that!

As we are aware, medical science certainly plays a role in recovery; however, it is vitally important to remember that you have a part to play as well. As I have been saying, reliance solely upon the medical profession for a total healing and permanent cure is simply wishful and faulty thinking. Unless you have realized it yet, medical professionals—to the best of my knowledge and research—have never claimed to be anyone's higher power and, therefore, should not unfairly be relied upon to be miracle workers. Once the medical professionals do their part to treat and help one to overcoming and defeating any life-threatening condition, affliction, adversity, or other serious event, then the person themself must then perform their part, like I and others have done, if they are determined to overcome whatever their diagnosis or illness is. Unless this is done, they can expect the possibility of a continued steep climb with whatever their affliction they have. This point has been repeated several times thus far but needs to be emphatically reinforced.

Far too many of us, as I continue to point out, place the total responsibility of our recovery from illnesses or other adverse conditions, physical or nonphysical in nature, on the medical profession and others. But rarely, if at all, do we stand on our own shoulders. We even go so far as to place the entire burden for our recovery upon a higher power, regardless of any particular religious belief. Instead, what should be taking place is gratitude for expected healing and being willing to take full responsibility for your own recovery and survival, during and following when medical science has done all they can. I did—as have others—and I survived serious medical and nonphysical conditions by doing what I have written in this book, in conjunction with the knowledge of medical science.

From years of observing people who found themselves in a serious life-changing or life-threatening situation, many were pessimistic and rarely optimistic when it came to these conditions and related circumstances. An illustration of this is when I was hospitalized. As I recall, I found myself surrounded by a number of pessimists who were also afflicted with cancer of various types and stages. To make matters even grimmer, many were surrounded by family members, friends, and others—the majority of whom I labeled as award-winning pessimists instead of life-enhancing optimists. At best, in my opinion, this was very sad, upsetting, and, above all, depressing to other patients to witness.

Not only did I encounter this type of mind-set with people whom I never met but also among family members who were involved with life-changing or life-threatening illness situations. Unfortunately, many just plain gave in to their conditions and illnesses and never considered the possibility of a recovery or the opportunity of long-term survival. Hence, the end result was even more concerning and disappointing. Now, I've been criticized for being too harsh at times when it comes to people having a life-changing or life-threatening illness. Well, do we really want to continue to accept and believe that a table full of prescribed medications and a line of surgeries keeping one in a depressive state are the entire answer to a full recovery and eventual permanent cure?

The power to heal anything that may possibly be disabling you is already yours because, as I said before, you own the power; it lies in being confident and grateful that you already know you do. It is a matter of placing your total trust in yourself—self-reliance versus reliance upon others than yourself.

Although I've alluded to this before, in my opinion, it merits saying again. Many people who idolize famous people believe that they are invincible, not realizing that they too are human beings and susceptible to everything you and I are and are not immune to any life-changing adversities, event, or illness. Believe it or not, no one is bulletproof or invincible when it comes to overcoming most adversities in life.

It completely baffles me to read about or see stories on television about the rich and the famous who spend obscene sums of money on every type of alternative treatments in search of a permanent cure from a life-threatening illness or condition, physical and/or nonphysical. They will even travel across the globe to foreign countries for various kinds of treatments and remedies, without much success and millions of dollars lighter.

In my travels, I have witnessed that, by nature, many people are short-term optimists and long-term pessimists when it comes to life-altering illnesses, physical and nonphysical alike. More often than not, when it comes to serious illnesses and/or events, as previously identified, most people permit other people's opinions to dictate the path they choose to follow instead of trusting their own natural instincts or intuition. Of course, I am taking into consideration that a person is mentally capable and not comatose or afflicted with any other condition that would prevent one from being cognizant of who or where they are and unable to make any decisions for themselves. Considering that a total healing and ultimate cure begins with focused thoughts and envisioning overcoming any adverse condition, it simply is not good enough to accept a "one day at a time" attitude.

If one is going to trust themselves to be able to bring forth a complete healing and ultimate cure, one absolutely must—as I've already described—be able to see themselves completely healed as it has already happened. Above all, be grateful for your healing and enjoy a normal and healthy life completely free of any illness, adversity, or undesirable event, serious or otherwise. It may be a good idea to highlight this and write it down and put it where you can see it all the time until it becomes a part of your every waking moment.

Today, you or someone you love or care about deeply may be in good condition; however, life offers none of us any guarantees of continued excellent health or absence of a grave illness or life-changing event to come into our lives.

You see, only we, as individuals, can bring forth a healing and eventual permanent cure. For anyone or any medical professional or those involved with alternative remedies to state otherwise may be misleading. Now, I am almost certain this statement may draw some criticism; however, it is what it is—the will to survive any adversity can be found deep within where one's all-knowing, unquestionable, inner guidance resides and is a necessary collaboration.

I absolutely know that by tapping into and choosing to trust my all-knowing inner guidance, its indisputable power was the reason I overcame each and every adversity; and I continue to rely upon it. Therefore, you too can discover its immense authority.

As I also stated before, the words *hope* and *faith* have no power in themselves. The strength they have can only come from the fuel *you* provide to them, which are unwavering belief, expectancy, and, above all, expressing gratitude in advance of a healing of any adversity.

We continue now to identify how your undesirable circumstances and adversities can change for good in your life once you decide they will.

18

YOUR CIRCUMSTANCES WILL CHANGE

That is, when you decide it will. Do you wish to know when your present suffering will begin to change? The answer is when you are ready to change it. All it takes is rediscovering the switch within, and it can change sooner than expected. This is especially true for life-threatening nonphysical conditions one may be aware of or could be waiting to enter your life.

It is important to be aware that you and only you are the author and the architect of your designs—all of them. Hard to accept, isn't it? This does not mean that a person in the advanced stages of a life-threatening illness may change this condition instantly; it means that one's personal attitude, strong belief, and expectation of recovery can change, allowing one's inner all-knowing guidance the opportunity to begin the healing process, having received the full trust and confidence of the person who may be the recipient of such a condition. However, if one has already reached a stage of total denial and unbelief and has given up entirely, chances are that they may have lost total connection with their all-knowing inner guidance.

First and foremost is trusting that you and only you have the power to overcome or avoid any life-threatening illness or event, no matter what it may be, physical or nonphysical. Unless you take this first step, anything else would more than likely be futile. Following the norm—by placing one's full and complete trust in today's remedies for treating life-threatening illnesses—is, in my opinion as a survivor, worthy of scrutiny. Why? Because you owe it to yourself and all those whom you love and who love you and those who care about you to do some very thorough research about alternative treatments that are devoid of some of the side effects of the current measures commonly used in attempting to manage some serious illness.

Advances are being made to improve medications that destroyed the body's immune system to the point of rendering it ineffective and unable to defend the body as it was intended to do naturally. Progress has been made in revising mutilating surgical procedures. Robotics have introduced new methods for survival intervention. Antibiotics have been modified to assist in the corrective aspects of controlling some of the complications of treating disease. Medical centers have been allocated for the treatment of specific cancer diagnoses, and technological advances have been made in medical equipment for the detection of malignancies. So there is an array of specialized prevention, treatment, and research facilities.

There are medical professionals, along with medical science as a whole, who are making amazing headway in helping heal people who have very serious, devastating illnesses. Quite sadly, however, many die despite these efforts. It may be important to note—for your own information, if you are not already aware of this—that deaths related to cancer have only dropped 5 percent since 1950 through 2005 (*The New York Times*) and have not improved that dramatically through 2010. The medical profession's opinion is that early detection and preventative measures, as well as pharmaceutical and technological advances, have caused this decrease in mortality rates. What this says about conventional science's record to be able to successfully treat cancer is not a statistic that would give many people much comfort if you are not among the 5 percent. As for me, this not only solidifies my bold decision to have refused heavily recommended chemotherapy treatments but seals that option permanently.

Of course, I cannot and will not recommend or make any attempt to lead anyone in any direction concerning their personal choice when it comes to their personal health care treatment choices. However, I will boldly state once again that one owes it to one's self to also consider credible alternatives prior to embarking upon any treatment program when it comes to treatment for any life-threatening illness or condition.

It's all about how your life will be by trusting that you can change it and being absolutely convinced that you can, and be very clear about this. Then, no matter what, no outside interferences should be allowed at this point. You need to make this your primary focus pertaining to this issue until you achieve whatever it is you are seeking for good. In addition, my suggestion would be to cease all negative thoughts, especially thoughts of despair and hopelessness, and never be pessimistic from this point forward and not allow anyone to tell you differently. This is your life we are discussing here and not someone else's.

Whatever you do from this point forward, reject every fear you may have about anything whatsoever. Train your mind to do this. You may be saying to yourself that this may be virtually impossible. Well, think about how adept you were training your mind to not do it!

Once you have begun this process, then begin to verbalize these commands coming from you internally—your all-knowing inner guidance—by saying these aloud to yourself, which will call them forth into your life. Do not do this at an office meeting or around a lot of people but alone by yourself, in your car, your room, your hospital bed (if you are having to be hospitalized for any reason, it is preferable at night when it is mostly quiet), your quiet place, or anywhere you can be alone without any interference. By doing so, you are literally calling forth your "inner knowing power." And no, this is not a religion, voodoo, or wishful or positive thinking; instead, it is the *outer* you talking to the *real inner* you, your all-knowing guidance.

This real you is always attempting to communicate with the conscious you (the physical you, your conscious mind) constantly. Whether you know it or not, this is what you have been doing all your life unconsciously. You surely have heard you say to yourself something like, "Uh, this might not be such a good idea, maybe I should not do this" or "I know this is a bad decision, but what the heck, I'll take the chance" or "this relationship is not going to work, but I'll find a way to make it work" or "I know I need to get another opinion, but I'll just go ahead anyway and trust those I feel comfortable with" or "I don't think that allowing these chemicals to be put into my body is what I want my body to be subjected to" or "I sense there is a better way to cure this problem naturally," etc. I am almost certain you can add many more of your own.

Your inner intuitive self is where your most empowering decisions have and will continue to come from—not from others, only you—because no one is, can, or will ever be able to live your life but you. We all have these intuitive feelings, don't we? But how often do we go against them and why? Far too often (in my case, anyway). Almost every time I did, I paid the price, which was not a comfortable place to wind up for me. These were followed by regrets and what-ifs. You most likely heard the term "Monday morning quarterbacking"; it is quite common among people familiar with the game of American football, also known, as second-guessing after the fact.

The most scoffed-at solution to knowing the correct options to consider for anyone needing to deal with the treatment of any life-threatening physical or nonphysical illness or condition and/or serious negative event is your very own inner guidance that is one with the all-knowing infinite mind. "What, is he kidding me?" you may be saying to yourself as you just may have jumped out of your chair. No! Quite the contrary, I'm not kidding you; as a matter of fact, I am very serious—more serious than a heart attack.

Am I saying that this is how I overcame two extremely serious back-to-back cancers and numerous life-threatening nonphysical illnesses and events? I not only believe it—I absolutely know that I survived every single one of those events and serious life-threatening illnesses due to this wonderful gift of my all-knowing inner guidance connected with the infinite intelligence that had given and continues to give me the answers, methods, and solutions necessary to make a reliable decision each and every time. Do I give credit to medical science? Absolutely I do. However, as I've been saying, medical science alone cannot bring forth a permanent healing and eventual cure, yet they certainly can and often do contribute to the healing process—of this I have no doubt.

I believe that medical science as a whole, dating back thousands of years, came to discover all that it has brought about pertaining to medical advances, as a result of an all-knowing infinite source that is connected with this inner guide I speak of that resides within each and every person currently living and those who lived many years ago.

It has been said that knowledge is power. There could be no truer statement, as far as I am concerned—especially when it comes to one's lifesaving choices that only a person alone can make for themselves when armed with the knowledge that comes from one's inner guidance that is one with the infinite intelligence. For me, the choice was to follow my inner power and not just what it was telling me but directing me to the right path I should be following. Personally, I cannot comprehend anything more valuable than this.

I easily could have followed the direction of the medical doctors who were all leading me to and recommending chemicals be placed into my veins through chemotherapy. Instead, I elected to go with my inner power that had given me the answers, methods, and solutions. I needed to be able to feel confident that I could overcome the life-threatening illnesses and events I personally had experienced. Once that decision was made, nothing could have altered my decision, which to this very instance I continue to follow my inner guidance that has yet to fail me. Why would I not continue to follow what my inner guidance is telling me to do?

"What is new about this inner power"? Absolutely nothing. As a matter of fact, it has been around long before the entire universe, which to this point in time, man has not yet been able to learn the universe's true origin. Probably, as I pointed out, even ancient cave people and most of humanity long ago, utilized their inner mind to be able to survive and avoid dangers of every conceivable type and had no medical science or modern technology to rely upon whatsoever.

These ancient civilizations were without the aid of modern day technology, computers, GPS systems, Doppler radars to detect weather conditions and oncoming severe storms, or any other means of instant communication humanity relies upon today. Yet they built the pyramids and other wonders of the world that, to this day, modern man has been unable to solve the mystery of how they accomplished what they did, without the aid of modern heavy equipment and other technologies used in modern societies worldwide.

In addition, every time I had ignored my inner guide in the past, I wound up on the wrong side of a situation. This includes personal as well as business matters. If I had it to do over again during that point in my life, I certainly would have gone with my inner guidance and not consider any other alternative.

I know that what is coming from deep within me is definitely more informative and powerful than what anything outside could ever possibly deliver that would be in my best personal interest as well as in the best interest of all concerned, relating to any given matter or situation that would be affected by any decision I may make.

Let me be even much clearer here about this very important issue concerning inner guidance. My greatest life's regrets, when it came to one's intuition, were when I went against my inner feelings by listening to outside advice pertaining to whether or not I should have the two surgeries. The other regrets I have are that I should have obeyed my inner guidance when it came to some business decisions I had made. Had I listened to my inner directives, I am more than certain that I would have avoided some extremely painful and embarrassing situations.

I have been asked many times if I regretted my decision to undergo these surgeries occurring within a year of one another. My answer to this question is always a resounding yes! I say this because, at the time, I had not rediscovered my all-knowing inner guidance; and therefore, like so many others facing such a critical decision and never having been face to face with such a serious life decision, I took the advice of those whom I trusted implicitly, including my medical doctors. I also took the advice of close business associates, people who had personal and professional knowledge of serious cancer matters, and even close family.

It has been said to me that it is easy for me to say this because you overcame both serious illnesses and whether or not I know for sure that it was not the surgeries themselves that had saved my life. This is a very good point and certainly deserves elaboration. Therefore, here is my answer: "Having reconnected with my inner power I was able to clearly dwell on all the situations that I could recall when I had unconsciously relied upon my inner guidance to make lifesaving decisions, and those decisions rarely, if ever, failed me."

I went back as far as I could remember, which took me back to my grammar school days and can remember making decisions based upon what I strongly felt. I never sat down with a piece of paper and a pencil to draw a line down the center of a page to list all the pros and cons of a decision because many of those decisions needed to be made quickly and not over a period of time. This is precisely what one's inner force does—the ability to reach a quick and accurate decision. Therefore, I placed my trust in my all-knowing inner guidance to provide me with the answers, methods, and solutions I was seeking.

It would be inconceivable to me that any person alive today can say that they never had a gut feeling about something, be it good or not so good—whether a relationship, a job, other people, a travel decision to go or not to go, etc. Most of us have made these types of decisions through our intuition, haven't we?

The question really becomes how often we pay attention to our intuitive feelings and innate wisdom, as opposed to how often do we heed outside influences instead—whether it is other people, medical advisors, business associates, well-meaning family members, friends and acquaintances, etc. I will venture to go out on a limb here to state that many people have regrets for not listening to their inner feelings. Had they done so, certain situations or circumstances in their lives may have had a more positive result for them. Could I be wrong? I do not believe I am.

I pride myself on being a well-educated person, having had a well-rounded business career, being fortunate to have had the opportunity to travel extensively and have had the privilege of meeting a number of interesting people worldwide. That said, I can honestly say that of the numerous people with whom I have been fortunate enough to meet and speak, many have said that they had regretted not following their first instincts. Some who did not follow their intuition are living with the calculated decisions they chose to rely on instead or the advice they had taken from those in whom they had placed most of, if not all, their trust.

Is it a mistake to take outside advice? Not particularly. However, this also depends upon what and who is giving the advice! For me—

and I am certain many people—my inner intuitive guide is what has and remains to guide me.

For those who may reject the idea of an inner guidance, tell me, has everything else you've tried thus far worked for you without having relied upon this inner wisdom that is connected with the all-knowing infinite intelligence? If your answer is yes, as I said earlier, then stop here. Apparently, you do not require this knowledge at this time. However, hold on to this book, should any life-threatening illnesses or serious life-changing event show up in your life in the future and current remedies fail you. At the very least, be kind enough to pass this book on to someone who may not be as fortunate as you. Just because we cannot see a thing does not mean it does not exist.

People who have been diagnosed with life-threatening illnesses, terminal or otherwise, have and do survive. None of them had any more options or special opportunities than anyone else has. Think about it!

What is it that we may all have had in common that skeptics possibly may not be considering? Why would you or anyone not even remotely consider that maybe—just maybe—these survivors really discovered something skeptics cannot detect? And maybe one day this something could possibly benefit you or a member of your family; a dear friend; a colleague; an acquaintance; a deprived, underprivileged person; or one of millions who cannot even afford to go to a doctor or hospital to receive any medical care whatsoever because they cannot afford out-of-reach, ever-skyrocketing medical coverage, let alone a doctor or medication. And, oh yes, let's not forget the financially wealthy; they too have nowhere to hide from any life-threatening illness or serious life-changing event as money cannot buy anyone a permanent healing or cure.

Have skeptics ever considered any or all of this or are they so blinded by having been so controlled by what they've read, learned, statistics, TV, medical science, and the huge pharmaceutical corporations that they are totally unwilling to wake up and open their eyes to the possibility that there may be other options than what mankind thinks they know about solving the rampage of serious diseases that I have been describing thus far?

However, having now passed the halfway mark, plus a few more years of a century on this planet and still in good health, raising a teenage son, in the process of writing two more humanitarian-related books, soon to launch my speaking engagements related to the information contained in this book, I absolutely know that I discovered something of tremendous value (not materialistic) that I am more than willing to share with anyone who cares enough about their life and the lives of others they care about and/or love. Crazy? No, let's just call it reconnected (not religiously intended), and you can be as well.

You may possibly be saying that you do not believe in any such thing that could possibly have been responsible for all the so-called survival miracles experienced by cancer survivors and survivors of other life-threatening and terminal illnesses and a myriad of other diseases throughout the world for centuries. Maybe you may also be saying you cannot be convinced otherwise. I say maybe you're right—for the moment, anyway—in your way of looking at things that may however possibly change in the blink of an eye, should you ever be faced with a diagnosis of any life-disrupting or life-threatening disease, condition, or illness.

My grandfather once told me when I was very young that knowledge is only useful if you decide to take the initiative and action and use it; otherwise, it is useless. I myself regret that it took me so many years to finally realize how true that advice was.

I cannot and do not ask or recommend that anyone follow or do anything I have done to rid myself of life-threatening physical and nonphysical illnesses and other serious life-changing events I personally encountered. This account is not about me and my survival; instead, this is about you and your survival and those whom you love and/or care and all mankind who is willing to embrace their all-knowing inner guidance that is one with the infinite intelligence.

Let's take a much closer look at why I say this and why acting on your inner visions and dreams is so vital to achieving your deepest desires.

19

BE THE INNER VISION AND DREAM

> Visualization is daydreaming with a purpose.
>
> —Author

This subject of overcoming life-changing adversities, physical or nonphysical, is my life's passion; and I will continue to be relentless in my pursuit in helping people worldwide to overcome self-induced problems and to understand that they need to become their inner visions/dreams for good and not to just dream the dream and do nothing with it! Unless you do, you become part of those who hope nothing more than wishful thinking without intention and action. Now, as I said earlier, there is certainly nothing wrong with the word *hope*; however, this has no place in the subject of life-threatening illnesses (again, an opinion of one, mine!) unless—as I just stated—acted upon.

First and foremost, you need to become the inner vision/dream! This is the primary reason why I chose not to place much emphasis on the word *hope*. You need to rely instead upon the gift you came into this world with—one's inner guidance, which is all the knowledge you will ever need to be victorious over most any type of serious life-changing events that you may possibly encounter in your lifetime.

No one—and I mean *no one*—on this planet will ever get out of here without having experienced at least one, if not more, life-disrupting nonphysical disorders. History itself confirms this to be a fact with all the persecutions, genocides, inhumane treatment by many of this world's governments and dictators; racial inequality and prejudices; etc.; causing any number of life-challenging nonphysical conditions, led by stress and extreme anxiety at every level.

The word *dream* means "a visionary creation of the imagination"; or "a strongly desired goal or purpose." The reason why this subject is so vital is because the difference between envisioning a desired episode in a dream and acting upon that dream is day and night. I believe envisioning, which is a very strong form of dreaming, is in the forefront of the methods I have been discussing thus far.

The wonderful state of dreaming and envisioning is what most people are familiar with, but far too many people allow this unique ability to dream and envision go to waste. Although we recognize that we all dream and that our imagination creates a vision of a scenario, there is a vast difference between envisioning a desired situation that is vital to achieving and actually acting on your deepest desires for good.

Life is not about hoping; it's about envisioning, imagining, dreaming, and believing, coupled with strong inner emotions, feelings, and unwavering expectation. Unless you can envision, imagine, dream, and feel it with a burning passion, chances are greater that hope, positive, and wishful thinking alone may—and all too often do—fail most of us. Why? Because far too many people do not practice envisioning and imagining, let alone follow their strong intuitive inner feelings for any significant period of time. And when they do not see any immediate visible results, they generally will revert to their negative and doubting ways.

I compare the words *hope, positive*, and *wishful thinking* to the word *luck*. After all, isn't this what it is? I realize that the word *faith* is firmly entrenched in many religions; however, unless you become the vision or dream, then faith is not going to be of much help. "Faith without works is dead," the Bible says in James 2:14–26 (KJV). In other words, you need do something and not just place the healing process in the lap of a higher power to do it for you. You just might be asking yourself this, "Where does inner vision and strong feelings come from and how do I access them?"

PREVAILING OVER INSURMOUNTABLE ODDS

Do you remember at any point in your personal life that you once had a vision or dream followed by a strong feeling for something that you wanted or to be something so bad that that was all you could dream about and that your every waking moment was consumed with a strong feeling? Where did it come from? It was certainly something that you could not see, smell, hear, or touch; yet it was always there. It was an all-consuming, burning desire, crying out for a need to be fulfilled. Remember, ego demands, opposed to inner visioning/dreaming and inner feeling that silently and gently nudges one to take action to have manifest their burning desire.

Some people feel the desire to become a famous person one day; others feel they will become a doctor and help people; and others feel destined for the clergy. Others deeply feel the burning desire for a certain significant other in their lives and had that feeling long before that person eventually became their significant other. Again, I ask you, where did those feelings come from?

Although you cannot touch, see, smell, or hear it; yet you have an intense desire for whatever it is you feel. It is far removed from your understanding or even your ability to perceive; over time, as that feeling consumes you from within, eventually you become or achieve whatever it is you so passionately have been feeling. There is no logical explanation to this powerful feeling—it just is!

It is right here many people would like to give it a name. Some will call it God, Jehovah, Jesus, the Light, Allah, the Universe, and other names and references far too numerous to list here. However, when this feeling surfaces or appears, it did so only because you summoned it into being. It has always been there with you since the day of your birth. You have no physical control over it because you have been predestined to be it—that is, your inner wisdom.

If you can firmly convince yourself that you—your physical self, through your conscious mind—is all the power that you will ever need to bring forth a permanent healing for anything in this life that you may encounter, the only reliance that you are then left with is hope and faith, in addition to medical science, none of which is a path to a complete healing and permanent cure. Never has been and never will be. In the medical community's defense, they never claimed to be able to.

These power words, *hope* and *faith*, however, require action and total dedication on your part and your unwavering belief in them and lots of patience. So do not blame them, should you fail to be healed of whatever it is that you are personally encountering in the way of a life-threatening illness or life-changing physical or nonphysical event—the only blame that can be directed is to yourself.

What is it I am risking by telling you this? Is it criticism, being labeled as a kook, and maybe even worse, only because I offer no scientific proof, I have no medical degree, PhD or MD, etc., after my name. Possibly the world's medical masterminds may one day attempt to discredit deep inner visioning/dreaming and feeling and becoming the vision/dream as the key and path to the beginning of the healing process of every type of life-threatening event. So be it and have at it. However, as I stated, the medical profession, having come a great distance, has never yet claimed to bring forth a total and permanent cure. Instead, it can and will continue to treat the symptoms and the result of the already-manifested, self-create physical and nonphysical conditions and illnesses.

The one thing I have learned in my personal encounter with people so far is that those who do all the doubting and naysaying (remember skeptics?) are those who are among the unfortunate self-elected group of incurables. Unless they can prove a thing via the senses or medical science, to them, it does not exist. I can sympathize with them; however, because as I said before, it was not too long ago I myself was a card-carrying member and in good standing with this worldwide group (a fictitious organization used for illustrative purposes only by the author). However, what they fail to recognize and admit to is the fact that many people globally have survived and have been self-healed from numerous life-threatening illnesses and conditions, physical and nonphysical—yours truly for one—and not solely through the knowledge of medical science entirely but instead through and by what they themselves chose, which came from what they called their inner wisdom.

Remember, there simply are no quick fixes for any serious life-changing or life-threatening event or illness, physical or nonphysical that I am aware of. (Yes, I realize that I have said this several times earlier.) However, if you choose to apply anything in this book to your life, be certain that you make a life commitment to yourself to continue to call forth your all-knowing inner guidance that is one with the infinite intelligence. This should be preceded by and following with, sincere and heartfelt gratitude, in advance, for your expected permanent healing, without which you can rest assured you will not be rewarded with much of a benefit.

Remember this as well: If your problems are associated with the economy but you achieved many of what had appeared to be insurmountable objectives in your life—up until the point circumstances became the present economic and financial hardships—nothing about who you really are has changed. What has changed is the sudden shift in the world's economic condition that has affected people all over the globe which has nothing to do with who you really are. If you will take a deep breath and think about it, you will once again begin to vision/dream and feel that indeed you have not changed and have the same drive to succeed you always have had deep inside. You absolutely know this, and furthermore, you already know that you can overcome any negative event or circumstance that has or may enter your life. The mere fact that you have made it this far in this highly competitive world is all the proof you need that confirms this fact to yourself.

Among some of the most amazing things I have ever witnessed in my life is the arrogance we all seem to be carrying within us—the nerve we have to believe that anything that happens to us is the fault of anyone or anything but ourselves. The exception, of course, is violent crimes; and even in these, some may have played somewhat of a role attracting persons or situations into their lives with very few exceptions.

Understand that maintaining a permanent healing for any life-threatening illness or event is a lifelong process and not to be considered a temporary freeing of any life-threatening illness, condition, or event. If one lives long enough, eventually he/she will wake up one day and finally realize that everything that has ever happened to them, good or bad, was the end result of their very own personal creation and design. You don't believe it? Then think this over for a while. Everything you have done in your life to date has all to do with the personal choices you made—no one else's!

What comes into your physical life is a direct result of what you have continuously dreamt about, dwelled on for a period of time, and deeply felt internally. Here are just some brief examples of what I mean:

Have you ever felt even slightly depressed? Why? Because you chose to be in that state of mind! The matter of what is concerning or had disturbed you in the past is what you have dwelled on for a considerable period of time. Have you ever felt unloved? Why? Because you envisioned and chose to feel unloved at that point in time. You focused and envisioned upon your false belief that no one can love you, and when you dwelt on this thought, you invited this condition into your life. You must first focus on loving yourself and who you really are inside and not continuously dwell on the outside world. Anyone who is seeking to fall in love with someone who has a seemingly perfect outer appearance all too often finds that the person they may have chosen for this reason alone turns out to be a terrible disappointment.

If you love the person who lives inside you first, then you certainly will attract the right person for you who can see this lovely person who lives inside the outer you and falls deeply in love with the person you really are. Always remember this about yourself, and you will be able to pick and select the right person for you because your inner wisdom is never wrong.

If you do not love yourself, then how can you possibly expect to attract anyone else to love you? Be the dream you see yourself to be and not the hope. *Hope* is a wish; however, a *continuous vision/dream* of the person you really are and will eventually become actually is different. All you have to do is to absolutely know it to be true, and what you are seeking always will follow.

Have you ever had deep grief for an extended period of time? Why? Because you chose to continue to grieve for whatever extended time period you grieved. You may have known or heard of people who grieved for years over the loss of a loved one and even go as far as to wish that they would also die. And some did. Why? Because they made the choice to die. Why? Because this is what they envisioned and dwelled upon day after day, and eventually, what they continued to envision and focus upon showed up in reality. Their most dominant

PREVAILING OVER INSURMOUNTABLE ODDS

desire materialized, and what they had visioned and dwelled upon for a considerable period of time was delivered to them.

Have you ever felt deeply upset because you could not get that car you wanted, that outfit you had your heart set on, or that special someone in your life you may have lost to another? Why? Because you chose to place yourself in that position, no other reason. You wound up in these circumstances because you envisioned, daydreamed, night-dreamed, and focused on these situations and for no other reason. These became your primary visions and thoughts, and because they were all negative, then negative is what you got. The chef deep inside of you, so to speak, prepared precisely what you ordered and delivered it to you as you had requested along, with all the trimmings that go with it.

Become the good dream you want to materialize in your life and not just the vision. Hoping and wishing is good, but becoming and envisioning the dream is the ultimate result. You do not have to assume a yoga position and have to place yourself in a meditative trance (although yoga is a very good practice and has its benefits). All it really takes is to change what you continuously focus upon and strongly feel.

Before you retire in the evening, as you begin to slowly drift off to sleep, make whatever it is you desire to become a burning desire. Try to imagine what it is that you desire, the only thought you're dwelling on, and hold this thought and vision as long as you can. Once you fall into a deep sleep, your all-knowing inner guidance will take over and will begin to put people and circumstances on your path and remove all the obstacles in your physical world. When you continue to do this, in time, you will begin to bring into reality what you are dreaming and focusing upon to manifest in your physical world as it must. Many people know this phenomenon as the law of attraction, one of the great universal laws.

Laws of the Universe

The laws of the universe go by many names. Here are some of its names:

1. *Law of Divine Oneness.* Everything is connected to everything else. What we think, say, do, and believe will have a corresponding effect on others and the universe around us.
2. *Law of Vibration.* Everything in the universe moves, vibrates, and travels in circular patterns. The same principles of vibration in the physical world apply to our thoughts, feelings, desires, and wills in the etheric world. Each sound, thing, and even thought has its own vibrational frequency, unique unto itself.
3. *Law of Action.* Must be employed in order for us to manifest things on earth. We must engage in actions that supports our thoughts, dreams, emotions, and words.
4. *Law of Correspondence.* This universal law states that the principles or laws of physics that explain the physical world, energy, light, vibration, and motion have their corresponding principles in the etheric or universe—"As above, so below."
5. *Law of Cause and Effect.* Nothing happens by chance or outside the universal laws. Every action (including thought) has a reaction or consequence—"We reap what we sow."
6. *Law of Compensation.* The universal law is the law of cause and effect applies to blessings and abundance that are provided for us. The visible effects of our deeds are given to us in gifts, money, inheritances, friendships, and blessings.
7. *Law of Attraction.* Demonstrates how we create the things, events, and people that come into our lives. Our thoughts, feelings, words, and actions produce energies which, in turn, attract like energies. Negative energies attract negative energies, and positive energies attract positive energies.
8. *Law of Perpetual Transmutation of Energy.* All persons have within them the power to change the conditions of their lives. Higher vibrations consume and transform lower ones;

thus, each of us can change the energies in our lives by understanding the universal laws and applying the principles in such a way as to effect change.

9. *Law of Relativity.* Each person will receive a series of problems (tests of initiation or lessons) for the purpose of strengthening the light within each these tests/lessons to be a challenge and remain connected to our hearts when proceeding to solve the problems. This law also teaches us to compare our problems to others problem into its proper perspective. No matter how bad we perceive our situation to be, there is always someone who is in a worse position. It's all relative.

10. *Law of Polarity.* Everything is on a continuum and has and opposite. We can suppress and transform undesirable thoughts by concentrating on the opposite pole. It is the law of mental vibrations.

11. *Law of Rhythm.* Everything vibrates and moves to certain rhythms. These rhythms establish seasons, cycles, stages of development, and patterns. Each cycle reflects the regularity of God's universe. Masters know how to rise above negative parts of a cycle by never getting too excited or allowing negative things to penetrate their consciousness.

12. *Law of Gender.* The law of gender manifests in all things as masculine and feminine. It is this law that governs what we know as creation. The law of gender manifests in the animal kingdom as sex. This law decrees everything in nature is both male and female. Both are required for life to exist.

However, I know it to only be the all-knowing inner guidance, the gift with which you came into this world and which you already own and possess that is needed to bring into your physical life anything good that you desire, as long as it benefits everyone concerned in a wholesome way. Remember, that it is not your problem or concern to know the *when*, the *how*, the *where*, or the *why*—just trust in the dream/vision that you turn over to your all-knowing inner guidance and allow this all-knowing inner power to do the rest. Be patient and never doubt that the result you desire will manifest, as it will when you trust that it will.

This also goes for preserving the dream as well. Once the dream is allowed to fade, it may give way to any or a combination of the nonphysical conditions. To allow any of this will negate the power of your inner guidance, thereby diminishing what you desire to be accomplished.

Think about this. Before you gained anything you have materially or possibly are in the process of losing or have already lost, no matter what the circumstances may be at that point in your life, ask yourself how you were able to obtain it in the first place. So whatever it was deep inside of you that brought it forward and lit the pilot light of your burning desire to have whatever it is you had achieved up to this point, do not allow that light to be extinguished for any reason whatsoever.

I myself was a self-ordained, so-labeled victim. If it were not for rediscovering and then acting upon my inner guidance deep inside me, I would never have been here today; this book—my vision and dream—would never have been possible.

How do I know all these things? I know because, as mentioned earlier, I was personally involved with almost every nonphysical condition and other extreme events, causing me to deal with an entirely different and much higher level of emotional storms and trauma. The likes of which I experienced could never be explained in words alone, unless one had personally known this experience and level of extreme trauma. Beyond these traumas, I even overcame these conditions that I elaborate in my forthcoming speaking engagement, through the incredible power of my all-knowing inner power.

Most people I know who have combined negative life situations do not even come close to what I have endured in my lifetime in the way of nonphysical conditions, life-threatening physical illnesses, and related events. However, that said, I believe that despite all my horrendous personal experiences thus far, there are some people in this world who have far exceeded my very serious life-changing scenarios whom I have yet to meet and who are also warriors and incredible self- healed survivors.

Visualization

People continue to ask me how I was able to overcome all that I have, most of which was deemed to be insurmountable. Among those who believed this were members of the medical profession who were treating me for cancer. However, little did they know I—like everyone ever born—already had been blessed with the methods, answers, and solutions necessary to overcome most life-disrupting illnesses and events, as well as a number of life-changing crises and related circumstances occurring at the same time. To make matters even worse, I was subjected to these simultaneously—all of which I believe may dwarf what most people would ever come close to experiencing in their lifetimes.

Among these methods is one that I had employed during my business career as a self-employed entrepreneur, which I began from the bedroom of my apartment with only a one hundred dollars in the bank, and ultimately achieved every goal I had established for myself, which included very successful businesses and prosperity on every conceivable level. So what does this brief history have to do with devastating crises? As I've just discussed, I accomplished all this and much more through the method of visualizing precisely what I wanted to achieve in my life and saw myself enjoying and possessing what I was visualizing in my conscious mind, transferring these visions directly to my inner guidance to bring forth what I was envisioning into my physical life.

Now you may be asking yourself, "What exactly does visualizing have to do with a method for what you may desire?" Visualizing—i.e., *imagining*—is not only an important method; it is among the most important methods one can employ. This very important method is all about actually envisioning yourself already owning and enjoying precisely what you have with an intense desire to realize your success. Although a well-known method that dates back centuries, not many people will spend the time to use this method, even though they are aware of it.

In addition, if they will actually discipline themselves to practice this technique instead, they will choose to give up when their desires do not manifest in their lives within a short period of time.

Therefore, if they do make an effort to use this powerful method, they are unwilling to exercise patience, which is the key to securing whatever is being visualized.

The question then becomes "How much time will it take for me to be able to obtain what I visualize?" The short answer is, it depends on how much time you are willing to dedicate to this visualizing method in order to be able to actually have what it is you desire to attain and the depth of your belief that it already has. It is important to understand that one needs to actually feel the excitement of really receiving whatever it may be desired to appear and to strongly continue to believe—without any doubt, wavering, or skepticism—that it will happen. If you do this, in time, it can materialize.

I have been asked by many people how one goes about visualizing whatever it may be that is desired for good, not evil. Visualization is actually seeing and actually having the end result in one's conscious mind (known as formulating a mental picture and holding on to this picture) and visualizing yourself actually possessing what is deeply desired to manifest. It is like playing a movie in one's mind over and over again and keeping that movie playing until whatever it may be eventually does show up in one's physical life.

If you choose to employ this method and continue to do so, what you continue to visualize can—with any doubt in my mind—become reality in your life in time.

This visualizing technique, coupled with unwavering belief and expectation, is well documented. It is known to have worked what is said to be miracles for those who truly believed in the power of visualizing in one's mind anything for achieving what they wish to occur when there is no doubt in this process.

Doubting and being skeptical, without fail, will neutralize the desired manifestation, and therefore, neither will happen that was visualized nor should it expected to be. Should this occur, you would have to begin again visualizing the desired results—however, this time, without wavering, being skeptical, or doubting. In short, visualizing is no more than seeing oneself actually receiving what has not yet happened (picturing in one's conscious mind as having already received, doing whatever it may be that is being sought) in the present and having successfully achieved the desired result. The key to this method is to imagine in your mind that whatever it may be you are seeking is actually taking place at that very moment and actually visualizing, envisioning, and picturing whatever it may be that is desired. Not only did I use this method to defeat two cancers, but I continue to rely upon it to develop into reality anything I desire for positive benefits where all are concerned. And it has not failed me even once, neither will it fail you.

There are several excellent books available on this subject. One of my favorites is a book written by American spiritual teacher, author, and philosopher Vernon Howard (1918–1992) titled *Psycho-Pictography: The New Way to Use the Miracle Power of Your Mind*.

It is important to understand that the mental pictures you focus on and predominantly think about eventually become like an architect's drawing of a project that has yet to be constructed. These exist first as a vision (imagining) in the architect's mind, which is seen as very real, already constructed, and inhabited by its intended tenants.

This example depicts that if you dedicate yourself to visualizing and imagining your goals and expected outcomes as if they are already taking place, what is being visualized can appear. Whatever the desired outcome may be, it must also feel real and accompanied with a joyful emotion and be as detailed as it can possibly be. You must also see yourself possessing whatever your desires for good are and implant this vision in your mind to be recalled often—very often— in the form of a habitual, dominant thought that overpowers the thousands of thoughts that go through your mind on any given day.

This process must be done without fail—at the very minimum, once a day, if not more often—as there is immense power in repetitive dominant thoughts that, when believed as true, will then be transmitted from your conscious mind to your inner guidance; and what is being desired to occur, believed, and visualized will be brought forth. Please keep in mind that this method needs to be done with total dedication until whatever is sought is eventually manifested in reality.

The only way this process can fail to bring forth the desired result is if this is not done as described. As I said, procrastinating, doubting, being negative and skeptical, being impatient, wavering, or choosing to listen to others who may possibly wish to convince you that this method is not worth your time. If you choose to accept these debilitating thoughts, this will nullify developing whatever it may be that you are seeking to effect. I should know because I did that myself in the beginning—until I finally realized what a misguided choice that was.

Should any of these negative thoughts take hold, you can rest assured that whatever it is you are seeking for good will not be achieved. How do I know this visualization method works? Because I personally achieved positive results and continue to use it for whatever I want to produce for my benefit in my life, and many other people do as well.

Utilized in the manner described, this visualization and imagining technique is one of the most powerful faculties a person possesses, and anyone in any adversity or undesirable life-changing event should seriously consider utilizing this method. It should not be a matter of concern with how the results being sought will appear—just trust the process and allow it to go to work to bring forth the desired result. You will be led to the right actions, decisions, answers, and desired results at the right time.

It is natural for anyone to look for immediate results and answers before being willing to do what is necessary to achieve them. Who wouldn't want to be able to see the results before they materialize and be able to see how this process unfolds and precisely what is happening for us every inch of the way? However, the *how* and *when* are not revealed to us, as the result will appear when we least expect it in ways we would not have imagined. When this method is utilized, it is necessary to trust in it, put into immediate action what comes into your mind from your inner guidance, and then strongly believe and expect that the desired result will appear in your life.

I adopted this method and further enhanced it by following what was clearly outlined in Vernon Howard's remarkable and incredible book *Psycho-Pictography*, within which he shows us precisely how to create a clear "mental picture" for each and every possible event one wants to produce. This book has become the centerpiece for me, concerning the subject of visualization and imagination and has worked marvelous wonders in my life and continues to do so, in conjunction with other very powerful methods I also adopted described in this chapter and those that you will find throughout the remainder of this book, in addition to the incredible method of communicating with the infinite intelligence through the method I outlined earlier.

As I said, I am not stating that once you begin to visualize and imagine a desired outcome or result that it will materialize within a day or a week or a month or that someone may come into your life and hand you a pile of money, offer you the world, and fix all your problems overnight. What I am stating is that the methods and the answers you may be seeking can come your way and can lead you to the desired results you are seeking, as they have and continue to do for me.

Therefore, I know for a fact, deep inside myself, this inner guidance is the primary reason that people who believe in their inner wisdom and this infinite intelligence I write about survived life-threatening adversities and have moved on with their lives today, knowing that this inner guidance will never abandon or fail them.

Through my personal testimony, I am living proof that one's all-knowing inner guidance will never fail you once you make a personal commitment to it for life. It is at this point when one's life can take a turn for a tremendous and wonderful experience of joy, happiness, and prosperity on every conceivable level.

Another pertinent question is this: Why do some people make it through a life-threatening episode and/or life-changing events and others do not? This is a great question and certainly deserves to be addressed.

Why Some People Make It and Some Don't

Why do many people become successful in life and others never even come close? Because they chose to be. That's right! You see, very successful self-made multimillionaires—not the ones who inherited their fortunes or were born with a silver spoon in their mouths, so to speak—have the same twenty-four hours at their disposal that anyone else has. The difference between them and unsuccessful people is what the successful people do with the very same twenty-four hours you and I have. (This includes what they vision, dream about, dwell, and focus upon continuously.)

"Yeah right!"—you certainly must have heard these remarks from skeptics, but he or she was born into a wealthy family and environment! Okay, maybe some were. But somewhere along their family line, someone only had a wooden spoon or a piece of shale or a clam shell to eat with, and chances are they never experienced financial wealth either! The simple truth is that we—no one or nothing else—chose our very own life path. Did I know or wish to accept this truth when I was a very young know-it-all? The answer is a resounding *no* and is also *no* for most people.

I have witnessed more self-pity in this world than I care to remember. Such questions like "why did this have to happen to me?" really get to me. It didn't! The real question is, *Why did you bring whatever it is upon yourself?* Another that gets me is the classic "Why me? I've done nothing to deserve this!" Really! You worked long and hard to bring whatever it is into your life, good or bad—we all did!

At this point, I can hear you saying, "This guy is really cynical!" You might also believe that I am coldhearted, self-centered, egotistical, etc. Maybe and maybe not! What I do know, however, is that I am here writing about these circumstances and sharing them with you in an honest and sincere effort to fulfill my life's mission, which is to reach out to people everywhere in an effort to bring them the methods, answers, and solutions and source of what I know that can bring them whatever they may be seeking for good. I have no ax to grind with the world—or anyone, for that matter—as all the undesirable events that came into my life were all my own doing and no one else's.

Perhaps you and others may pass this information on to someone else who can also benefit from the information contained in this book written by a true survivor of numerous life-threatening illnesses and serious, traumatic conditions and events, physical and nonphysical. If I could have survived all this as one of the most negative persons I have known—until I chose to change all that—then you and those with whom you may choose to share this information also can! Only you can tell yourself that you cannot do anything because only you can pilot your own destiny, as there is not one human being on this planet who can walk on your life's path because that path was designed solely for you and you alone!

In my sole opinion, the only obstacle preventing you from doing this and also being successful at overcoming most—if not every nonphysical condition, physical illness, and undesirable event in your life—is you! Know that it is you and others who control the overwhelming nature of your ailments. I firmly believe that should you choose to utilize any information contained within this book, at your sole and independent discretion to do so, you just may stand more than a fighting chance to overcome whatever life throws at you, as I and other survivors have done against the odds. And therefore, there is absolutely no reason you can't either, unless you convince yourself you can't.

Once again, I do not recommend, advocate, or suggest that you do anything that I did, as whatever I have chosen to do for myself to bring about permanent healing was and remains my individual choice. Therefore, before embarking upon anything that you may choose to do, should you come face to face with any life-changing illness or event, it will also be your personal choice too. However, first seek out the advice of a medical professional or any other credible professional before embarking upon any alternative choices such as I have thus far described.

I once read this fabulous quote by George Bernard Shaw that inspired me beyond words can possibly describe: "We have not lost faith, but instead we have transferred it from God to the medical profession" (or whatever a higher power would be to you). No truer words could have been uttered, as it relates to the lack of trust we have in ourselves, and we go out of our way to demonstrate this every day, don't we? Oh, you might be thinking, "This is not so!" Then ask yourself this: "How many times a day or a week—or for some, an hour—do you ask someone their opinion about something?" I am willing to state that the manufacturers of aspirin have yet to manufacture enough aspirin to match how many times in people's lifetimes throughout the world do this frequently (a slight exaggeration, but you get the point, right!). Don't feel singled out because even the geniuses also do it and quite often!

Another favorite saying of mine is by William W. Watt: "Do not put your faith in what statistics say until you have carefully considered what they do not say." Brilliant, isn't it? This is the motto I have lived by since experiencing nonphysical conditions and physical illnesses and events and one of the many keys as to why I have "successfully" defeated every life-destructive event that most people possibly may never face in their entire lifetimes.

You may be asking yourself, "How is it that you can still be standing, having encountered such incredible life-threatening odds?" As you have realized, I not only survived serious, life-damaging physical events that, according to medical science, I should not have survived without further invasive treatments. I also had survived numerous serious life-disrupting events that most people more than likely may possibly not have. (As far as the physical events are concerned, I have provided in the appendix of this book a copy of a medical document concerning my odds of surviving cancer without electing chemotherapy treatments that confirms this experience.)

Ask yourself this: "Why haven't I been able to overcome my exposure to life-changing events as well?" The answer may be that you have become accustomed to your condition or have developed an "it will pass" attitude. It more than likely may not, unless you personally decide to take total control, beginning right where you are and right now!

The Importance of Taking Immediate Action

Let's direct a few terms first. The word action means "the accomplishment of a thing usually over a period of time, in stages, or with the possibility of repetition." *Direct action* means "action that seeks to achieve an end directly and by the most immediately effective means."

Anyone faced with a harmful physical condition, situation, or other circumstance should certainly be seeking the most expedient resolution to their circumstance or situation. I realize that a number of life-threatening illnesses can take time to be medically controlled or arrested. However, as identified previously, by dependency upon medical science alone, many people fail to take any personal responsibility or appropriate action on their own, placing the entire responsibility, dependency, and weight on their medical providers while they wait for these medical providers to perform a so-called miracle on their behalf. It's going to be a very, very long wait—and possibly never—because, as I've been saying, medical science does not claim a complete and permanent cure for many severely damaging diseases or causes leading up to illnesses.

Yes, I realize this sounds harsh, and it is! However, I have had enough "personal experience" with this subject of direct action and taking personal responsibility to be able to state without any reservation whatsoever that taking direct responsibility and immediate direct action on your part is not only vitally necessary but, in many cases such as mine, can be lifesaving.

If I did not take direct and immediate action by deciding to reconnect with my gift of inner wisdom that is connected to the infinite intelligence I am almost certain I would not be in this world today. We must first be willing to change how we think, and then we must be receptive to alternative ways to help ourselves and accept the fact that our medical providers are in the business of treating us. They provide us with the best medical care they are capable of, refer us to other medical professionals who are specialists in treating specific diseases and life-compromising illnesses, and follow up with us as we progress with their recommended or prescribed medical treatments, prescription medications and/or therapy, medical counseling, etc.

Therefore, when a subject like inner guidance is presented, it does not lead to immediate change in our way of looking at things (a possible alternative way toward the achievement of a thing—i.e., "a cure"); it simply remains in the mind of one who is looking at it as a concept—and possibly a very interesting one, at that—but to that person, just the same, it is one among numerous other concepts as well. However, when an accepted learned thing takes root in one's mind, it follows that direct action will also take place almost simultaneously because the conscious mind accepts it to be true and will begin to immediately act upon it.

Once we begin to accept the possibility that a certain method just may be one among several other methods, we may choose to consider it as another option. It is at this exact point in our lives that we finally awaken to the fact that we have an almost inexplicable power to create everything and anything in our lives, consciously and subconsciously, positive or negative. We then begin to finally realize that we know how much we are directly responsible for what occurs in our lives, especially this present moment in time.

Upon realizing this, we then begin to understand how creative we really are. And by taking immediate direct action, we can obtain even more positive results. Realizing and accepting that accountability and personal responsibility are the primary keys to reclaiming your inner power, along with being willing to acknowledge and recognize that we had been aware of in our lives up until now, whatever it was and is today.

How important it is to every single person on this planet to clearly understand that they had something to do with everything that they have or ever will experience in their lifetime. This includes any circumstance they may currently have or may possibly have in the future.

Unless or until we are able to accept and take responsibility that we attract and have had and always will have some role to play in whatever occurs in our lives, positive or negative, then we will continue to live in the sad world of denial. Therefore, what acknowledgement and responsibility really come down to is that we are acting with knowledge or, better said, "we do what we do knowingly." Simply put, all you have to be able to be willing to do is to admit the validity of your part in whatever that has come into your life, be it a positive or a negative event, and to take personal responsibility for whatever it is, good or bad.

When I was finally able to clearly see the circumstances that had come into my life, I was able to truthfully admit to myself that I had something to do with whatever was affecting me at the time. Did I know exactly what I may have done to have played a role in those circumstances? No, not precisely. However, when I began to look back on those situations, I was able to find a number of things that may have contributed to those circumstances and that I could certainly have done or chosen differently. And when it came down to denial, I certainly was an award-winning member of that group as well, prior to accepting responsibility and acknowledging my role in "attracting" each and every event that had come into my life.

What this did for me was to keep me alert for all future events and be able to carefully weigh all my choices and options before making any important decisions. From that point forward, I realized that I had control over my decisions. By doing so, I found that I have and continue to be able to live being more aware of things that could possibly cause me to attract any negative event into my existence and every positive event I want to exist.

My acknowledgement does not mean that I am condemning all my actions and criticizing almost everything I have done with my life—quite the contrary, I might add. Instead, it is my willingness to take full responsibility for my actions and being able to recognize the role these played in allowing any negative event or circumstances to enter into my daily interactions, including the positive ones as well. We all selectively choose to deny things; it is human nature to do so. It is also human nature to attempt to lay blame on something or someone else for our hardships, as no one wants to believe that they had any role in attracting any serious negative event into their lives.

Unless you are willing to acknowledge and to take responsibility for your role in anything you attract—negative or positive (especially negative)—it will be difficult for you to reach the point of being able to connect or reconnect with the incredible gift that has been given to you—your all-knowing inner guidance. Being in a constant state of acknowledgement and taking personal responsibility is precisely what your inner guidance actually is about, and the sooner you can accept this truth, the sooner you will be able to connect or reconnect with your gift of an all-knowing inner guidance. How do I know this? I credit my permanent healing of all the negative events that I have been aware of in my life to this inner knowing power—that is, the infinite intelligence one with my inner guidance.

I want you to know one more thing about this act of taking responsibility. In no way is this to be misconstrued as a "who is to blame for my condition or who made this happen to me and at whom can we point the finger or such arrogance as to whom can we sue for everything they've got for this" idea. No! What this responsibility is and how you need to approach it is in choosing everything that is going to bring you into accepting your personal role in whatever you may be experiencing. It is of utmost importance not to continue to add additional stress, anxiety, and concerns, which may add more fuel to your situation or circumstance, causing you to sink even deeper into that condition.

There is a time for everything; however, this is neither the time for any adversity or negativity to take over nor should it ever be. What you are seeking is a healing, not a war! Therefore, eliminate from your life all the blaming and all the soldiers who wish to join the "blame and revenge brigade"—this includes yourself as their leader! If you are bitter, angry, or wish to lay blame, I suggest you surround yourself instead with caring and loving people who will support your inner courage to overcome whatever it is that may be plaguing you. I mean *anything* that includes a nonphysical illness or undesirable life-changing event or circumstance that can change into a serious life-damaging physical illness, if it is not arrested by you and prevented by you from continuing to grow.

Think about What You Choose to Say before Saying It

I cannot impress upon you enough the importance of what you choose to let come out of your mouth and how this precisely dictates the condition you create for yourself at any given time. Consider that we create everything that happens to us every moment of our lives. With this in mind, "absolutely know" that what you continue to focus upon and speak out, more often than not, will eventually materialize in your life, be it positive or negative. It represents to your inner guidance what you truly believe and therefore what your inner guidance will transmit to the infinite intelligence for you to eventually realize.

In a nutshell, only say what you really want to occur in your life and never continuously say, think, focus, or dwell upon what it is you do not want. If you will do this beginning right now, I can tell you from my very own knowledge (as I cannot speak for another's personal experiences) that in a short period of time, you will begin to personally witness circumstances and events changing in your life in a very positive direction. Begin first with small things for a while, and as these begin to materialize into your physical life, slowly graduate to more challenging situations. Do not overwhelm yourself with wants or dwell upon what it is you don't want in your life. If you do, that is precisely what you will attract and invite into your life. Trust what I am saying as I was an expert at inviting and attracting a myriad of experiences into my life that I did not want—illnesses were just some of them. Practically everything else I did not want to enter into my life did!

I am not going to expand on any religious beliefs, as every one of us were born with the gift of free will; thereby, we have the freedom to choose silently and openly what we trust and believe when it comes to the subject of any unseen intelligence beyond man. It really does not matter what anyone may choose to label such intelligence.

As for myself, my strong trust in the gift of my all-knowing inner guidance and what I have personally been able to witness during my lifetime thus far is more than enough to have convinced me that a very powerful unseen force and intelligence does exist. I believe that no one can either create or bring forth a total and absolute permanent healing for anything for any prolonged period of time; only a more powerful guidance and intelligence can accomplish this for humanity. Why else is medical science baffled when someone diagnosed with a terminal or irreversible life-threatening illness survives and is, in many cases, later found to not even have a trace of the disease remaining in their physical body?

I found that the events I had personally participated in had strengthened me so much mentally that I absolutely refused to allow anyone near me who was the bearer of any negative news or thoughts concerning my condition or about statistics about how few people survived them. That was a lot of eliminating, and I possibly offended some people along the way; however, it was my physical person that was under serious attack by these physical and nonphysical events, not theirs.

As you can possibly imagine, it did not take long before I found myself surrounded by only just a few true supporters who may not have agreed totally with how I chose to handle my circumstances but who respected my choices to do what I trusted to be the correct path to choose for me to bring forth a total and permanent cure for these circumstances and events. A path that I absolutely know brought forth the answers and the methods that allowed me to overcome numerous undesirable life-changing events that seemed to be bombarding my physical life continuously for a number of years. I found that by speaking out for what I preferred to exist in my life and by adopting this verbal exercise regularly when I was alone—i.e., my car, at home, walking, bicycle riding, exercising, etc.—that everything negative began to take a wonderful turn for the positive. This is when I began to be aware of what I truly wanted in my life, and to this very moment, I continue to do this and have not once ever considered abandoning these outward desires by speaking them versus just occasionally thinking about them.

What am I really saying here? I am saying that I quickly learned how to endure the circumstances and negative events that I had personally attracted into my physical life. I learned from my inner guidance how to reverse any and all undesirable, life-affecting events that occurred. I firmly trust that, had I not had these negative events and circumstances enter my life when they did, I may never have had the opportunity to reconnect with my gift.

Am I saying that we have to endure pain, suffering, and everything that is associated with these events? I trust that anything that we may possibly have to endure can only make us stronger and not necessarily physically. If we wish to become stronger physically, then we should exercise our bodies, even if it means deciding to walk half an hour a day, if we are physically able.

As I see this topic of endurance, I relate it to how humanity chooses to deal with it. Of course, there are varying levels and degrees of endurance, such as physical, loss, suffering, pain, failing relationships, etc. However, we should realize that almost every level of endurance is based upon where a person chooses to set the bar for their individual level of tolerance in any given circumstance or situation in which they may find themselves having challenges.

I have been asked on a number of occasions if I truly believed that this gift of inner wisdom is the answer to all our undesirable, life-altering negative events and circumstances that we may encounter. Had I been asked this question before I reconnected with this gift, my quick answer would have been a flat *no*. However, having been given the opportunity to reconnect with this gift and having had vast personal participation with its immense power soon after I decided to reconnect with this inner force, my answer now is—and will always remain—a resounding *yes*!

Please be reminded that this book is not a pitch to get anyone to accept this gift. This is and will always be a personal decision to either make this connection or reconnection or to not make it and continue on with life as is. What you choose to acknowledge thus far is entirely up to you. There is no one alive who can make this decision for you. I for one, however, am extremely pleased that I decided to reconnect with my all-knowing inner power because, as a result of making that decision, my life has changed and improved dramatically and positively. For me, this was and remains my acceptance of what I know to be real, perpetual, and incredibly reliable.

High on the list of what I deemed necessary for my survival was to be able to accept my circumstances and the negative, undesirable life-transforming events that I had attracted into my life.

Among the many downfalls in life was my strong need to always have to be in control of everything that was going on in my life. Talk about a task made for a superhero! If I was not in control of a given situation, I would become discontented, irritable, and frustrated among other feelings that certainly was not productive for me—or anyone else, for that matter, who was around me at the time.

What I learned over time was that people will always do what they are going to do according to the life path they have chosen. There is not much anyone can or even should do to change them, unless they choose another path for themselves, especially if the one they are on is not working for them. Definitely, this "always having to be in control" problem was among one of the key negative behaviors that contributed to my life-threatening physical and nonphysical illnesses.

When I refused to accept something in my life and continued to dwell on the matter, eventually, I could actually feel myself getting frustrated, anxious, nervous, and felt a great deal of pressure building up in me. This is one of the worst things a person can do to themselves. Keeping this type of frustration pent up deep within for any sustained period of time can lead to a nonphysical illness and eventually can manifest into a physical illness. And if not controlled, this may develop into a life-threatening illness and possibly death.

The Serenity Prayer is classic in advising acceptance, offered by many to God (or whatever unseen power preferred):

Serenity Prayer

God grant me the serenity to accept the things I cannot change,
courage to change the things I can,
and wisdom to know the difference.

For me, it became an obsession to try to change things, circumstances, and people around me; and all I got back from this futile effort was illness, frustration, and off-the-chart anxiety and stress while those around me were not affected at all. When a relationship came to an end, I found myself unprepared to accept the reality of that event. When a substantial business deal fell through, I found myself ill prepared to accept the reality of the loss of all the time and effort that went into getting it past the finish line. When I lost a substantial sum of money, after having spent years building a successful business, I was ill prepared to accept this event in my life as well. And when I attracted the physical and nonphysical illnesses into my life, I refused to accept those events as well. As a matter of fact, during that period of time, I became the poster boy of nonacceptance, ten years in a row, and have the battle scars to prove it.

As I reflect on that point in my life, the humor in all this is that I could not even control myself—the only thing in this world I believed I had any control over—let alone all the circumstances I was futilely attempting to control. The huge piece of the puzzle that I was missing was that by failing to be able to control my very own thoughts, emotions, and how I reacted to things going on around me, how could I possibly even imagine that I could control others or events that were overwhelming me?

Can we control the forces of Mother Nature? Not likely. Nature will do what it has been doing for millions of years, which is to be what it is. So we accept nature for what it is, and we deal with it now, don't we? Can we control what is going on in the universe? Not likely. And the universe has been doing what it has and continues to do for billions of years now, doesn't it? So what's to control? You are! You control the real you who resides deep within your physical body that houses the real you. You cannot possibly control much else, can you? And unlike me back then when I was how I just described, you have every opportunity to do just that—by being willing to accept these truths and to take full control of your life right here and right now.

If we truly wish to change anything, especially ourselves, we must first begin with acceptance. Once we do, we move on from this point. Unless we do, we will remain stagnant. We must first be willing to accept ourselves before we are ready to tolerate what is going on all around us and to verbally claim this approval. This is right in line with the saying "watch what you say to yourself, aloud or silently." Most people speak to themselves continuously, silently, for fear that if they spoke aloud, others may label them insane or headed in that direction.

As for myself, I always have a place to go where I can find solitude and where I can be alone with my all-knowing inner guidance that is one with the infinite intelligence, so I may have my private conversations and ask questions and expect the answer will come. And with patience, the answer always does. If you choose to try reconnecting with your gift of inner power, I strongly suggest that you also find a quiet place where you can be away from the sounds of the outside world for a while, to be alone and be able to connect with your inner guide as often as you can in this manner.

You will be pleasantly surprised that when you come to trust this gift, how remarkable a turnaround your life will take if you allow it to work for you. Do not ever doubt that once you become to trust this inner power, it will bring forth the methods, answers, and solutions. When they come, acknowledge them, even if they are not precisely what you requested. Your inner guide knows what path to take to bring forth all the happiness, joy, and abundance you deserve in this lifetime. So never doubt you will receive the answers because the answers will come as they must.

This is the process of being led from deep within one's inner self and not from outside, your physical self. To do this, you first must approve of yourself for who you are right at this moment and come to terms with the world around you for what it is right now. Do not try to change it. Instead, only concentrate on changing yourself inside. This will result in reality in the form of joy, happiness, and abundance at all levels of your life, including your physical appearance.

Remember, acceptance is not good enough unless you are willing to continuously practice it every day of your life. This does not mean that you need to accept people running all over you. Being flesh and blood on the outside, we are going to do things and act in ways we do not necessarily like. This includes how we think sometimes and how we feel; therefore, you will need to include all this when you choose to endure everything that comes into your life. By all means, know that you cannot be selective when it comes to tolerance. There are no exceptions when it comes to approval. You either allow everything for what it is or you don't. But to make a feeble attempt to be selective in what you will or will not readily permit is not acceptance, but your deciding to be selective in what you will and will not accept in your life is.

Although this is anyone's prerogative, it also can be a road map to eventual self-destruction for all the reasons and more that I have already outlined. Toleration does not mean you are to become anyone's lapdog or allow others to control and/or walk all over you, for that matter. This is not acceptance—this is being a victim of others. Approval is saying to you, "This is how the world is right now, or how businesses are at this point in time, or how people are at this time in mankind's evolution on this earth." If instead you chose to fight what is natural change, then you can rest assured you may one day wind up with any one of the nonphysical illnesses, worrying about what you cannot change, or—even worse yet—a possible nervous breakdown.

I had to learn to understand all the things I did in my life that I am not proud of and some of which I cannot believe I even would have considered. I also had to accept all the things I did not do but wish that I had. I had to accept all my not-so-good thoughts and my good thoughts, my negative thoughts and my positive ones, my losses and my gains, my poor choices and my great ones, my private thoughts and my verbal ones, my sadness and my joys, etc. I had to understand that these are all part of one's life, whether poor, well off, or not-so-well-off financially. I had to accept being at the bottom, climbing to the top and returning to the bottom, and once again, finding myself looking up toward that steep climb back up once again. And when stricken with very serious physical events in my life, I had to also learn how to accommodate these events in my life as well.

I've been asked, "What do you mean when you say that there is no exception when it comes to tolerating everything?" By not being able or willing to accept what is going on all around you, it just may eventually lead to negative events that you invite into your life through nonacceptance, including but not limited to possible eventual physical and nonphysical conditions and illnesses.

I firmly trust that had I failed to learn how to adapt to these things, I would have punched my clock and have been out of here a long time ago and never have had the privilege of being able to raise my young son who was only six months old when I was diagnosed with cancer twice in one year. Acceptance assists in making clear where you are at all times in terms of reality, what your role is in the scheme of life, and the options available that will neither simplify nor complicate the road ahead. Therefore, you see it was my willingness to embrace reality that brought me to this point in my life. It was what brought me back to reconnecting with my gift of inner instruction, and it will be yours, should this be the direction you choose to pursue.

We come now to the methods I employed to overcome each and every one of the adversities I had experienced that I identified. I continue to rely upon these methods to this very day since they were given to me by this unseen infinite intelligence that is connected with one's all-knowing inner wisdom.

20

THE METHODS THAT CAN REVERSE LIFE-CHANGING ADVERSITIES

I believe that among the primary reasons I was able to overcome all that I have was my choice to employ certain key methods that were identified to me through my ongoing conversations with this infinite intelligence I continue to speak of that is connected with one's inner guidance. By doing so, without fail, I habitually used these methods to defeat not only serious nonphysical conditions but life-threatening physical illnesses that could have ended my life as well.

The following are the key methods I continue to use and rely upon to bring forth whatever I may desire to utilize for not only good in my personal life but for the good of all I care about as well. That also includes everyone because I am convinced that there is not a person alive who does not have a strong need—whether a return to or maintenance of good health, coupled with enjoying prosperity on every conceivable level. Not only do I believe this is possible, but I am certain it is. I not only personally continue to utilize these measures but also achieve beneficial results. I am convinced that by choosing to adopt these methods, almost anyone can have the same opportunity I continue to have to develop, whatever good they may be seeking, provided they do not allow doubt and skepticism to interfere and employ unwavering expectation.

Keep in mind that coupled with any beliefs one may have, religious or otherwise, individually and collectively, these methods are extremely powerful, if one decides to make them a part of their lives and willing to exercise patience and, above all, firmly maintain unwavering belief in their positive influence.

The following are the primary methods I relied upon to achieve and overcome all that I have identified thus far.

Focused Thought

Chief among all the methods I identify are focused thoughts, without which nothing desired for good can possibly be obtained. I consider this method so important, and I cannot emphasize strongly enough its significance and importance in your life and the lives of everyone.

As I have identified, most take for granted that whatever they may have accomplished in their lives thus far was of their own doing; however, nothing can be further from the truth. The fact and reality is that any accomplishments and successes you may have acquired thus far in your life were the result of your habitual focused thoughts on whatever it was you wanted to explore at the time. The thoughts that you chose to not let go of and instead cultivate and nurture eventually materialized in your physical life: Earning a degree in the field of your endeavor. Landing that position you had always dreamed of. Finding the partner you had pictured in your mind over and over again. Living in that home you had always dreamt of owning. Visiting or studying in a foreign country you always envisioned in your mind that one day you would go to. And actually everything else, for good, you had always wanted to exist in your life.

Therefore, absolutely anything you had ever wanted in your life came about by way of the thoughts you focused on and remains to be the reason why you experience whatever it is for good or for your detriment. It is important for you to understand that the thoughts you choose to habitually focus on are communicated to your inner guidance that eventually will show up in your life.

It is important to know that we all are residing in two separate but very significant worlds—the world within from where your feelings, emotional state, attitudes, intuition, and wisdom come; and what manifests in your physical life for you to experience, the places you have gone and will go to, the people you have met and will continue to meet during your life's journey, the events you have witnessed thus far, and countless other realities you have had and will continue to have. Whether they are for your good or for your disadvantage, all is dependent on the thoughts and choices you choose to make that will eventually show up in your physical world.

The reality of these separate worlds rarely even comes close to being understood—let alone recognized by the majority of people—and therefore, they are unable to tell the difference or be able to separate these two worlds. Therefore, the consequence is that they generally become controlled solely by their outer world, the one they see and are aware of every day. They pay little, if any, attention to their world within where the manifestation of whatever people come to distinguish for good or whatever detrimental situations that may happen to them begin, depending on the thoughts that are transmitted from the conscious mind to the all-knowing inner guidance/inner mind.

Thoughts are always seeking to find form and a place to appear, meaning they are seeking to materialize in physical life to be produced, whether good or evil. However, like the millions of sperm attempting to ultimately be born to realize that process, only one succeeds. Considering this analogy, thoughts are doing the very same thing; therefore, it is only a single predominant thought that is focused upon that will win out over the thousands of thoughts created or are influenced every day. This is solely due to the fact that it is the thought that has been given the most attention and is repeated over and over and over again in the conscious mind until that thought is manifested in reality and eventually surfaces in the outer world.

The significance here is to recognize the fact that your predominant thoughts have a tremendous amount of power and influence over you and your resulting actions. The rest of the thousands of thoughts you will reflect upon every day will come and go with little attention given to them by you or you being influenced by them. That is because you choose the thoughts you want to concentrate on and allow all the others to escape your conscious mind as they have no significant impact on what you desire to actively pursue in your life.

Keep in mind that the thoughts you focus on are your choice—they can be either beneficial or harmful to you, depending on what you focus on for any significant period of time that will become your predominant habitual thoughts. You also need to understand that any embedded beliefs you harbor that contain fear all have an effect on what you bring into reality and are presently concentrating on as well as the effect they will have or are having on others.

It has been my observation over the years that many people will meander through life never realizing or paying any attention to what they think or how their inner guidance works and what it is attempting to tell them and what it disregards. I am convinced that what we focus on through our habitual thoughts affects our lives in a very dramatic way, positive or negative; and if people would come to realize this, they may possibly begin paying much closer attention to what they are thinking and begin to direct and control their thoughts more carefully. Much more enthusiasm for what they desire to appear for good would discard those thoughts that would not offer a thing of value or that could not enhance their lives with prosperity on every level.

It should be important to you that you begin to do so without further hesitation because prosperity on every level can begin to happen in your life, once you make a commitment to yourself to do just that. Being aware of this or not, understand that you are self-creating each and every one of your life experiences by what you habitually think about.

Keep this in mind. Although I emphasized this before, every time you are about to make an important choice, realize that you are the creator of all your experiences and no one else. Therefore, it is imperative that you begin to look at your life seriously and take a closer look at how you are living it. I have heard people say that they lack the finances they need to do the things they would like to accomplish, but rarely—if ever—do they do a thing to improve their lack of finances. Others complain about the insurmountable debt they had accumulated and believe that they will never be able to find the job they want and need that will pay them enough to be able to surmount these obstacles and prefer to worry about it instead of making a serious effort to resolve it. Even though they were seeking a way out and looking for financial abundance because their mind was in a worry and doubting consciousness, they never were going to be able to overcome their self-created circumstances.

The more they think and dwell upon the insufficiencies in their life and keep reminding themselves of the condition they are subjected to and put themselves down, the more they dig an even deeper hole for themselves. By thinking weakness instead of strength, they just fool themselves to believe they would never discover the answers and the strength they need to overcome their deprivation.

Many people want to enjoy prosperity (the key word for having abundance on every conceivable level); however, wishing and hoping will not bring forth what is being sought, and neither will hard work or by working two or three jobs. What can, however, is to make the decision to alter your thinking and begin focusing on what it is you truly want. Concentrate on making those thoughts as your habitual and predominant thoughts, with full expectation of their manifesting in your physical life to be processed without doubting, worrying, or wavering—which would nullify those thoughts—and instead proceed with strong, unwavering expectation; belief; and, above all, patience.

I will tell anyone who asks what is absolutely necessary in order to achieve whatever one may be seeking for their life (including the return to good health and possessing prosperity on every level of their life) to begin to commit themselves to developing a new consciousness and focus on the fact that if they are seeking success, then they need to develop a consciousness of success. If seeking financial wealth, then they need to develop a consciousness of wealth. If seeking a return to or maintaining good health, then they need to begin developing a good health awareness, like I did, and so many more like me have and continue to do so. If you or anyone is seeking any or all of this, then this is precisely how you need to start thinking. Anything or anyone else should be disregarded that attempts to continue to interfere with whatever it is you are seeking.

I've had people tell me that it was easy for me to give them this advice because I was no longer in their situation and have returned to good health and experiencing prosperity on every level. The fact that they remarked that they were not me and their situation is much different and that they cannot see themselves ever being able to elevate themselves to the level I am talking about here—not only is this faulty thinking, but this is a perfect example of what a true defeatist attitude is. There need not be any such thing as perpetual deficiency on any level, ranging from financial lack, all the way out to absence of good health. And in response to "I'm no longer in their situation" argument, the response to this is that I chose to change the way I was thinking and began to focus only on the empowering thoughts that would bring me what I wanted to bring into my life.

The one constant and reliable thing that separates anyone from insufficiency on any level or anything that they wish to be realized is how they choose to think. By choosing to do so, any self-defeating thoughts presently stuck in one's conscious mind will change; and this can only happen when the decision is made to eliminate them and begin to commit to developing a new consciousness.

It is this new thinking that can free anyone from any undesirable situation to which they are exposed. This committed new way of thinking must take place first before any changes in your situation can possibly occur. This takes very little effort. All that is necessary is to make the decision to "just do it" and begin reflecting on what it is that you want to materialize in your life for good. Should you decide to begin changing your thoughts, without doubting or wavering, in time, they will. My mind-set changed and continues to do good for me and others. Therefore, there is no reason why it cannot do the same for you as well.

First, decide what exactly it is that you want to develop for good in your life. If it is better health, then focus on better health thoughts; if it is wealth, then focus on thoughts of wealth; if it is a better relationship, then focus on thoughts of better relationships; if it is prosperity on every conceivable level, then focus on thoughts of prosperity; etc. What is so comforting about changing thoughts is that regardless of circumstances or the number of failures occurring in the past or is currently being faced, by continuously focusing on your desires, you can change your situation for the better.

What is even more remarkable is that all it takes is a total commitment to self. No expense is needed to be incurred, and no special training is required to afford the desired effect that is truly wanted. The only requirement is to make the decision to commit to expending the effort necessary to develop a new consciousness. If you will do this, everything you are seeking can materialize into reality, as long as you continue to keep this commitment to yourself.

It is up to you. You can either choose to stay where you are in life right now or decide to change it by altering how you think and commit to never allowing yourself to regress, no matter what. By doing so, there should be no reason why you cannot participate in the joy of life you are seeking and prosper on every conceivable level.

Keep in mind that the predominant thoughts you continuously hold in your mind are a very powerful force communicated to your inner guidance that can produce whatever your desires, if you do not doubt or waver and believe with unwavering expectation.

Intuitive Feelings

Feelings are another very important and extremely powerful source concerning the method of visualization and imagination. What you visualize in your mind must be accompanied with excitement, elation, joy, and absolutely knowing what you have been visualizing is real.

Feelings are sometimes identified as having a gut feeling that comes from your intuitive inner power. The mere feeling that a result you are seeking is on its way to you—by way of what you have been visualizing in your mind—already exists and is being produced is a sure sign that it is. As I had emphasized before, it is imperative that you do not allow any anxiety, doubt, or worry to destroy your desires for good and that you must visualize that it will and already has arrived, even though you have not yet actually perceived whatever you are seeking to have manifest in reality for you. Just trust that if you claim it as yours, it can be. The strong feeling that it is on its way is evidence that everything is already in the process of going well and that whatever is being desired is already beginning to be demonstrated in your physical life; and if applicable to you, any adversity and/or undesirable set of conditions is soon to be done with.

Keep in mind that feeling accompanies visualizing (i.e., mental pictures). What you are seeking through the method of intuitive feelings is the actual physical sensation that is accompanied with excitement, palpitation of the heart, goose bumps, and an uplifting sensation that can also be accompanied with tears of joy.

Understand that having a strong inner feeling is not akin to what people refer to as hoping for a thing to occur in their life or wishing for a thing for personal benefit. Instead, as I said, the process of intuitive feeling is staking a mental claim on whatever it may be you are seeking to bring forth. I personally can attest that, along with visualization (imagining) and strong feelings, the sensation of the beginning of what is being desired to be become reality for good is very real.

The writing method I have described, coupled with visualization, and engaged in every day without fail for not less than fifteen minutes, preferably more, focusing upon the same predominant thought of what you desire to conceptualize, will produce an even stronger inner feeling of confidence, self-trust, and excitement like you possibly may never have felt before. It is important for me to state that the habit of repetition cannot be overemphasized. Like anything else, engaging in something one wants to accomplish for good in life, no matter what it may be, if done inconsistently, will produce the anticipated results.

How I accomplished and overcame all that I have thus far was done by establishing a regular routine by engaging the methods I describe in this chapter and throughout this book. I kept to this daily routine without fail and allowed absolutely nothing to interfere. The key here is to actually live your life as though whatever you are seeking already belongs to you. To feel excited and take full possession of it in your conscious mind in turn will transmit this feeling to your all-knowing inner guidance, and eventually, you should be surprised at the positive results you can expect to materialize.

Believe me, I know what I am talking about, having accomplished for good all that I have and continue to do so by utilizing the other powerful methods described as follows.

Acknowledging Your Past Accomplishments and Victories

Acknowledging the success and victories achieved in life thus far is all too often forgotten, thereby leaving behind all the good feelings derived from the achievements and instead moving on to new goals and desires. These new desires then become a primary focus, allowing the feelings of past achievements to fade into the past to never be recalled again into their memory. This is not only a total abandonment of what were once strong intense desires and goals and the feelings of realization but how they were attained. Few people ever even consider this fact or give it any thought, thereby failing to understand the tremendous power these past achievements hold for them.

The power I am talking about is reusing over and over again the very same success energies, thoughts, ideas, and, above all, strong feelings with the same powerful results that had brought forth these previous successes and accomplishments. Therefore, they can and should be tapped into without any reservation whatsoever as they are still there within you to be called upon again, and again, and again. Nothing you accomplished has changed other than your age, which is insignificant where acknowledging and tapping back into your past successes and positive results are concerned. This is precisely what I did concerning my reliance upon the methods I am identifying for you and others who have brought me all the good I was seeking and continue to have.

The problem appears to be that once we have achieved what we desire, we instantly forget that accomplishment and, most of all, how and what we did to accomplish it and quickly move on to new goals and desires that also pose the very same challenges that our previous desires did when they were a priority in our life. This is precisely where many people fail in their quest to achieve their present wants and desires.

PREVAILING OVER INSURMOUNTABLE ODDS

By not taking advantage of what it was that you did to bring forth what you had previously wanted to materialize in your life, you forfeit a tremendous source of power you relied upon to bring forth your past achievements, wants, and burning desires for good. What you should be doing instead of wishing and hoping is bringing forth the belief, feelings, and excitement you once had felt when you accomplished what was once very important to you in the past.

This method of acknowledging continues to work very well for me and others when seeking to accomplish certain desires and results. It is that former feeling and exuberance that occurs when I think of all I had achieved in the past and recall the former elation that becomes a powerful driving force among the other methods that I continue to employ in my life.

This book is an excellent example because it came about by my calling forth all my past attainments and successes and how I felt at the time about them, when others believed these were close to almost impossible to reach. Despite their beliefs, I did. Why? Because I was more than determined and armed with an army of methods and answers and past successful results necessary to be able to do all that I did and to fulfill the desires I wanted. I never allowed those past good results and how I carried out solutions to them to ever leave my mind. My past successes, coupled with my inner guidance, were and remain to be among the driving force that allows me to develop whatever I have recently actualized; and they will continue to accomplish the same in the future. Therefore, in my opinion, there should be no reason why you cannot achieve your desires as well.

This very valuable method of acknowledgement teaches that you should always congratulate yourself about what you have thus far achieved in your life, whether recent or past victories, regardless if these were monumental or small. Always recall how you obtained them and recall whatever it was that made you feel victorious, happy, and good about yourself. Be certain to utilize the memories of these successes for what it may be you are seeking in the present to achieve, overcome, and/or occur in your life, which, once recalled, are certain to begin to attract even greater successes.

By focusing on the progress you had in the past, what you did to achieve that status, the recognition and praise you have received from others for having the specific knowledge and skills you have developed and applied to do so, and the continued advances you made in your life—you have proven to yourself there are no obstacles to prevent you from achieving any challenge, goal, desire, or overcome any adversity or undesirable life-changing event that may come your way. Therefore, continue to explore and never cease searching for everything to acknowledge that you find that you have moved forward. Do not neglect to do this, as it is one of the strongest methods you can rely upon because *you* accomplished them—no one else did it for you—and it will be you who will do so for yourself in the present and the future. Of this, you can be rest assured.

Allow me to share with you what I have done and continue to do always to keep my past and most recent developments in mind and in front of me where I can reference them at any time I desire. These remind me continuously of who I really am, what I have already obtained, and what I am capable of reaching and even more—much more.

What I did—and I offer this suggestion for you to consider—was to continue to *feel successful* and extremely proud of all that I have done, especially in the past, and allow my mind to reflect on all that I have achieved and succeeded in doing thus far. The achievement of having the privilege to work for prestigious, well-known corporations in high-profile positions; my extensive, successful career as a self-employed business owner and related successes; all the assets I acquired; achieving all my short-term and long-term goals; the dates I initiated my thoughts of what I wanted to accomplish and the dates that they were completed to my complete satisfaction; those I was able to help and to teach my methods and the realization of their successes and when; overcoming serious life-threatening adversities, the dates they occurred, and the dates they were overcome, etc.—these are just some of my successes. To this point in time, I continue to add to my extensive written list of accomplishments and continue to record all my present achievements, which include having written this book so you and others can reach your heartfelt desires and goals.

The following is an example of what I also do that you may wish to also consider that keeps me in a prosperous mind-set. Deciding to act and think in this manner can greatly enhance this and the other methods I identify.

I suggest that you obtain a legal pad or notebook and begin recording each and every one of your strengths that you can think of. Take about fifteen minutes to reflect on these very important strong points. Having done so, begin to write them down, as I do, and continue to add to this list as you develop even more. As you continue to review this growing list, your inner guidance will make absolutely certain that your conscious mind continues to enhance and multiply even greater strengths that you will acquire that can eventually bring prosperity on every conceivable level, as it has for me and others.

Here are some examples for you to get an idea of what I am suggesting:

- I dress very well.
- I have talent and can teach others.
- I am very good at what I do.
- I am compassionate.
- I am a person who is creative and can envision my desires being manifested.
- I have an optimistic outlook on life.
- I see everyone as equal and never less than that.
- I am courteous to everyone I meet and those I know.
- I am thoughtful of others.
- Among my objectives is to assist others to also accomplish their goals.
- I am educated and willing to share that knowledge with others.
- I am a good father, partner, husband/wife, friend, companion, etc.
- I never quit or give up.

This list could go on and on; however, I trust you get the idea.

I cannot express enough how important listing and seeing your strengths in written format is, opposed to having to recall it in your mind. You can also utilize this list for furthering your career by listing a number of your strengths and accomplishments on your résumé, as prospective employers seek people who are proud to identify their strengths, skills, and accomplishments as they identify your true character and added value to them. Here are some examples to consider:

- I am reliable.
- I am excellent with people.
- I get along with almost everyone.
- I am very organized.
- I am meticulous in my work habits.
- I motivate others.
- I am a good manager.
- I have excellent communicating skills.
- I have excellent references and list of past accomplishments.

Always remember this: *nothing in life succeeds like success.* And if you will take the time to reflect on your past results thus far, you will clearly see that this describes you because you have already succeeded in many areas of your life now, haven't you? Therefore, there should be absolutely no reason why you cannot duplicate and surpass those successes right now and in the future.

The key point here is, whatever you do, absolutely never, ever cease acknowledging and believing in yourself and never wait for things to come to you. Instead, through this and the other powerful methods as identified that you may need to overcome adversity, create your own opportunities and whatever else you want to be produced. Nothing or no one else can or ever will do it for you because you are the architect of all you are, have been, and ever will be.

Eliminating Self-Destructive Beliefs

This method is extremely important. I recommend that you pay very close attention to it as it is imperative that you do so if you truly want to develop the manifestation of your desires.

Belief is something we all have that are formed and accepted by us as being true as far back as our early childhood. Beliefs have not only been etched into our minds, but we have also adopted and continue to defend them because once we have a belief firmly implanted in our minds, we rarely ever question them. This is because we will always assume that they are correct and true. For example, if we think that all men with full beards are the type who are always hiding something, having lots of money is difficult to achieve, hard work is the only way to get ahead in life, you are not worth much and will not get anywhere in this world, you will never go to college, you will never be good enough for the girl or guy of your dreams, you will not find the job you really want because you do not have the right skills, you will never get over this illness, there is no cure for your attitude toward others, you will never make that team, etc.—we will continue to hold on to and to formulate even more of these types of beliefs and will begin to tear down every aspect of ourselves, including our entire life for that matter, and never come to realize that our beliefs are almost the last thing we will ever consider challenging or changing.

This method is very powerful because, if you were not aware before, what you choose to continue to believe and accept in your mind that something is true is precisely what you will eventually cause to occur, good or bad. You need to clearly understand this because your status in life, your health situation, your relationships, your career, your marriage, and your overall well-being relies on it.

The fact is, many of us will use our beliefs to harm ourselves, usually without even realizing it at the time. Evidence of this can be found by taking a moment to take a very hard look at any problem that you may possibly be having at this point in your life. More than likely, you will discover that most, if not all, your problems are rooted in wrong and very limited beliefs. By *limited*, I mean you have few life-enhancing beliefs when it comes to a number of areas of your life, thereby leaving you without many options.

If you are undergoing serious problems plaguing your life, perhaps it is high time that you examine precisely what you believe what these problem areas are, especially your overall health, relationships, and financial condition. Having done this, take an even deeper look about what your embedded beliefs are in these very important areas of your life, keeping in mind that disempowering beliefs are life destructing and must be eliminated without fail—if you seriously want to change any problem areas for the better that may be disrupting your life.

After having examined your present beliefs about any problematic areas in your life, you will find that you literally have declared war on your inner guidance. You are in a battle with a myriad of self-ordained limiting beliefs that keep haunting and telling you that you are not going to be able to surmount the problems that you are living with constantly in your own mind.

Having mentioned your subconscious mind earlier (*subconscious mind*—"the mental activities just below the threshold of consciousness" or "existing in the mind but not immediately available to consciousness"), which is actually your all-knowing guidance that is connected with the infinite intelligence, it is important to understand what is contained and stored there is very important to you. Any negativity that is communicated to your inner guidance by your conscious mind will be immediately absorbed and accepted as true by your inner mind. Therefore, your inner mind will immediate begin to work on bringing forth these conditions and beliefs to become realities in your life and see to it that they are manifested and experienced—e.g., an ongoing state of poverty and want, inability to find the right relationship, failure to get further in life, failure in almost everything you do, constant troubles in many areas of your life, etc.

Consequently, be acutely aware that whatever is communicated to your inner mind will eventually be brought forth as the actuality that can be either your empowering or your self-limiting beliefs that come about by way of your habitual thoughts about such firm opinions.

It is equally important to understand that, upon accepting any self-limiting beliefs, ideas, or habitual thoughts—whether they are true or false in nature—your conscious mind will begin and continue to process thoughts that correspond and support these self-limiting beliefs and ideas that are now etched in your inner guidance and accepted as truth. An example of this may be the following mind-sets: "I will never beat this disease"; "this relationship/marriage will

PREVAILING OVER INSURMOUNTABLE ODDS

never work out"; "I'll never amount to nothing, living in want seems to be my lot in life"; "no one seems to ever care about me or what I have to say"; "I will never find someone to love me, so why bother trying?"; "I'll never be respected"; "my past will continue to cost me lost opportunities"; etc. Therefore, believing any of this, your inner guidance will work day and night relentlessly to see to it that these and any self-limiting beliefs will be supported by the proof you supply to it by way of your confirming thoughts that support these beliefs.

However, if you believe the contrary, you will actualize the reverse—your beliefs that your health, financial situation, marital issues, or relationships with others are improving every day and that your problems are dissipating. You will then begin to develop and witness that the former debilitating beliefs will be remarkably improved and eventually will no longer exist.

Here is something important you also need to pay close attention to: most problems, illnesses, and undesirable life-changing events that are disturbing you are often the result of your beliefs and disempowering thoughts. *You* are the problem and not the problem itself, and *you* are also the solution. "Why?" you may be asking yourself. Because the problem areas of your life are not emanating from any sources in your physical world; instead, these are coming directly from deep inside of you—more specifically, your faulty beliefs that emanate from your unconscious mind that have been deeply embedded there for quite some time as a result of the disempowering thoughts your conscious mind has been allowed to accept as true and to transmit to your inner mind. They will remain there until you decide to replace them with new and more constructive and healthy beliefs. When this is done, then and only then can any new empowering thoughts begin to enter your conscious mind, thereby replacing your self-defeating beliefs with powerful, supportive new beliefs that are totally contrary to those that have been affecting you negatively for far too long.

When this change occurs in your conscious mind, empowering beliefs and accompanying thoughts will ultimately become the result, making room for the beneficial effect you are seeking to manifest in your life. How do I know this? Because this is precisely what I did and can say, without a shadow of a doubt or regret, that I am extremely pleased that I did. By doing so, I was able to overcome every problematic area that was plaguing my life, the result of which literally stunned most people who had witnessed my remarkable recovery and turnaround.

Having said this, understand that you—not anyone else—needs to take personal responsibility for your life and the realities that surround it on a daily basis. If you are willing to be honest with yourself, you should be able to see that this is true. I did. Once I accepted this truth, I was then able to clearly see that it was in fact me who was causing myself all the problems, illnesses, and other undesirable life-changing adversities and events I experienced.

Therefore, taking personal responsibility; changing your beliefs, thoughts, and attitude; and realizing that it is you who needs to change from the inside out, if you truly want to eradicate problem areas from your life are the keys to your new and improved life.

I am going to challenge you right here and now to begin to create the new you by empowering yourself with supportive beliefs. Keep in mind at all times to never discount the fact that you can plant any empowering, beliefs, thoughts, ideas, wants, and burning desires in your inner guidance. Once planted and allowed to go unmolested by negativity, doubting, skepticism, wavering, and lack of confidence, you will begin to accept and begin to go to work almost immediately to bring these new empowering beliefs, thoughts, ideas, wants, and your burning desires for beneficial effect in your life. Keep in mind that this has to be done with strong feeling and with continuous, habitual predominant thoughts of whatever you are planting your inner mind, including ridding of anything you no longer want to harbor that may be plaguing your life.

Let me ask you this: *are you able to see yourself in any of the brief examples of debilitating beliefs listed below?*

- I cannot overcome _____.
- There are no opportunities for me.
- It's no use because _____.
- It's too hard to get _____.
- People will never except me because _____.
- I'll never find the right person for me.

- My life will always be filled with deficits.
- Opportunities continue to allude me.
- I have tried _____, but it never seems to work out for me
- Things seem to always never go my way.
- Life is never going to be okay for me.
- I was born under an unlucky star.
- I have no idea what to do about _____.

Were you are able to recognize yourself among any these or related disempowering beliefs or others you may be having? If your answer is *yes*, you absolutely must begin to change them and do it soon—not a day, a week, a month or a year from now—that is, if you want to live in the disempowering, self-defeating world you have created for yourself. Yes, as I said, you are the architect of the majority of your circumstances yourself. Therefore, becoming aware of this, it's time to do something about it or choose to continue living your life never really having whatever you truly want.

I too finally had come to realize that I had to give up living in the comfort of my many self-constructed excuses for harboring self-defeating, disempowering beliefs and related thoughts that were responsible for all the problematic areas in my life.

Having discovered this, I learned that I was not alone in this regard. There are countless people everywhere who are living with similar disempowering beliefs who seemingly are more than content to stay as they are. Those who refuse to make any attempt whatsoever to change prefer to live with the problematic areas that are plaguing them—among these troublesome areas are various illnesses, life-threatening conditions, and other adversities and events—simply because they believe that their situation is hopeless. Therefore, they choose to tolerate these conditions and problems, truly believing that this is their fate in life.

Does this describe you or someone one you may know? If so, don't you think it is time you made the decision to change your beliefs and turn your boat around and stop heading in the direction of the menacing, life-threatening storm and instead steer toward shore where you know you will be safe?

I believe this method of eliminating self-destructive beliefs is so important that I am going to ask you to do the following for yourself. I want you to take any problematic areas of your life and write what it is that you feel deep within about them but not think about them. What you are looking for is if they are limiting beliefs versus empowering beliefs. If you are honest with yourself and will take a brief amount of time (a few minutes out of your day to write these down), you will soon see for yourself how revealing this process will be for you and how the self-destructing inner feelings are literally holding you back from whatever you truly want to accomplish.

Now list your new empowering beliefs. You can take some inspiration from the list below:

- I can overcome _____.
- There are countless opportunities for me.
- It's worth believing that I can because _____.
- Nothing is too hard for me to achieve_____.
- People accept and like me, because _____.
- I'll definitely find the right person for me.
- My life will always be filled with opportunities I am seeking.
- Opportunities never elude me.
- Everything I want to experience for good is waiting for me to discover.
- Things always seem to go my way.
- Life is always going to be okay for me.
- I was born under a lucky star.
- My inner guidance always supplies me with the right answers, methods, and solutions in any situation.

Having listed your new empowering beliefs, repeat them to yourself silently several times a day. By doing so, you will be actually transmitting these new empowering beliefs directly to your inner mind, within which, if you are consistent, you will begin to accept them as true and begin working on these beliefs. In time, whatever it is you are now believing can appear in your life. Keep in mind that you cannot insert any doubt, lack of patience, or give up on your all-knowing inner power. The key here is repetition several times a day, especially before you retire for the evening. This action on your part ensures that your inner mind will begin believing your new empowering beliefs, which in turn will begin to produce the results you are seeking.

A word of caution here is important when transmitting new ideas, desires, and goals to your inner guidance coming from your conscious mind. When planting new beliefs, you must be absolutely certain that you continue to drive these new beliefs deep into your all-knowing inner mind by repeating them to yourself, silently, as often as possible, to be certain the inner mind believes them. Like anything else, when you actualize what is new—e.g., a new car, new house, new job, new relationship, etc.—the emotion and excitement cannot be sustained for a significant amount of time, unless the initial enthusiasm is kept alive. No matter how great that feeling is in the beginning, it is certain to fade and eventually dissipate, along with the excitement it was initially accompanied with when first conceived. Therefore, more than likely, you may regress to your former disempowering beliefs and thoughts.

This is precisely where contemplation and unwavering expectation plays a significant role in your conscious mind. Coupled with your new beliefs, ideas, desires, and goals said to yourself often every day with strong feeling, these can be conceptualized by you, keeping in mind to not allow any contradictory thoughts that will negate your empowering new beliefs that will be transmitted by your conscious mind to your all-knowing inner power. Remember, your new beliefs were just born and need to be handled as though it were a newborn infant and protected against harm. In particular, do not ever allow your former disempowering beliefs to make a recovery to regain control of your conscious mind.

Think of your new empowering beliefs as newly planted seeds. Like any plant, your new beliefs will not grow without being properly cared for in order to begin their journey to grow into your new outlook. Without continued attention and care, you can rest assured that your former disempowering beliefs will return and crowd out your new empowering beliefs. Like any plant, your new beliefs must go through their natural growing stage before they will eventually become a suitable factor in your physical world. Always keep in mind that any new empowering beliefs require this natural growing stage to mature into an accepted belief by your inner guidance before they can begin to bring forth your desires to produce a positive effect. The key point here is to realize, like any new seed, it will take time and, above all, patience. And if you follow these suggestions, you can rest assured, in time, they will grow.

Understand you are transmitting new beliefs to your inner mind which, more often than not, will conflict with your old disempowering beliefs. Therefore, know that no new empowering beliefs will be able to enter your inner mind unless you truly intend to repeat them to yourself each and every day—as often as you can and silently to yourself—and prepare to continue to do so for up to several months, if necessary. Keep in mind that the disempowering beliefs you relied upon took quite some time to develop, which you now lived with, that more than likely have gotten you into your present undesirable situation.

If you truly want to acquire whatever you are seeking for good, know that it will take your total dedication to yourself if you are serious about what you wish to possess. Be aware that this must be done without hesitation, procrastination, or any halfway attempts. In other words, you need to become totally dedicated to your commitment to secure your intense desire. If you are ready to commit yourself to this method, begin today and do not allow another day pass you by. If begin to plant your new beliefs and desires in your all-knowing inner guidance, once accepted, your inner power will remove every obstacle to bring forth your desires. I know this for a fact and continue to use this method and can tell you that without it, I would never have been able to have overcome and achieve what I have. I trust that you now realize how important this method is and that you will not hesitate to make it an important part of your life in order to achieve your desires.

In continuation are methods that will assist in recreating your powers, as they are reflected in the conscious mind's association with the inner guidance and play a significant role in the process.

21

THE METHODS THAT CAN DEVELOP CREATIVE THOUGHTS

Recreating Yourself

This method of recreating yourself is equally as important as empowering beliefs. The reason I say this is because most people today believe they are not creative. Consequently they rarely allow themselves to be creative, thereby permitting themselves to live the same "follow the leader" life that far too many people choose to do. More often than not, this condition, along with complacency, is akin to being lost in a cave without any light to guide one's way, thereby having no idea where they are going.

People who do not explore their creative nature rarely, if ever, allow themselves to come close to exploring new avenues, ways, and beliefs that can greatly enhance their lives on every conceivable level imaginable. When people say that they have no reason to spend the time trying to be creative, quite sadly, they have no intention to become the next famous painter, composer, writer, athlete, or surgeon. Most people who think this way believe that they have nothing new to contribute because everything that could ever have been thought of already has been thought of already or that they do not have the required training, education, or skills to be able to create anything new that could benefit them or others. In comparison to these types of thoughts, there are those who believe the complete opposite and act in accordance with their belief that they can create new opportunities for themselves and are excited by the thought of being creative and having the opportunity to be able to contribute useful new ideas for mankind's benefit.

For anyone who has such a noncreative mind-set, it is important for them to consider that before deciding to stay in such a frame of mind, they must take a moment to really take a good look all around them. If they will do this, they will begin to notice the results of someone else's creative thoughts, imaginations, and ideas—someone who is no different than they are. All they did was to begin to believe in themselves and to envision whatever it was they knew could be accomplished. Some very brief examples include the average chair, windows, buildings, elevators, cars we drive, airplanes we fly in, surgical instruments doctors depend upon, all the fabulous machines used to diagnose diseases and serious illnesses, machines that make all these things and even the tiniest pin used to hold new apparel together, and thousands—no, millions—of related objects.

Where did you think they all originally come from? They came from someone's ideas, envisioning, and imagination, empowering thoughts, unwavering belief, expectancy, self-confidence, and self-trust. All mankind's conveniences came into existence as a result of someone's creative mind.

Why is being creative so important? To begin with, if one believes they are not creative and have no desire to be, this is like being in a vehicle stuck in mud. The more one tries to get out of it, the more they just spin the car's tires and get nowhere, thereby creating an even deeper rut that only ensures staying stuck in the very same place. This is precisely where so many people find themselves and why they get no further in life. Most people will rarely own up to this reality. Even though they truly believe they are not creative, the fact is, we are all creative. Everything we have ever produced in our lives, we created, as we all are the architects of our own reality.

What does "recreating yourself" mean? It means that if you believe you do not have creative powers, it is time that you come to realize that you should begin believing in yourself and your creative powers, regardless of whether you choose so your new beliefs believe you do or not.

PREVAILING OVER INSURMOUNTABLE ODDS

If you are among those who may believe they are not a creative person, know that you can awaken your creative powers and should do so without further hesitation. If you feel that you are stuck in a rut, perhaps it may be because at some point in your life you were led to believe that you were not a creative person. Should this be the case, it is time that you come to realize the truth that we all have within us a great deal of creativity because we were all born with creative ability. If we are not taking advantage of it, then it is only because we choose not to and not because you may believe you don't. All you need to do to begin to believe you have creative ability is to take a moment to think back in time, and you should see how creative you were in school as a child and how your creative gift had been used to achieve the results you wanted. We all did.

The problem with so many people is that they were either told or convinced at a very young age that they were not creative. Hence, they swallowed this misrepresentation hook, line and sinker, so to speak, and commenced their life actually believing this falsehood, thereby repressing their creative powers for years—even to this very moment in time for some. Having said this, the good news is, you can awaken your creative powers and begin to put them to work for you right now.

Allow me to share with you precisely how my creative powers benefited me—and continue to do so—as they relate to the numerous successes and adversities I overcame.

I first discovered my creative powers when I was very young. It was during this time I became very curious about how I could accomplish the things I wanted to achieve as I grew older. Therefore, I embarked upon a mission to learn all I could about the things I wanted to experience and created a plan for myself of how I was going to obtain them.

One of my earliest burning desires was to be a drummer in a band, but I did not have a set of drums at the time and had no way of getting them as my parents back then simply were not in any financial position to purchase them for me. So what did I do? I decided to be creative. I arranged an entire set of my fantasy drum set in my backyard from used metal garbage pails (back then garbage pails were made out of metal and aluminum, not plastic) and carved drumsticks out of tree branches from the tree in our back yard and used a tree stump for a seat. I then began to practice on this set of homemade garbage drums.

In time, I became quite proficient at playing on these garbage drums, and one day the grammar school band teacher heard of my garbage can drum set and came to see them and watched me play to music coming from my mother's Victrola (that is what they called a record player back then) that I dragged from the house and connected with my dad's long extension cord to where my makeshift drum set was. The band teacher was so impressed that he asked me to come to a rehearsal and learn how to read drum music.

Well, it was from that point that I graduated from garbage cans to real drums, to later becoming the lead drummer in the school orchestra, all the way out to becoming a well-known drummer in real bands in the '60s, '70s, and '80s, which I credited to my creative ideas that came from my burning desire to become a well-known drummer one day. And I did just that. No matter what your age, you too can certainly realize your dreams!

From this point, as I grew older, I created in my mind the belief and thought that I would also find a way to work for prestigious corporations in the field I loved, which was finance at the time. Therefore, I designed a plan to create this reality. Although my parents could not put me through college, I created a way to go to college part time. It was then I created a small business for myself helping students with homework assignments, and I also began teaching young kids drums lessons in their homes. Between these two businesses, I was able to pay for my college courses and eventually achieved my goal to work for prestigious corporations in senior financial management positions with such companies as Pitney Bowes Corp., Wilson Sporting Goods Corp., Levolor Blinds Corp., Beneficial Finance Corp., and other well-known public corporations.

From there, I created my own financial service company and began working as an independent financial risk analyst, offering my company's services to lending institutions and commercial lending companies. Over time, I created my life dream to have a prestigious home in an area I always wanted to live and accomplished just that.

Following all this, I created the idea of becoming a writer and seminar speaker. This book is a result of my continuing to be creative.

One's creative gifts are not only useful for accomplishments such as I just described but surmounting life's unexpected, life-changing experiences that include adversities on every conceivable level imaginable, including life-threatening adversities, as well. I know because I did this by creating what I wanted and transmitting those dominant thoughts to my all-knowing inner guidance to bring forth what I was seeking to become reality.

What I have just identified is how I utilized my creative powers to overcome all that I have and other accomplishments I created thus far. However, this is not all I overcame and accomplished utilizing my inner creative powers. As I have described, there were many other life-changing events that I also overcame by utilizing my inner creative powers. I believe that by employing this creative method, anyone can go about awakening their creative powers that can serve them well throughout their lives to achieve almost anything for good they may desire. Here's what I did:

1. Being creative includes being aware that you have many other options available to you that you should explore before settling for the very first solution or answer you may come across. Succeeding at whatever you are seeking to accomplish should not include following others and what they did. Instead, you must discover your own creative way to acquire what it is you are seeking to incorporate into your reality. This includes anything beneficial, not just overcoming or ridding yourself of problem areas in your life.
2. Dare to be different by finding your own way to deal with any problem areas you may be having and do what others refuse to do by first doing some research to learn as much as you can. Become as informed as possible before you set out to create your plan to achieve whatever you are seeking to overcome or eliminate from your life. You were never meant to have to live a life full of stress, anxiety, despair, pain on any level, or any related adversities.

3. Begin to challenge the status quo and begin to inquire on your own by querying everything, as I did, if you truly want to live a creative life. I found that to be in an essential, continuous learning environment as you move forward on this creative path to your continued creativity growth during your lifetime, never take anything whatsoever for granted, regardless of who may annoy, upset, or who may think you are out of line or naive. Go past what anyone else may think about your new probing ways and do it anyway, despite what others may say. Always get a second, third, fourth, and even fifth opinion where a serious illness or life-changing nonphysical event may show up in your life. Even then, as I just stated, take the time to do some valuable research yourself. By all means, do not have anyone at all do it for you, unless you are medically incapable, and even then, only have someone you totally trust to do it for you. After all, it's your life we are discussing, isn't it? The questions you should be asking yourself are those that ask the *why, where, when* and *I* questions, such as the ones below:

- Why is my life going like this?
- Why can't I live the life I always wanted to experience?
- Why am I suffering when I can do something about it?
- Why am I allowing others to dictate to me how I should live my life?
- Where have I gone wrong in my life?
- Why have I chosen to put up with all this?
- Why have I not ventured out and begun to explore all the opportunities out there for me?
- Why should I continue to live with this uncomfortable situation any longer and just do something about it?
- Why do I allow myself to be taken for granted all the time?
- When am I going to stop feeling sorry for myself and instead begin to help myself?
- When am I going to stop depending on others?

- When will I ever learn my lesson and stop doing things that disturb me?
- When am I going to do my own research on my condition and cease taking advice from others?
- Why am I always concerned about resolving the problems of others and never considering myself for once?
- I wonder what would happen if I started to explore alternative solutions for my problem.
- I wonder what benefits I would derive if I just began to wean myself off of over the counter medication.
- I wonder how my life would improve if I would just begin to believe I can find a loving and caring person.
- I wonder how much better I would feel if I would just stop eating all the wrong foods.

One word of warning here. Never suppress yourself, regardless how ridiculous or out of line any question you may ask may seem to you or others—just ask it! I asked plenty of questions before I made the decision to permit any surgeon to operate on me when I had the two cancer events. They weren't too happy about it, of course. Neither would I have been had I been in their shoes, having spent the majority of my life studying and working inhumane hours to get as far as they have. However, even realizing this, I forged ahead and just asked away. And I am better off for it today because I did and have absolutely no regrets because, as I said, it's your life we are talking about here and no one else's.

By asking a myriad of questions, including asking myself questions concerning almost everything to do with my life, I was able to reveal to myself some very dark corners where I had never looked before about my life that were responsible for a number of undesirable occurrences. Had I asked probing questions sooner, I may have been able to avoid some very unpleasant situations and saved myself a lot of grief. In addition, by asking questions, I was able to clearly see numerous opportunities I had repressed and missed, which I regretted.

I believe not asking probing questions is among the primary reasons why most people find themselves continuously at a dead end and in undesirable situations they are finding a difficult time getting out of. Serious problems in one area of our life have an adverse effect on other areas of our lives, resulting in an extremely difficult position to find oneself in. Begin asking yourself and others penetrating questions if you seriously intend to live the life you deserve in which your creative powers can serve you well in most, if not all, areas of your life.

Begin formulating mental pictures containing alternative opportunities, thoughts, and, above all, ideas aside from just settling on one resolution to any problem areas in your life. It is right here where most people fall off the cliff, so to speak. What do I mean by this? What I mean is that the one resolution choice pertaining to problem areas in one's life appears to be an acceptable way of thinking for most people—i.e., surgery is the only solution, chemotherapy is needed in an attempt to rid the body of cancer, diverting the water in this direction may resolve the flooding issue, etc.

The issue here is that few people will ever look for alternative solutions to a problem they may be troubled with and will instead go with the very first one with which they are familiar or what others have been doing for years and years. They use outdated solutions that are no longer workable but still utilized and do not use their imagination and creative ability to find other solutions to resolve or to overcome problem areas in their life.

Why is this so important? It is important because by seeking other solutions to problematic situations, there may be another alternative that can resolve the issue being addressed. However, most people will not take the time to question it or are literally stuck in a habitual way of thinking and living. They will not seek out other solutions and miss the opportunity to resolve problem areas in their life by choosing to just settle for the very first answer they think of or that others have been following and doing for years.

This is important pertaining to medical issues and diagnoses. If you insist upon only having one resolution to your problem areas of your life, stop and think first to ask yourself if you have neglected to call upon your creative inner mind that contains countless options and alternative solutions from which to choose. All you have to do is to reprogram your mind to seek out these alternative solutions, each and every time you are seeking other possible options for resolving any problem areas of your life.

I cannot possibly emphasize strongly enough how being a creative being is absolutely essential if you intend to live a self-rewarding life filled with opportunities on every conceivable level, which you may desire to explore and can be manifested in your life. Keep in mind at all times that your creative powers have and will always exist within you, for you to call upon at any point in time—should you choose to access them to resolve any issues that may be concerning you—in ways that will astound you. They can help you discard conventional ways that are not serving you to resolve issues you may encounter or are presently disturbing you and can provide you with continuous access to other opportunities, answers, solutions, and new ideas that far surpass former antiquated methods.

Since achieving all that I have thus far and overcoming very serious life-changing conditions and events, I have never relinquished or abandoned my creative powers. If you are serious about greatly enhancing any areas of your life, then you too should seriously consider allowing your creative powers to transform your life into a wonderful opportunity from this point onward.

Befriending Your Inner Guidance

The simple dictionary definition of the word *befriend* is "to become or act as a friend to." However, to befriend one's inner guidance goes much deeper than the common dictionary definition. It reaches the furthest depth of this inner force, which provides not only the capability of being able to control the healing process (pertaining to whatever ailments or other adversities that may encounter) but also goes as far as being able to completely heal the body, when you decide to befriend their inner guidance. The conscious mind is interconnected with the all-knowing inner guidance that I have identified as the key to becoming aware of every desire being sought for good and that can also prevent sickness and serious illnesses from returning and appearing in our lives.

Most people are unaware of the fact that their conscious mind and all-knowing inner guidance are interconnected. As a matter of fact, most people are unaware that they have an all-knowing inner force that can bring forth anything they believe in their conscious mind to be true, good or bad. Having become aware of this inner guidance, medical science has come to at least acknowledge that most diseases and adversities can be controlled by the person who has them and can even be reversed through the mind–body connection. Many people like myself have restored themselves back to good health, utilizing the inner guidance's power to heal and even surmount illnesses and/or adversities. What all this really comes down to is that people like me have begun to realize that they could achieve major changes for good in their lives on any conceivable level, especially those that are medically related, by befriending their inner guidance, coupled with other methods.

If you have never been made aware before, know that your body and conscious mind have the ability to heal and eventually overcome most illnesses and adversities. A doctor does not heal a serious wound, a broken bone, a skin disease, illness, etc.; a doctor treats the diagnosed condition and assists the body in its healing process, as does a mental health specialist who aids in the process of healing one's conscious mind. It is your inner power that knows precisely what to do in such events and whatever else that it may need to attend to, including serious illnesses.

You should also be aware that your inner mind works better concerning the healing process when you bring forth visions and continuous thoughts of good health, coupled with unwavering belief and expectation that the healing you are seeking for any illness, serious or otherwise, or other adversity has already occurred and that you have already been completely healed. This is precisely how I overcame serious illnesses, numerous adversities, and other undesirable life-changing events that could have otherwise taken my life.

I consider myself very knowledgeable concerning befriending one's all-knowing inner guidance and conscious mind and their combined self-healing power. Therefore, having healed myself from numerous serious life-threatening and life-changing events, I can personally attest to the fact that the mind itself, connected with one's all-knowing inner power, that can remove every obstacle if one chooses to, once the inner power is accepted by anyone who cares to learn how to apply this and the other methods I have identified. I have identified here that the inner guidance can resolve almost any adversity one may encounter when wavering, doubting, skepticism, and lack of self-confidence are not present in one's conscious mind. Not only do I teach these methods, but I continue to personally acknowledge experience in what they can do for one's life when coupled with the power of the all-knowing inner guidance. Medical science has come forth to support that proper medical advice and the mind–body connection can be a powerful healing team.

    I have had a number of people tell me that this could not possibly work for them and that they could not possibly believe that any of this works. They generally state that if the medical community could not bring forth a permanent cure for any life-threatening illness or other serious life-changing conditions, there is no way a person could do it on their own. Although I have no problem with anyone's opinion concerning what they have come to believe about being able to heal life's ever changing conditions, it is important to recognize that such beliefs are accompanied with fears and worries of expectations that a serious life-changing event may invade their body one day. Or if they are beset by a serious life-changing illness, they have been led to believe that medical science has the only answers to bring forth a complete healing and permanent cure.

    It is these types of thoughts that are combined with fear, denial, and a negative attitude that eventually aggravate physical illnesses as one's mind is receiving these thoughts, believing they are true and are transmitting them to one's inner guidance that in turn believes that is what one wants to acquire and will bring forth what is being asked to be produced. Therefore, it is important to recognize that when anyone begins to fear a disease or the possible eventuality of having an illness, they are more likely to contract or worsen a condition that is already being developed through their fearful and doubting thoughts and stress. These negative influences, extreme anxiety, and habitual worrying can interfere with the inner healing powers and help to prevent an otherwise unstoppable army of methods that not only can prevent illness but promote healing from coming to the rescue as well.

It is also very important to realize that most people have no clue or will even begin to explore the tremendous inner power they control, let alone all the other methods I have identified. If they would take the time to learn more about these powerful methods and begin to use them, they will find that by befriending their inner guidance, they can eliminate unnecessary worrying, anxiety, stress, uncertainty, doubting, lack of self-confidence, and, above all, fear that can result in a stranglehold on their life that instead could have been avoided.

It is vital that you understand and realize that your health is your responsibility, not your doctors' or other health care providers'—it is yours and yours alone. Therefore, you need to begin taking a very active role in your own health and above all your own healing as absolutely no one can play that role in your life other than you. That said, always remember, should you contract or may be presently suffering from a serious life-changing illness or event, you should never give into it, regardless of its nature or stage. Instead, personal responsibility for your recovery, prudent medical care, and becoming an active participant in overcoming and/or defeating whatever the event, condition, situation, or circumstance may be just may save you.

The best place on this planet where you are going to find a healing doctor is in your own mind, so begin now to befriend your conscious mind and inner guidance as they are the key, along with all the other methods I have identified, to healing almost any condition or adversity you may encounter.

Expectation

The *Merriam-Webster Dictionary* defines *expectation* as "to consider probable or certain." Expectation is another very powerful tool that I employed that was pivotal in the final stage in achieving whatever it was I seeking. Once I set my mind on this expectation, I then left it with my inner power to bring forth my desires, and over time, whatever I was expecting appeared in my life.

Why is *expectation* such a powerful word? Because once expectation is held in the conscious mind, it eventually becomes accepted as true. Therefore, it will be transferred to the inner mind to be retained and to appear in one's physical life, good or bad, depending upon which dominant thoughts convey, and are believed by both the conscious and inner mind.

Among some of the reasons why what is expected to occur in a person's life for good does not show up is the lack of patience and complete trust that it will. I have personally witnessed this on countless occasions in the lives of others, ranging from expectation of the continuance of a marriage or relationship, all the way out to the expectation of overcoming a serious adversity that included a life-threatening illness.

We expect many things to come our way in life, don't we? This is an instinctive part of human behavior. However, when it comes to our health and the ridding ourselves of the messes and nonphysical issues, conditions, and events we bring upon ourselves is quite another matter. This word *expectation*, when it comes to determining outcomes of good versus bad, is almost nonexistent in our conscious minds—let alone our all-knowing inner mind—when it comes to overcoming and removing them from our lives.

The one thing I learned early during the numerous adverse conditions I faced was that failure in others to heal began occurring as soon as they placed the thought in their conscious mind that they will not be able to overcome whatever it may be they are dealing with. By holding that thought in their conscious mind for any extended period of time, it becomes a habitual thought. Therefore, once the conscious mind accepts that thought as truth, it will be transmitted to the all-knowing inner force. In turn, the inner mind will accept it as truth and will begin to bring forth the end of an adverse condition or whatever it was that the conscious mind believes it wanted to maintain. Not only can this be dangerous, it can also possibly be fatal if they are continuous disempowering thoughts.

GARY DEBELLONIA

Unwavering Self-Trust

The word *self-trust* means "self-confidence in oneself and in one's powers and abilities," according to *Merriam-Webster*.

Am I some miracle as some people have labeled my survival of numerous serious adversities to be? No, not even close. My survival of all that I have overcome emanated from self-trust and self-reliance, coupled with my complete and unwavering trust in my inner guidance that is one with the all-knowing infinite intelligence.

As for miracles, who am I to say that they do not exist? However, if I am to be considered a miracle due to all I have survived, I reject this premise. I believe my survival of these physical experiences could only have taken place because I was totally reliant upon myself and completely trusted in the guidance I was receiving from my inner guide—and nothing else—for the decisions I made.

The key point I am attempting to make here is that you need to start becoming—if you are not already—self-reliant, self-trusting, and self-aware of your inner guidance's objective concerning the opinions of others, when it comes to serious matters that affect your life to such a degree as any serious life-changing adversity and related situations.

This is not to be interpreted as to shutting anyone out and not listening to them. Instead, it's about taking control of your own situation and circumstances and relying upon yourself to make important and critical decisions as they pertain to life-changing adversities. Choosing to do so, you have everything to gain and nothing to lose by developing an impenetrable and unwavering self-trust.

Based upon my observation, most people do not seem to trust themselves much, which I find astonishing. Instead, they appear to continue to place their blind faith in governments, others, and everything and everyone else other than themselves for information and knowledge. Know this: everything you feel and experience through your emotions, intuition, and inner feelings, connected to the all-knowing infinite intelligence, are all that you really need to trust because they are the real you within. I am not speaking about or for any religion; I am referring instead to your inner guidance, which every human being was born with that resides deep inside us all.

Quite sadly, far too many people go through life not knowing (or if they do know, fail) to trust their inner self. Instead, they seem to place their trust in everything else—their leaders, medical science, medical providers, and countless others are a good example of this.

Most people seem to be totally oblivious of having placed their self-trust and self-confidence on the shelf and transferred total reliance to others. The more you transfer your trust and reliance to others, the more you become removed from your very own wise inner counsel. This just more reason you need to turn or return to your never-failing, all-knowing inner guidance. I cannot begin to tell you how many people I have known who have become so falsely convinced by others of their unworthiness and chose to rely on others to lead them, thereby causing themselves to become seemingly totally reliant upon others for almost everything. The result is their not being able to move ahead on a clear, self-trusting path in any phase of their lives. This is primarily caused by not trusting in their all-knowing inner guidance.

That said, understand completely that you must be willing to embrace and commit yourself to living your life full of self-confidence. This includes trusting the intuitive inner messages that are continually being sent to you from your all-knowing inner guidance. Their presence is expressed as your instincts, emotions, strong feelings, and, most of all, your dominant thoughts.

Why is self-confidence or self-trusting so important? Because only you can point yourself in the right direction and choose the life path you want to follow. No one on this planet can live your life for you, and no one can make your decision as to what path you choose to follow as well. Many people seem to believe that they have no control over the adversities that come into their life and allow themselves to become overwhelmed by them. There is no doubt that fear plays a major role here and is the culprit that appears to block out the gift of self-confidence and self-trust that one can call upon at any time. Instead, they will ignore their gift and trust that, by doing so, whatever they are seeking will be resolved whether it is a serious illness or any serious life-changing event, they believe will be healed by relying upon others or some source other than themselves.

I place a great deal of emphasis on this method because it is right here where one is going to find what they are really made of and how much they really believe that they play a major role in overcoming whatever adversity in life.

This becomes the pivotal point concerning either having or lacking self-confidence or self-trust in one's ability to play a major role in surmounting a serious life-changing event. In many instances, it can also be the deciding factor as to whether one will be able to overcome a serious life-changing adversity. The primary reason is that rarely, if ever, would any source one may decide to rely upon ever guarantee a permanent healing or resolution of whatever the matter may be for which one is seeking relief.

I have yet to meet any credible medical professional who would go so far as to guarantee a permanent healing and/or cure of a life-threatening illness or a psychologist or psychiatrist who would guarantee a complete resolution to one's serious life-changing situation. As I have pointed out, the only source that can assist in possibly contributing to overcoming any serious life-changing event, once it has been treated by medical science and/or professional counseling, is one's total self-confidence and self-trust in their all-knowing inner guidance that is connected to the infinite intelligence. To my knowledge, that has a proven track record of being the only factor that can actually be totally relied on, coupled with one's own determination to surmount any serious life-changing event or adversity.

You are here on this planet to advance in your life, not to be or remain stagnant or to live in deprivation, illness, or ongoing strife—all of which are unnatural circumstances. Instead, you were meant to be prosperous on every level of life, happy, joyful, and free from disease or any life-threatening illnesses or negative events.

As you continue on your journey through life, you will come to learn that indeed you are more powerful and unique than you ever realized. The mere fact that you are in this world at all proves that you are not just a physical being; you are also a very powerful, one-of-a-kind spiritual being as well. (I will not be delving into the worlds of the numerous religious beliefs, which is not the intent of this book.) Know this, believe it, and, most of all, feel it with deep emotion. You've even possibly heard and/or may have read what I just said somewhere before; but for some reason, most people have either forgotten this or may have chosen to disregard it entirely or never knew this at all.

Understand that this book is in no way meant to replace proper medical care and advice but instead to be used in conjunction with proper medical attention and credible professional advice. Never disregard prudent and trustworthy necessary medical advice. I didn't. By combining credible medical advice with your self-reliance, self-confidence, self-trust, and your all-knowing inner wisdom, there should be no reason that you can't embark upon or return to the path of totally trusting in your intuitive inner guide, deep feelings and emotions, strong beliefs, and, above all, self-confidence and self-trust.

Understand completely that you need to approach the information in this book with full expectation and complete confidence and trust in your inner guidance, your *real self.* You must be willing to embrace and commit yourself to living a life full of self-confidence and trusting your inner intuitive messages that are continually being sent to your from your all-knowing inner guidance—which are connected to your emotions, strong feelings, and, most of all, your dominant, empowering thoughts.

We have now seen the tremendous role that self-confidence and self-trust play in one's life and how, by putting these methods into action, the opportunity is created to be able to heal oneself from any unexpected life-changing problem or adversity and, like myself and many others, have a very strong possibility of overcoming even a life-threatening illnesses and other serious life-changing event.

The Extraordinary Power of Giving

Giving is among one of the most powerful methods that you need to always be aware of. When put this into action, giving is another method that brings forth what is desired to be contributed for good. What you are saying by giving is that you have more than enough to share with others even if it is only a morsel of food. It is a well-known fact that the wealthiest people in the world maintain their monetary wealth by giving away vast sums of money. (I am not referring to political contributions.) And by this act of giving, they attract even greater financial wealth into their lives.

The more this gift of giving is shared with others, the more you will receive an abundance of the good things you desire for your life, as the law of giving cannot help but return to you tenfold what you give to others. No, it does not have to be in the form of monetary or material assets. Just the mere act of sharing with others what you have either discovered for the first time or rediscovered in this book regarding what you have deep inside—your all-knowing intuitive inner guidance that is one with infinite intelligence—so others too can make the choice of coming to know this extremely powerful force that can bring forth their innermost desires for good to be shared as well.

It amazed me to learn how most people do very little giving during their lifetime and instead, find a myriad of ways to spend and invest their time in the accumulation of "stuff." They build a vast inventory of material things which, and over a period of time, wind up in some storage place or at a garage sale instead of being given to those less fortunate.

It further amazes me how anyone can expect to achieve prosperity on all levels without returning anything back through the wonderful gift of giving. No matter how little or small, the giving of your time or material possessions that are no longer useful or needed can and will begin to bring forth an abundance of good into your life.

Do you have a desire to make a positive difference in the world but don't feel you can because you believe you can't? You are probably thinking of a person that gives millions of dollars to charitable causes who has the wherewithal to do so. Let's take a look at what Roger B. Carr, author of *Mentor to the Rich of Heart*, has to say about that:

> An Everyday Philanthropist is someone who gives unselfishly everyday *toward the good of their fellow man [and woman]*. Giving money is not the only way to show

love, benevolence and good will. *There are many other ways for you to do this that requires little or no money.* So don't let your lack of being a multi-millionaire keeps you from improving the world we live in. *You don't have to be rich, famous or retired to make a difference in the world every day!* [my emphases]

I have also chosen several interesting quotes from *The Prophet* by poet Kahlil Gilbran (1883–1931) that I believe to be germane to what I am attempting to get across to you about giving:

> Then said a rich man, "Speak to us of Giving." And he answered: You give but little when you give of your possessions. It is when you give of yourself that you truly give for what are your possessions but things you keep and guard or fear you may need them tomorrow?
>
> And tomorrow, what shall tomorrow bring to the over prudent dog burying bones in the trackless sand as he follows the pilgrims to the holy city? And what is fear of need but need itself? Is not dread of thirst when your well is full, the thirst that is unquenchable?
>
> *There are those who give little of the much which they have and they give it for recognition and their hidden desire makes their gifts unwholesome. And there are those who have little and give it all. These are the believers in life and the bounty of life, and their coffer is never empty. There are those* who give with joy, and their joy is their reward. And there are those who give with pain, and that pain is their baptism. And there are those who give and know not pain in giving, nor do they seek joy, nor give with mindfulness of virtue: They give as in yonder valley the myrtle breathes its fragrance into space. Through the hands of such as these God speaks, and from behind their eyes He smiles upon the earth. It is well to give when asked, but it is better to give unasked, through understanding: And to the open-handed the search for one who shall receive is joy greater than giving. And is there aught you would

withhold? All you have shall someday be given: Therefore give now, that the season of giving may be yours and not your inheritors'. You often say, "I would give, but only to the deserving". The trees in your orchard say not so, nor the flocks in your pasture.

They give that they may live, for to with-hold is to perish. Surely he who is worthy to receive his days and nights, is worthy of all else from you. And he who has deserved to drink from the ocean of life deserves to fill his cup from your little stream. And what desert greater shall there be, than that, which lies in the courage and the confidence, nay the charity, of receiving? And who are you that men should rend their bosom and unveil their pride, that you may see their worth naked and their pride unabashed? See first that you yourself deserve to be a giver, and an instrument of giving. For in truth it is life that gives unto life- while you, who deem yourself a giver, are but a witness. And you receivers- and you are all receivers- assume no weight of gratitude, lest you lay a yoke upon yourself and upon he who gives. Rather rise together with the giver on his gifts as on wings: For to be over mindful of your debt, is to doubt his generosity who has the free-hearted earth for mother, and God for father.

I believe that these two well-written excerpts alone say volumes about the most important subject of giving. I cannot express enough the importance of this subject of giving. It doesn't take a separate book to try to impress the importance of a subject as important as this one is and how it can affect one's life in a dramatic way, either positively or negatively. What it takes is common sense.

It should also be expressed again that "giving" is not necessarily the giving of assets or any material items; instead, the giving of one's time to others is one of the most important of all the things one can do. Imagine for a moment and reflect on what you do with your time every day, week, month, and year. Certainly you have some time to spare to give of yourself to the less fortunate, children, the elderly, and others who may need some of your time, talent, or just attention.

PREVAILING OVER INSURMOUNTABLE ODDS

As busy as I was as a self-employed businessman, I always made time as a teacher's aide, volunteering to donate my time to children at my son's elementary school who were slow learners and ESL (English as a second language) students who came mostly from one-parent families. I did this at least three to four days a week for a number of years; was a volunteer soccer coach for a coed under-eight soccer team; an assistant scout leader for a cub scout troop; took time to take neighborhood kids on field trips; spent time playing football, basketball, and baseball with neighborhood children on weeknights and weekends, despite having many pressing projects to accomplish; assisted my three stepdaughters and my son with homework and school projects; instructed kids in the discipline of martial arts as an assistant martial arts instructor; volunteered as a professional musician in a church orchestra; and much more. As I look back on all this giving, had I the opportunity to do it over again, I certainly would.

My giving gift has yet to cease, as I am still giving every chance I get to those in need and those not in need—if it's not, then a lending ear just to be there for someone who just needs someone to listen to them. Also it's my continuing to donate my time to others who need my help or assisting my son and stepdaughter with their homework, taking a carload of kids here and there, volunteering as an assistant football coach for my son's American football team, or whatever someone else needs. I always make the time, even though I too have numerous things that I need to accomplish.

So what about you? Are you truly so busy that you cannot find the time to give some of your time to others in need? No, I am not suggesting that you become someone's lapdog or slave—far from it. Instead, truly give some of your time to reach out to help others who need your help. There are a myriad of things you can do for people in need right in your town, let alone the nation or world.

It is difficult for me to try to understand why anyone may say "I simply do not have the time with all the things I have to do every day." Really? You might say you do not have the luxury of reaching out to others either. Why? You can believe that by not giving of your time to those who need you, you can rest assured that the blessings you are silently seeking may be a long time coming, if they do at all. Is this a scare tactic? Not at all! It is a fact of life.

Why do you think some of the wealthiest people on this planet stay that way? They stay that way and their wealth continues to grow and grow and grow because they have made giving to others in many ways, which is a very important part of their life plan to do just that and they are not hard to identify. Therefore, you do not have to give sums of money or assets; instead, the giving of portions of your time to your fellow man, woman, young person, or family is all it will take.

Yet how many among us spend our weekends entertaining ourselves, watching sports, playing golf, going to the beach, going shopping, and just focus on our immediate family's needs and desires daily, year after year, and, rarely— if ever—volunteer even one day, evening, or weekend a month to others (not including extended family or close friends) who need your help.

I can remember like it was just yesterday when I was volunteering my time to special needs children and ESL (English as a second language) students at my son's elementary school that despite the efforts of the school's administration reaching out for volunteers, only a handful of parents ever volunteered for any number of the school's needs. Year after year, it was always the same parents who volunteered, and it was the same situation with the children's soccer league.

Not only did this shock me, it appalled me as well. Many would use work responsibilities as their reason, and others would not volunteer at all who had the time to do so. Most of the matters needing volunteers required not more than an hour of someone's time, and others were, at most, a few hours one or two evenings a week. I too had business obligations and deadlines to meet, yet I made it my personal responsibility to give my time and to stand out in the harsh winter cold and rain at night to coach kids in soccer several nights a week, as well as Saturday games, and never missed one practice or game, even if I was not feeling well.

Am I looking for an "attaboy" from my readers? Not at all, quite the contrary. What I am seeking is, if you are not giving, for you to think about becoming a giving volunteer who can begin to recognize the tremendous feeling giving to others in need will come over you. The benefits will surely come to you tenfold as you continue to reach out and give some of your time to others who so desperately need your help, especially in today's serious economic disaster that has swept across this nation.

I know—and always knew—that for me, giving was the absolute right thing to do.

I continue to give to others through this book by reaching out to mankind everywhere, introducing or reintroducing them to the existence of one of the greatest gifts ever given to all of us, which is the gift of one's inner guidance and all-knowing infinite intelligence.

Keep in mind that all your material possessions are temporary. Absolutely nothing we believe we own do we ever own because no one has ever or will ever be able to take their accumulated stuff with them upon departing this earth. These temporary possessions becomes outdated or lose their usefulness, and we usually will either get rid of them or store them in a places I call the "forgotten pits." We dare enter these rarely visited places when we feel like mountain climbing, so to speak, in some attic or in a dark cellar or moving mountains of stuff buried in a storage facility we donate to monetarily each month but really do not know why, as we rarely use or even visit these stuff, for the most part, more than three times a year, instead of giving it to others who cannot afford to buy these castaway possessions who can possibly make use of these outdated items.

What better gift can one give to themselves than by sharing this most precious gift of giving with others in need so they too may one day have the opportunity to share with others who also may want to share with others, so on and so forth, this wonderful gift of giving?

I sincerely believe that most people are giving in nature, even if they truly do not have any material assets to give. I also believe that, considering the circumstances most people are finding themselves in today due to the seriousness of the economic condition worldwide, many people are focused upon their survival, finding a way to keep their homes, paying their financial obligations, and holding on to their jobs. These are very concerning and real issues; there is absolutely no denial of this fact. However, what I am telling you is that despite these uncomfortable circumstances and the financial storms that assail you, you may possibly find that one still needs to include the time or way to reach out to others who very likely may be exposed to even more severe hardships and truly need your help.

Keep in mind that it is the combination of all these methods and those that I have identified and your all-knowing inner guidance that brings forth whatever you are seeking for good and for the good of all concerned and to seriously consider making these methods a significant part of your daily routine.

We now will explore the remarkable power of your gift of inner intuition.

22

THE INCREDIBLE POWER OF YOUR INNER INTUITION

> By choosing reliance upon one's inner intuition versus learned outer experiences, mankind can change the outer aspects of their lives.
>
> —Author

Having been subjected to a number of life-threatening illnesses and by working with and through my intuitive all-knowing inner guidance, I was able to identify and am convinced that the root causes that I listed in the beginning of this book and related events are among the reasons for most, if not all, diseases and life-threatening conditions. Medical science is slowly recognizing that many illnesses are linked to these root causes.

People whom I have interviewed and those I have known who wound up with serious heart conditions and other serious life-changing illnesses had spent the majority of their lives in stressful situations such as working environments and highly stressful family circumstances. Over time, these and related conditions escalated which added to their emotional and psychological problems.

In addition to the these conditions, many people allow themselves to dwell on the past and continued to carry on family and other feuds dating back years and other past issues that they refused to let go of and move on with their life—i.e., bad memories, a failed marriage, some painful event that had occurred such as a loss of a loved one, losing a job, financial difficulties resulting in the loss of material possessions, and countless other situations. Some people had also carried this baggage with them into a new relationship.

The cumulative result of all this was a complete draining of their energy, which, when depleted, leaves one wide open for a nonphysical illness that could eventually manifest into serious life-compromising physical illnesses and even death—if allowed to go unresolved. Most people do not recognize these conditions building up in their bodies and mind until one day they are staring a very serious physical condition in the face. Such was the case with me.

The human body, like the universe we are surrounded by, works on energy; and like any automobile, when the operator of the vehicle pays little attention to the gas, they soon find themselves all alone on some highway, miles away from assistance in a precarious situation. In comparison, for the most part, we rarely pay attention to the amount of energy we siphon from our own bodies every day, let alone mentally, going through our self-imposed stressful routines like robots giving minimal thought to the eventual future consequences of the energy we are depleting.

What I noticed about many people who were undergoing these conditions was that they had either lost complete touch with their intuitive inner guidance entirely or never knew that it existed. Therefore, they had no idea that they were born with this inner power and consequently never even knew that the answers they were seeking to their negative circumstances had been with them throughout their entire life in the form of their inner guidance that they could call forth, had they been aware that this inner power existed.

In addition to this, as I had discovered and acknowledged for myself and went on to connect with others who had as well, I learned that all humankind shares similar feelings such as fear of abandonment, being left alone, loss, disease, a diagnosis of a terminal illness or mental illness, the unexpected and unknown, betrayal, etc. These are just a mere sampling of the many types of fears shared by everyone. Rarely do people realize that fear at any level and feelings of deep anger can escalate into a serious psychological crisis.

In order to avoid this from taking place, one must be able to rely upon their inner intuitive guidance. The only way for this to be done is for one to quiet their conscious mind and allow this inner guidance to communicate with you through intuition and strong inner feelings. When it does, you should begin to feel a warm feeling throughout your entire body emanating from deep within you and calmness like you had never felt before in your lifetime. This is when you will finally realize that you have made a direct connection with the real you that contains the methods and solutions to resolving every undesirable situation and circumstance you had been exposed to and where you will find the answers you have been seeking, unless one is unwilling to firmly believe that they do possess an incredible power deep within themselves.

People I have spoken with—and there were many—had an array of topics they were seeking assistance with, ranging from health issues to a sincere desire to learn more about their own all-knowing intuitive inner guidance. These people varied from everyday ordinary people and even people in the medical field who, despite their individual religious beliefs and faiths, expressed a need to understand more about their inner power.

Not being a member of any denominations myself, I certainly am not one to give anyone spiritual guidance related to a higher power. However, what I am able to do with the highest possible level of confidence is to share my personal experience related to the awesome resources that one's intuitive inner guide possesses—having myself realized not only the incredible healing and curing power that one's inner guide can demonstrate and receiving the answers and methods to every need anyone may have for whatever serious life-changing situation they may be facing.

I have and continue to rely solely upon my intuitive guidance for all my needs, including matters that I myself may not have the answer to. It makes very little difference how much we are able to educate ourselves here on this planet. That type of education is light-years away from being able to even scratch the surface of what this intuitive inner guidance can do in a person's life. To continue to ignore this, in my opinion, is one of the worst decisions anyone can ever make in their very short stay on this planet.

I have also spoken with people from all walks of life and professions during my travels that have one common thread that runs through their conversation, which is to be able to know what this unseen power really is and how they can utilize it for their own personal gain. If this is truly their intention to attempt to use their intuitive inner guide for their personal gain, greed, or deception—no answer at all will ever come forth for them. Just dead silence. One may as well just turn their heads toward their other shoulder where that little fella with pointed ears, dressed in red, and a pitchfork in his hand is perched, ready to give one its misguided advice. I cringe to even imagine anyone being that foolhardy to choose that option, but quite unfortunately, there are those who will continue to choose that option, regardless of the outcome, which quite often, is not the one expected.

I have had a number of medical people share with me their frustration about patients who were spiritually connected as were they, but they were prohibited from sharing their spiritual experiences with them or to cross that line due to strict ethics attached to their profession. Others have offered that they intuitively believed that a number of their patients relied heavily upon their inner powers for healing conditions they were having physically. My opinion is that knowing about one's intuitive inner guide and its ability to heal physical, psychological, and nonphysical illnesses is not confined to just people suffering from certain ailments but is available to everyone who occupies space on this planet. Frankly, I look forward to being able to witness the day where medical science finally agrees that there is a very good and beneficial reason to incorporate one's inner power with medical science for the benefit of their patients and begin offering an optional remedy for their patients' ailments.

It was not until I became intuitively aware that many physical illnesses are given birth through nonphysical illnesses and conditions that I had allowed to violate my body and mind and to literally take over my life that I learned that they ultimately manifested themselves into full-blown physical illnesses. I am thoroughly convinced that I could certainly have avoided my conditions, had I reconnected with my inner intuitive guidance much earlier than I did.

PREVAILING OVER INSURMOUNTABLE ODDS

There are simply no words sufficient enough in any language that can adequately describe this experience to anyone, unless one has been through it and can relate to such a situation. Believe me, if you haven't been through anything like I have, make it your primary mission to never have a future date checked off on your calendar to have to undergo such a circumstance.

Here is where your inner intuitive guidance can alert you far in advance of any oncoming nonphysical condition that has the opportunity of eventually developing into a physical illness, which is attributable to today's fast-paced lifestyle that most people engage in every day, believing this is what it is going to take to get ahead. Ahead of what? I have no idea. Unless it is to stay ten paces ahead of the cardiologist, followed by the mortician—both of whom would eagerly love to have your business.

If this were not enough, throw in the high-tech equipment people expose themselves to each and every day for more than eight hours a day, including both at the work environment and in their homes. This includes computers that emit electromagnetic energy, our high-tech cellular telephones that are said to be able to cause brain cancer, high tension wires we live close to, and every type of electronics we allow ourselves to be exposed to constantly and whose cumulative effects are unknown. This does not even include what new devices that are disguised as being beneficial to mankind that will be coming around the corner, polluting the places we live, and yet collectively are a mass conglomeration of some of the deadliest weapons humanity can use against themselves.

Why then is this inner intuition so valuable to you concerning these and many other related matters? Because what use is it to anyone to have already attracted a serious illness when, by paying attention to their intuitive guidance, they could have avoided any such condition to show their lives. Treating a serious medical condition after the symptoms have already arrived in one's body is like closing the barn door after all the horses have already escaped.

I have known and interviewed people who admittedly were so fatigued and drained from most of their energy that they had no clue how they would be able to endure another year of the incredible pace they had chosen by allowing themselves to get on that life-depleting treadmill in the first place. For me, this was very easy to understand because I spent the greater part of my adult life chasing the golden goose myself, only in the end to find out that there was no golden goose all along. Does this mean that one should seriously consider ending their career or seek another type of work? No, not at all. What it means is that one needs to be able to begin to listen to what their intuitive inner guidance is telling them continuously.

Sometimes it may be leading you to changing your career or it may be giving you the answer to how you can avoid all the stress and tremendous pace you have created for yourself. Consider how to more effectively manage your current situation and recapture all the energy you have been depleting from yourself every day and to shed any depression you possibly may have begun to feel or possibly are developing.

Why is it so worth it to begin to listen to one's intuitive inner guide and to begin following its prodding? The alternative is a nightmare that most sane people should want to avoid at all costs, in addition to speeding up the aging process and taking an emotional toll that may take years to overcome. This begs the question, "Was it all worth it?" As for me, the answer is a blunt *no*. It certainly was not worth it because once one loses their health—or, worse, their sanity—what did it matter anyway? In the end, we may have gained some wealth, maybe some notoriety, possibly some fame, climbed the corporate ladder, and achieved many material assets. Although we won the battle, we undoubtedly, ultimately lost the war. Although this sounds grim, the fact is that it is happening in real time, every single day at a record pace in America and all over the world.

Here is a fact that you may wish to consider what most people do unconsciously in their everyday life. (Notice I said "some people," not "all people.") In order to accomplish whatever it is they are desiring to achieve in their life, they cannot just say they are going to do something to secure whatever it may be they intend to do; instead, they actually move in the wrong direction toward the objective. To achieve it, one must take the right action in addition to thought. Short of taking the appropriate action, you can do all the contemplating and planning you wish; however, the desired goal will never be reached by simply contemplating.

PREVAILING OVER INSURMOUNTABLE ODDS

The same holds true for ridding oneself from reaching a point of no return by remaining in the rut they steered themselves into over a period of years. Unless a person is willing to take the appropriate action, the likelihood of remaining in that self-created condition increases dramatically. The action I am describing is following what their intuitive inner guide has been directing them to take for some time. Unfortunately, however, most people find themselves far too busy attempting to create their earthly utopia that they choose to totally ignore the methods and solutions from their all-knowing infinite intelligence, which are communicated to their inner guidance—even at the price of working at a job, career, or a relationship that they have come to dislike or even possibly despise immensely yet choose to plod on, day after day, even though they may sense this will ultimately just add to their growing discontent.

Perhaps you or someone you know who is in a similar situation who feel trapped in their self-constructed cage. Some people who are living in these conditions—or worse—will begin to seek an escape or an outlet somewhere to bring them temporary relief. Such ways include alcohol, drugs, and sex; withdrawal from others, including family, becoming unapproachable; or just ignoring their self-created circumstances altogether, allowing them to escalate to a future serious condition.

The news is full of horrific stories where some people finally come apart and wind up destroying the lives of fellow employees, significant others, innocent people, entire families, and often even themselves in the process. However, it does not ever have to reach this height of frustration, despondency, hate, and/or anger if one would begin to listen to their inner guide and begin to take the appropriate action to begin to remove themselves from any potentially explosive situation. I marvel at the so-called TV psychologist who will allow people, who are in a very high-distressed condition, to air their problems for millions to see and then offer their textbook advice to those less knowledgeable. How is it possible that a person, a couple, or a family absorbing such advice, who have been living with whatever the condition is for years, could be able to have it resolved or even be expected to take this advice and to act on it as though this is the answer to their very serious issue? The fact of the matter is, it's not!

I am willing to wager that if these people were followed up within a year later, the majority would not have improved from the date they appeared on such a show.

In addition, in today's wicked economic disaster, possibly the rich and the famous may be able to afford ongoing sessions with a psychiatrist or psychologist or be able to check into a rehabilitation facility. However, the average person or household may only be able to do so for several sessions before it becomes financially out of reach, not inclusive of the expense of prescribed mind-altering medications that will only temporarily mask the condition before it comes roaring back.

This may upset some professionals out there; however, the fact remains that unless a person is so far gone mentally and they need to be institutionalized for years or are deemed to be a threat to society, themselves, or their families—if that may be the case—the majority of these conditions need never reach this point in anyone's life. Because all the advice and right direction one will ever possibly need is already within them, giving them the answers they are seeking for whatever the situation or circumstances troubling them. I am a firm believer that the only one that can heal anyone from a serious life-changing event and/or illness and also bring about a permanent cure is the one undergoing the condition and/or symptoms and only through a deep connection and personal relationship with their inner intuitive guidance.

Medical science is helpful up to a point; however, after that, until and unless the individual themselves are willing (assuming they are capable mentally, cognizant, and aware) to take control of their healing and eventual expected cure by taking the action their intuitive inner guide is instructing them to take—the likelihood of this positive outcome is remote at best. Always keep in mind that advice does not heal, but taking right action directed by one's intuitive guide can.

Nothing would make me more pleased than you fully comprehending this by way of my sharing my incredible experience with this inner power with you. A person once challenged the word *gift* and also proceeded to tell me that intuition is not a gift but, instead, a learned discipline. The word *intuition* is described as "a natural ability or power that makes it possible to know something without any proof or evidence"; and "the power or faculty of attaining to direct knowledge or cognition without evident rational thought and inference." Now, what about the word *gift*? This is described as "special favor by God or nature." These definitions certainly remove these opinions.

Now here is where it gets even more interesting. You see, the word *god* these days appears to offend many people for some strange reason unbeknownst to me and probably millions of others as well. So be it. However, there would be no religions on this planet whatsoever if they did not believe and teach the worshiping of some unseen power by whatever name mankind decided to attach to it.

Let's look at this for a moment, shall we? As a mass of humanity, are we to believe that man or woman is, has been, and forever will be the superior power that had incarnated and evolved on this planet beginning from a tadpole, to an ape, to prehistoric man, and, eventually, modern man? Are we not smart enough to realize that a greater power had to put that tadpole here in the first place? Isn't it odd that people all over this planet worship or believe in something far superior to themselves, even a symbol of a serpent that they pray to, sing songs to statutes of ancient gods, and will even spend days and weeks in meditation and even attempt to summon forward? Simultaneously, they still try to disprove and deny that a superior—even possibly a supernatural—power exists.

That said, the person, whom I just mentioned and who honestly believed that intuition is a learned discipline, must have been somewhat out of touch with their senses, as intuition emanates from deep within a person and not from some textbook written by someone who learned it from someone who also learned it from someone. This remains an unknown event to scientists who have yet prove the origin of the universe itself and are still, after all these years, relying upon experimental research, opinions, and conjecture to solve the still unresolved mysteries of the universe and still will be, long after the next one hundred generations come and go.

There even are people who believe in that guy in the red suit who has pointed ears, blows fire out of his mouth, has a pointy tail, carries a pitchfork and lives in someplace supposedly called hell. Why then do millions of people globally believe as they do? What is it then that the Inca, the Egyptians, the Mayans, the Asians, the American Indians, tribes in Africa, etc., worshipped? Certainly, all these people cannot be insane! No, they all believe in a superior power much greater than they. I personally witnessed an atheist call out for Jesus just before he passed away. How remarkable is that? Therefore, even if one does not believe in the Christian God, millions upon millions cannot be so out of touch as to not believe that there certainly exists a much greater unseen power that maintains control over common earthly beings such as us.

Now, as I had said before, I am not a person who has dedicated himself to any particular religion. Instead, I do believe that we are not alone and that we came to earth with much more power than we realize or are even willing to admit. That power happens to lie deep within each and every one of us and all those who have gone before us and who will come long after us. Denying this is to say the we are simply creatures with a brain learning from other creatures with a brain who learned what they know from other creatures with a brain. Yet no one has been able to verify beyond the shadow of any doubt, scientifically or otherwise, how that very first brain came about that contained all that hand-me-down knowledge. Until that happens, if ever, I choose to rely upon the unseen power that has more than proven itself to me—and millions of others, I am certain—over and over again to be the inner all-knowing power and guide that is one with infinite intelligence, which cannot be disproven. Everyone owns this power, whether they choose to use it or not, even the naysayers and skeptics.

Far too many people in history have healed themselves from terrible diseases, terminal illnesses, near-death experiences, traumatic situations, what were deemed medically or physically impossible, and much more that was inconceivable to have been accomplished. Yet the persons involved in any one or more of these unexplained phenomena who healed themselves were able to overcome them when no one else or any technology known to man or science could.

In order not to tread on anyone's religious beliefs, this book does not delve too far into this very sensitive area because I am of the belief that one's choice of religion is a very personal matter. One's religious preference should never be debated or ridiculed by anyone for any reason because to what, how, or whom a person may choose to believe in does not matter. In the final analysis, each person is placing their belief in something, someone, or someplace superior and more powerful and knowledgeable than themselves. To deny this is to be totally lost. However, if one is lost, all it takes is to look inward for answers and cease to rely on any outward solutions for any situation or circumstances at any point in time.

I have heard people involved in holistic health refer to intuition as a science. Let's look at the meaning of the word *science*.

Science, as defined in *Merriam-Webster*, is the "knowledge or a system of knowledge covering general truths or the operation of general laws, especially as obtained and tested through scientific method"; "such knowledge or such a system of knowledge concerned with the physical world and its phenomena: Natural Science"; or "a system or method reconciling practical ends with scientific laws (cooking is both a science and an art)."

Now let's look at the word *intuition* again: "quick and ready insight"; "immediate apprehension or cognition"; "knowledge or conviction gained by intuition"; and "the power or faculty of attaining to direct knowledge or cognition without evident rational thought and inference."

Now let's look at the word *insight*: "the power or act of seeing into a situation"; or "penetration: the act or result of apprehending the inner nature of things or of seeing intuitively."

Now let's explore the word *faculty*: "ABILITY, POWER: as an innate or acquired ability to act or do"; "an inherent capability, power, or function"; or "any of the powers of the mind formerly held by psychologists to form a basis for the explanation of all mental phenomena."

I trust you possibly may agree that intuition is far removed from science as it is defined in layman's terms and, therefore, is innate. *Innate* means "existing in, belonging to, or determined by factors present in an individual from birth."

I am of the firm belief that intuition cannot be taught as a science but can be taught to others how to reconnect with their all-knowing inner guidance and what to do with the answers, methods, and directions being received and how to filter outer noise from the physical brain and only hear what one's intuitive guide is telling them on a continuous basis. I do not know about you, but I for one do not ever want to be a passenger but instead be the pilot, always knowing the correct course I am heading on to my desired destination, versus wondering or guessing where I am and in which direction I am headed. How about you? Is someone or something else piloting your life? If it is, take full control of your destiny and get in the pilot's seat. And when you put on your headphones, all you will hear from that point forward will be your inner guide directing you safely to wherever you wish to become reality that is for your highest good and the highest good of all concerned.

Please try to clearly understand, inner intuitive direction shows up first as a feeling and cannot be taught from any textbook or lecture. Feelings come from deep within a person—one's all-knowing inner guidance—and are not the interpersonal type that originates from the outer self as heartfelt feelings for another person. Therefore, a person's inner feelings belong solely to them, which no one else can hear, sense, or feel. This is what makes one's inner intuition so dynamic, awesome, and personal.

One's inner guidance, however, after having sent the response to the problem, situation, or circumstances, expects the person to take immediate action and follow the path it has directed toward the desired results and to not put off the answers and/or directions for some future date, which could possibly result in no results whatsoever. This inner guide knows precisely when action needs to be taken by the person receiving the answers in order for the expected results to appear in time in reality.

I have also heard others state they intended to teach how to use intuition as a common part of one's perceptive skills. I am not looking to discredit anyone; however, here is what perception says about itself: "awareness of the elements of environment through physical sensation [color perception: physical sensation interpreted in the light of experience]." I now refer you back to the definitions I had provided for you for *intuition, insight,* and faculty, which clearly state what inner intuition is and is not.

PREVAILING OVER INSURMOUNTABLE ODDS

This is not a war of interpretation; instead, I am merely but setting the stage properly regarding what inner intuition is and making it perfectly clear that it cannot be taught. It must be understood, and one must know how to tap into their intuitive power. Anything short of this is an effort in futility and setting oneself up for immediate failure—in my opinion as a recipient.

I do not know about you; however, I am not a person who wishes to wait for an undefined and indefinite period of time for answers and proper guidance to anything that may be impacting my life and the lives of others who may also be concerned. Call me impatient—I guess that's a description that fits millions of humankind on this planet. However, if I am needing to take prompt action in order to bring forth the desired positive results, I certainly need to know what that action on my part needs to be as well as *where, when,* and *how* and be able to rely upon the outcome that would be in my highest, best interest and all concerned.

I've done enough studying in my lifetime and, therefore, can see absolutely no reason why what I need to know, which is already available to me through my personal all-knowing inner guidance, or that understanding this power would require that I would have to attend any sermon to learn what I was already born with through my marvelous gift of the all-knowing inner guidance. Talk about peace of mind.

There is no better feeling of confidence that one could have than knowing that all the methods needed for whatever one needs to know—considering it is for good and not for evil—can be found right where one is at the moment. All it takes is a continuous awareness of the fact that one's inner guide is always with them, ready to communicate the right direction and path to be taken each and every time.

I am convinced that countless people worldwide are not aware that they even have an intuitive inner guidance ready and more than willing to resolve their problems, issues, illnesses, and much more. They possibly have never even been exposed to what their inner guidance is and how it works for the highest good of everyone concerned as well as the person requiring their inner guidance's knowledge.

Although I regret that I had not rediscovered my inner guidance until after having experienced very serious physical and nonphysical events in my life, my focus and mission is to make every attempt to reach out to others what I absolutely know will bring forth methods, answers, and solutions to problems that people have. The traditional methods and conventional resources that are so heavily relied upon by the majority of humanity alone cannot bring forth or guarantee a complete healing or a permanent cure from any grave illness.

I challenge anyone to visit any hospital, nursing home, and related health care facilities if one is concerned enough about how they can heal themselves from a myriad of life's physical and nonphysical illnesses, unexpected negative situations and circumstances, or events occurring either presently or that may one day may happen and witness how many people there are hooked up to every conceivable medical apparatus known to medical science and the looks of confusion and despair—and for some, fear—on their faces.

Even when I spoke with patients when I was in the hospital, for the most part, they could not cease dwelling on their inevitable demise. They were basing this assumption on what their medical practitioners were telling them and that was being reinforced by others. Despite my efforts to talk to them about the contrary, many of them were absolutely convinced that they would never walk out of that hospital, and, if they did, would soon pass away at home. Allow me to tell you what you most likely have heard a gazillion times before: *what you sincerely believe, you will eventually achieve.* How true a statement this is?

If you convince every cell in your physical body that it is going to die away and you continue to send that message to your inner guidance day after day, it is like ordering what you wish to actually exist from life's menu. Therefore, you will eventually achieve the desired result because you are sending a command to all your cells, instructing them to cease functioning as they were designed and meant to. I call this type of mind-set "the predemise trance."

Had I not reconnected with my all-knowing inner guidance, it is very possible that I as well may have become a member of this "predemise choir." Had that been the case, my family would have been visiting a person in the cemetery who left this world long before his time. No matter how strong one is informed about the awesome power of their all-knowing intuitive guidance, that person cannot break through a closed mind-set that is convinced that nothing or no one is going to dissuade them from their desire to self-destruct.

The point I am moving toward is that, one who has not undergone a serious life-changing event, physical or nonphysical, and has not reconnected with their all-knowing inner guidance needs to become very aware that now is the time to begin to resurrect a relationship with your inner guide. Why do I say you need to reconnect? Because your inner guidance never left you, although you possibly may have abandoned it temporarily, having been distracted by the physical world's remedies for whatever you needed to deal with up to the point in your life that just may not be working for you as well as you had hoped.

Remember, you have relied upon your inner guidance on many past occasions, unknowingly telling you that something was either right or not right for you. You know, that inner intuitive feeling you get when faced with something you need to decide about or are seeking a resolution for? Everyone everywhere has been unconsciously aware of this at one time or another in their life—and even more often than that—when their inner guidance was and is attempting to communicate to them the direction in which they should or should not pursue an action.

Now that I have said this, absolutely know that once you have made this reconnection with your inner guidance, you are then more than prepared to handle any problem, situation, or circumstance life throws at you. You can rest assured that absolutely no one gets through life without having had at least one negative nonphysical event come into their life, not discounting the possibility of a life-threatening physical event.

From my personal experience, I can tell you that, after having reconnected with my inner guidance, I have never come to regret it; instead, I have been astonished what it has accomplished in my life for me right up to this present time. I am convinced that my inner guide will continue to lead me to correct decisions, people, places, and the correct path to take when needing resolution and methods for the positive outcome of whatever it may be I know outer-world sources cannot provide for me. The best part of this relationship with one's inner guidance is that the answers and direction needing to be taken arrive on a timely basis; therefore, I never have to wait for months to know absolutely *what* I need to know and *when* I need to know it.

So many people have asked me, "So why don't I heal?" The reason some people do not heal is that they have allowed a lifetime of negativity and disbeliefs to take the place of their all-knowing inner guidance. It is almost as though they have built a wall between their outer selves and their inner selves, ten thousand miles thick and twenty thousand miles high. (A slight exaggeration, but you get the point, I trust.)

In order to be able to reunite with one's inner guide one must be willing to stand back and take a deep look at their life as it has been up to this point and be willing to admit to themselves that their futile attempts to control their life's circumstances, situations, negative events, illnesses, etc., will and possibly have worked for them for a while. However, relying on outer sources and conventional remedies is, at best, temporary.

Therefore, one must also be willing to see the truth that they cannot possibly permanently heal their serious life-changing events through the use or reliance upon any outer source and will, sooner or later, need to rely upon a power much greater than their physical selves and brain—neither of which has the ability to bring forth a permanent healing, proper direction, the right path to follow, and the methods and answers to the myriad of questions they will continue to have as their life progresses.

Conventional sources have their place; however, when they have reached their limits of knowledge and advice of what to do and when you have shelled out a serious amount of money for these services, then where do you go for additional advice or assistance?

Our inner guidance has a wealth of endless information; correct methods; proper guidance; the right paths to take; and the answers to where, what, when, and even who. And the bonus is that one never has to open their wallet—not even once—as the information coming from our inner guidance that is one with the infinite intelligence is free of charge and is available twenty-four seven for life. If I had to pay for all that my inner guidance has done for me so far, I am certain my bill would be somewhere in the high millions of dollars by now because the quality and wealth of knowledge of what I continue to receive from my inner guide is immeasurable by any standard.

Nonphysical life-threatening illnesses such as depression, stress, anxiety, psychological and emotional problems, etc., have contributed deeply as to why a person eventually develops any number of physical and mental illnesses. Especially within the past six years when people in this country primarily are involved in unprecedented life-changing circumstances that most everyone was and still is ill prepared to be able to handle.

The internet and TV with barely many regulatory controls any longer are permeated with trash that young people globally seemingly worship that dictates the way they dress, speak, behave, and act. The internet itself has opened a cesspool of filth for older youth and little children to delve into at will with minimal, if any, monitoring or control over what they are exposed to. Therefore, it's no surprise why so many minors are already on a path leading to any number of nonphysical illnesses and conditions by the time they reach ages thirteen. And the parents of these children are already on a destructive path themselves because many appear to be far too busy with their own personal lives to be concerned with such matters. Until, of course, one day they come face to face with a serious nonphysical illness problem that they were totally unprepared to deal with, in addition to their offspring.

Now, I know that what I just described here is not going to be popular with most people who have young children who are middle school and high school ages. With the exception of those parents out there who do have their pulse on what their children are involved with and keep tight controls on what they are exposed to, there are parents, who don't seem to be aware and to whom this applies, who need to brace themselves for the inevitable backlash that will come eventually. When it does, keep in mind that not only are youngsters going to be deeply affected but so will the parents, which could very well expose everyone involved to eventual serious nonphysical illnesses and conditions. If not kept in check, these may very well possibly lead to physical illnesses, emotional distress, severe stress and anxiety, and possibly some level of mental disorders.

I mention this only because this is precisely how the younger generation is involved at this point in time. Not every young person, however, but enough that it is very noticeable everywhere one looks. Did parents in the '60s up through the '90s have similar problems? You bet they did! However, this is not to the extent as parents today do. Today, all the events I just outlined are just the tip of the iceberg, as these issues go much, much deeper than what I have just briefly described. Today, it's all about the money, the fame, sexual promiscuity, the provocative way and style of dress, the drugs, the restrictions placed upon teachers barring them from being able to control what goes on in their classrooms, and the administration in schools everywhere having their hands tied due to bureaucratic and government interferences, both local and federal.

These observations and statements are neither going to win me any praise nor am I expecting them. What I am expecting, however, is to open the eyes of not only the parents of this generation's young people but to their own lives as well and to take a good hard look at what they are allowing and believe. What controls, if any, do they have to establish within their own households to be able to monitor what their children are exposing themselves to and who they are associating with every day? I am not making any attempts to play the role of child or family psychologist, as heaven knows that I certainly am not one; but I am a parent of a teenage boy and raised three stepdaughters as well and know from my own personal experience the dedicated and caring parental work that needs to go into keeping children far away from self-destructive behaviors and associations that may possibly come to revisit them in the future and could very well possibly lead to passing these very same traits on to their children—the next generation.

This now leads me back to what I was saying earlier about the outer self versus one's inner self. We all are aware of this all-knowing intuitive inner guidance. It is this inner guidance that is constantly telling us what we should be and not be doing. It tells us the correct direction in which to go and to avoid. It gives us the answers to every perplexing question, problem, or event we may ever be face to face with. It shows us how to avoid and to eliminate stress and anxiety and a myriad of other life-destructive nonphysical illnesses, conditions, and events from our lives for good. It shows us how to stay on the right path, to be able to avoid any undesirable factors life may have to throw at us. It gives us a very clear path to how our future lives can and will be—by following the life path that had already had been laid out for us (one's purpose in life). And above all, it delivers the peace, confidence, and certainty we all need to survive and to live a healthy and prosperous life on all levels, as it was meant to be, and not a life of what-ifs, grief, anxiety, stress, depression, worry, etc., and teaching our children these almost-forgotten values so they can pass them on to their children and their children's children as well.

One can choose to consider all this or choose to ignore it instead. Of course, the choice is up to the chooser. However, before deciding to ignore the foregoing, which most of you are already aware of, consider the consequences of selecting the other direction. Remember, inner guidance never leaves you and is constantly leading you in the right direction because this is the unseen force that is working deep within each and every one of us every moment we are alive. Therefore, one needs to take a serious look at their life; and if you do have children, you certainly owe it to them to consider what I have just outlined about our younger generation and you, their parents.

This now leads me to what begs these questions: "Have you ever taken a moment out of your life to ask yourself or to contemplate the origins of illnesses and why they develop in the first place?" and "Have you ever wondered what will it take to heal a serious illness, physical or nonphysical?" and "What severe stress, anxiety, depression, trauma, and distress can do to trigger severe physical illnesses?"

Let's say that is current and most everyone is familiar with if they are paying any attention at all to what is happening in America today as well as almost every civilized country in the world. In the USA, since the Great Depression, a period of economic decline in the industrialized nations, Americans are witnessing the greatest economic downward spiral and unprecedented unemployment and rapid movement by its government toward socialism.

Millions are out of work, the country's government appears to have lost total sight of the serious effect that this condition is having on the American public, unprecedented home foreclosures, millions of small business owners losing their sole source of income, material assets disappearing right in front of the middle class every day. A myriad of additional consumer and small business taxes are on a fast-track increase, consumer spending is at an all-time low while government spending is out of control, and confidence in government and its elected representatives has dwindled to its lowest point ever. Savings accounts have declined substantially, investments are suffering, residential and commercial real estate investments and purchases are virtually stagnant, business and real estate lending has been reduced to a trickle, venture capital has all but diminished. Gas and heating oil prices and gasoline have gone through the roof, and socialism has raised its ugly head as a very distinct possibility. The USA appears to be rapidly heading towards a European-style society; world strife, wars, terrorism are on the incline; and the younger generation appears not to have a clue to what is happening in their own country or seem to even care.

All of what I just outlined and more is as current as this morning's news. That said, let's answer the last of the questions I just outlined: "Have you ever thought about what severe stress, anxiety, depression, trauma, and distress can do to trigger an entire society to experience severe physical illnesses?"

Now, relating back to the circumstances that millions of people have found themselves facing within the past six years and seeing no apparent relief on the horizon, the possibility of becoming susceptible to any number of life-threatening nonphysical illnesses is not just a possibility but a reality. One can be in great physical condition, eat all the right foods, and take care of themselves physically; however, if one abuses themself through continuous stress, anxiety, depression, trauma, distress, or any one or combination of the life-threatening nonphysical illnesses—they can very well lead to these illnesses and/or prevent one from healing from any illness that they may already be developing.

If one is interconnected with their inner guidance, on the other hand, they can have the opportunity to restore one's energy and power entirely and also eliminate any and all negative thoughts and beliefs. The entire ceiling can fall down around you, and you would not be affected by it and would come away with and an "oh well, at least I was not hit in the head by anything" attitude. Be grateful and ready to move on with your life, regardless of whatever your situation may be, which is not to continue to dwell on any misfortune or loss that could only eventually prove to be even more disastrous.

You may be saying to yourself right now, "But you are not in my shoes." Yes I am. I am not immune to any of what I have been describing, and I was in those shoes not too long ago. I can tell you that long before this serious economic situation occurred, I had gone through what most people on this planet would more than likely never face and brought myself out of it with absolutely no help from anyone on this planet, and neither did I reach out for any help as well. I had many of the life-threatening nonphysical illnesses on the chart I have provided in this book, and then some. Had I not made the reconnection with my inner guidance when I did, I can assure you that I would more than likely not be here today.

Therefore, I am more than convinced that if I could have survived all that plus cancer and having the extreme confidence in my intuitive guidance to even have refused chemotherapy treatments, then it certainly may be possible, in my opinion, for others to overcome anything that they may be exposed to now or possibly in the future. And yes, I am being redundant; however, I am just one person among thousands of others who have overcome much more than I and have gone on to live productive, thankful, and prosperous lives. If these people all over the world and I could have achieved what was deemed by others, including medical science, to be insurmountable, then there is the probability—despite the seriousness of their present circumstances or situation—that others can also.

I certainly believe that healthy food choices and exercise are very helpful when it comes to warding off diseases. However, coupling this with listening to one's inner guidance may aid in preventing and even overcoming some of this planet's deadliest illnesses. Of course, nothing in life when it comes to one's quality and longevity of life and good health is etched in stone as a guarantee. However, having a choice to just maintain a healthy lifestyle versus combining this type of lifestyle with one's inner guidance can greatly enhance the chances of avoiding a serious life-threatening illness, physical or nonphysical—thereby setting the stage for being able to overcome any serious illness, negative event, or circumstance that may enter one's life. Certainly this would be light-years ahead of those who choose otherwise when it comes to overcoming and bringing forth a permanent cure from any life-threatening illness that one may possibly encounter in the future.

When you begin to receive an intuitive message, always be certain to pay very close attention to what your inner guidance is telling you, whether it is about yourself, someone you know, a situation you are in, or any event that you may be involved with. Seeking a safe harbor instead of a healthy insight and attempting to deny any images that may come in the way of your intuition that you may wish to reject—never dismiss them because you are seeking a preview into the unknown future. Even though an intuition does not at first meet your desires, wishes, or hopes, do not toss it out, because your inner guide is sending you something else; this intuitive message that you are receiving is an integral part of the answers you are seeking.

Your inner guide will never lead you in the wrong direction and will always place you on the correct path, if you do not reject whatever it is that your inner guide is telling you. Be patient and receptive at all times because the desired answers and proper directions will come. All you need to do is to trust that they will and allow yourself to be pleasantly overwhelmed with joy when they do.

One more thing, know that your inner guidance does not wear a watch; therefore, all expected outcomes will come in your inner guidance's timing and not yours. This is precisely where extreme patience on your part becomes very critical.

Sometimes it is necessary for your inner guide to have to delve back into your past in order to be able to retrieve the root causes of whatever it is you desire. More often than not, this possibly may be somewhat painful when your inner guide brings these events to your attention, which is only for the purpose of achieving a total healing and/or resolution or proper direction to be taken. I did not like many of the events and things that I had to revisit in my life in order to understand and be able to deal with, including what brought about the root causes that introduced so many nonphysical and eventual serious life-threatening physical illnesses into my life before the solutions were revealed to me by my inner guidance. It is very important that you never lose sight of this and open yourself to being totally receptive to the truth of whatever it is that brought forth whatever it may be you are seeking. By allowing this revealing process to occur, you then begin with the truth and end up with the truth and the results you are seeking, as long as those results benefit not only you but everyone concerned in a good and positive way as well.

    I could not help but notice that when I speak to people about their concerns, among one of the very first things I can feel from them is their resistance to be able to face their innermost fears. The majority of these people were either unwilling or unable to act on the messages that their inner guide was desperately attempting to get to them. What their inner guidance was attempting to do was to awaken them from the false beliefs and feelings of hopelessness they were harboring. They actually had convinced themselves that, by choosing to ignore whatever it was that was so deeply concerning them, it would eventually just go away. However, after years of living with these conditions, matters only became worse, not better and never did disappear.

    Obvious to me, this was their safe haven or safe place which was constructed of false walls and soundproof interior where they believed they could hide. Once they learned that this was not only damaging to their mental health but to their overall health as well, eventually, they were able to develop an entirely different mind-set. They then were finally free to be able to become open to what their inner guide was telling them and able to live a healthier and more assured life.

    Far too many people I have had the opportunity to visit with and people in general I have observed in business, everyday life, and even abroad when I used to travel, as well as extended family members, seem to walk around with blinders on. Consequently, not being able to see that life at times can be painful; and that pain, quite unfortunately—be it physical or emotional—is a part of life that no one can escape, no matter what they may attempt to try and do. Every person before us, alive today, and to follow all had and will have a specific purpose in life to complete; and with that purpose will come pain, disappointments, trauma, and illness, nonphysical and/or physical. It will never always be comfortable or trouble free—maybe in the hereafter but certainly not on this planet—as history and everyday life very clearly support this to be true.

What I also am very aware of is that no one I have ever known or met, including myself, ever received a document attached to their birth certificate that stated, "This is to certify and guarantee that this person born here today will never have any painful or uncomfortable experiences or illnesses during their entire lifetime on planet earth," and signed by a higher spiritual power.

Yet countless people everywhere actually believe that they will get through the gauntlet of life without any of these adverse conditions. It begs asking, when these things do eventually show up in their lives, that the common statement seems to be "Why me?" What? "Should it have been someone else instead?" So if you happen to be among the people who do believe this way, I hate to be the bearer of bad news—if you have not yet endured any painful situation in your life (not necessarily physical illnesses or diseases), then you need to know that you will not leave this life without at least having one painful event in your life that you yourself can resolve without assistance, be it conventional or through your inner guidance or a combination of both. This I can assure you. The good news is that if and when any painful event does enter your life you are never alone, even if you live alone or are a recluse. Your inner guide is constantly with you and will bring forth the resolution, direction, and answers you will need to know when you need them and will be right on time—never too early or too late.

I am so confident about this that I live my entire life completely trusting my intuitive guidance and very little dependence on others, as they can neither be able to permanently heal me nor cure me of anything physical, nonphysical, or otherwise that may find its way into my life. I can assure you that I am not alone and that there are thousands of people of all ages out there right now who know and rely upon their inner guidance for proper guidance in all that they do in life. Therefore, this is among the primary reasons it is so important that one learns how to develop and to connect—or reconnect—with one's inner guidance.

It was once—or probably still is—considered by some in medical science that for one to talk to themselves is a sign of some level of mental illness. Well then, if talking to my all-knowing inner guidance had saved my life on more than one occasion and brought forth a complete healing and permanent cure of very serious illnesses and life-changing events, I am willing to live with whatever label medical science wishes to place on me; and I am certain I am not alone in that regard.

People have asked me for the steps they need to take to be able to tap into or connect with their inner guidance. My response is that there are no specific steps, manuals, or instruction that can assist anyone to connect with their inner guidance that is one with the all-knowing infinite intelligence other than a direct dialogue through the written method I have described earlier. It is not a subject that is taught; instead, it is developed and refined by choice concerning the type of lifestyle one chooses to live in order to be able to receive the answers, methods, and desired results of whatever it may be they are seeking.

Being intuitive means to have knowledge that is independent of thought. The experience of being intuitive is considered to be able to have information about reality without input from the conscious mind. Therefore, it is not having to *have* to think about it but, instead, considered as real and the message came from being able to be objective and receptive to the answers one is receiving from their intuitive inner guidance received from the infinite intelligence.

The majority of my intuitive impressions come to me in the way of mental images or a very clear instruction, accompanied by a strong feeling, having no emotional components attached to them—just the message, image, and feeling. You must also keep in mind that you should not make any attempts to connect with this infinite intelligence when you are very tired or have anything that is pressing on your mind. Wait until you are rested and have no trauma interfering with the answers, methods, and solution you are seeking to receive from this infinite force.

I have found that anytime I was attempting to receive images or messages from my inner guidance that I was unable to make the connection until I was calm, rested, and away from all outer interferences. Patience is always best and advisable.

I cannot emphasize enough that you are aware that inner intuition has also been described as one's inner feeling. Not too many people could honestly state that they never had a certain feeling about something that told them to either go forward with something or to avoid it altogether. No matter what the subject of that inner feeling is, it is always right and never wrong—whether we chose to trust it or not—because it comes directly from your inner guidance. The choice to accept what this inner guidance is attempting to communicate is ours alone to make either way.

My mission is to share my personal incredible communication experience with this infinite all-knowing intelligence with others, knowing that this source of infinite intelligence can bring forth any desire one wishes for their highest good and for the benefit of all concerned. Once one makes a decision to open an ongoing dialogue with this unseen intelligence and believes, without wavering or doubting or being impatient, that whatever it is one desires for good can be realized in one's physical life. I am living proof of this, as are others throughout the world who have the same connection with this infinite intelligence.

The chapter that follows is about this book having no ending—instead, it's the beginning of the rest of your life—and is a summary of important topics that were presented for your attention and continued interest.

23

THE BEGINNING OF THE REST OF YOUR LIFE

I wish to extend my sincere gratitude to you for caring as much as you do for not only yourself but for all those who have come into your life and even those you have yet to meet. You know precisely who you are internally and also sense that what you have learned thus far from your outer world does not even begin to scratch the surface of what you already know that can bring you the benefits you desire for the optimal outcome that you seek.

Through the pages of this book, you have learned why so many people have more failures in life than successes. You learned about the root causes of most nonphysical conditions and physical illnesses and why so many people succumb to them when the possibility to survive through their inner guidance was within their grasp all along, had they only made the decision to tap into it. You learned why medical science, although very valuable to serving humanity, is not the total answer to one's survival of serious life-threatening events such as cancer and why it is so important that the medical community seriously consider that it is the patient, not medical science, that can bring forth their healing.

You learned that one's all-knowing inner guidance has been around since humankind inhabited this world and why people who refuse to call upon it do not do so well when they encounter a life-threatening illness/event and why many of those who do survive go on to live their lives. You learned why religions of every conceivable type are not separate, despite their desire to give the world that perception, and that they all actually worship the very same unseen power, and that the only difference between them are the names they attach to this unseen power that cannot be contacted through sight or touch but, instead, resides within each and every person fortunate enough to have been born on this planet.

You learned about my story and what I did to overcome what was deemed by medical professionals and others not to be survivable. You learned how you can be the one who goes far beyond anyone's expectations, including the power of inner guidance, if you have or ever develop any serious life-changing event or life-threatening illness and so much more through your unseen all-knowing infinite intelligence—the very same unseen force I used to rid myself of two cancers and other serious life-threatening events—to be able to achieve my life's purpose and every desire for my highest good that I chose and continue to possess.

I also want to leave you with this: all the positive or negative occurrences in your life thus far have been a result of your very own self-suggestion, *no one else's*. If they are happy and prosperous, you are among that unique group of humanity who has found their life's path and purpose for your life.

As I've been repeatedly bringing to your attention, all there is to know can be found in the vault deep within you that contains all the knowledge, answers, methods, and solutions you'll ever need to know. This vault, to which you hold the only key concerning your life, contains your all-knowing inner guidance that is one with the infinite intelligence that contains the answers, methods, and solutions to anything and everything you care to know and is available to you at any time you choose to connect with it.

This much I do know about this unseen force for certain— it's the intelligence far greater than humankind could ever fathom that can materialize any desire meant for your highest good, if you thoroughly believe that it can. How I know this for certain is because I have personally witnessed the positive results of its power in my life countless times and can attest to the fact that it is not only real; it is as real as you are. It is more powerful than all the minds combined that have ever existed or exist now and will go on existing long after mankind is no longer. In other words, it is perpetual, just like the spirit (your inner guidance) that resides within each and every one of us—the real you and me—because it is one with the creator of everything humankind has and will ever experience.

As the title of this chapter states, this book is the beginning of the rest of your life. All you need to do to be aware of this power within is to thoroughly believe in this tremendous gift with which you were born. I can assure you that if you choose to do this, with unwavering confidence, trust, and expectation, you can also have the opportunity to begin to live your purpose for being here as I am doing at this very moment, as a result of my unwavering belief and trust in this all-knowing unseen power and inner guidance that is one with the infinite intelligence.

It is my sincerest wish that, like me and others, you too will also choose to realize your innermost desires for good. If you never before believed in an unseen, inner all-knowing power, then now is your opportunity to reunite with the greatest gift of all that can bring forth every desire and level of prosperity you'll ever want to experience that is for your highest good and for the highest good of all concerned.

Remember this: Anyone can pick up a book and read it. However, reading is one thing; taking what one has read and turning it into the knowledge and action required is quite another thing altogether. That said, I encourage you to take immediate action pertaining to whatever you may have found to be helpful to you in this book.

I wish to thank you for sharing my thoughts and also want to extend my sincerest best wishes to you for a prosperous life on every conceivable level—in addition, for believing and trusting in yourself and for your sincere desire to surmount any adversity you may be facing or may encounter. I trust that you found the information contained in this book to have been very helpful and encouraging and further wish to extend my sincerest wish and prayers for you to achieve all that you desire for good from this moment forward.

Acknowledgments

I wish to first acknowledge my wonderful and dedicated son, Nick, who has been my inspiration from the time he was a very young child and the one person in my life who has been my rock and whose presence in my life was among the primary reasons for my burning desire to overcome several cancers and numerous traumatic, life-threatening nonphysical adversities and events. It was through my son Nick's total and undying dedication, support, and encouragement that I was led to write this book for every person worldwide who may presently be suffering through a serious life-threatening condition and/or undesirable life-changing situation of any type, be it physical or nonphysical, and those who have been fortunate to not have a serious life-threatening condition so far.

My son Nick's encouragement for me to share my incredible, serious, life-changing experiences with everyone who is willing to open their minds and understand that adversarial episodes can be overcome and defeated and are self-imposed was among the driving forces to write this book that identifies that it is we—all of humankind—who are the creators of most adversities and undesirable events we face during our brief stay on this planet. However, we can also have the opportunity to change what we create through the methods provided in this book.

This book also could never have been made possible if it were not for my dear friend, Ernie Garcia, a man I met under some of the most adverse conditions anyone could possibly ever imagine. Without his steadfast dedication, ideas, and ongoing encouragement to get this book to everyone who needs to know what and how I overcame every life-threatening adversity I encountered, this book would possibly never have been written. Words could never sufficiently express my deepest appreciation and gratitude to you, Ernie, and thank you for always being there for me and picking me up and placing me back on the path to get this book done for all those who could possibly benefit immensely from its content.

I also wish to recognize my cousin Manny. Manny has been a paraplegic for well over forty years and, despite his very serious physical handicap caused by an unfortunate automobile accident, had fought the most courageous battle to continue to hold on to life and who somehow was never seen without a huge smile for everyone, despite his ongoing battle, in and out of the hospital for years. Thank you, Manny, for giving me the encouragement to stick with it, despite all odds against me during all those adverse circumstances my readers will find within the pages of this book and by being a role model for me. You encouraged me to never give up—and even more, to never quit—no matter what the odds may be against you. I will always be forever grateful to you for your words of encouragement and support, without which I just may have allowed the countless adversarial, life-changing events I had been subjected to overcome me.

Then there is Juanita Civello, a very dear friend and who has been on this planet for ninety-two years who chose to dedicate her entire life to aiding and caring for her fellow man, woman, and child as a registered and teaching nurse and whose relentless, ideas, assistance and dedication for me to get this book out of the computer and out to all those who needed to learn how I overcame all that I have despite the insurmountable odds against my ever being able to prevail over them. I will never forget all your encouragement and the myriad of ideas you gave me that greatly enhanced the contents of this book. I will also never forget you and thank you from the depths of my heart for always being there for me as a very special friend and confidante.

I also wish to recognize my stepdaughter Mayra for her tremendous turnaround in life by going from a young lady who at first did not see much hope for her life or saw the value of an education, to becoming a star student at her high school, achieving many awards, including the principal's award for excellence and achievement in her final year of high school; to go on to work in politics; become a fashion model in Las Vegas, Nevada; secure important positions with well-known Las Vegas hotel restaurants; a management position with a very well-known, high-profile fashion house; and to pursuing her dream to eventually work in the legal profession as an attorney today. I am very proud of you, Mayra, as you have established yourself as a great role model for the younger generation by showing them that despite any adversity they may encounter in their young life, there is absolutely no mountain too high that they cannot conquer—if they decide they will, despite the odds, as you have done. You are an incredible young lady, and I am proud of you and grateful that you have graced my life, and for being a very important part of my life.

Then how can I forget my wonderful Aunt Santa and Aunt Gloria who both never left my side from childhood and all during my darkest days? They were there to hold me up when I was literally giving up on life while I was going through the most horrific and unspeakable times in my life. I cannot thank you both enough for always being there for me and for your spiritual encouragement. It was both of you who also encouraged me to get this book out, as you truly believed that people everywhere must read what is contained in these pages. Thank you and know I will always love you both.

I would also like to dedicate this book to my mother who, when I was a young boy, had always instilled in me that there was never such a word as *quit* and always told me that that word could only be found in a fool's dictionary. She was there to make certain that her two sons never walked away from any of life's challenges and faced up to our adversities and taught us that they were only temporary speed bumps and that we could achieve anything we decided to accomplish, despite anyone's opinion to the contrary. And she was right. Thank you, Mom, for all you did for me and my brother during your lifetime—you have never been or ever will be forgotten.

To my brother, Wayne, you taught me what perseverance really was and how one can always come back in a big way, despite any adversity, if only they will take a good look at all one had accomplished in their life, regardless of any setbacks one may face. Wayne had to also overcome some of life's most difficult experiences, and he conquered everything life had to throw at him and survived it all. He is still a master scuba dive instructor and continues to encourage the younger generation, as well as the elderly, that there is absolutely nothing they cannot conquer and accomplish if they truly want to. And by example, he has brought many people back from self-inflicted trauma, lack of self-confidence and trust, deep depression, and a myriad of other life-changing situations. Thank you, bro, for being such a great example for me and for all the lives you touched.

Then there is my lifelong friend Billy Mac whom I have known for many years, whom I met when I was a young musician, and with whom I enjoyed working in a number of musical groups over those years. Billy, you taught me patience and, above all, how to never throw in the towel and just continue on with an optimistic attitude, despite all the disappointments that may come one's way. Your training as a proud veteran and retired member of the US Navy was evident by how you treated everyone with fairness, and you were always ready to help others when they were down and needed support, which was and remains also evident by how you and you wife Shirley raised your girls and your long-term marriage. And most of all, Billy, thank you for your ideas for this book for which I give you credit and for your inspiration to get this book out to share the message that is contained within its pages. I will always remember you and Shirley for your deep and dedicated friendship over all these years, and thank you both so much for all your encouragement and support.

This book is also dedicated to the those public figures who, despite their battles with very serious physical life-threatening illnesses—regardless if they survived or not—raised the bar for every living member of humanity to let them know that they too can conquer whatever adverse situation one may face during their lifetime that the height to which that bar can be lifted, if they would just convince themselves that they not only can but will. They are certainly to be commended for never quitting and never throwing in the towel. Instead, they went the extra mile and found a way to prolong their battle when others gave in. And those who completely overcame their very serious physical illness, you know who you are, and I also wish to dedicate this book to all of you for being such an inspiration and role model for all those who follow who may be having a serious physical and/or nonphysical life-threatening event or possibly may have in the future.

PREVAILING OVER INSURMOUNTABLE ODDS

I am also dedicating this book to each and every current and retired member of the United States Armed Forces, living and deceased, who have faced tremendous life-threatening situations, circumstances, and events with courage that goes far beyond what mere words could ever have the power to describe. These are the men and women and their families who are the role models for anyone anywhere need to look up to, as they have suffered the most horrendous injuries, major life-changing events, and even death.

I wish to thank all those warriors and their families who overcame their ordeals with a life-threatening and/or life-changing condition of any type. I sincerely respect what you had and/or may presently be experiencing that may have changed your lives substantially. It is to all of you that I salute. I am so grateful for your courage and unwavering, unconditional, and unselfish dedication to your country. Millions throughout the world owe all of you more than a debt of gratitude—they owe you their lives because you not only preserved and ensured their freedom but their children's freedom and that of their children for generations to come.

May God (or whatever unseen power you may believe in) always keep all of you well, safe, and prosperous on every conceivable level, and I thank you for giving me this opportunity—through your courage, dedication, and bravery—to write this book for all humankind and to recognize your dedication to all who respect freedom and for your unselfish sacrifice.

I am also dedicating this book to each and every cancer survivor and survivors of any serious life-threatening physical illness and all those who have survived unspeakable, life-changing nonphysical adversities for their courage and perseverance that, in turn, gives the encouragement needed to everyone everywhere to know that they too can overcome any undesirable life-changing condition.

I also dedicate this book to you, my reader, who had the foresight to seek out answers, methods, and solutions concerning the possibility of overcoming any possible life-disrupting adversity and/or event that you personally may be enduring or affecting a significant other, family member, or anyone whom you may deeply care about.

www.ingramcontent.com/pod-product-compliance
Lightning Source LLC
Chambersburg PA
CBHW021422070526
44577CB00001B/11